S0-CFP-060

Elementary Japanese

Elementary Japanese

Volume Two

by Yoko Hasegawa, Ph.D.

in collaboration with

Wakae Kambara
Noriko Komatsu
Yasuko Konno Baker
Kayo Nonaka
Chika Shibahara
Miwako Tomizuka
Kimiaki Yamaguchi

TUTTLE PUBLISHING
Tokyo • Rutland, Vermont • Singapore

Published by Tuttle Publishing, an imprint of Periplus Editions (HK) Ltd.,
with editorial offices at 364 Innovation Drive, North Clarendon, Vermont 05759
and 130 Joo Seng Road, #06-01/03, Singapore 368357.

LCC Card No: 2003110213
ISBN 0-8048-3506-3

Distributed by:

North America, Latin America & Europe
Tuttle Publishing
364 Innovation Drive
North Clarendon, VT 05759-9436
Tel: (802) 773 8930; Fax (802) 773 6993
Email: info@tuttlepublishing.com
www.tuttlepublishing.com

Japan
Tuttle Publishing
Yaekari Building, 3rd Floor
5-4-12 Osaki, Shinagawa-ku
Tokyo 141-0032
Tel: (03) 5437 0171; Fax: (03) 5437 0755
Email: tuttle-sales@gol.com

Asia Pacific
Berkeley Books Pte. Ltd.
130 Joo Seng Road, #06-01/03
Singapore 368357
Tel: (65) 6280 1330; Fax: (65) 6280 6290
Email: inquiries@periplus.com.sg
www.periplus.com

10 09 08 07 06 05
10 9 8 7 6 5 4 3 2 1

Printed in Singapore

– Contents –

– Preface –

Elementary Japanese is designed for people beginning their study of the Japanese language at the basic level. Because of its ample grammatical explanation, it can also serve as a grammatical reference. It is suitable for college courses as well as individual study. It consists of 27 lessons: 14 in Volume I and 13 in Volume II. One possibility is to cover Volume I in the first semester, and Volume II in the second semester, using the first week of the second semester to review Volume I.

Lessons typically contain:

(i) A dialog
(ii) Usage notes
(iii) Grammar notes
(iv) Exercises
(v) New kanji (Chinese characters) and explanation
(vi) Kanji review exercises
(vii) New vocabulary

(i) The dialog is the core of each lesson as it contains all of the grammatical constructions to be studied in that lesson.

(ii) Usage notes elaborate dialog expressions and include social and/or pragmatic explanations, e.g. politeness.

(iii) Grammar notes are linguistically oriented, although technical terms are avoided as much as possible. They attempt to explain the rationale behind grammatical constructions and their usage, rather than introducing them as mere facts. Historical changes and morphological processes, e.g. sequential voicing, are occasionally mentioned, making explanations more readable and comprehensible. Whenever appropriate, Japanese and equivalent English expressions are compared and contrasted, enabling students to utilize their already acquired knowledge of language use.

(iv) The exercises evolved from extending and expanding the materials developed in the Japanese Language Program at the University of California, Berkeley during several recent decades. Virtually all exercises emulate actual uses of the language rather than imposing mechanical drills. They are designed primarily for use in classroom activities, emphasizing interaction among students. They can also be used for self-testing at the end of each lesson, in which case, the user is advised to play two (or more) roles if necessary.

(v) The study of kanji (ideographic Chinese characters) is one of the greatest obstacles in learning Japanese; acquisition of more than 1,000 kanji is needed to read Japanese texts, e.g, newspaper articles. While introducing a total of 313 basic kanji, *Elementary Japanese* explains the fundamental differences between ideographic (primarily representing ideas) and phonographic (representing sounds, e.g. English) writing systems.

(vi) This textbook considers that the acquisition of kanji is of pivotal importance to any effective Japanese language program; it therefore provides additional exercises designed for both learning and retaining kanji. Moreover, it utilizes kanji while an increasing number of people today use hiragana, e.g. 下さい, 分かる, もらった時, かも知れない. There are two reasons for this choice. First, repetitive exposure to and frequent utilization of kanji help learners to retain them. Second, while the use of hiragana for such words has become conventionalized, many people still prefer to use kanji. If students do not learn, for example, ください is written as下さい, they will have difficulty deciphering it. For these reasons, *Elementary Japanese* employs kanji whenever plausible.

(vii) In addition to a vocabulary list for each lesson, comprehensive vocabulary lists (both Japanese-to-English and English-to-Japanese) are provided as appendices.

Cultural information and proverbs are interspersed. The importance of inclusion of contemporary interests and the continuing need for sex/gender neutrality in concepts, words, and images are recognized.

Abundant and innovative uses of illustrations and visual aids are provided throughout *Elementary Japanese*. The dialogs employ comic strip format, a method that enables learning sentences strongly associated with actual daily life situations. When a grammatical particle or a kanji radical is introduced, it is signaled by a clear visual marking, enabling students to locate relevant paragraphs quickly and at the point of need. The dialogs are illustrated by Neil Cohn; other drawings are by Neil Cohn, Yoko Katagiri, Joyce Nojima, Natsuko Shibata Perera, Virginia Tse, and Hiromi Nishida Urayama.

Upon completing the activities provided in *Elementary Japanese*, students can expect to be able to

(a) describe themselves, their families and friends,
(b) talk about daily events, using basic vocabulary and grammatical constructions,
(c) understand conversations on those topics as well as classroom instructions,
(d) read and write short, simple compositions.

Many people have helped with *Elementary Japanese* and its accompanying CDs over the last ten years of its creation. Acknowledgement is due to our colleagues and students at the University of California, Berkeley who provided valuable feedback and/or participated in numerous recording sessions. They include Kate Chase, Ramon Escamilla, Momoe Saito Fu, Anthony Higgins, Alex Highsmith, Yoko Katagiri, Seiko Kosaka, Wesley Leonard, David Malinowski, Yasuhiro Omoto, Mischa Park-Doob, Kazumi Yahata-Pettersson, Tatsuo Saile, Keiko Sakatani, Shoichi Tamura, Angela Tiao, Masayoshi Tomizuka, and Hiromi Nishida Urayama. We appreciate the generous support of the Berkeley Language Center, where all audio materials were recorded. The recording engineer was Gina Hotta. Special thanks go to Flavia Hodges and Doreen Ng of Tuttle Publishing Company for bringing this work to publication.

This project was supported in part by grants from the Department of East Asian Languages and Cultures and the Center for Japanese Studies at the University of California, Berkeley.

Yoko Hasegawa
Berkeley, California

日本とうちゃく
Arriving in Japan

日本では、くつをぬいでから家に上がることになっています
In Japan, people take their shoes off before they enter a house

9
さあ、どうぞ上がって下さい。
はい、しつれいします。
10
あっ、ミラーさん、くつ。日本では、くつをぬいでから、家に上がることになっています。
11
あ、すみません。日本のしゅうかんは日本語のじゅぎょうで習ったり、友達に聞いたりしましたが、うっかりくつをぬぐのをわすれてしまいました。アメリカでは、くつをぬがないで家に入るので……。どうもすみませんでした。
12
だいじょうぶですよ。日本のしゅうかんをたくさん勉強して下さい。
はい、ありがとうございます。よろしくおねがいします。

会話

(くうこうで)

1 いさお ： ミラーさんですね。秋山いさおです。いらっしゃい。

You're Miller-san, aren't you? I'm Isao Akiyama. Welcome.

2 ミラー ： あっ、秋山さんですか。始めまして。ジミー・ミラーです。おせわになります。よろしくおねがいします。

Oh, Akiyama-san? Nice to meet you, I'm Jimmy Miller. Thanks for taking the trouble (to invite me).

いさお ： こちらこそ、どうぞよろしく。

Nice to meet you, too.

3 いさお ： 飛行機はどうでしたか。ゆれましたか。

How was the plane (trip)? Was there turbulence?

ミラー ： いいえ、あまりゆれませんでした。それで、ずっと音楽を聞きながら本を読んでいました。

No, there wasn't much. So I (just) read books while listening to music the whole way here.

4　いさお：それはよかったですね。それじゃ、家でみんなが待っていますから、行きましょう。リムジンで新宿(しんじゅく)まで行って、新宿からタクシーにのりましょう。
That's good. Well, everyone is waiting for us at home, so let's go. We'll take a shuttle bus to Shinjuku, and then take a taxi from there.

(秋山さんの家で)

5　いさお：ただいま。
I'm home.

6　ゆりこ・まゆみ・いちろう: お帰りなさい。
Welcome back.

7　いさお：ミラーさんがつきましたよ。
Miller-san has arrived.

8　ミラー：ジミー・ミラーです。始めまして、どうぞよろしく。
I'm Jimmy Miller. How do you do. Nice to meet you.

ゆりこ：ゆりこです。どうぞよろしく。
I'm Yuriko. Nice to meet you, too.

9　ゆりこ：さあ、どうぞ上がって下さい。
Please come in.

ミラー：はい、しつれいします。
Thank you.

10　いさお：あっ、ミラーさん、くつ。日本では、くつをぬいでから、家に上がることになっています。
Oops, Miller-san! Your shoes! In Japan, people take their shoes off before they enter (step up into) a house.

11　ミラー：あ、すみません。日本のしゅうかんは日本語のじゅぎょうで習(なら)ったり、友達に聞いたりしましたが、うっかりくつをぬぐのをわすれてしまいました。アメリカでは、くつをぬがないで家に入(はい)るので……。どうもすみませんでした。
Oh, I'm sorry. I learned about Japanese customs in my Japanese class, and I heard about them from my friends, but I was careless and forgot to take them off (to my regret). In America, we enter a house without taking off our shoes, so .... I'm very sorry.

12　いさお：だいじょうぶですよ。日本のしゅうかんをたくさん勉強して下さい。
That's all right. I hope you'll learn many Japanese customs.

ミラー：はい、ありがとうございます。よろしくおねがいします。
Yes, thank you in advance for your help.

使(つか)い方

Title とうちゃく is the verbal noun which is a Sino-Japanese equivalent to つく "to arrive". For *verbal noun*, see 第四課, **4k**; for *Sino-Japanese equivalents*, see 第五課漢字ノート.

2 おせわになる literally means "X (addressee) is going to care and/or trouble for Y (speaker), and therefore Y will be much indebted to X". You may need to use it when you stay overnight at someone's home, or when someone offers you a tour of some place, etc. At the end of such an occasion/event/activity, you say おせわになり[ました], rather than おせわになり[ます].

よろしくおねがいします (literally "please favor me") is a general and polite expression for making a request. It is used frequently in Japanese conversations, but there is no equivalent expression in English.

こちらこそ literally means "it's this (my) side (rather than yours)" and can be translated as "I should say that". Here, ミラーさん says *Please favor me*, and 秋山さん responds *It's I who must ask for your favor.*

3 ずっと is an adverb, meaning "continuously/all the time". It normally occurs with ～ている or adjectives that denote temporary states or conditions.

飛行機では、ずっと本を読んでいました。
(Lit.) On the plane, I was continuously reading books.
I read books the whole time on the plane.

朝から*ずっと頭がいたいです。
(Lit.) Ever since morning my head is painful.
I've had a headache since this morning.

今学期(こんがっき)はずっといそがしいです。
I've been busy all the time this semester.

1998年からずっとアメリカに住んでいます。
I've been living in the United States continuously since 1998.

> *NOUN から "since N"
> 昨日から，来週から，六月から, etc.

4 There is an interesting difference between Japanese and English here. While the past tense is used in Japanese それは[よかった]ですね, the use of the past tense, *that **was** good*, is strange in English here; you need to use the present tense, *that **is** good*. Conversely, the use of the non-past tense, それは[いい]ですね, sounds strange in Japanese. (See **15g** for this use of それ.)

新宿: This place name consists of 新 "new" as in 新しい and 新聞, and 宿 "inn／accommodation" as in 宿題. 新宿 was established in 1699 (Edo era) as the final outpost on the road from Nagano prefecture to Edo.

5, 6 ただいま (literally "right now") is used when one enters one's home, company, office, etc. The family members or colleagues respond by saying お帰りなさい (literally "come home (respectful)").

9 As the 漢字 suggests, 上がる literally means "move upward". Typically, Japanese houses have an entrance area called the げんかん, where you take off your shoes. All rooms beyond the げんかん are raised 1-2 steps. Therefore, to enter a Japanese house is to step up into the house. (After taking your shoes off, you should arrange them neatly so that they face the door with their heels against the steps.)

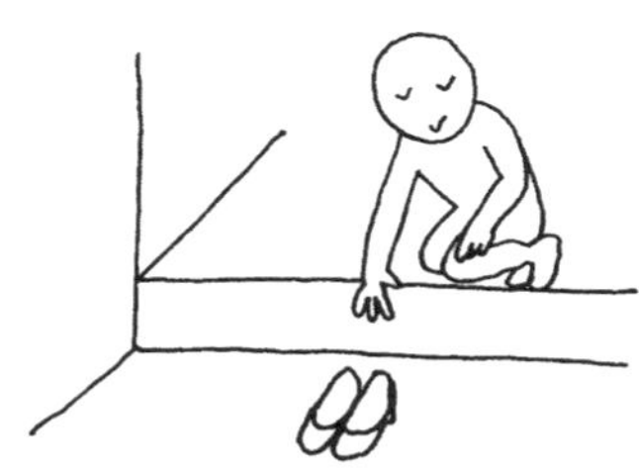

11 See **15e** for うっかり.

12 日本のしゅうかんをたくさん勉強して下さい literally means "Please study many Japanese customs".

文法 (ぶんぽう)

15a	**VERB1 Pre- ますフォーム + ながら VERB2**	**"X does V2 while doing V1"**
15b	**CLAUSE1 て CLAUSE2**	**"C1, and C2"**
15c	**CLAUSE1 てから CLAUSE2 = てフォーム + から CLAUSE2**	**"After C1, C2"**
15d	**VERB1 Negative フォーム + ないで VERB2**	**"X does V2 without doing V1"**
15e	**てフォーム + しまう**	**"finish VERB-ing"**
15f	**VERB1- たり VERB2- たりする**	**"do V1 and V2, among other things"**
15g	**Anaphoric それ**	

15a VERB1 Pre-ますフォーム + ながら VERB2　　"X does V2 while doing V1"

ます

「V1 (Pre- ますフォーム) + ながら + V2」means that the person (subject) does two actions (V1 and V2) simultaneously with an emphasis on V2 (V2 is the main verb). Both actions must be controllable and performed by the same person. That is, verbs denoting uncontrollable events — e.g. かかる, しぬ, わすれる — cannot be used in this construction. Furthermore, V1 must designate an action which lasts over a period of time during which V2 is performed; thus such punctual verbs as かぜをひく, 来る, つく cannot appear as V1.

(1) 音楽を聞きながらへやをそうじしました。
I cleaned the room while listening to music.

(2) いつも、うんてんしながらたんごを覚(おぼ)えます。
I always memorize vocabulary as I drive.

In English *while*-sentences, the emphasis can be on either V1 or V2, depending on the context. That is, the main action is not so specified in English. In the ながら construction, on the other hand, the emphasis is **always** on V2; V1 must denote an **accompanying**, rather than the main, action.

(3) 私はいつも、歌(うた)を歌(うた)いながらおふろに入ります。
I always take a bath while singing. / I always sing while taking a bath.
(*Sing* meant as the accompanying action.)

(4) コーヒーを飲みながら話しませんか。
(Lit.) Why don't we talk while drinking coffee?
Shall we talk over coffee?

(5) テレビを見ながら話したので、あまりよく覚えていません。
(Lit.) I talked while watching TV, so I don't remember (the conversation) well.
I was watching TV when we talked, so I don't remember (the conversation) well.

While all the English sentences in (6)-(7) would be acceptable, the Japanese b-sentences are strange. In (6), because writing a composition is clearly the main activity and looking into a dictionary secondary, (6a) is natural and easy to comprehend, but (6b), which treats looking into a dictionary as the main activity, is unnatural and it is difficult to envision. The same reasoning applies to (7a) and (7b).

(6a) ○　じしょをひきながら作文(さくぶん)を書きました。
　　 ○　*I wrote a composition while consulting a dictionary.*
(6b) ×　作文を書きながらじしょをひきました。
　　 ○　*I consulted a dictionary while writing a composition.*

(7a) ○　レシピを見ながらてんぷらを作りました。

○　*I made* tempura *while keeping an eye on (Lit. watching) the recipe.*

(7b) ×　てんぷらを作りながらレシピを見ました。

○　*I kept an eye on the recipe while making tempura.*

15b　CLAUSE1 て CLAUSE2　"C1, and C2"

て

Japanese lacks an invariant word corresponding to the English coordination* conjunction *and*. While nouns require と or や for coordination (e.g. 本と新聞, 英語や日本語), い -adjectives use ～くて, and な -adjectives + で (cf. 第七課, **7d**).

(1) カレーライスはおいしいです。
カレーライスは安いです。

→　カレーライスはおいしくて安いです。
Curry rice is delicious and inexpensive.

(2) 日本語のじゅぎょうはにぎやかです。
日本語のじゅぎょうはおもしろいです。

→　日本語のじゅぎょうはにぎやかでおもしろいです。
Japanese class is lively and enjoyable.

* Coordination: The clauses in coordination are independent of each other, so that each clause can form a sentence by itself. Although the final clause normally has slightly more weight than the other(s), coordinated clauses carry equal significance.

(Contrast with)

Subordination: A subordinate clause is dependent on the main clause, so that it cannot form a sentence by itself. Semantically, a subordinate clause supplies additional information to the main clause, e.g. *when I was a child, before the class begins, although she is smart, if you want to read it*, etc.

In fact, the て and で appearing in adjective phrases (e.g. おいしく[て], にぎやか[で]) are two instances of the connective particle て, which can coordinate all types of predicates: adjectives, nominals, verbs, or a combination thereof.

A　い -Adjectives

(3) さいきん、いそがしいです。
さいきん、映画を見に行けません。

→　さいきん、いそがしくて映画を見に行けません。
Recently, I've been busy and can't go to see movies.

B な -Adjectives

(4) 先週のテストはかんたんでした。
いいてんが取れました。

→ 先週のテストは かんたんで、いいてんが取れました。
Last week's test was easy, and I got a good grade.

C Nominal Predicates

(5) 山本さんは留学生です。山本さんは日本から来ました。

→ 山本さんは 留学生で、日本から来ました。
Yamamoto-san is a foreign student, and (he) came from Japan.

D Verbs

(6) リムジンで新宿まで行きました。それからタクシーにのりました。

→ リムジンで新宿まで行って、それからタクシーにのりました。
I/We went to Shinjuku by shuttle bus and then took a taxi.

And-Linkage て-Linkage

In both *and*-linked and て-linked clauses, the meaning relationships between the two clauses can be interpreted in various ways (temporal sequence, cause-effect, means-end, etc.) because *and* and て are very general (and vague) connectives that do not contradict most meaning relationships. As a rule, if two clauses suggest a certain relationship without *and*/て, that relationship persists through *and*/て coordination. For example, if you hear "Recently, I'm busy; I can't go to the movies," you normally interpret the utterance in such a way that the speaker cannot see movies recently because s/he has been busy. So, in (3) and (4), the first clause is naturally understood as the reason for the second clause. In (1), (2), and (5), on the other hand, such cause-effect relationships are logically inappropriate, whereas in (6), the natural interpretation is of temporal sequence. In short, *and* and て do not specify cause-effect or temporal relationships in these cases, but they do not prevent the listener from interpreting the utterance in such a way.

While subordination is restricted to combining two clauses, coordination can combine more than two. Like *and*, the て form coordinates, so it can conjoin more than two clauses.

き むら
木村さんは留学生です。木村さんは頭がいいです。木村さんはしんせつです。

→ 木村さんは留学生で、頭がよくて、しんせつです。
Kimura-san is a foreign student and smart and kind.

明日は、大学へ行きます。明日は、友達と昼ごはんを食べます。明日は、六時ごろ家へ帰ります。

→　明日は、大学へ行って、友達と昼ごはんを食べて、六時ごろ家へ帰ります。

Tomorrow, I'll go to college and eat lunch with a friend and go home around 6.

行って　　食べて

When C1 Denotes a Change

Many verbs denote a change of location (e.g. 行く, 来る, 帰る), a change of posture (e.g. たつ, すわる, 寝(ね)る "to lie down"), or a change of appearance (e.g. ふくをきる, ぬぐ, めがねをかける, ふとる). When such a verb appears in C1, the natural interpretation is not a mere temporal sequence, but, rather, that the resultant state of C1 continues during the period when C2 occurs.

ダウンタウンへ行って映画を見ます。

I'll go downtown and see a movie (there).

今日は、早く帰って寝ることにします。

Today, I'll go home early and go to bed (at home).

あそこにすわって* 話しませんか。

Why don't we sit over there and talk?

> * The location of すわる is marked with に, e.g. いすにすわる "sit in a chair".

私は目がわるいので、めがねをかけてうんてんします。

Because I have poor eyesight, I wear glasses and drive (= I wear glasses when I drive).

日本では、くつをぬいで家に上がります。

In Japan, people remove their shoes and (only then) enter (a house).

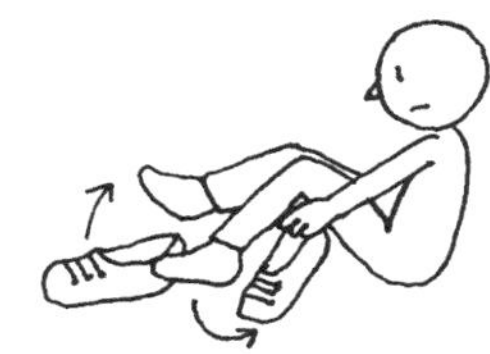

Different C1 & C2 Subjects

Note that て can link not only predicates (i.e., the subjects of the conjoined predicates are necessarily identical) but also clauses, where the subjects of the conjoined clauses may be different.

友達があそびに来て、(私は) 宿題ができませんでした。

A friend of mine visited me, and I couldn't do my homework.

コンピューターがこわれて、(私は) こまりました。

(My) computer broke down, and it was a real pain (for me).

この字(じ)はむずかしくて、(私は) 読めません。

This character is difficult, and I can't read it.

When C1 and C2 have different subjects, the interpretation frequently pertains to a cause / reason relationship.

15c　CLAUSE1 てから CLAUSE2　"After C1, C2"
= てフォーム + から CLAUSE2

The verb of C1 must be in the てフォーム. Because this construction is similar to 「C1-て C2」, the two clauses can also frequently be connected by only て, without から. The use of ～てから, however, expresses the event sequence more clearly. Do not confuse this から with the から indicating "because" (cf. 第五課, **5f**). The "because" から takes the polite or plain form, whereas the sequential から takes the てフォーム.

大学をそつぎょうしてから日本へ行ってみるつもりです。
After graduating from college, I plan to go to Japan (to see what it is like.)
家へ帰ってから宿題をしました。
After I got home, I did my homework.
きっさ店でお茶を飲んでから映画を見に行きませんか。
Would you like to go see a movie after having tea at a café?
電話してから来て下さい。
Please call and then come over. (= Please call before coming over.)

The subjects of C1 and C2 can be different.

春川さんが来てから、すずきさんが来ました。
Harukawa-san came, and then Suzuki-san came.
雨がやんでから、家へ帰りました。
I went home after the rain stopped.
しゅじんがでかけてから、母に電話しました。
I called my mother after my husband left home.

While ～て creates coordination, ～てから creates subordination. So, ～てから cannot be used more than once per sentence.

○　朝おきて、ごはんを食べて、家をでました。*
　　I got up in the morning, ate breakfast, and left home.
×　朝おきてから、ごはんを食べてから、家をでました。
×　*(Lit.) After getting up in the morning, after eating breakfast, I left home.*
○　朝おきて、ごはんを食べてから、家をでました。
　　I got up in the morning, and after eating breakfast, I left home.

* でる has two meanings: "to attend" and "to leave". When it is used as "to attend", に marks the event; when used as "to leave", を is needed.
じゅぎょうにでる　*attend class*
家をでる　*leave home*

○　朝おきてから、ごはんを食べて、それから家をでました。
After getting up in the morning, I ate breakfast and left home.

15d　VERB1 Negative フォーム + ないで VERB2 "X does V2 without doing V1"

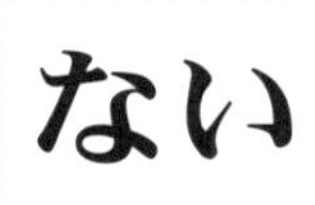

This construction implies that while V1 and V2 are normally performed together, in a particular case mentioned V1 does not accompany V2. V1 must be in the Negative フォーム, and like ～ながら, V1 and V2 must share the same subject.

(1) 昨日は、はをみがかないで寝ました。
Yesterday, I went to bed without brushing my teeth.

(2) アメリカでは、くつをぬがないで家に入ります。
In America, (people) enter a house without taking off their shoes.

(3) とけいをはずさないでおふろに入りました。
I took a bath without taking off my watch.

Note that unlike ～てフォーム and *and*-coordination, e.g. (4), ～ないで and *without* constructions create subordination and thus cannot appear more than once in a sentence, e.g. (5).

(4) ○　ブラウンさんは、テニスをして、シャワーをあびて、買い物に行きました。
○　*Brown-san played tennis, took a shower, and went shopping.*
○　ブラウンさんは、テニスをして、シャワーをあびないで、買い物に行きました。
○　*Brown-san played tennis, didn't take a shower, and went shopping.*

(5) ×　ブラウンさんは、テニスをしないで、シャワーをあびないで、買い物に行きました。
×　*Brown-san went shopping without taking a shower without playing tennis.*

15e　てフォーム + しまう　"finish VERB-ing"

て

The VERB てフォーム + しまう indicates that some activity or event has been completed. Because it emphasizes irreversibility or finality of the resultant state, this construction often implies a sense of regret.

お金を全部つかってしまいました。
I've spent all my money.

かぜをひいてしまいました。

I've caught a cold.

夏目さんは大学をやめてしまいました。

Natsume-san left college.

電車(でんしゃ)の中にかさをわすれてしまいました。

I forgot my umbrella on the train.

かぎをもたないで、家をでてしまいました。

(Lit.) (To my regret,) I left home without carrying the keys.

I left home without my keys.

電気(でんき)をけさないで、寝てしまいました。

I fell asleep without turning off the light.

勉強しなかったので、しけんにおちて*しまいました。

Because I didn't study, I failed the exam.

村山(むらやま)さんはおくさんとけんかして**しまいました。

Murayama-san had a quarrel with his wife.

* The event of おちる 'fail' must be marked with に.

** けんかする "to quarrel" requires と "with" to mark the other person.

*** X に Y をはる "put Y on X".

うっかり "carelessly/absentmindedly" frequently occurs with ～てしまう. うっかりわすれてしまう is sometimes abbreviated as うっかりする.

うっかり、ふうとうにきってをはらないで***、手紙を出してしまいました。

Carelessly, I sent out a letter without putting a stamp on the envelope.

すみません。{ うっかり、わすれてしまいました。/ うっかりしてしまいました。}

I'm sorry. Carelessly, I forgot about it (to my regret).

This construction can be used with verbs that denote uncontrollable events, for example:

いぬがしんでしまいました。

My dog died.

とけいがこわれてしまいました。

My watch broke.

毎日いそがしくて、つかれてしまいました。

I've been busy everyday and got tired.

The negative counterpart of ～てしまう, i.e. ～ないでしまう, is rarely used.

15f　VERB1-たり VERB2-たりする　"do V1 and V2, among other things"

「V1 (た Form) + り + V2 (た Form) + り + する」 means (i) the same person sometimes does V1 and sometimes does V2, among other activities, within a limited period of time, or (ii) in a given group of people, some do V1 and others do V2, among other activities. (This pattern parallels the partial listing construction for nouns 「X や Y など」 "X and Y, among other things".)

日曜日には、せんたくしたり、へやをそうじしたり、テレビを見たりします。

On Sundays I do the laundry, clean my room, watch TV, etc.

日本では、京都へ行ったり奈良(なら)へ行ったりしました。

In Japan I went to Kyoto, Nara, etc.

昨日は、本を読んだりひるねをしたりしました。

Yesterday I did things like reading books and taking a nap.

こども達(たち)はテレビを見たりそとであそんだりしています。

Some children are watching TV, and others are playing outside.

私が東京大学へ行った時、学生は図書館で勉強したりジムでスポーツをしたりしていました。

When I visited the University of Tokyo, some students were studying in the library, and others were playing sports at the gym.

昨日のこうぎで本を読んだり話をしたりしている人はいましたが、寝ている人はいませんでした。

During the lecture yesterday, although some were reading books and others chatting, no one was sleeping.

The second V- たり can be left out when its implication is obvious.

日曜日にはせんたくしたりします。

I do the laundry (among other things) on Sundays.

～たり～たりする can also be used to describe repetitive changes of situation.

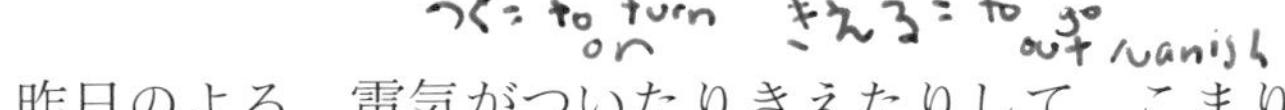

昨日のよる、電気がついたりきえたりして、こまりました。

I was bothered by the light going on and off last night.

今朝から雨がふったりやんだりしています。

It's been raining on and off since this morning.

15g Anaphoric それ

Up until now, we have used それ to refer to a thing located close to the addressee, contrasting against これ and あれ. In the following conversation, the それ in いさおさん's speech does not refer to any tangible object, but rather to what is expressed in the preceding utterance by ミラーさん.

ミラー：いいえ、（飛行機は）あまりゆれませんでした。それで、ずっと音楽を聞きながら本を読んでいました。
No, there wasn't much turbulence. So I just read books while listening to music the whole way.

いさお：それはよかったですね。
That's good.

This use of それ is called *anaphoric* (which means "referring back to or standing for preceding words"). The anaphoric use of それ is very close to the anaphoric use of "that" in English.

第十三課

ミラー：私は冬休みに、日本へホームステイに行くんです。
I'm going to Japan for a homestay during winter break.

山本：へえ、日本へ行くんですか。それはいいですね。
Oh, you're going to Japan? That's great.

第十四課

ソン：チョコレートはくうこうで買えますよ。
You can buy the chocolates at the airport.

ミラー：それは楽ですね。
That'll be easy, then.

A: 今学期は、中間しけんが四つあります。
This semester, I have four midterm exams.

B: それは大変ですね。
That's tough.

れんしゅうもんだい
練習問題

I.　ビンゴゲームです。クラスメートに聞きましょう。

れい
例　Q:　X さんは歌を歌いながらシャワーをあびますか。

A:　はい、歌を歌いながらシャワーをあびます。

(or) いいえ、歌を歌いながらシャワーはあびません。

例	1.	2.
＿＿＿＿＿＿さん	＿＿＿＿＿＿さん	＿＿＿＿＿＿さん
3.	4.	5.
＿＿＿＿＿＿さん	＿＿＿＿＿＿さん	＿＿＿＿＿＿さん
6.	7.	8.
＿＿＿＿＿＿さん	＿＿＿＿＿＿さん	＿＿＿＿＿＿さん

　　え
II.　絵を見て文を作りましょう。「～て」をつかって下さい。

例

テープを聞いて学校へ行きます。

1.

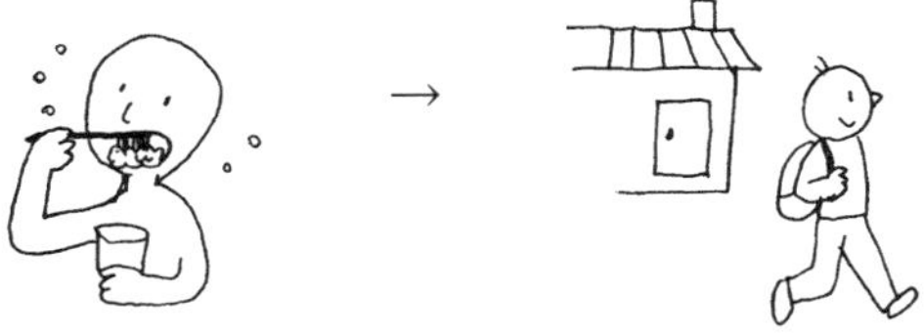

＿＿＿＿＿＿＿＿＿＿＿＿＿＿＿＿

＿＿＿＿＿＿＿＿＿＿＿＿＿＿＿＿。

2.

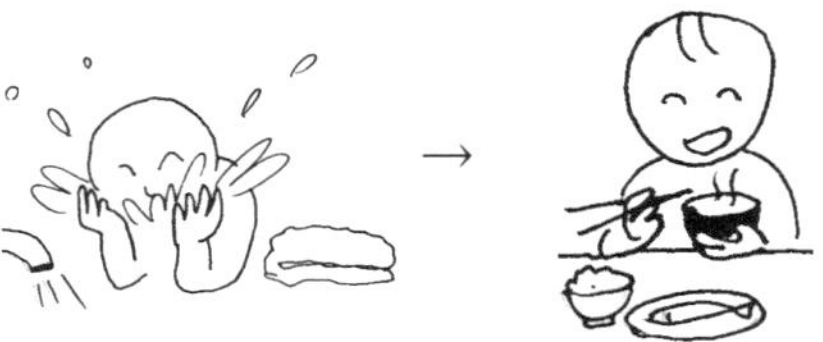

＿＿＿＿＿＿＿＿＿＿＿＿＿＿＿＿＿＿＿＿

＿＿＿＿＿＿＿＿＿＿＿＿＿＿＿＿＿＿＿＿。

3.

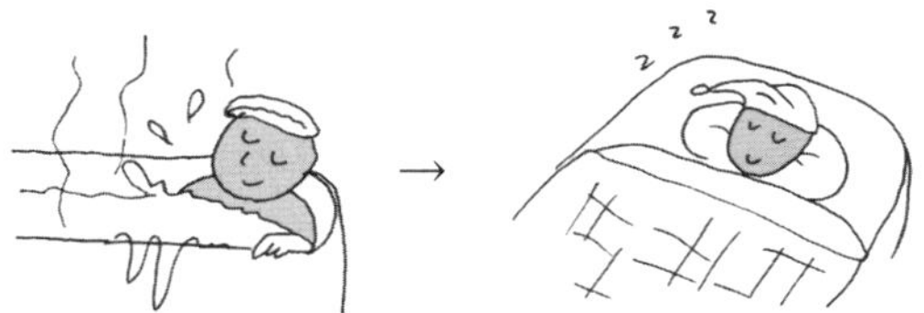

＿＿＿＿＿＿＿＿＿＿＿＿＿＿＿＿＿＿＿＿

＿＿＿＿＿＿＿＿＿＿＿＿＿＿＿＿＿＿＿＿。

4.

＿＿＿＿＿＿＿＿＿＿＿＿＿＿＿＿＿＿＿＿

＿＿＿＿＿＿＿＿＿＿＿＿＿＿＿＿＿＿＿＿。

5.

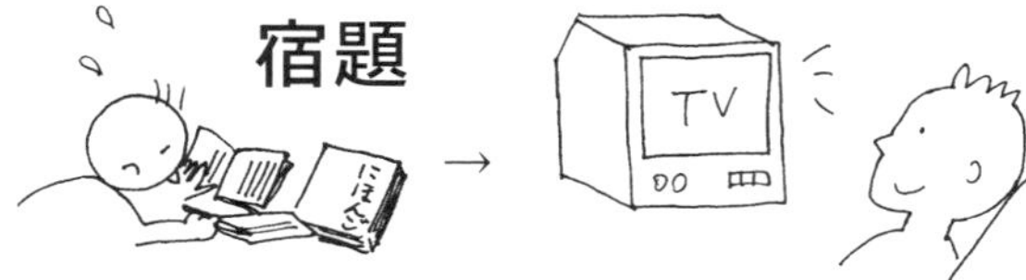

＿＿＿＿＿＿＿＿＿＿＿＿＿＿＿＿＿＿＿＿

＿＿＿＿＿＿＿＿＿＿＿＿＿＿＿＿＿＿＿＿。

III.　絵を見て文を作りましょう。「〜て」をつかって下さい。

例（れい）

朝おきて、はをみがいて、かおをあらいました＿＿＿＿＿＿＿＿＿＿。

1.

＿＿＿＿＿＿＿＿＿＿＿＿＿＿＿＿＿＿＿＿＿＿＿＿＿＿＿＿＿＿＿＿。

2.

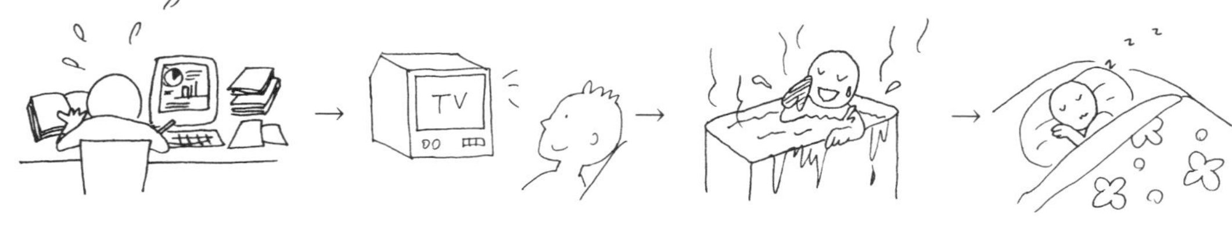

＿＿＿＿＿＿＿＿＿＿＿＿＿＿＿＿＿＿＿＿＿＿＿＿＿＿＿＿＿＿＿＿。

IV.　パートナーは何をさきにしますか。聞きましょう。Circle the appropriate arrow.

例　A:　Bさんはシャワーをあびてから朝ごはんを食べますか。

　　B:　はい、シャワーをあびてから朝ごはんを食べます。

　　　　(or) いいえ、朝ごはんを食べてからシャワーをあびます。

V.　パートナーに聞きましょう。「〜てから」をつかって下さい。

Sheet A

1.　これはスミスさんのスケジュールです。パートナーはスミスさんのスケジュールを知りません。絵を見てパートナーのしつもんにこたえて下さい。

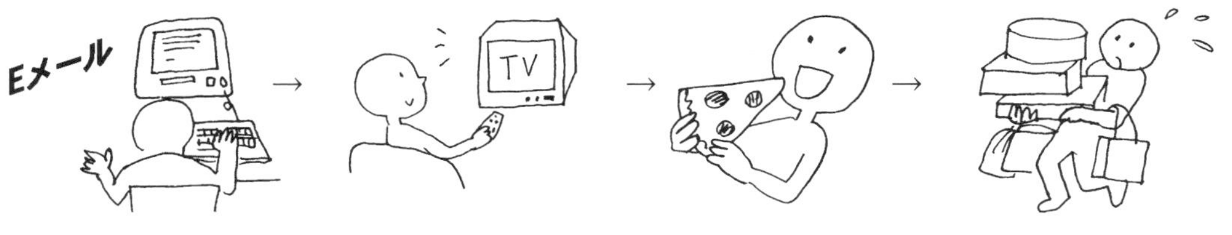

2.　パートナーは木村さんのスケジュールを知っています。パートナーにインタビューして木村さんのスケジュールのじゅんばんを書いて下さい。

　　Q:　木村さんは勉強してから何をしますか。

(1)　　(　)　　(　)　　(　)

Sheet B

1. パートナーはスミスさんのスケジュールを知っています。パートナーにインタビューしてスミスさんのスケジュールのじゅんばんを書いて下さい。

   Q:　スミスさんはEメールをチェックしてから何をしますか。

(1)　(　　)　(　　)　(　　)

2. これは木村さんのスケジュールです。パートナーは木村さんのスケジュールを知りません。絵を見てパートナーのしつもんにこたえて下さい。

VI. 「～て」か*「～てから」をつかって、しつもんにこたえて下さい。

> * か here means "or". か can be used to conjoin only nouns.

1. 昨日、家へ帰ってから何をしましたか。

   ____

2. 今朝、何をしてから大学へ来ましたか。

   ____

3. 何をしてから寝ますか。

   ____

VII. 絵を見て文を作りましょう。「～ないで」をつかって下さい。

例(れい)

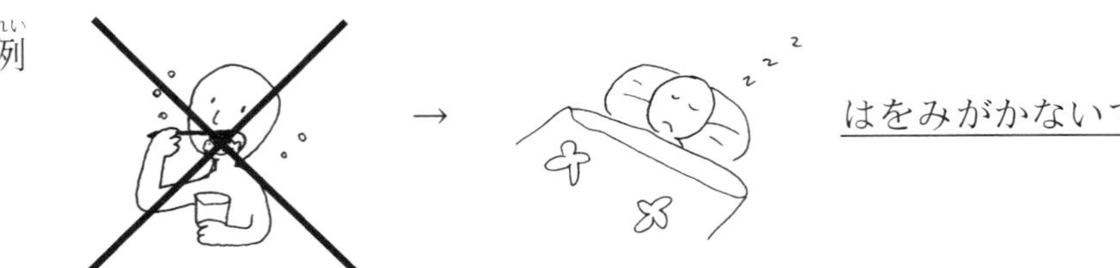

はをみがかないで寝ました。

1. →

2. →

3. →

4. →

5. →

6. →

7. →

友達の家

VIII. 絵を見て話しましょう。「〜てしまう」をつかって下さい。

例　A:　もう、宿題をしましたか。

　　B:　はい、もうしてしまいました。

1.　昨日

A:　もう、漢字をれんしゅうしましたか。

B:　はい、＿＿＿＿＿＿＿＿＿＿＿＿＿＿＿。

2.　A:　もう、たんごを覚えましたか。

　　B:　はい、＿＿＿＿＿＿＿＿＿＿＿＿＿＿＿。

3.

A:　もう、全部食べましたか。

B:　はい、＿＿＿＿＿＿＿＿＿＿＿＿＿＿＿。

4.　A:　ミルクを全部飲みましたか。

　　B:　はい、＿＿＿＿＿＿＿＿＿＿＿＿＿＿＿。

IX. ブラウンさんは何をしますか。AとBの絵を見て、1と2のしつもんにこたえて下さい。3と4には、あなたのこたえを書いて下さい。「〜たり〜たりする」をつかって下さい。

1. ブラウンさんは週末、何をしますか。

____。

2. ブラウンさんはこうえんで何をしますか。

____。

3. あなたは週末、何をしますか。

____。

4. あなたはこうえんで何をしますか。

____。

X. 絵を見て話しましょう。「〜てしまう」をつかって下さい。

例　A:　どうしたんですか。

　　B:　おさけをたくさん飲んでしまいました。

1. A:　どうしたんですか。

　　B:　______________________________。

2. A:　どうしたんですか。

　　B:　______________________________。

3. A:　どうしたんですか。

　　B:　______________________________。

4. A:　どうしたんですか。

　　B:　______________________________。

XI. 「〜たり、〜たりする」をつかってこたえましょう。

例　Q:　あなたは家へ帰ってから何をしますか。

　　A:　私は家へ帰ってからテレビを見たり、宿題をしたりします。

1. あなたは冬休みに何をしましたか。

____。

2.　学生は図書館で何をしますか。

______________________________。

3.　コンピューターで何をすることができますか。

______________________________。

4.　日本へ行った時に何をしてみたいですか。

______________________________。

XII.　読みましょう。

私は冬休みにりょうしんといっしょに日本へ行きました。東京では、品川(しながわ)のりょかんにとまりました。さいしょの日(ひ)はりょかんで休みました。そして、つぎの日に銀座(ぎんざ)へ行ってかぶきを見ました。それから、日本料理のレストランでおすしを食べました。レストランはとてもにぎやかでした。

日本はとても寒かったです。私はコートをもたないで日本へ行ってしまったので、大変でした。それで、三日目(みっかめ)に新宿へ行ってコートとスカーフを買いました。

四日目(よっかめ)に、りょうしんは上野(うえの)のびじゅつ館(かん)へ行きました。私は東京に留学している友達に会って、いっしょにひるごはんを食べました。ひるごはんを食べながらいろいろな話をしました。とても楽しかったです。

私達は京都にも行きました。京都はとてもきれいでした。おてらやじんじゃをたくさん見ました。あるきながらしゃしんをたくさんとりました。奈良(なら)へも行きたかったですが、時間がなかったので、行けませんでした。こんど日本へ行った時には奈良へ行って、有名なだいぶつが見たいです。

りょこうはとても楽しかったです。

一日目(いちにちめ)	*first day*
二日目(ふつかめ)	*second day*
三日目(みっかめ)	*third day*
四日目(よっかめ)	*fourth day*
五日目(いつかめ)	*fifth day*
六日目(むいかめ)	*sixth day*
七日目(なのかめ)	*seventh day*
八日目(ようかめ)	*eighth day*
九日目(ここのかめ)	*ninth day*
十日目(とおかめ)	*tenth day*
十一日目(じゅういちにちめ)	*eleventh day*
十二日目(じゅうににちめ)	*twelfth day*

しつもんにこたえて下さい。

1.　この人はいつ日本へ行きましたか。
2.　この人はだれと日本へ行きましたか。
3.　この人は新宿で何を買いましたか。どうしてですか。
4.　この人は友達と何をしましたか。
5.　この人は京都で何をしましたか。
6.　この人は奈良(なら)でだいぶつを見ましたか。

新しい漢字

歌（うた）	歌（うた）う	絵（え）	映画（えいが）	覚（おぼ）える	木村（きむら）
今学期（こんがっき）	電気（でんき）	電車（でんしゃ）	電話（でんわ）	習（なら）う	寝（ね）る
始（はじ）める	飛行機（ひこうき）	村山（むらやま）			

新しい使（つか）い方

上（あ）がる	会話（かいわ）	きっさ店（てん）	こども達（たち）	作文（さくぶん）	字（じ）
新宿（しんじゅく）	入（はい）る	春川（はるかわ）	日（ひ）	びじゅつ館（かん）	三日目（みっかめ）

Radicals: 木（き）へん・ノ木（ぎ）へん

木 in 木曜日 means "tree, wood". Its 音（おん）読み is モク; its 訓（くん）読み is き. 木 can also appear as a へん radical and is called きへん, e.g. in 校, 村. 木（き）へん漢字 generally designate the notions of wood, tree, building, etc.

The radical 禾 in 私 and 秋 is called ノ木（ぎ）へん (カタカナ「ノ」＋木（き）へん; き → ぎ by sequential voicing, cf. 第十一課, **11f**). Unlike 木（き）へん, ノ木（ぎ）へん does not indicate clear semantics for the 漢字.

上 ジョウ・うえ・あ(がる)	丨　ト　上
	top, up: 上手 *good at*
歌 うた・うた(う)	一 … 哥　哥　歌　歌
	to sing, a song
絵 え	𠃋 … 糸 … 絵　絵
	picture

映	エイ	*reflection, projection:* 映画 *movie*
画	ガ	*picture:* 映画 *movie*
覚	おぼ(える)	*to memorize, to remember*
会	カイ・あ(う)	*to meet:* 会話 *conversation (meeting and talking)*
話	ワ・はなし・はな(す)	*to talk, to speak:* 会話 *conversation,* 電話 *telephone (electric conversation)*
店	テン・みせ	*shop:* 店員 *store clerk,* きっさ店 *café*
木	モク・き	*wood:* 木曜日 *Thursday (the day of wood),* 木村 *Kimura*
村	むら	*village:* 木村 *Kimura*
達	たち・だち	*plural marker:* 私達 *we,* 友達 *friend(s),* こども達 *children;* (達 generally makes the noun plural, but 友達 can be used as a singular noun, e.g. 友達が一人あそびに来ました.)

期	キ	*term, season:* 学期 *academic term*
作	サク・つく（る）	*to make:* 作文 *composition*
宿	シュク・ジュク	*inn:* 宿題 *homework,* 新宿 *Shinjuku*
電	デン	*lightning, electricity:* 電気 *electricity,* 電車 *electric train,* 電話 *telephone (electric conversation)*
車	シャ・くるま	*car:* 電車 *electric train*
習	なら（う）	*to learn*
寝	ね（る）	*to go to bed, to lie down*
始	はじ（める）	*to begin*

飛 ヒ							飛	飛	飛	
	to fly: 飛行機 *airplane (flying machine)*									
機 キ	一	十	才	木						
				機	機	機				
	machine: 飛行機 *airplane (flying machine)*									

漢字の復習(ふくしゅう)

I. 読みましょう。

1. 今日から春学期です。
2. 先週、木村さんと電話で話しました。
3. この中国の映画はとても有名です。
4. 姉は絵をかくのが上手です。
5. 小学校の時に手紙の書き方を習いました。

II. つぎのたんごを読んで下さい。それから (1) から (10) の ＿＿＿＿＿＿ にたんごを書いて下さい。Change the verb form if necessary.

上がる	覚える	習う	始める	働く
休む	教える	住む	作る	入る

1. 私は毎日六時間 ＿＿＿＿＿＿ います。でも、私の仕事はかんたんです。
2. 山本さんのお父さんは東京に ＿＿＿＿＿＿ います。
3. 私はいつも車をうんてんしながらたんごを ＿＿＿＿＿＿ ます。
4. 来週、姉があそびに来ます。クラスを ＿＿＿＿＿＿ たいので、先生に手紙を書きました。
5. おふろに ＿＿＿＿＿＿ 寝たので、よくねむれました。
6. ミラーさんはくつをぬがないで家に ＿＿＿＿＿＿ ました。
7. 小学校の時に、ピアノを ＿＿＿＿＿＿ ました。でも、れんしゅうしなかったので、わすれてしまいました。今はピアノはひけません。
8. 私はアメリカ人です。日本人の友達にアメリカのしゅうかんを ＿＿＿＿＿＿ ました。
9. 私達は七時にパーティーを ＿＿＿＿＿＿ ました。
10. ルームメートのたんじょう日なので、ケーキを ＿＿＿＿＿＿ ました。

新しい語彙(ごい)

アイスクリーム	*ice cream*
上(あ)がる ㋒ ⓘ	*to step up*
一日目(いちにちめ)	*first day*
五日目(いつかめ)	*fifth day*
うっかり	*carelessly*
うっかりする Ⓘ ⓘ	*to forget to do something carelessly*
(しけんに) おちる ㋸ ⓘ	*to fail (an exam)*
か	*or*
会話(かいわ)	*conversation*
かお	*face*
かぎ	*key*
かぶき	kabuki
から	*since*
きっさ店(てん)	*café, coffee shop*
きって	*postal stamp*
けんか(する)	*quarrel*
げんかん	*entrance*
こうぎ(する)	*lecture*
コート	*coat*
九日目(ここのかめ)	*ninth day*
こたえる ㋸ ⓘ	*to answer*
こども達(たち)	*children*
こまる ㋒ ⓘ	*to get in trouble*

こわれる ㋸ ⓘ	*to break (intransitive)*
今学期(こんがっき)	*this semester*
さいしょ	*first*
さきに	*ahead, before*
作文(さくぶん)	*composition, writing*
字(じ)	*letter, character*
じゅんばん	*order*
スカーフ	*scarf*
ずっと	*continuously, all the time*
(お)せわになる ㋒ ⓘ	*to be cared for*
だいぶつ	*great statue of Buddha*
ちかてつ	*subway*
つぎ	*next*
つく ㋒ ⓘ	*to arrive*
でかける ㋸ ⓘ	*to go out*
でる ㋸ ⓣ	*to leave*
X てん	*X point(s)*
十日目(とおかめ)	*tenth day*
とうちゃく(する)	*arrival*
七日目(なのかめ)	*seventh day*
は	*tooth*
(おふろに) 入(はい)る ㋒ ⓘ	*to take (a bath)*
はずす ㋒ ⓣ	*to take off (accessories)*

ひ	*day*
(じしょを)ひく (ウ)(t)	*to look up*
びじゅつ館(かん)	*art museum*
ふうとう	*envelope*
二日目(ふつかめ)	*second day*
みがく (ウ)(t)	*to brush, polish*
三日目(みっかめ)	*third day*
ミルク	*milk*
六日目(むいかめ)	*sixth day*

やむ (ウ)(i)	*to stop (raining)*
ゆれる (ル)(i)	*to jolt*
八日目(ようかめ)	*eighth day*
四日目(よっかめ)	*fourth day*
よる	*night*
リムジン	*airport shuttle bus*
りょかん	*Japanese-style inn*
レシピ	*recipe*
わすれる (ル)(t)	*to forget*

名前

うえの(上野)	*Ueno*
ぎんざ(銀座)	*Ginza*
しながわ(品川)	*Shinagawa*

新宿(しんじゅく)	*Shinjuku*
春川(はるかわ)	*Harukawa*
村山(むらやま)	*Murayama*

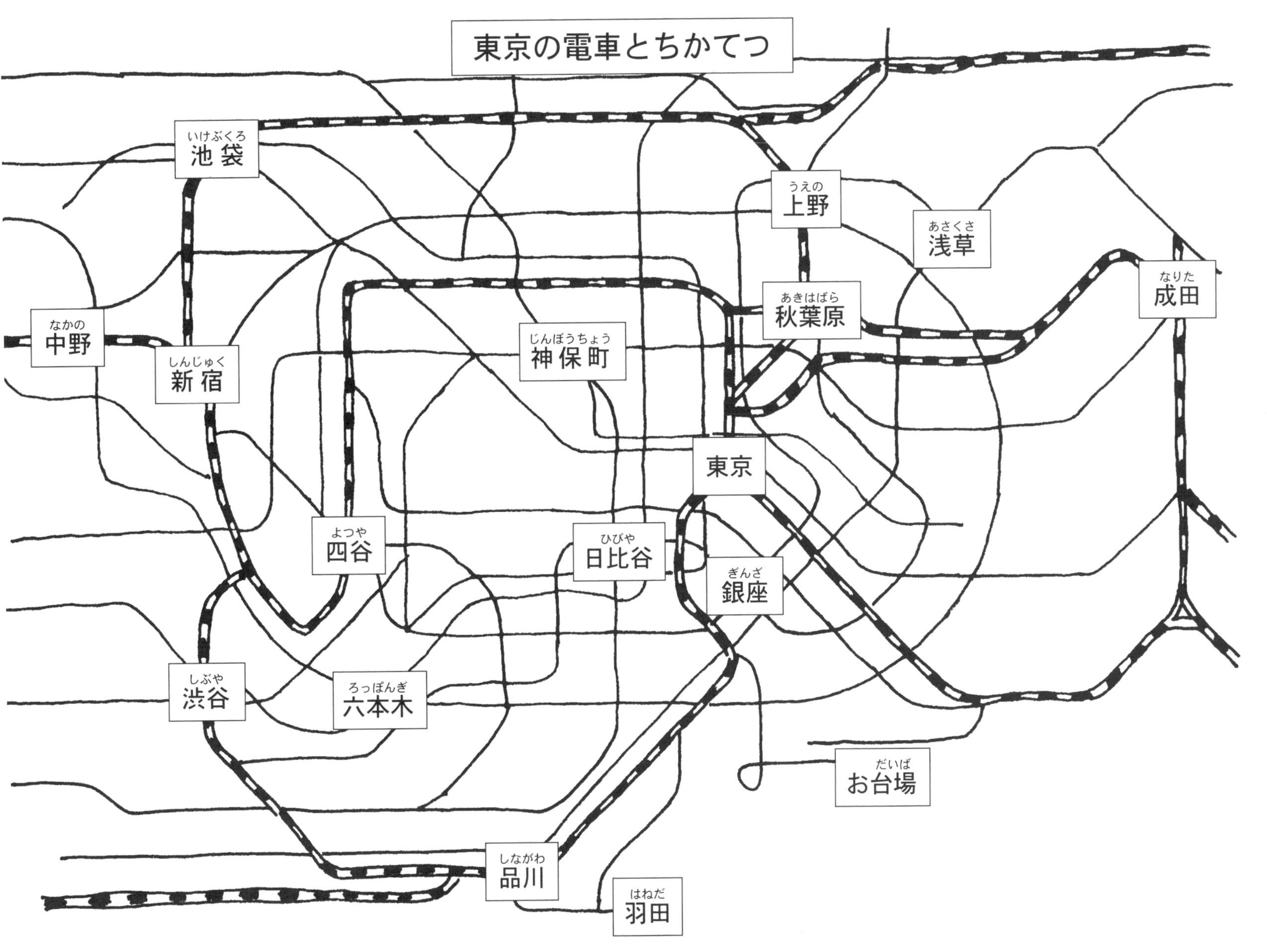
東京の電車とちかてつ
いけぶくろ 池袋
うえの 上野
あさくさ 浅草
なりた 成田
なかの 中野
しんじゅく 新宿
じんぼうちょう 神保町
あきはばら 秋葉原
東京
よつや 四谷
ひびや 日比谷
ぎんざ 銀座
しぶや 渋谷
ろっぽんぎ 六本木
だいば お台場
しながわ 品川
はねだ 羽田

一年生の漢字 by Stroke Count

In the following table, the 漢字 in dark black have been learned in Lessons 3-15.

①	一	②	二	七	八	九	十	人	入	③	三	千	土	上	小
山	下	川	大	女	々	子	口	夕	④	五	六	日	月	火	水
分	木	今	中	父	円	手	方	文	元	少	午	友	化	予	切
犬	心	天	内	介	不	反	⑤	四	本	半	生	石	広	古	目
兄	母	去	冬	仕	外	末	出	白	左	右	写	田	用	正	冊
⑥	百	行	先	会	安	早	好	年	多	字	気	名	米	全	休
毎	有	色	忙	自	当	両	耳	同	回	考	地	伝	肉	死	成
次	⑦	何	来	私	見	車	弟	男	作	住	図	花	利	返	村
言	赤	近	足	医	社	困	冷	初	対	⑧	金	明	学	英	長
姉	妹	東	京	国	知	物	店	事	雨	取	画	始	受	供	使
夜	青	歩	卒	法	味	所	者	門	枚	招	注	泣	泳	⑨	昨
食	茶	待	後	音	背	前	便	秋	春	室	変	映	飛	洗	屋
度	急	単	乗	思	科	専	相	故	計	送	持	昼	客	⑩	時
家	留	高	帰	校	書	紙	院	員	料	夏	勉	酒	病	降	真
眠	旅	配	借	個	案	弱	笑	⑪	閉	部	理	都	週	教	宿
強	習	雪	終	授	転	動	問	符	魚	紹	悪	族	婚	⑫	買
晩	間	飲	番	開	朝	寒	達	絵	覚	期	葉	晴	復	運	貯
答	痛	着	暑	最	短	貸	遊	然	落	結	⑬	新	暗	話	漢
楽	働	電	寝	試	業	意	遠	辞	鉄	数	⑭	語	読	銀	聞
静	歌	練	駅	説	様	⑮	質	熱	調	談	⑯	館	頭	機	親
薬	⑰	濯	績	⑱	曜	題	験	顔	難	⑲	願				

第十六課 LESSON 16

東京見物(けんぶつ)
Sightseeing in Tokyo

晩ごはんまでに帰らなくてもいいですか
Is it okay if I don't get back in time for dinner?

1
あのう、シャツを洗わなくてはいけないんですが、洗濯機を使ってもいいですか。
ええ、もちろん。いつでも使って下さい。家の洗濯機は使いやすいですよ。
2
ミラーさん、今日は何をするんですか。
今日はまず、浅草でおてらを見て、お台場でひるごはんを食べて、それから銀座へ行くつもりです。
3
へえ、ミラーさんは、いろいろなところを知っていますね。
4
じつは、インターネットでしらべたんです。東京で外国人に一番人気があるところは浅草でした。
Asakusa
5
そうですか。たしかに、浅草にはおもしろい店がたくさんあって、とても楽しいですよ。
6
あのう、今日、晩ごはんまでに帰らなくてもいいですか。夜、日本に留学している友達といっしょに六本木へ行きたいんです。
7
もちろんいいですよ。夜の六本木には、わかい人がたくさんいて、とてもにぎやかですよ。
へえ、そうですか。
8
ところで、もんげんは何時ですか。
やあ、もんげんですか。ミラーさんはむずかしい言葉を知っていますね。もんげんはありませんよ。

会話

1　ミラー　：あのう、シャツを洗わなくてはいけないんですが、洗濯機を使ってもいいですか。

Excuse me, I need to wash my shirts; may I use the washing machine?

ゆりこ　：ええ、もちろん。いつでも使って下さい。家の洗濯機は使いやすいですよ。

Yes, of course. Please use it any time you like. Our washing machine is easy to use.

2　いさお　：ミラーさん、今日は何をするんですか。

What are you going to do, Miller-san?

ミラー　：今日はまず、浅草でおてらを見て、お台場でひるごはんを食べて、それから銀座へ行くつもりです。

Today, I plan to see the temple in Asakusa first, eat lunch in Odaiba, and then go to Ginza.

3　ゆりこ　：へえ、ミラーさんは、いろいろなところを知っていますね。

Gee, you know a lot of places, don't you.

4　ミラー　：じつは、インターネットでしらべたんです。東京で外国人に一番人気があるところは浅草でした。

To tell the truth, I checked things out on the Internet. The most popular place in Tokyo among foreigners was Asakusa.

5　いさお　：そうですか。たしかに、浅草にはおもしろい店がたくさんあって、とても楽しいですよ。

Is that so? Definitely, there are many interesting shops in Asakusa, so it's very enjoyable.

6　ミラー　：あのう、今日、晩ごはんまでに帰らなくてもいいですか。夜、日本に留学している友達といっしょに六本木へ行きたいんです。

Uh... would it be okay if I didn't get back in time for dinner? I want to go to Roppongi tonight with a friend who's in Japan as a foreign student.

7　ゆりこ　：もちろんいいですよ。夜の六本木には、わかい人がたくさんいて、とてもにぎやかですよ。

Yes, of course, that's fine. Roppongi at night is full of young people, so it's very exciting.

ミラー　：へえ、そうですか。

Oh, is that so?

8　ミラー　：ところで、もんげんは何時ですか。

By the way, what time is the curfew?

いさお　：やあ、もんげんですか。ミラーさんはむずかしい言葉を知っていますね。もんげんはありませんよ。

Whoa ... curfew? You know some pretty sophisticated vocabulary, don't you. There's no curfew.

9　ミラー　：あ、そうですか。分かりました。じゃあ、行ってきます。

Oh really? Okay. I'll be on my way then.

いさお・ゆりこ：行ってらっしゃい。気をつけて。

Bye! Take care.

使い方

Title As the 漢字 suggest, 見物 literally means "see things"; it is the standard term for "sightseeing".

1 As explained in 第一課, **1g**, the vowels [i, u] are normally devoiced when they occur between voiceless consonants (i.e. [p, t, k, s, sh, h]). So, the [u] in せんた[く]き becomes devoiced and the preceding consonant [k] is not even released, resulting in [sentakki] せんたっき.

いつ "when", いつも "always", いつでも "anytime/always/whenever"

If something belongs to the house/family, 家の is more natural than 私達の, e.g. 家の車, 家のコンピューター, 家の電話. If a computer, telephone, etc. are exclusively for your use, then use 私の, e.g. 私のけいたい (電話) "my cellular phone".

2 The adverb まず means "first (of all)".

例 (レストランで)

A: 何にしますか。

What are you going to have?

B: のどがかわいていますから、まず、ビールが一ぱい飲みたいです。

I'm thirsty (my throat has gotten dry), so first I'd like to drink a glass of beer.

例

先生: まず、きょうかしょのせつめいをよく読んで下さい。それから宿題をして下さい。

First, please read the explanations in the textbook carefully. Then, do the assignment.

浅草 is the oldest temple town and one of many commercial and entertainment districts in 東京. お台場 is a newly developed seaside recreational resort. 銀座 is the most expensive shopping district in Japan; its name comes from the silver mint which was built there during the Edo period.

4 X は Y に人気がある means "X is popular among Y".

例 このハンドバッグはわかい人に人気があります。

This handbag is popular among young people.

6 Having numerous embassies in its vicinity, 六本木 (Lit. "six trees") is the most international town in 東京. Clubs and bars are packed until the first morning train.

9 行ってきます is a salutation when you leave your territory (home, office, etc.). It consists of 行く and 来る, meaning "going and coming back".

行ってらっしゃい is a casual version of 行っていらっしゃい, which is an expression used to respond to 行ってきます. 気をつける means "be careful / take care":

例 (when making an error)

すみません。これからは気をつけます。

I'm sorry, I'll be more careful in the future (from now on).

気をつけて is an adverbial expression, meaning "cautiously".

例

先生: この漢字はむずかしいですから、気をつけて書いて下さい。

Because this kanji is difficult, please write it carefully.

文法

（ぶんぽう）

16a	**てフォーム + もいいですか**	**"May X do ~?; Is it okay to do ~?"**
	てフォーム + もいい	**"X may do ~; It's okay to do ~"**
	てフォーム + はいけない	**"X may not do ~; It's not okay to do ~"**
16b	**Negative フォーム + なくてはいけない**	**"X must do ~"**
16c	**Negative フォーム + なくてもいい**	**"X need not do ~"**
16d	**Pre- ますフォーム + やすい**	**"easy to do ~"**
	Pre- ますフォーム + にくい	**"difficult / uncomfortable to do ~"**
16e	**X までに**	**"by X (time)"**

16a てフォーム + もいいですか "May X do ~?; Is it okay to do ~?"
てフォーム + もいい "X may do ~; It's okay to do ~"
てフォーム + はいけない "X may not do ~; It's not okay to do ~"

This construction consists of:

VERB てフォーム	+	も	+	いい	+	です	+	か
		also		*good / okay*		*is*		*?*

Literally, therefore, it means "Is it also okay to do ~?' (there are many things you are allowed to do) and can be used to ask for permission, "May I do ~?" ("Can I do ~" is frequently heard in American English.) To answer such a question, you can say ～てもいいです "It's also okay to do ~" or ～てはいけません "It's not okay to do ~". But these expressions sound highly authoritative in many situations, so people normally use ～て下さい, rather than ～てもいいです, and ～ないで下さい, rather than ～てはいけません. Note that ～て下さい and ～ないで下さい here are used for granting or denying permission, rather than making a request.

どうぞ食べて下さい。　*Please eat it.* (Request)

- vs. -

もっと食べてもいいですか。　*May I eat more?*

ええ、どうぞ食べて下さい。　*Yes, please do.* (Granting permission)

= *Yes, you're welcome to eat more.*

この本を読まないで下さい。　*Please don't read this book.* (Request)

- vs. -

この本を読んでもいいですか。　*May I read this book?*

いいえ、読まないで下さい。　*No, please don't.* (Denying permission)

The particle よ frequently accompanies 〜てもいいです to soften the authoritative tone.

洗濯機を使ってもいいですか。
May I use the washing machine?

Softer ↓

はい、使ってもいいです。	いいえ、使ってはいけません。
Yes, you may.	*No, you may not use it.*
はい、使ってもいいですよ。	いいえ、使わないで下さい。
Yes, go right ahead.	*No, please don't use it.*
はい、どうぞ使って下さい。	いいえ、使わないで下さいませんか。
Yes, please go right ahead.	*(Lit.) No, would you please not use it?*
	Actually, if you could, please don't use it.

If you have authority to grant permission, the use of 〜てもいいです or 〜てはいけません would be appropriate.

店員: すみません。ようじがあるので、早く帰ってもいいですか。
(Lit.) I'm sorry. Because I have an engagement, may I go home early?
I'm sorry, but may I go home early? I have an engagement.

マネージャー: 今日はひまですから、早く帰ってもいいですよ。
Because business is slow (not busy) today, you may go home early.

いいです, だいじょうぶです "It's okay" and, to a lesser extent, だめです "It's no good" are also used to answer 〜てもいいですか questions.

あのう、今晩電話してもいいですか。 — *Uh… Can I call you this evening?*
ええ、いいですよ。 — *Sure, you can.*

すみません、電話を使ってもいいですか。 — *Excuse me. Can I use the telephone?*
はい、どうぞ。 — *Sure, go right ahead.*
外国(がいこく)へ電話してもいいですか。 — *Would it be okay to call overseas?*
外国ですか。外国はちょっと……。 — *Overseas? Well, that would be a little …*

びじゅつ館でスケッチしてもいいですか。 — *May I sketch in the museum?*
はい、だいじょうぶです。 — *Yes, that's okay.*

びじゅつ館でしゃしんをとってもいいですか。 — *Can I take pictures in the museum?*
いいえ、だめです。 — *No, you cannot.*

びじゅつ館で絵にさわっても* いいですか。

May I touch the pictures in the museum?

いいえ、ぜったいにだめです。

No, absolutely not.

パーティーに弟をつれて来ても** いいですか。

Would it be alright to bring my (younger) brother to the party?

はい、どうぞつれて来て下さい。

Sure, feel free to bring him.

お手洗(てあら)いでタバコをすってもいいですか。

May I smoke (Lit. inhale a cigarette) in the restroom?

いいえ、だめです。外(そと)ですって下さい。

No, you may not. Please smoke outside.

お酒(さけ)を少し飲んでうんてんしてもいいですか。

Can I drive while / after drinking a little sake?

ええっ。もちろんだめですよ。

What? Of course not!

* さわる "to touch"
X が Y にさわる
X touches Y.

** つれて来る "to bring"
つれる "take" + 来る "come"
X が Y を Z につれて来る
X brings Y to Z.

Y = person(s), animal(s)

16b Negative フォーム + なくてはいけない "X must do ~"

This construction requires the Negative フォーム of a verb, and it literally means "It won't be okay if X doesn't do ~".

明日しけんがあるので、夜中(よなか)の二時まで勉強しなくてはいけません。

Because I have an exam tomorrow, I have to study until 2 o'clock tonight.

日本語のクラスでは、いつも日本語を話さなくてはいけません。

We must always speak Japanese in our Japanese class.

めがねをなくしてしまったので、新しく作らなくてはいけません。

(Lit.) Because I've lost my glasses, I need to make (them) newly.

Because I've lost my glasses, I need to have a new pair made.

そつぎょうするためには、百二十たんい取らなくてはいけません。

In order to graduate, (students) must earn 120 units.

お金がないので、銀行からかりなくてはいけません。

Because I have no money, I have to borrow from the bank.

毎週ミーティングにでなくてはいけません。

I/We have to attend the meeting every week.

日本語コースの学生はまじめに勉強しなくてはいけません。そして、毎日きょうかしょを読まなくてはいけません。

All students in (this) Japanese course must study seriously. And you must read the textbook every day.

教室に来てから読んでもいいですか。

Can we read it after we come to class (Lit. classroom)?

いいえ、教室で読んではいけません。家で読まなくてはいけません。

No, you must not read it in class. You have to read it at home.

図書館で友達と話してもいいですか。

May I talk with friends in the library?

はい、いいです。でも、静かに話さなくてはいけません。

Yes, you may. But you have to talk quietly.

学生:　作文をもう一ど出(だ)さなくてはいけませんか。
　　　Do I have to turn in the composition once more?

先生:　ええ、もう一ど出して下さい。
　　　Yes, please turn it in one more time.

16c　Negative フォーム + なくてもいい　　“X need not do ~”

Neg

This construction takes the verb Negative フォーム and literally means “It'll also be okay if X doesn't do ~”.

店員:　週末(しゅうまつ)も仕事しなくてはいけませんか。
　　　Do I have to work on weekends too?

マネージャー:　いいえ、週末は仕事しなくてもいいです。
　　　No, you don't need to work on weekends.

ミラー:　今晩、早く帰らなくてもいいですか。
　　　Would it be alright if I didn't come home early this evening?

ゆりこ:　ええ、いいですよ。
　　　Sure, that would be fine.

学生:　来週、宿題を出さなくてもいいですか。
　　　Is it okay if I don't turn in the assignment next week?

先生:　いいえ、毎週宿題を出さなくてはいけません。

No, you have to turn in assignments every week.

学生:　期末(きまつ)しけんを受(う)けなくてもいいですか。

(Lit.) Is it all right not to take the final exam?

May I be excused from taking the final exam?

先生:　いいえ、受けなくてはいけませんよ。

No, you must take it.

びじゅつ館に入る時、お金をはらわなくてはいけませんか。

When we enter the museum, do we have to pay a fee?

はい、大人(おとな)ははらわなくてはいけません。でも、子供(こども)ははらわなくてもいいです。

Yes, adults have to pay, but children don't.

16d Pre-ますフォーム + やすい "easy to do ~"
Pre-ますフォーム + にくい "difficult/uncomfortable to do ~"

ます

These constructions accommodate only verbs in their Pre- ますフォーム.

石川先生はしんせつで、話しやすいです。

Ishikawa-sensei is kind and easy to talk to.

山本さんのテレビは大きいので、見やすいです。

Because Yamamoto-san's TV is large, it's easy to watch.

ビートルズの歌は、覚えやすくて、歌いやすいです。

The Beatles' songs are easy to remember and sing.

キムさんの作文は、字が小さいですから、読みにくいです。

Because the characters in Kim-san's composition are small, it's difficult to read.

とうふはとてもやわらかくて、はしで食べにくいです。

Tofu is very soft and difficult to eat with chopsticks.

このくすりはにがいので、飲みにくいです。

This medicine is bitter, so it's difficult to take.

あのう、ちょっと言(い)いにくいんですが……。

Uh… this is kind of hard to say, but …

Both やすい and にくい are い-adjectives, so the past tense is ～かった.

秋山さんのけいたい電話は、ボタンが大きくて、使いやすかったです。

Akiyama-san's cellular phone had large buttons and was easy to use.

秋山さんからかりたようふくは、きやすかったです。

The clothes I borrowed from Akiyama-san were easy to wear.

今朝のこうぎは分かりにくかったです。

The lecture this morning was difficult to understand.

昨日の夜はゆきがふったので、うんてんしにくかったです。

It snowed last night, so it was difficult to drive.

16e Xまでに "by X (time)"

X can be a time expression or an event that is known to occur at a certain time.

夜、十時までに電話して下さい。

Please call me by 10 P.M.

明日までに宿題を出さなくてはいけません。

You must turn in your homework by tomorrow.

しけんまでに漢字を三十覚えられますか。

Can you memorize 30 kanji in time for the exam?

クリスマスまでにプレゼントをおくります。

I'll send the gift by Christmas.

おそく帰ってもいいですか。

(Lit.) Would it be alright if I came home late?

May I come home late?

いいえ、十時までに帰らなくてはいけません。

No, you must come home by 10 o'clock.

練習問題 (れんしゅうもんだい)

I. びょうきです。おいしゃさんに聞きましょう。

例(れい) あなた: タバコをすってもいいですか。

いしゃ: いいえ、(タバコを) すってはいけません。

(or) はい、(タバコを) すってもいいです。

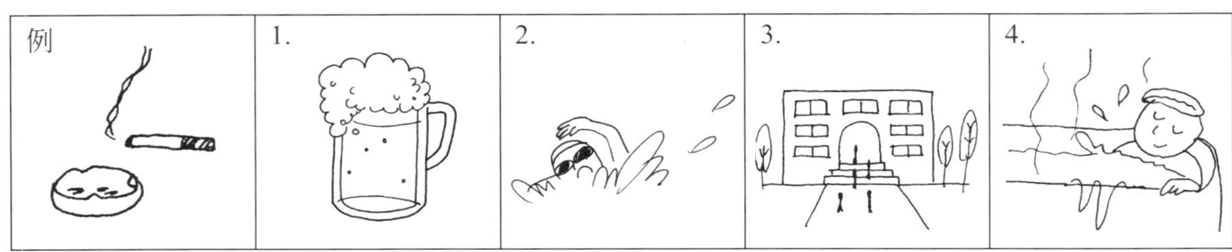

II.　ホストファミリーに聞きましょう。

例　A (学生)　　B (ホストファミリーの人)

A:　明日の晩、友達の家で晩ごはんを食べてもいいですか。

B:　はい、いいですよ。

(or) いいえ、(明日の晩、友達の家で晩ごはんは) 食べないで下さい。

III.　週末、こうえんでパーティーをしたいです。ちかくにこうえんが二つあります。さくらこうえんとふじこうえんです。どちらのこうえんでパーティーをしましょうか。パートナーと話して下さい。まず、Aさんはさくらこうえん、Bさんはふじこうえんの絵を見て、してもいいこと (activities) に○、してはいけないことに×を書いて下さい。そして、しつもんしましょう。パートナーのこうえんで何をしてもいいですか。何をしてはいけませんか。こたえをよく聞いて、○か×を書いて下さい。

例 1 B:　さくらこうえんでじてんしゃにのってもいいですか。

A:　いいえ、(じてんしゃに) のってはいけません。

例 2 A:　ふじこうえんでじてんしゃにのってもいいですか。

B:　はい、(じてんしゃに) のってもいいです。

	例	1.	2.	3.	4.	5.
さくら こうえん	×					
ふじ こうえん	○					

A　さくらこうえん

B　ふじこうえん

IV.　あなたは今、びじゅつ館にいます。いろいろなことがしたいです。びじゅつ館の人に聞きましょう。

例1. 絵にさわる。

例 1

あなた:　絵にさわってもいいですか。

びじゅつ館の人:　いいえ、(絵に) さわってはいけません。
(絵に) さわらないで下さい。

例 2

あなた:　有名な絵をスケッチしてもいいですか。

びじゅつ館の人:　はい、(有名な絵を) スケッチしてもいいです。
どうぞ、(有名な絵を) スケッチして下さい。

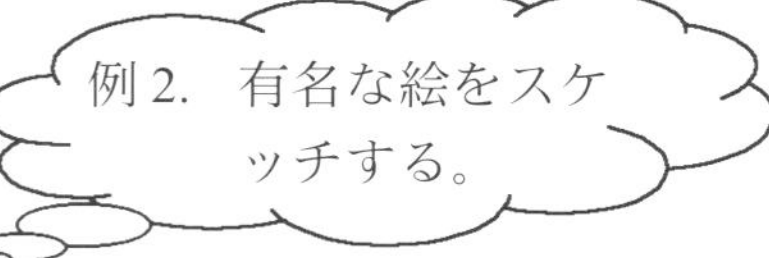

V.　日本語のクラスは宿題が多いので、しめきりの日に出すのは大変です。ほかの日に出したいです。先生に聞いてみましょう。

例1　あなた:　先生、聞き取りの宿題を金曜日に出してもいいですか。

　　先生:　いいえ、だめです。月曜日の三時までに出さなくてはいけません。

例2　あなた:　先生、漢字の宿題を火曜日に出してもいいですか。

　　先生:　はい、火曜日に出してもいいですよ。

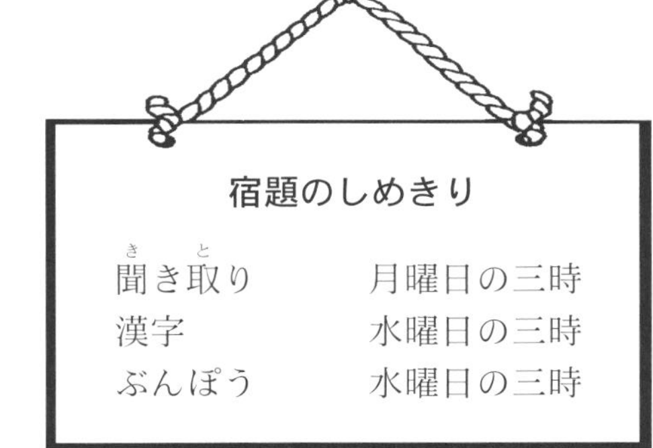

VI.　今日は金曜日です。木村さんは明日パーティーをします。木村さんは何をしなくてはいけませんか。聞きましょう。

例　あなた:　明日の朝、六時におきなくてはいけませんか。
　　木村:　はい、明日の朝、六時におきなくてはいけません。
　　　　　(or) いいえ、明日の朝、六時におきなくてもいいです。

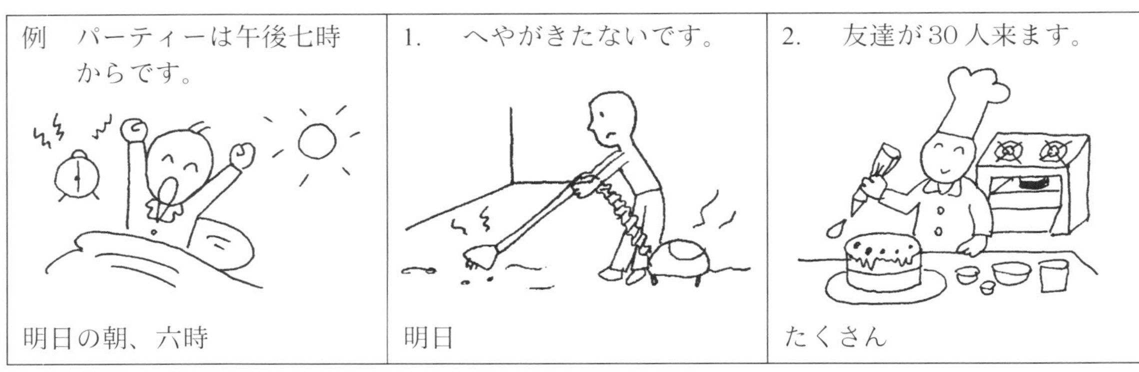

例　パーティーは午後七時からです。　明日の朝、六時

1.　へやがきたないです。　明日

2.　友達が30人来ます。　たくさん

3.　家に飲み物がぜんぜんありません。　今日

4.　月曜日にしけんがあります。　今晩

5.　家にいい音楽のCDがたくさんあります。　今日

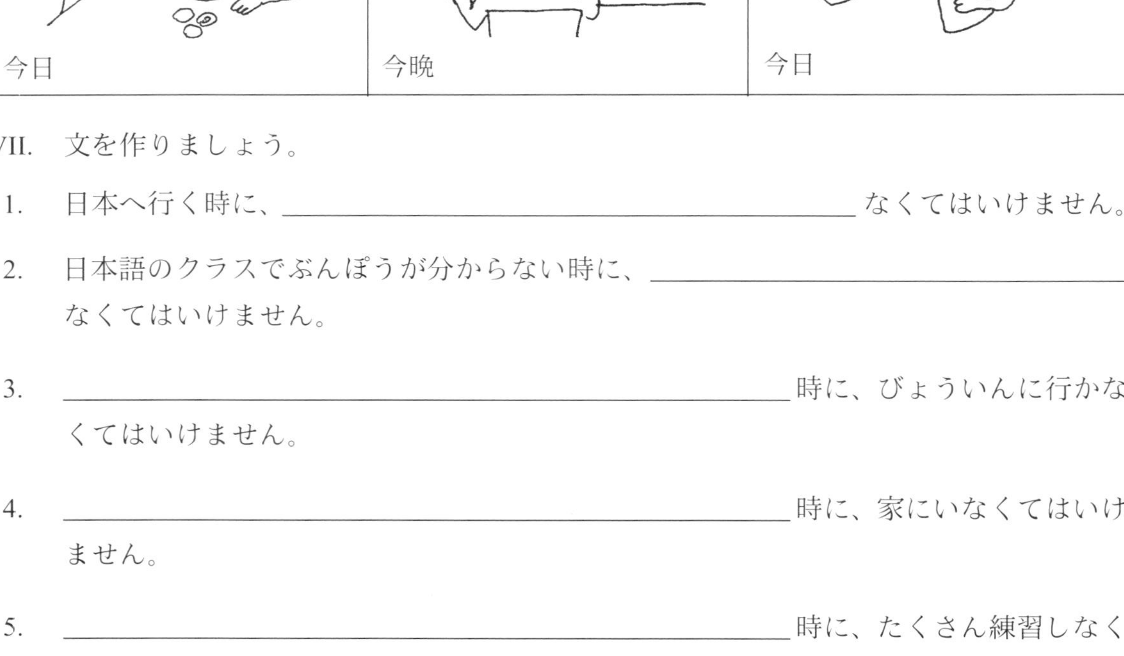

VII.　文を作りましょう。

1.　日本へ行く時に、＿＿＿＿＿＿＿＿＿＿＿＿なくてはいけません。

2.　日本語のクラスでぶんぽうが分からない時に、＿＿＿＿＿＿＿＿＿＿＿＿なくてはいけません。

3.　＿＿＿＿＿＿＿＿＿＿＿＿時に、びょういんに行かなくてはいけません。

4.　＿＿＿＿＿＿＿＿＿＿＿＿時に、家にいなくてはいけません。

5.　＿＿＿＿＿＿＿＿＿＿＿＿時に、たくさん練習しなくてはいけません。

VIII.　日本語のコースで、学生は何をしなくてはいけませんか。グループで話しましょう。

IX.　絵を見て言いましょう。

例 1.　このくつはあるきにくいです。

例 2.　この車はうんてんしやすいです。

X.　つぎのしつもんにこたえて下さい。

1.　カリフォルニア／アメリカ／etc. は住みやすいですか。
どうしてですか。

2.　マッキントッシュと PC とではどちらの方が使いやすいですか。
どうしてですか。

XI. 読みましょう。

日本語のクラスでは毎週、月曜日の三時までに聞き取りの宿題を出すことになっています。そして、水曜日の三時までに漢字とぶんぽうの宿題を出すことになっています。今日は水曜日です。ですから、聞き取りの宿題は出さなくてもいいですが、漢字とぶんぽうの宿題を出さなくてはいけません。

私は昨日、宿題をしましたが、こたえが二つ分かりませんでした。それで、ブラウンさんに電話してみましたが、ブラウンさんは家にいませんでした。ホームズさんにも電話をしましたが、ホームズさんもいませんでした。

今日、一時ごろ、もう一どブラウンさんとホームズさんに電話をしましたが、今日もいませんでした。私は一人でもう一どもんだいをかんがえてみましたが、分かりませんでした。それで、オフィスアワーに行きました。先生はとてもしんせつでした。そして、三時までに宿題を出すことができました。

先生のせつめいはとても分かりやすかったので、来週また、オフィスアワーに行くつもりです。

しつもんにこたえて下さい。

1. いつまでに聞き取りの宿題を出さなくてはいけませんか。
2. 今日、どの宿題を出さなくてはいけませんか。
3. この人は、昨日、だれかに電話をしましたか。
4. ブラウンさんは今日一時ごろ家にいましたか。
5. この人はどうして、日本語のオフィスアワーに行ったんですか。
6. 先生のせつめいはどうでしたか。

新しい漢字

洗う（あら）	言う（い）	受ける（う）	お手洗い（て あら）	外国（がいこく）	外国人（がいこくじん）
期末しけん（きまつ）	言葉（ことば）	子供（こども）	酒（さけ）	週末（しゅうまつ）	洗濯機（せんたくき）
外（そと）	出す（だ）	使い方（つか かた）	使う（つか）	夜中（よなか）	夜（よる）

新しい使い方

大人（おとな）	気（き）	聞き取り（き と）	見物（けんぶつ）	人気（にんき）	六本木（ろっぽんぎ）

Radicals: さんずい

The カタカナ「シ」-like へん radical appearing in 洗, 濯, 酒, and 漢 is called さんずい. Generally, さんずい漢字 represent ideas related to water. In fact, this radical was derived from 水 "water".

Weird Conventions

Traditionally, 漢字 dictionaries use radicals to organize 漢字. That is, 漢字 are listed under a radical they contain. Radicals are, in turn, organized according to their stroke counts. 亠 (なべぶた) and 亻 (人べん) are listed as two-stroke radicals, 女 (女へん) and 广 (麻だれ) as three-stroke radicals, 日 (日へん) and 木 (木へん) as four-stroke radicals, and so forth.

When counting the strokes of a radical, it is frequently the case that the strokes of the original 漢字 from which the radical was derived are counted, rather than the strokes of the derived radical itself. So, さんずい (氵), which clearly consists of three strokes, is categorized as a four-stroke radical because the original 漢字「水」consists of four strokes. For another example, 草かんむり (艹, cf. 第十二課) is written with three strokes, but it is considered a six-stroke radical because the original 漢字「艸」consists of six strokes. By contrast, 囗 (国がまえ) is counted as three strokes (丨・冂・囗), while the original 漢字「国」consists of eight strokes.

Another peculiar convention in 漢字 dictionaries concerns which radical the 漢字 is listed under when it contains more than one radical. 酒, for example, consists of two radicals: さんずい and 酒づくり「酉」, and it is traditionally listed under 酒づくり, not under さんずい.

洗	セン・あら(う)	*to wash:* 洗濯 *laundry,* 洗濯機 *washing machine,* お手洗い *toilet/restroom*
言	こと・い(う)	*to say:* 言葉 *language, word*
受	う(ける)	*to receive*
手	て	*hand:* お手洗い *toilet, restroom,* 上手(じょうず) *good at,* 手 *hand,* 手紙 *letter,* 下手(へた) *bad at*

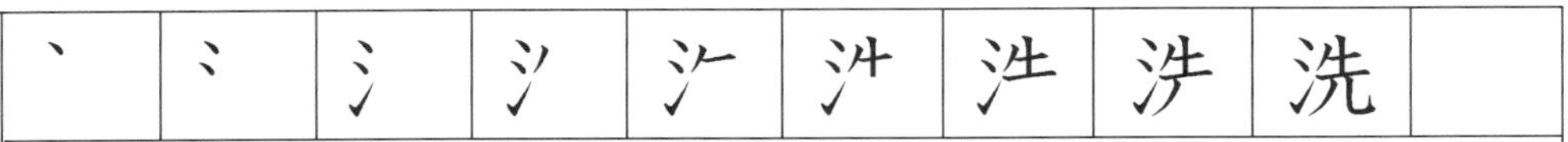

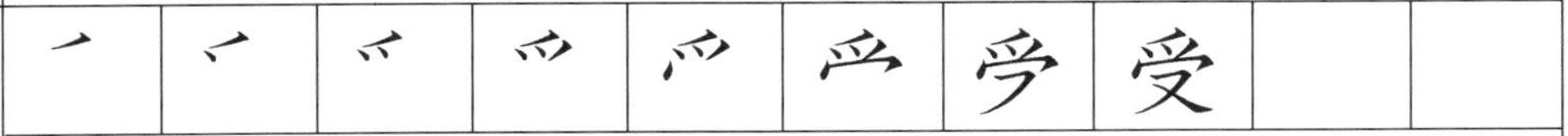

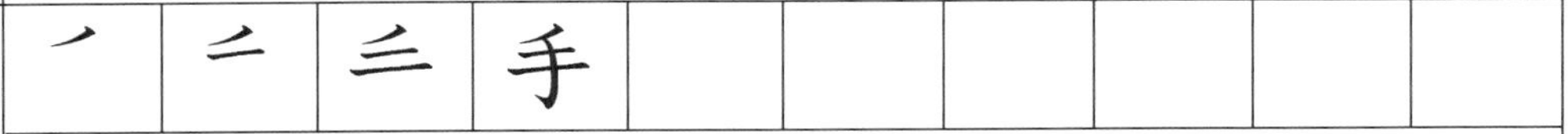

外	ガイ・そと	*outside:* 外国 *foreign country,* 外国人 *foreigner*
国	コク・ゴク・くに	*country:* 中国 *China,* 外国 *foreign country,* 外国人 *foreigner*
気	キ	*spirit:* 元気 *energetic,* 電気 *electricity,* 人気 *popularity*
期	キ	*term, season:* 学期 *academic term,* 期末 *end of an academic term*
末	まつ	*end:* 期末 *end of an academic term,* 週末 *weekend*
見	ケン・み(る)	*to see / look:* 見物 *sightseeing*
物	ブツ・もの	*thing;* this word is frequently combined with the Pre-ます form of a verb, e.g. 買い物 *shopping,* 食べ物 *food,* 読み物 *something to read.* When 見物 is read as みもの, it means "something to see"; when it is read as けんぶつ, it means "sightseeing".
葉	ば	*leaf:* 言葉 *language, word*
子	こ	*child:* 子供 *child*

供	ども	*companion:* 子供 *child*
酒	さけ	*liquor*
濯	タク	*to wash, to rinse:* 洗濯 *laundry,* 洗濯機 *washing machine.* The right hand side (tsukuri) is the same as 曜 as in 日曜日.
機	キ	*machine:* 洗濯機 *washing machine,* 飛行機 *airplane (flying machine)*
出	だ（す）	*to submit / send out*
使	つか（う）	*to use:* 使い方 *usage*
夜	よ・よる	*night:* 夜中 *middle of the night*

漢字の復習(ふくしゅう)

I.　読みましょう。

1. このアパートは、ひるは静かですが、夜はうるさいです。
2. この漢字はもう勉強しましたが、読み方は覚えていません。
3. 私の妹は洗濯も料理も下手です。
4. 友達に手紙を出しましたが、まだ返事が来ません。
5. この言葉を使って、文を作って下さい。

II.　漢字のクイズです。□に漢字を書いて、読んで下さい。

例(れい)　女　＋　子　＝　[好]　　[好]き（すき）

1.　タ　＋　ト　＝　□　　□（　　　）

2.　タ　×　2　＝　□　　□い（　　　）

3.　水　＋　先　＝　□　　□う（　　　）

(You have to change 水 into a radical.)

4.　日　＋　月　＝　□　　□るい（　　　）

5.　日　＋　音　＝　□　　□い（　　　）

6.　人　＋　木　＝　□　　□む（　　　）

(You have to change 人 into a radical.)

新しい語彙(ごい)

いしゃ	*medical doctor (as a job description)*
いつでも	*anytime*
おいしゃさん	*medical doctor*
大人(おとな)	*adult*
外国人(がいこくじん)	*foreigner*
かわく　(ウ)(i)	*to get dry*
聞(き)き取(と)り	*listening*
期末(きまつ)しけん	*final examination*
気(き)をつける　(ル)(i)	*to be careful*
くすり	*medicine*
くすりや	*drug store*
けいたい電話(でんわ)	*cellular phone*
見物(けんぶつ)（する）	*sightseeing*
こたえ	*answer*
こと	*matter, affair*
言葉(ことば)	*language, word*
さわる　(ウ)(i)	*to touch*

しめきり	*deadline*
すう ㋒ⓣ	*to inhale*
スケッチ（する）	*sketch*
ぜったいに	*absolutely*
せつめい（する）	*explanation*
洗濯機（せんたくき）	*washing machine*
たしかに	*undoubtedly, definitely*
出（だ）す ㋒ⓣ	*to submit, send out*
タバコ	*tobacco, cigarette*
たんい	*unit(s)*
つれて来（く）る Ⓘⓣ	*to bring (person, animal)*
X ど	*X time(s)*
ところ	*place*
なくす ㋒ⓣ	*to lose*
にがい ㋑	*bitter*
人気（にんき）	*popularity*
のど	*throat*
はらう ㋒ⓣ	*to pay*

ハンドバッグ	*handbag*
PC（ピーシー）	*PC*
びょういん	*hospital*
ボール	*ball*
ボタン	*button*
ホテル	*hotel*
まず	*first of all*
X までに	*by X (time)*
マネージャー	*manager*
ミーティング	*meeting*
もう一（いち）ど	*once more*
もっと	*more*
もんげん	*curfew*
もんだい	*problem*
ようじ	*business, errand*
ようふく	*(Western-style) clothes*
夜中（よなか）	*middle of the night*
わかい ㋑	*young*

名前

インターネット	*Internet*
おだいば（お台場）	*Odaiba*
クリスマス	*Christmas*

マッキントッシュ	*Macintosh*
六本木（ろっぽんぎ）	*Roppongi*

第十七課 LESSON 17

京都で
In Kyoto

春になると、さくらがさきます
When spring comes, cherry trees blossom

1
わあ、きれいなにわですね。
2
ええ、このにわは一年中きれいなんですよ。毎年、もう少し寒くなると、雪が降ります。雪が降ると、もっときれいになりますよ。
3
それから、春になると、さくらがさきます。夏は、みどりがとてもきれいです。そして、秋になると、木の葉が赤やき色になるんです。
4
へえ、それはきれいでしょうねえ。
5
ミラーさん、「お花見」を知っていますか。
6
日本では、さくらがさくと、さくらの木の下でごはんを食べたり、お酒を飲んだり、歌ったりするんです。
7
へえ、それは楽しいでしょうね。私もお花見がしてみたいです。
じゃあ、ミラーさん、春にまた来て下さい。
8
ちょっと寒くなりましたね。
そうですね。ヒーターをつけて、部屋をあたたかくしましょう。
9
私、おなかがすいた。
ぼくも。
そうね。もう六時だから、晩ごはんを食べに行きましょう。

会話

1 ミラー：わあ、きれいなにわですね。

Wow, what a beautiful garden!

2 ゆりこ：ええ、このにわは一年中(じゅう)きれいなんですよ。毎年(まいとし・まいねん)、もう少し寒くなると、雪(ゆき)が降(ふ)ります。雪が降ると、もっときれいになりますよ。

Yes, this garden is beautiful all year round. Each year, when it gets a little colder, snow falls. When it snows, the garden becomes even more beautiful.

3 いさお：それから、春になると、さくらがさきます。夏は、みどりがとてもきれいです。そして、秋になると、木(こ)の葉(は)が赤(あか)やき色(いろ)になるんです。

Then, in spring cherry trees blossom. In summer, the green of the trees becomes remarkably vivid. And when autumn comes, the leaves turn red and yellow.

4 ミラー：へえ、それはきれいでしょうねえ。

Boy, that sounds really beautiful.

5 ゆりこ：ミラーさん、「お花見(はなみ)」を知っていますか。

Miller-san, do you know about ohanami*?*

6 ゆりこ：日本では、さくらがさくと、さくらの木(き)の下でごはんを食べたり、お酒を飲んだり、歌ったりするんです。

In Japan, when the cherry trees bloom, we eat, drink sake, and sing songs under the trees.

7 ミラー：へえ、それは楽しいでしょうね。私もお花見がしてみたいです。

Wow, that must be fun. I want to try out ohanami *myself.*

いさお：じゃあ、ミラーさん、春にまた来て下さい。

Well then, please come back in spring.

（りょかんで）

8 ミラー：ちょっと寒くなりましたね。

It's gotten kind of cold, hasn't it?

いさお：そうですね。ヒーターをつけて、部屋(へや)をあたたかくしましょう。

Yes, indeed. Let's turn on the heater and warm up the room.

9 まゆみ ：私、おなかがすいた。
I'm hungry.
いちろう：ぼくも。
Me too.
ゆりこ ：そうね。もう六時だから、晩ごはんを食べに行きましょう。
Alright. It's 6 o'clock now, so let's go eat dinner.

使い方

2 きれいな[ん]ですよ is a casual version of きれいな[の]ですよ and means the same as きれいですよ (cf. 第六課, **6g**). When a statement is a well-known fact, ～のです is more commonly used than ～です. In fact, all sentences in **2** can be in the ～のです form: もう少し寒くなると、雪が降るんです。雪が降ると、もっときれいになるんですよ. 歌ったりするんです in **6** is another instance of this construction.

3 木(こ)の葉: here, 木 is pronounced as こ, instead of き.

5 お花見 consists of the beautifier お + 花 "flower" + 見 "viewing". Here, 花 means さくら "cherry blossoms", the flower of flowers. In Japan, さくら is a metaphor for life: a brief, brilliant blooming, followed by the inevitable rapid fall. It symbolizes beauty, transiency, melancholy, and dainty resignation. When the buds blossom in early spring, there is a custom of having a picnic-like party under full-bloom cherry trees, known as お花見.

9 Plain speech like おなかがすいた, instead of more formal おなかがすきました, is normally used among family members.

ぼく is a first-person pronoun used mainly by boys.

そうね is a casual feminine equivalent of そうですね.

> 日本のことわざ
> Japanese Proverb
>
> 花よりだんご。
> *Dumplings are of more use than cherry blossoms.*
>
> だんご "rice dumplings"
>
> It emphasizes the importance of practical things over what some would deem "frivolous aestheticism".

文法（ぶんぽう）

17a	**ADJECTIVE / NOUN + なる**	**"become ADJECTIVE / NOUN"**
17b	**List of Professions**	
17c	**ADJECTIVE / NOUN + する**	**"make X ADJECTIVE / NOUN"**
17d	**CLAUSE1 と CLAUSE2**	**"When / If / Whenever C1, C2"**
17e	**Plain フォーム + でしょう**	**"It's probably the case that ~"**
17f	**NOUN 中**	**"throughout NOUN; in the middle of NOUN"**
17g	**色 (Color Terms)**	

17a　ADJECTIVE / NOUN + なる　"become ADJECTIVE / NOUN"

A　With an い-adjective, use the stem + く + なる.

もうすぐ、寒くなります。

It'll become cold soon.

木村さんはさいきん、やさしくなりました。

Recently, Kimura-san has become (more) considerate.

およいでいる時に、おなかがいたくなりました。

(Lit.) When I was swimming, my stomach became painful.

I got a stomachache while I was swimming.

B　With a な-adjective, use the stem + に + なる.

たくさんれんしゅうしたので、ギターが上手になりました。

Because I practiced a lot, I got good at the guitar.

春川さんは本を書いて、有名になりました。

Harukawa-san wrote a book and became famous.

近くにスーパーができて*、便利になりました。

A new supermarket opened in my neighborhood, so it's become convenient (to shop).

> *The verb できる (sometimes written as 出来る) has several meanings.
>
> 1.　to be able to, can
>
> 小山さんはスキーができます。
>
> *Koyama-san can ski.*
>
> 試験（しけん）がよくできませんでした。
>
> *I couldn't do well on the exam.*
>
> 2.　to come to being
>
> 近くにスーパーができました。
>
> *A new supermarket has opened in my neighborhood.*
>
> 3.　to be done
>
> 晩ごはんができました。
>
> *Dinner is ready.*

C　With a nominal predicate, drop です and add に + なる.

病気（びょうき）になりました。

I became ill.

スピーチコンテストで一番になりました。

I got (Lit. became) first place at the speech contest.

私はかいしゃいんになるつもりです。

(Lit.) I intend to become a company employee.

I plan to get a job at a company.

17b　List of Professions

actor はいゆう　俳優 *actress* じょゆう　女優	*accountant* かいけいし 会計士	*architect* けんちくか 建築家	*artist* アーティスト・ げいじゅつか 芸術家
astronaut うちゅうひこうし 宇宙飛行士	*athlete* スポーツせんしゅ スポーツ選手	*carpenter* だいく 大工	*company employee* *office worker* かいしゃいん 会社員
computer programmer コンピューター プログラマー	*cook* シェフ・いたまえ 板前	*designer* デザイナー	*economic analyst* けいざいアナリスト 経済アナリスト
engineer エンジニア	*farmer* のうぎょう けいえいしゃ 農業経営者	*fisherman* りょうし 漁師	*flight attendant* フライト アテンダント

* 先生 "teacher" is a respectful term, so it cannot be used to describe your own or your family member's profession.

〇　春川さんのお母さんは先生です。

〇　私はきょうしです。　　　×　私は先生です。

〇　私の父はきょうしです。　×　私の父は先生です。

17c ADJECTIVE／NOUN + する "make X ADJECTIVE／NOUN"

A **With an い-adjective,** use the stem + く + する.

部屋を明るくして下さい。

Please make the room bright(er).

ヒーターをつけて、部屋をあたたかくしましょう。

Let's turn on the heater and make the room warm.

ミーティングをもう少し早くして下さい。

Please make the meeting a little earlier.

このスキットは長いですね。ちょっとみじかくして下さいませんか。

This skit is a little long. Could you please make it shorter?

先生、試験をもっとやさしくして下さい。

Sensei, please make the exam easier.

B **With a な-adjective,** use the stem + に + する.

部屋をきれいにして下さい。

Please clean the room. (Lit. Please make the room clean.)

宿題をしているんですから、静かにして下さい。

I'm doing my homework, so please be quiet.

どうぞ、楽にして下さい。

Please make (yourself) comfortable.

C **With a nominal predicate,** drop です and add に + する. We have already studied this construction in 第九課, **9g**.

お茶にしますか、コーヒーにしますか。	*Tea or coffee?*
私はお茶にします。	*I'll take tea. (Lit. I'll make it tea.)*
ソンさんを一番にしましょう。	*Let's put Son-san first place.*
その話は、明日にして下さい。	*Please wait until tomorrow to talk about it.*
だれをリーダーにしましょうか。	*(Lit. Who shall we decide to be the leader?)* *Who shall we select as the leader?*
木村さんにしましょう。	*Let's decide on Kimura-san.*

17d CLAUSE1 と CLAUSE2 "When / If / Whenever C1, C2"

The predicate of C1 must be in the Dictionary フォーム or ない フォーム. This is one of the most interesting constructions in Japanese because its meaning differs significantly according to the tense of the sentence (i.e. the tense of the main clause C2).

A When C2 is in the past tense:

Both C1 and C2 refer to past specific events, and this ～と construction indicates that (i) C1 and C2 occurred consecutively, or (ii) C1 provides a background or setting when C2 occurred.

While ～時 (に) and ～て allow C2 to represent an event controllable by the speaker, C2 in ～と must not be controllable by the speaker (cf. 第十三課, **13b** for ～時 (に) and 第十五課, **15b** for ～て). Because C1 and C2 are conjoined by a mere temporal sequence relationship, ～と frequently implies unexpectedness and / or surprise.

(i) C1 and C2 occurred consecutively (by accident / unintentionally):

(1) 電車がえきにつくと、人がたくさんおりました。
When the train arrived at the station, many people got off.

(2) 今朝、図書館に行くと、木村さんに会いました。
When I went to the library this morning, I ran into Kimura-san.

The verb 会う means either "to meet" (controllable) or "to run into" (uncontrollable). In (2), 会う can mean only the latter because of the constraint of the ～と construction.

(3) 私が (村山さんに) その話をすると、村山さんはおこってしまいました。
When I told Murayama-san that story, he became angry.

(4) 私が電話すると、母はとてもよろこびました。
When I called (her), my mother was delighted.

(5) セーターを洗うと、小さくなってしまいました。
When I washed the sweater, it shrank (Lit. became small).

(6) 部屋をあたたかくすると、気もちがわるくなりました。
When I made the room warm, I became (feeling) sick.

(7) ぶんぽうがよく分かりませんでしたが、きょうかしょを読むと、すぐ分かりました。
I didn't understand the grammar well, but when I read the textbook, I understood it immediately.

Sentence (8) below is unacceptable because C2, returning books, is controllable by the speaker. However, the identical C2 is acceptable in (9), with which the speaker describes another person's actions (i.e. not controllable by the speaker). The same difference exists in (10) and (11).

(8) × (私は) 図書館へ行くと、本を返しました。
I went to the library and returned books.

(9) ○ 山本さんは、図書館へ行くと、本を返しました。
Yamamoto-san went to the library and returned books.

(10) × (私は) ドアを開けると、外へ出ました。
I opened the door and went outside.
(Going out of the room is a controllable action by the speaker.)

(11) ○ 山本さんは、ドアを開けると、外へ出ました。
Yamamoto-san opened the door and went outside.

(ii) When/While/During C1, C2 occurred. C1 is normally in the ～ている construction to indicate that when C2 occurred, C1 was in progress:

(12) 食事をしていると、村山さんがあそびに来ました。
While I was having a meal, Murayama-san came to visit me.

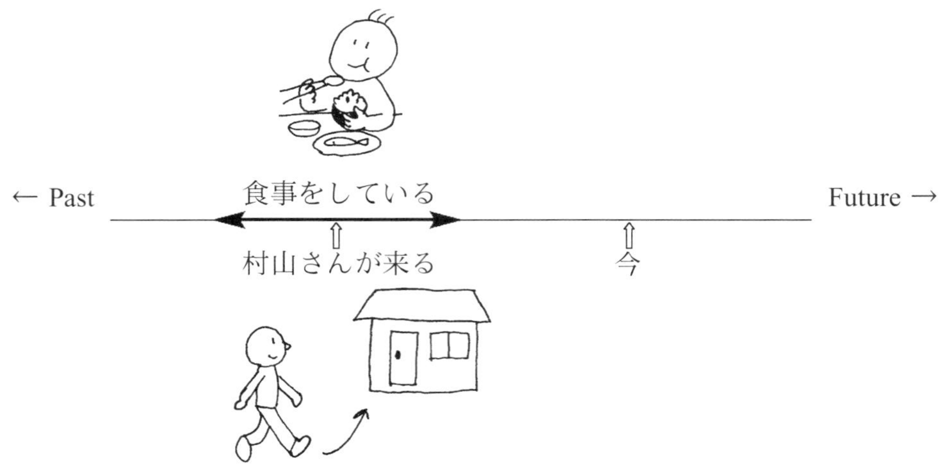

(13) とおりを* あるいていると、石川先生に会いました。
While I was walking along the street, I ran into Ishikawa-sensei.

> * Some moving verbs (e.g. あるく "walk" and はしる "run") require the location to be marked by を.
>
> みちをはしる
> *run down the street*

(iii) When C1 happened, the speaker discovered C2. In this usage, C2 is either an event in progress (〜ている), e.g. (14), or a state of affairs, e.g. (15)-(16):

(14) まどを開けると、雨が降っていました。
When I opened the window, (I found that) it was raining.

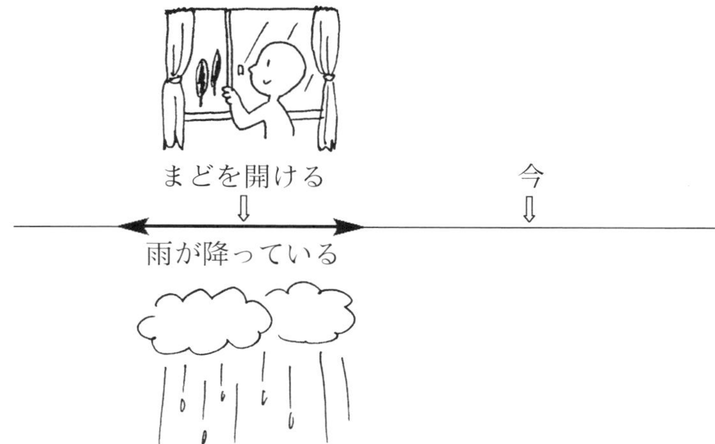

(15) 石川先生のオフィスへ行くと、ミラーさんがいました。
When I went to Ishikawa-sensei's office, (I found that) Miller-san was there.

(16) 目をさますと、雪国(ゆきぐに)*でした。
[In a train]
When I woke up, (I realized that) it was (I was in) snow country.

Sentences (17)-(18) below do not convey the intended meanings of discovery because they indicate that C2 occurred **after** C1.

(17) ×　まどを開けると、雨が降りました。
×　*When I opened the window, it rained.*

(18) ×　先生のオフィスへ行くと、先生はパーティーをしました。
×　*When I went to the sensei's office, she hosted a party.*

---

*『雪国』川端康成(かわばたやすなり)
Snow Country by Yasunari Kawabata

国境(こっきょう)の長(なが)いトンネルを抜(ぬ)けると雪国であった。夜の底(そこ)が白くなった。信号所(しんごうじょ)に汽車(きしゃ)が止(と)まった。(Opening sentences)
The train came out of the long tunnel into the snow country. The earth lay white under the night sky. The train pulled up at a signal stop (Translation by Edward Seidensticker).

国境 *a border*
トンネル *tunnel*
抜ける *go through*
雪国であった = 雪国だった
底 *bottom*
信号所 *a signal place*
汽車 *a steam train* (cf. 電車)
止まる *to stop*

(Lit.) When (the train) went through a long tunnel at the border, it was snow country. The bottom of the night became white. The steam train stopped at a signal place.

B When C2 is in the non-past tense:

When C2 is in the non-past tense, C1 and C2 do not refer to specific events. This construction indicates that C2 is a natural or conventional consequence of C1.

(i) C2 is a natural consequence of C1:

(19) 漢字を使わないと、わすれてしまいます。
If we don't use kanji, we'll forget them.

(20) コートをきないと、寒いですよ。
(Lit.) If you don't wear a coat, it's cold.
It'll be too cold if you don't wear a coat.

(ii) C2 represents a habitual consequence of C1. いつも "always" frequently appears in this construction. The controllability constraint on C2 does not apply:

(21) (私は) ごはんを食べると、いつもねむくなります。
Whenever I have a meal, I always get sleepy.

(22) 春になると、(私は) いつもヨセミテへ行きます。
When spring comes, I always go to Yosemite.

(iii) This construction can also be used for logical or timeless relationships:

(23) 二に三をたすと、五になります。
(Lit.) If you add 3 to 2, it (the result) becomes 5.
2 plus 3 is 5.

2 + 3 = 5
10 - 4 = 6

(24) 十から四をひくと、六になります。
(Lit.) If you subtract 4 from 10, it (the result) becomes 6.
10 minus 4 is 6.

(25) ボタンをおすと、電気がつきます。
If you push the button, the light turns on.

(26) そのかどを左(ひだり)に (へ) まがると、銀行があります。
(Lit.) If you turn left at that corner, there is a bank.

(27) 二つ目のかどを右(みぎ)に (へ) まがると、学校があります。
(Lit.) If you turn right at the second corner, there is a school.

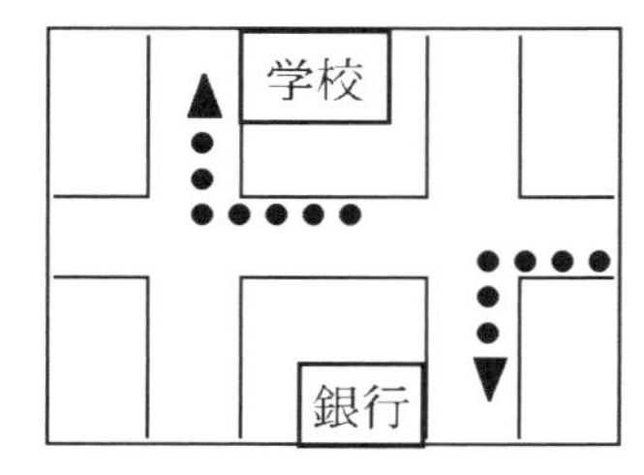

一つ目	*first*	四つ目	*fourth*	七つ目	*seventh*
二つ目	*second*	五つ目	*fifth*	八つ目	*eighth*
三つ目	*third*	六つ目	*sixth*	九つ目	*ninth*

Because the ～と construction is used basically to express a relationship between two observable events, C2 cannot be an intention, desire, permission, prohibition, request, or suggestion.

(28) ○ 春になると、さくらがさきます。
When spring comes, cherry trees bloom.

(29) × 春になると、ヨセミテへ行くつもりです。(～つもり)

(30) ○ 雪が降ると、子供達は雪だるまを作ります。
When it snows, children make snowmen.

(31) × 雪が降ると、スキーをするつもりです。(～つもり)

(32) × お金があると、りょこうしたいです。(～たい)

(33) × ひまがあると、家へ来て下さい。(～て下さい)

(34) × ひまがあると、映画を見ませんか。(～ませんか)

(35) × 日本語を知っていると、話してもいいです。(～てもいい)

(36) × お酒を飲むと、うんてんしてはいけません。(～てはいけない)

(37) × 分からないと、こたえなくてもいいです。(～なくてもいい)

(38) × お金がないと、働かなくてはいけません。(～なくてはいけない)

17e PLAIN フォーム + でしょう "It's probably the case that ~"

In this construction, verbs and い -adjectives must be in a plain form; な -adjectives and nominal predicates behave irregularly, i.e., だ does not appear. The adverb, 多分(たぶん) "maybe/perhaps" often accompanies this expression.

A Verbs: Plain フォーム + でしょう

今日は、一日中、雨が降ったりやんだりするでしょう。
It will probably rain on and off all day today.

ミラー　：ソンさんは、まだ、図書館にいますか。

Is Son-san still in the library?

小山　　：さあ、よく分かりませんが、多分、もう家に帰ったでしょう。

Well I'm not sure, but maybe she's gone home.

ソン　　：木村さんは今週の週末、どこかに行きますか。

Is Kimura-san going anywhere this weekend?

ミラー　：さあ、よく分かりませんが、多分、どこにも行かないでしょう。

Well I don't know for sure, but she'll probably stay home.

ソン　　：キムさんは昨日、クラスへ来ましたか。

Did Kim-san come to class yesterday?

ミラー　：さあ、よく覚えていませんが、多分、来なかったでしょう。

Well I don't remember well, but he probably didn't come.

B　　い-Adjectives: Plain フォーム＋でしょう

ミラー　：大学の図書館は新しいですか。

Is the University library new (newly built)?

ソン　　：さあ、よく知りませんが、多分、新しいでしょう。

Well I'm not sure, but it's probably new.

ミラー　：私達の大学のバスケットボールチームは強(つよ)いですか。

Is our college basketball team strong?

ソン　　：さあ、よく分かりませんが、多分、あまり強くないでしょう。

Well I'm not too sure, but it's probably not very strong.

ミラー　：小山さんが作ったケーキはおいしかったですか。

(Lit.) Was the cake that Koyama-san made delicious?

Was the cake made by Koyama-san delicious?

ソン　　：さあ、私は食べませんでしたからよく分かりませんが、多分、おいしかったでしょう。

Well since I didn't have any, I'm not too sure, but it was probably delicious.

小山　　：先週の試験はやさしかったですか。

Was last week's test easy?

山本　　：じつは、私は受けなかったんですが、多分、やさしくなかったでしょう。

To tell the truth, I didn't take it, but it was probably not easy.

東京は多分、寒くないでしょう。
It's probably not cold in Tokyo.

みんな早く出しましたから、試験はあまりむずかしくなかったでしょう。
Since everyone turned it in early, the test was probably not very difficult.

C　な -Adjectives: Plain フォーム + でしょう. When the sentence is non-past affirmative, use Stem + でしょう.

木村　：りょうは、週末、静かですか。
Are the dorms quiet on weekends?
ソン　：さあ、よく分かりません。りょうに住んだことがないんです。でも、多分、いつもより静かでしょう。(Non-past affirmative)
Well I don't know. I've never lived in a dorm. But I guess they're quieter than usual.

木村　：パーティーはにぎやかでしたか。
Was the party lively?
ソン　：さあ、私は行かなかったんですが、多分、にぎやかだったでしょう。
Well I didn't go, but I imagine it was (quite) lively.

木村　：村山さんはさかなが好きでしょうか。
Does Murayama-san like fish?
ソン　：さあ、おすしを食べませんから、多分、好きじゃないでしょう。
Well she doesn't eat sushi, so I guess she doesn't like it.

先生A：先週の試験はかんたんだったでしょうか。
Was last week's test easy?
先生B：いいえ、みんな試験のてんがわるかったですから、かんたんじゃなかったでしょう。
No, since everyone got a bad score, I guess it wasn't easy.

D　Nominal Predicates: Plain フォーム + でしょう. When the sentence is non-past affirmative, use Noun + でしょう.

ミラー：村山さんのせんもんは何ですか。
What's Murayama-san's major?
木村　：さあ、よく分かりませんが、多分、英文学でしょう。
Well I'm not sure, but maybe it's English Literature.

ミラー：ソンさんがいませんね。
Son-san isn't here, is she?
木村　：ええ、多分、病気でしょう。
No, she's probably sick.
(Pay attention to the mismatch of ええ and *No*, cf. 第六課, **6i**.)

ミラー：あの人達は学生ですか。
Are those people students?
木村　：さあ、よく分かりませんが、多分、学生じゃないでしょう。
Well I'm not sure, but probably not.

17f　NOUN 中　"throughout NOUN; in the middle of NOUN"

When 中 appears with a time expression, it is read as じゅう* or ちゅう and means 'throughout ~'.

一晩中(ひとばんじゅう)　*all through the night*
一日中(じゅう)　*all day long*
冬中(じゅう)　*all through the winter*
一年中(じゅう)　*all year round*
午前中(ちゅう)　*all through the morning*
今週中(ちゅう)　*all through this week*
夏休み中(ちゅう)　*all through the summer vacation*
学期中(ちゅう)　*all through the semester*
X月中(ちゅう)　*all through the Xth month*

> * じゅう is a result of sequential voicing (cf. 第十一課, **11f**).
>
> chū → jū
>
> Therefore, it was originally written as ぢゅう. However, in recent years, most people write じゅう instead.
>
> **午前中 is a common word, but 午後中 does not exist.

明日は、午前中**は雨ですが、午後は晴(は)れるでしょう。
Tomorrow there'll be rain in the morning, but it will clear up by the afternoon.

今日はいそがしくて、一日中、ぜんぜん休めませんでした。
I was busy today and had no break at all the whole day.

中 can also attach to a noun that indicates an activity (mostly verbal nouns, cf. 第四課, **4k**). In this combination, 中 is always pronounced as ちゅう and means "in the middle of ~".

試験中ですから、静かにして下さい。
Because an examination is in progress, please keep quiet.

食事中はテレビをつけないで下さい。
Please don't turn on the TV during meals.

電話しましたが、話し中でした。
(Lit.) I called, but (the people on the line) were in the middle of talking.
I called, but the line was busy.

ダイエット中ですから、あまい物は食べません。
Since I'm on a diet, I don't eat sweet things.

17g　色(いろ) (Color Terms)

	Noun	Adjective
Black	くろ	くろい
Blue	青(あお)	青い
Green	みどり みどり色	(みどりの) (みどり色の)
Red	赤	赤い
White	白(しろ)	白い
Yellow	き色	き色い (き色の)

> 早口言葉(はやくちことば)
> Tongue Twister
>
> 赤まき紙(がみ)、青まき紙、きまき紙
> *red, blue, and yellow rolled paper.*
>
> まき紙　"rolled (letter) paper"
> まき（ます）"to roll" +
> 紙 "paper"

練習問題(れんしゅうもんだい)

I.　「なる」か「する」を使って文を作りましょう。

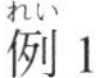
例(れい) 1

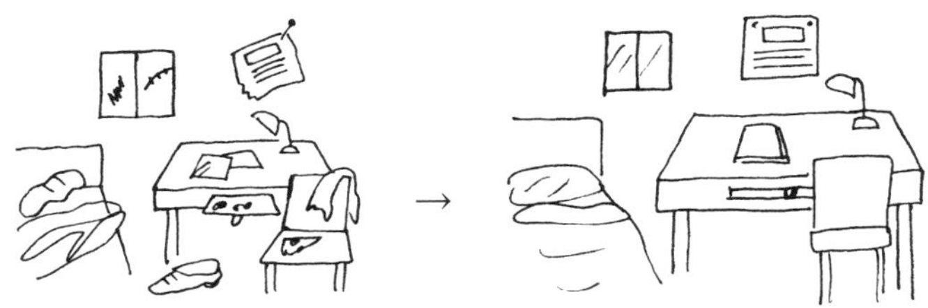

木村さんは部屋を<u>きれいにしました</u>。
木村さんの部屋は<u>きれいになりました</u>。

例 2

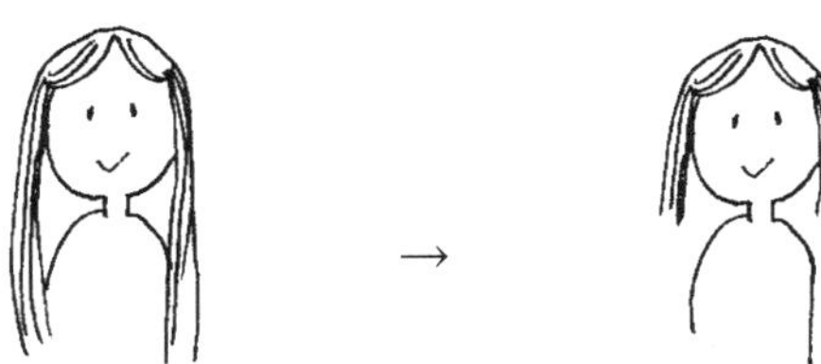

木村さんはかみを<u>みじかくしました</u>。
木村さんのかみは<u>みじかくなりました</u>。

1. 私は大学に入った時に、新しいコンピューターを買いました。
今、私は四年生です。私のコンピューターはもう ________________。

2. 教室が暗かったので、やまださんは電気をつけました。
やまださんは ________________。
教室は ________________。

3. 私は日本語が下手でした。それで、たくさんれんしゅうしました。
私は日本語が ________________。

4. りょうでパーティーをしたので、にぎやかでした。でも、もうパーティーはおわりました。
りょうは ________________。

5. 昨日、頭がいたかったです。それで、くすりを飲んで、一日中寝ていました。
私は ________________。

II. [ ] の中の言葉の Adverb フォームを ________ に書いて下さい。それから（　　）の中のただしい方に○をつけて下さい。

1. [古い] 私の車はとても ________________（なりました・しました）。

2. [大きい] コンピューターのスクリーンの字が小さかったので、字を ________________（なりました・しました）。

3. [むずかしい] 先学期(せんがっき)のクラスはやさしかったですが、今学期は ________________（なりました・しました）。

4. [暗い] もう六時です。外は ________________（なりました・しました）。

5. [きれい] パーティーをするので、部屋を ________________（なりました・しました）。

6. [さびしい] 友達が日本へ帰ってしまったので、私は ________________（なりました・しました）。

III. これはマジックキーホルダーです。例(れい)を見て、マジックキーホルダーの使い方を書いて下さい。

Magic Key Holder

例(れい)　(私が) キーホルダーのスイッチをいれると、キーホルダーはテレビになります。

1. (私が) キーホルダーをこすると、＿＿＿＿＿＿＿＿＿＿＿＿＿＿＿＿。

2. (私が) ＿＿＿＿＿＿＿＿＿＿＿＿ と、キーホルダーは音楽をえんそうします。

3. (私が) ＿＿＿＿＿＿＿＿＿＿＿＿ と、キーホルダーはけいたい電話になります。

IV. 文を作りましょう。

1. 昨日、家へ帰ると、＿＿＿＿＿＿＿＿＿＿＿＿＿＿＿＿。

2. オフィスアワーに行くと、＿＿＿＿＿＿＿＿＿＿＿＿＿＿＿＿。

3. ＿＿＿＿＿＿＿＿＿＿＿＿ と、コンピューターはこわれてしまいました。

4. ＿＿＿＿＿＿＿＿＿＿＿＿＿＿＿＿ と、まどが開いていました。

V. このコンピューターには『ファッション・トライ』のプログラムが入っています。『ファッション・トライ』を使ってスクリーンの人のようふくや色をかえることができます。例を見てマニュアルを作って下さい。

赤　青　白　くろ　き色　みどり

ズボン　シャツ　くつ　めがね　スカート　ネックレス　ソックス　ぼうし　セーター

例　青とズボンのボタンをおすと、青いズボンをはきます。

1. くろとめがねのボタンをおすと、＿＿＿＿＿＿＿＿＿＿＿＿＿＿＿＿。

2. ＿＿＿＿＿＿ と ＿＿＿＿＿＿ のボタンをおすと、＿＿＿＿＿＿＿＿＿＿。

3. ＿＿＿＿＿＿＿＿＿＿ と、＿＿＿＿＿＿＿＿＿＿＿＿＿＿。

4. ＿＿＿＿＿＿＿＿＿＿ と、＿＿＿＿＿＿＿＿＿＿＿＿＿＿。

5. ＿＿＿＿＿＿＿＿＿＿ と、＿＿＿＿＿＿＿＿＿＿＿＿＿＿。

VI. 1と2はあなたのこたえを書いて下さい。3と4は文を作って下さい。

1. Q: あなたのふるさとでは春になると、どうなりますか。
   A: ＿＿＿＿＿＿＿＿＿＿＿＿＿＿＿＿＿＿＿＿。

2. Q: あなたのふるさとでは冬になると、何をしますか。
   A: ＿＿＿＿＿＿＿＿＿＿＿＿＿＿＿＿＿＿＿＿。

3. 私は朝おきると、＿＿＿＿＿＿＿＿＿＿＿＿＿＿＿＿。

4. 私は一晩中勉強すると、＿＿＿＿＿＿＿＿＿＿＿＿＿＿。

VII. パートナーに聞きましょう。それからゲームをしましょう。まずパートナーに聞きましょう。

例(れい) Q: Aさんは何年生ですか。
A: 二年生です。

	(　　　　) さん
1. 何年生ですか。	
2. にくを食べますか。	
3. スポーツが好きですか。	
4. 何がとくいですか。	
5. 日本へ行ったことがありますか。	

つぎはゲームです。クラスメート三人にあなたのパートナーについて聞きましょう。こたえがただしい時は一てんです。

例 Q: Xさんは何年生でしょうか。
A: Xさんは多分一年生でしょう。

	(　　　　) さんのてん	(　　　　) さんのてん	(　　　　) さんのてん
1.			
2.			
3.			
4.			
5.			
Total	/5	/5	/5

VIII. ちずを見ながら言ってみましょう。Xは、あなたが今いるところです。

例　かどをまがります。

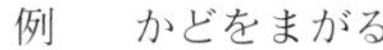
例　かどをまがる

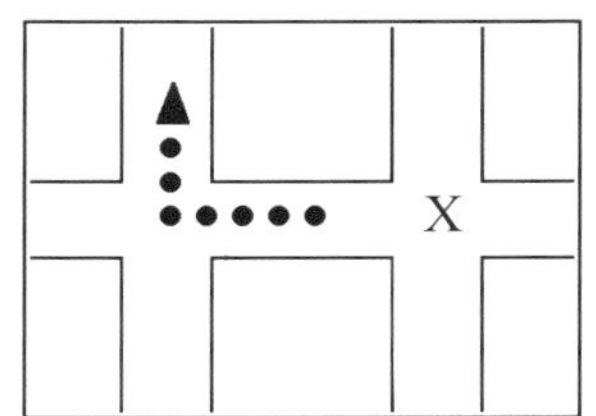

1.　かどを右に (へ) まがる
　　かどを左に (へ) まがる

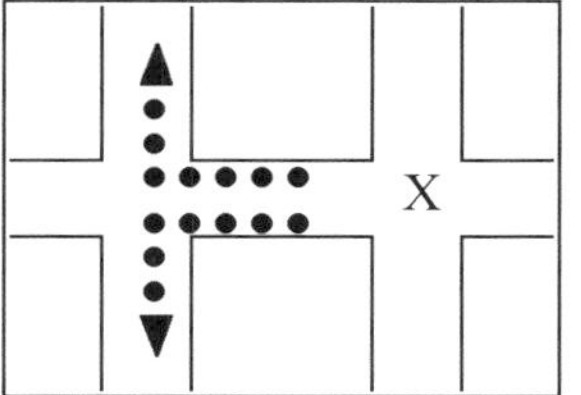

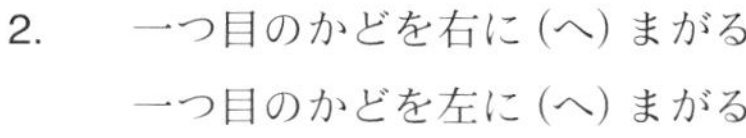
2.　一つ目のかどを右に (へ) まがる
　　一つ目のかどを左に (へ) まがる

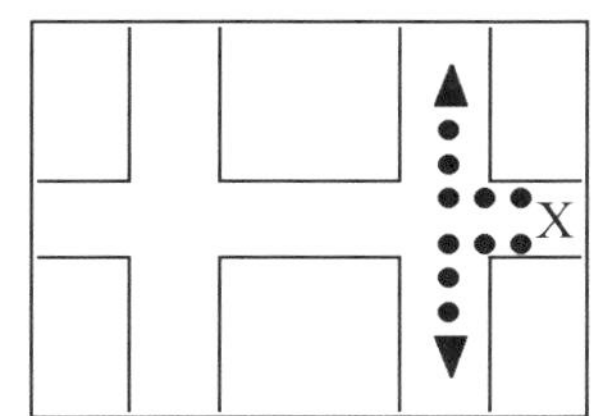

3.　しんごうを右に (へ) まがる
　　しんごうを左に (へ) まがる

4.　つきあたりを右に (へ) まがる
　　つきあたりを左に (へ) まがる

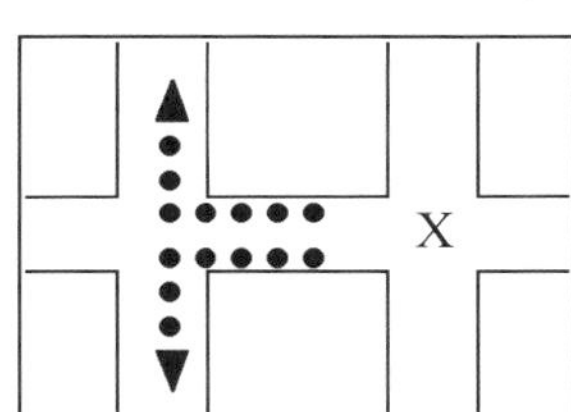

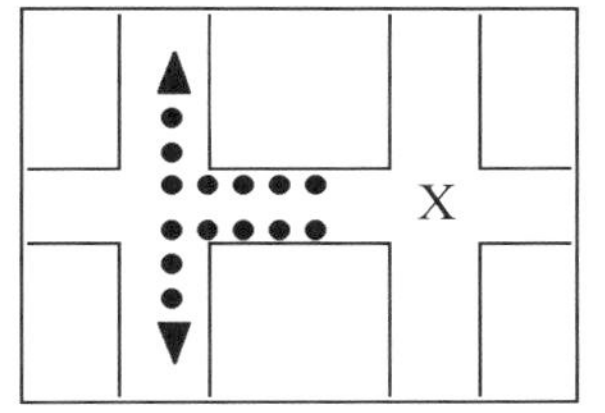

5.　まっすぐ行く

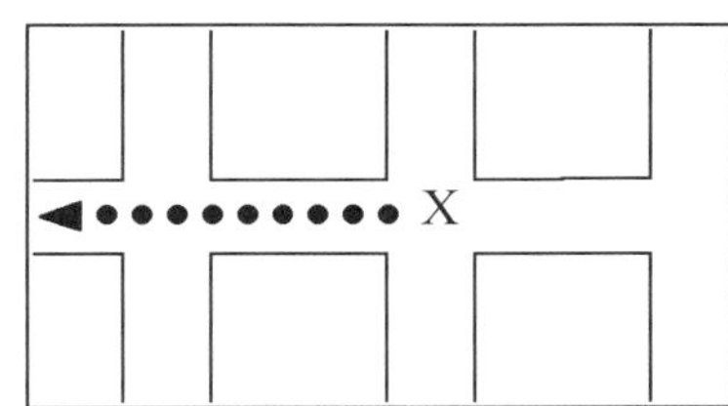

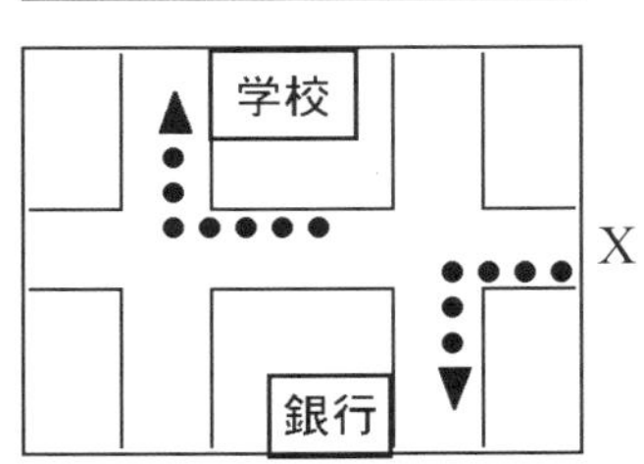

6.　一つ目のかどを左に(へ)まがると銀行があります。
　　二つ目のかどを右に(へ)まがると学校があります。

IX.　本屋(や)に行きたいですが、行き方が分かりません。「と」を使って、行き方を教えて下さい。(X: 今いるところ)

例

A.

B.

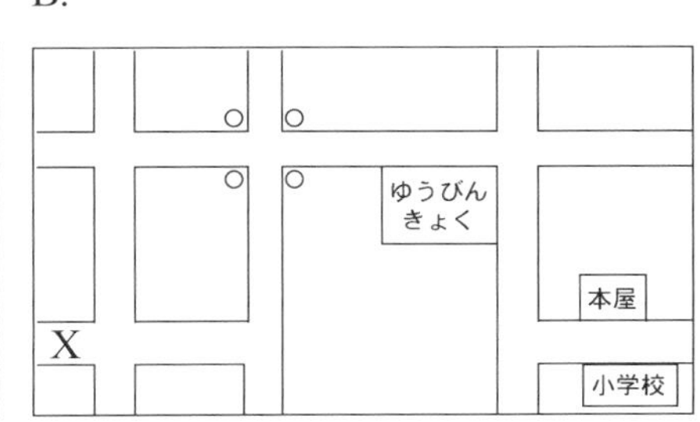

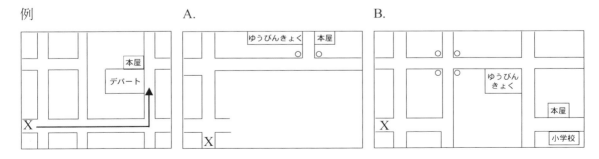

例　Q:　本屋はどこにありますか。

　　A:　まっすぐ行って下さい。三つ目のかどを左に (へ) まがると、デパートがあります。本屋はデパートのとなりにあります。

X.　行き方を聞きましょう。

Sheet 1

1　あなたは今、えきの前にいます。ゆうびんきょくとくすり屋へ行きたいですが、行き方が分かりません。でも、あなたのパートナーは行き方を知っています。ゆうびんきょくとくすり屋はどこにありますか。パートナーに聞いて下さい。

例(れい)　Q:　病院(びょういん)はどこにありますか。

A:　病院ですか。このみちをまっすぐ行くと、銀行があります。銀行のかどを右に(へ)まがって、一つ目のかどを左に(へ)まがると、病院があります。

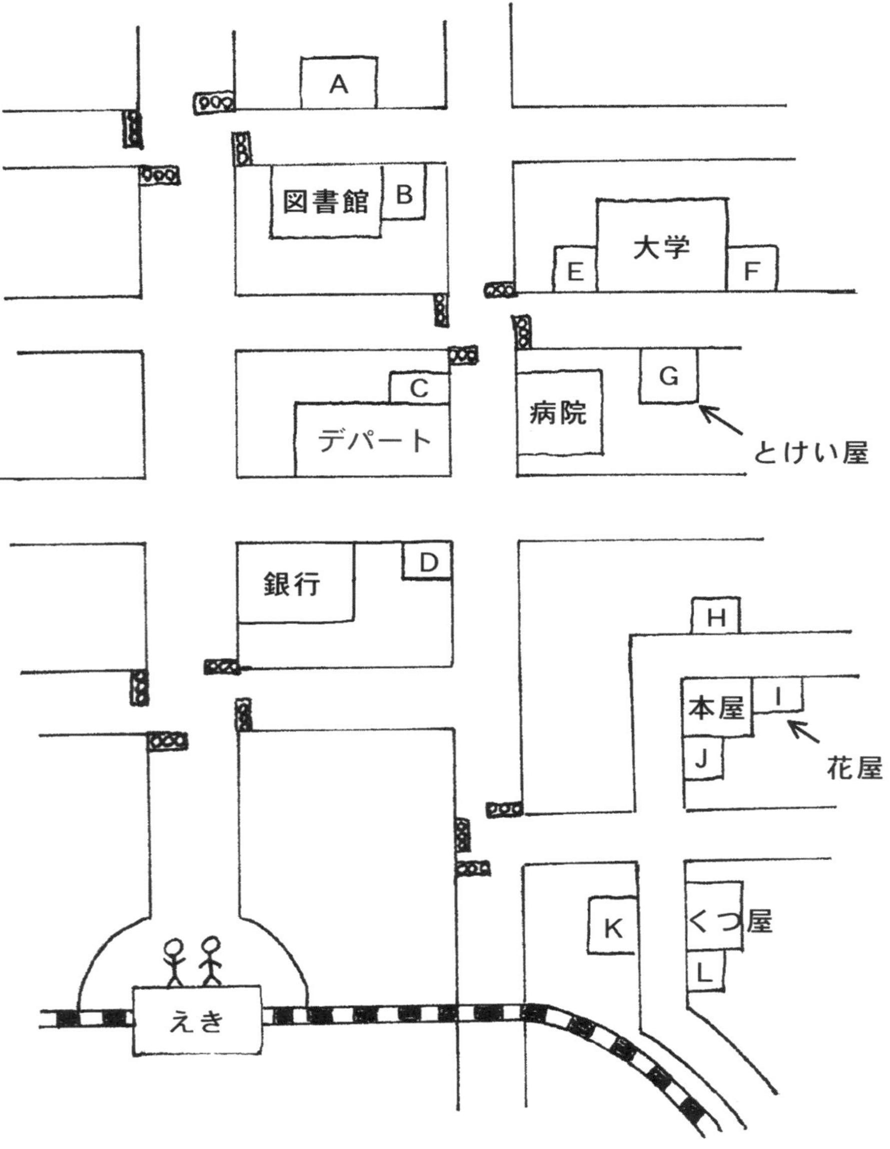

Sheet 2

2　あなたは今、えきの前にいます。花屋ととけい屋へ行きたいですが、行き方が分かりません。でも、あなたのパートナーは行き方を知っています。花屋ととけい屋はどこにありますか。パートナーに聞いて下さい。

例　Q:　病院（びょういん）はどこにありますか。

　　A:　病院ですか。このみちをまっすぐ行くと、銀行があります。銀行のかどを右に(へ)まがって、一つ目のかどを左に(へ)まがると、病院があります。

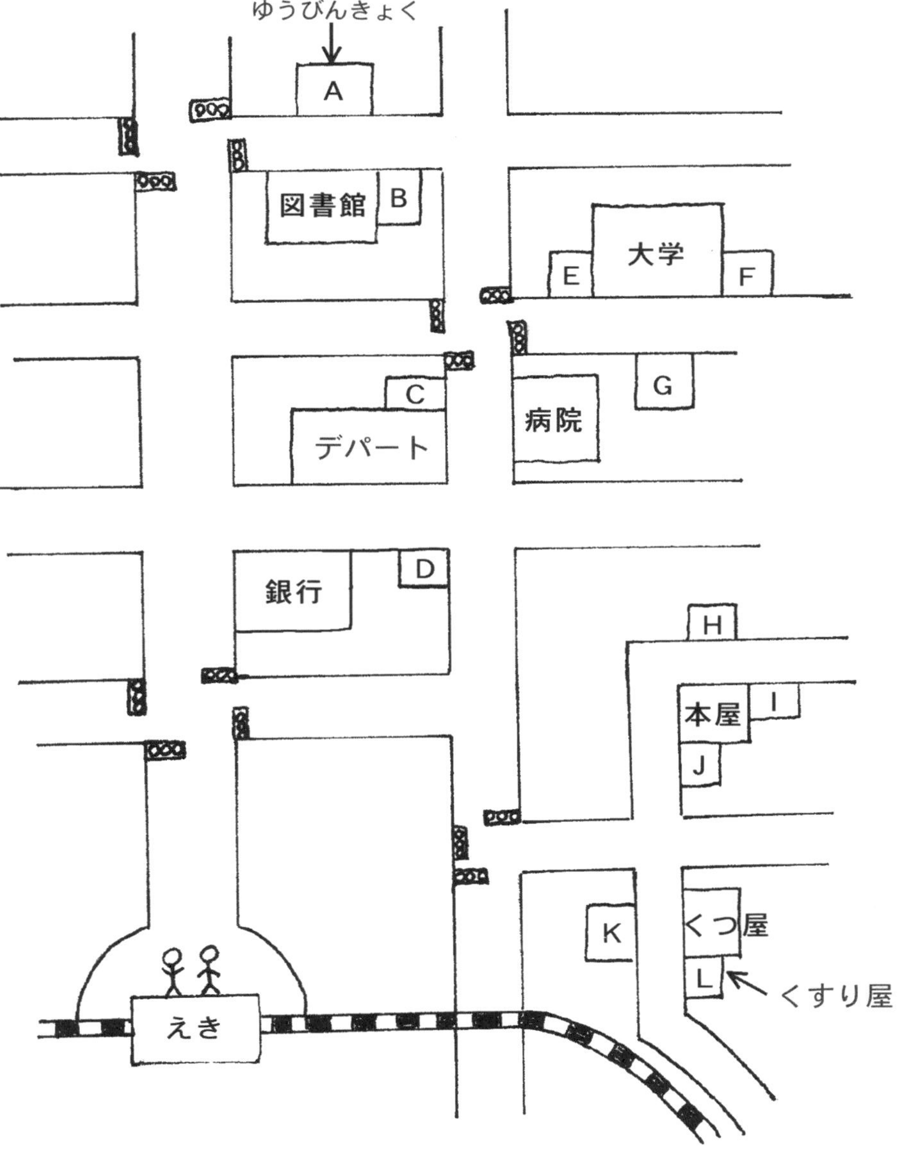

XI.　読みましょう。

私は中学生（ちゅうがくせい）の時、バスで学校へ行きました。でも、てんきがいい日は、あるいて帰ることにしていました。

私の学校の前のみちをまっすぐ行くと、大きいもりがありました。ある日 (one day)、私はもりの中に入ってみました。もりの中には小さい川（かわ）があって、その川のちかくに古いおてらがありました。おてらのよこのとをおしてみると、かんたんに開きました。中に入ってみると、たたみの部屋がありました。部屋のまん中に小さくてきれいな石（いし）が三つありました。青い石とみどりの石と赤い石でした。その石をずっと見ていると、気もちがおちつきました。

ちょっと暗くなったので、家に帰ることにしました。でも、みちが分かりませんでした。おてらの前のみちを右にまがったり、左にまがったりすると、広いにわがありました。にわには赤やき色の花がたくさんさいていました。とても静かできれいだったので、私はにわのベンチにすわって少し休みました。

とても寒くなったのでとけいを見ると、もう五時でした。それで、私はまたせまいみちを右にまがったり、左にまがったりしましたが、まだ帰るみちが分かりませんでした。私はとてもかなしくなりました。

やっと家へ帰ると、もう七時でした。私はとてもつかれたので、何もしないで寝てしまいました。つぎの日、またもりに行っておてらをさがしましたが、おてらはどこにもありませんでした。

しつもんにこたえて下さい。

1.　この人は中学生の時、毎日何で学校へ行きましたか。
2.　この日、この人はどこへ行きましたか。
3.　もりの中に何がありましたか。
4.　おてらの部屋に何がありましたか。
5.　この人は家へ帰ってから何かしましたか。
6.　つぎの日、おてらに行けましたか。
7.　どうしてですか。

新しい漢字

～屋（や）	青（あお）	赤（あか）	色（いろ）	試験（しけん）	白（しろ）
晴れる（は）	左（ひだり）	病院（びょういん）	病気（びょうき）	降る（ふ）	部屋（へや）
右（みぎ）	雪（ゆき）				

新しい使い方

開(あ)ける	石(いし)	一年中(じゅう)	～中(じゅう・ちゅう)	お花見(はなみ)	川(かわ)
木(き)	木(こ)の葉(は)	食事(しょくじ)	先学期(せんがっき)	多分(たぶん)	中学生(ちゅうがくせい)
強(つよ)い	出(で)る	一晩中(ひとばんじゅう)	毎年(まいとし・まいねん)		

Radicals: 雨(あめ)かんむり・こざとへん・おおざと

雨 appears as a かんむり "crown" radical in 電 and 雪; it is called 雨(あめ)かんむり (eight strokes). 雨かんむり漢字 are, of course, related to rain: e.g. 電 "lightning/electricity", 雪 "snow".

阝 as in 院 and 降 is called こざとへん, which was derived from the character 阜 "small village". Because 阜 consists of eight strokes, こざとへん (three strokes) is conventionally listed as an eight-stroke radical.

When 阝 appears as a つくり (right-hand part), as in 都 and 部, it is called おおざと or おおざとづくり (つくり → づくり by sequential voicing, cf. 第十一課, **11f**). おおざと is derived from the character 邑 "large village", which consists of seven strokes. As a convention, おおざと (three strokes) is listed as a seven-stroke radical in 漢字 dictionaries.

屋 ヤ	㇕	コ	尸	尸	屋	屋	屋	屋	屋	
	roof, house, shop: 部屋 *room,* くすり屋 *drug store*									
青 あお	一	十	丰	丰	青	青	青	青		
	blue; this 漢字 contains the moon.									
赤 あか	一	十	土	赤	赤	赤	赤			
	red									
開 あ(く)・ あ(ける)	丨	𠃌	門	門	門	門	門	門	門	門
	開	開								
	to open									

中	チュウ・ジュウ・なか	*middle, inside:* 中間 *midterm,* 中学生 *junior high school student,* 中学校 *junior high school,* 中国 *China,* 一年中 *all year around,* 食事中 *while eating,* 試験中 *exam in progress*
色	いろ	*color*
木	モク・き・こ	*wood:* 木曜日 *Thursday (the day of wood),* 木村 *Kimura,* 木の葉 *tree leaves*
葉	は・ば	*leaf:* 言葉 *language, word,* 木の葉 *tree leaves*
試	シ	*testing:* 試験 *examination*
験	ケン	*testing, an attempt:* 試験 *examination*
食	ショク・た(べる)	*to eat:* 食事 *meal*
白	しろ	*white*
多	タ・おお(い)	*abundant:* 多分 *perhaps, probably;* it consists of two カタカナ「タ」.

Kanji	Reading	Stroke order	Meaning
分	フン・プン・ブン	ノ 八 分 分	*minutes, portion:* 一分（いっぷん）*one minute,* 二分（にふん）*two minutes,* 多分 *perhaps, probably*
強	キョウ・つよ（い）	㇆ コ 弓 弘 … 強 強	*strong:* 勉強 *study (make efforts to become strong)*
出	だ（す）・で（る）	丨 … 出 出	*to go out, to send out*
晴	は（れる）	丨 冂 日 日 … 晴 晴 晴	*clear up;* this 漢字 consists of the sun (日) and blue (青).
左	ひだり	一 ナ … 左	*left;* note that this kanji is similar to 右 *right* below, but the order of the first two strokes is different.
病	ビョウ	丶 亠 广 … 病 病	*illness:* 病気 *illness, sickness*
降	ふ（る）	㇇ 阝 … 降 降	*to fall*
部	ブ・へ	丶 亠 … 立 … 音 音 … 部	*section:* 全部 *all,* 部屋 *room*
右	みぎ	ノ ナ … 右 右	*right*

雪 ゆき	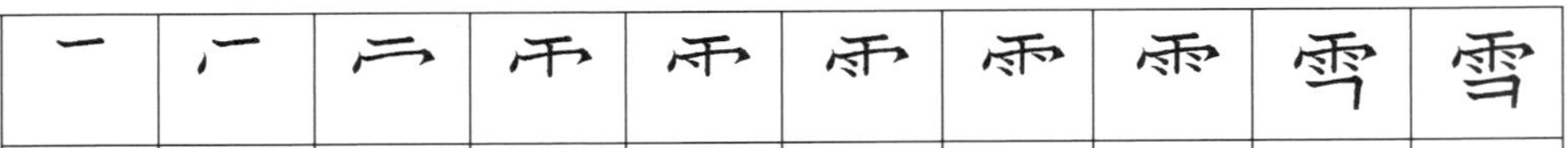
	雪
	snow

漢字の復習(ふくしゅう)

I.　読みましょう。

1. 夏になると、毎日、雨が降ります。
2. 冬になると、寒くなります。
3. 銀行は、朝何時に開きますか。
4. 明日の三時まで待ってみましょう。
5. 宿題を教えて下さいませんか。

II.　1-13を読んで下さい。そして、＿＿＿＿＿に［　　］の中の言葉のはんたい (opposite) のいみの言葉を書いて下さい。

1. ［左］	＿＿＿＿＿。
2. ［元気］です。	＿＿＿＿＿です。
3. ［大人］	＿＿＿＿＿。
4. 部屋に［入ります］。	部屋を＿＿＿＿＿ます。
5. ［雨が降って］います。	＿＿＿＿＿ています。
6. 先生は［試験をします］。	学生は試験を＿＿＿＿＿ます。
7. 夏は［あつい］です。	冬は＿＿＿＿＿です。
8. ［朝・ひる］	＿＿＿＿＿。
9. ［わすれます］。	＿＿＿＿＿ます。
10. アメリカ人の友達が私に英語を［教えます］。	私はアメリカ人の友達に英語を＿＿＿＿＿ます。
11. 部屋の［中］にいます。	部屋の＿＿＿＿＿にいます。
12. まどが［閉まって］います。	まどが＿＿＿＿＿います。
13. 毎朝八時に［おきます］。	毎晩十一時に＿＿＿＿＿ます。

新しい語彙（ごい）

青（あお）		*blue (Noun)*
青（あお）い	(イ)	*blue*
赤（あか）		*red (Noun)*
赤（あか）い	(イ)	*red*
開（あ）ける	(ル)(t)	*to open*
あたたかい	(イ)	*warm*
石（いし）		*stone*
一年中（じゅう）		*all year round*
五（いつ）つ目（め）		*fifth*
いれる	(ル)(t)	*to turn on (a switch), to put into*
色（いろ）		*color*
えんそう（する）		*music performance*
おこる	(ウ)(i)	*to get angry*
おす	(ウ)(t)	*to push*
おちつく	(ウ)(i)	*to calm down*
おりる	(ル)(i)	*to get off (a train, airplane, etc.)*
かいしゃいん		*company employee, office worker*
かえる	(ル)(t)	*to change*
かど		*corner*
かなしい	(イ)	*sad*
川（かわ）		*river*
木（き）		*tree*
キーホルダー		*key holder*
き色（いろ）		*yellow (Noun)*
き色（いろ）い	(イ)	*yellow*
気（き）もち		*feelings, mood*
くろ		*black (Noun)*
くろい	(イ)	*black*
九（ここの）つ目（め）		*ninth*
こする	(ウ)(t)	*to rub*
木（こ）の葉（は）		*leaf of a tree*
さく	(ウ)(i)	*to bloom*
（目（め）を）さます	(ウ)(t)	*to wake up*
シャツ		*shirt*
食事（しょくじ）（する）		*meal*
白（しろ）		*white (Noun)*
白（しろ）い	(イ)	*white*
しんごう		*traffic light*
スイッチ		*switch*
スクリーン		*screen (of a computer)*
先学期（せんがっき）		*last semester*
たす	(ウ)(t)	*to add*
ただしい	(イ)	*correct*
たたみ		tatami *mat*
多分（たぶん）		*perhaps, probably*
中学生（ちゅうがくせい）		*junior high school student*

つきあたり	*the end of a street*
強(つよ)い ㋑	*strong*
できる ㋸ ⓘ	*can do, to be done, to come to being*
と	*door*
七(なな)つ目(め)	*seventh*
(お)花見(はなみ)	*flower viewing*
晴(は)れる ㋸ ⓘ	*to clear up*
ひく ㋒ ⓣ	*to subtract*
左(ひだり)	*left*
一(ひと)つ目(め)	*first*
一晩中(ひとばんじゅう)	*all through the night*
二(ふた)つ目(め)	*second*
ふるさと	*hometown*
ベンチ	*bench*
ぼく	*I (typically by boys)*
毎年(まいとし・まいねん)	*every year*
まがる ㋒ ⓘ	*to turn*
マジック	*magic*
まっすぐ ㋤	*straight*
マニュアル	*manual*
まん中(なか)	*(dead) center*
右(みぎ)	*right*
みち	*way, road, street*
三(みっ)つ目(め)	*third*
みどり	*green*
みどり色(いろ)	*green color*
六(むっ)つ目(め)	*sixth*
もり	*woods*
X屋(や)	*X store*
八(やっ)つ目(め)	*eighth*
やっと	*finally*
四(よっ)つ目(め)	*fourth*

第十八課 LESSON 18

きこく
帰国
Returning Home (to One's Country)

そつぎょう　　　あと
卒業した後で、また来て下さいね
Please come visit again after you graduate

7
じゃあ、みなさん、しつれいします。
さようなら。お元気で。

会話

1 ミラー：みなさん、色々(いろいろ)とありがとうございました。

Well everyone, thank you very much for everything!

いさお：いいえ、どういたしまして。楽しかったですね。

You're welcome. It was a lot of fun, wasn't it.

2 ミラー：ええ、ほんとうに。おかげさまで、日本の文化(ぶんか)やしゅうかんをたくさん学(まな)ぶことができました。

Yes, it was. With your help, I was able to learn a lot about Japanese culture and customs.

ゆりこ：時間がある時に、手紙を書いて下さいね。

Please write us a letter when you have the time.

3 ミラー：はい、できるだけたくさん書くようにします。

Yes, I'll write as often as I can.

いさお：待っていますよ。私達も書きます。卒業した後で、また来て下さいね。

We'll be waiting for it. We'll write to you, too. Please come visit again after you graduate.

ミラー：はい。ありがとうございます。

Yes, thank you.

4 まゆみ：ミラーさんといっしょに練習(れんしゅう)したので、英語がちょっと分かるようになりました。ありがとうございました。

Because of practicing my English with you, I can understand it better now. Thanks a lot.

5 いちろう：あまりコンピューターゲームをすることができませんでしたね。もっとしたかったです。

(It's too bad) we weren't able to play computer games that much. I wanted to play more.

ミラー：そうですね。また今度(こんど)来た時にしましょう。

Me too. Let's do it again when I come back.

6 ゆりこ：あっ、ミラーさん。しゅっぱつまで後(あと)三十分ですよ。みんな飛行機に乗(の)り始めましたよ。急(いそ)いで下さい。

Oh, Miller-san, there's only 30 minutes left before departure. Everyone's started getting on the plane. Please hurry.

ミラー　：はい。

Yes.

7　ミラー　：じゃあ、みなさん、しつれいします。

Well, goodbye, everyone.

いさお・ゆりこ・まゆみ・いちろう：さようなら。お元気で。

Goodbye. Take care.

使い方

1 In Japanese, a repetition of certain words conveys plurality, e.g. 時々 (時＋時) “time + time → sometimes”, 人々 (人＋人) “person + person → persons/people”. When 色 “color” is repeated, it means “color + color → variety”: 色々な (な -adjective) “various”, 色々と (adverb) “variously”.

2 おかげさまで literally means “thanks to your shadow/shelter” and is used to express gratitude. The idea behind this expression is that our success, prosperity, progress, accomplishment, well being, etc. are often brought about by other people’s (or gods’) aid and support, although we may not be aware of it. A common situation in which to use おかげさまで is if you have recovered from an illness and someone asks, “Have you gotten well?” You respond to that person with おかげさまで、よくなりました. おかげさまで can also be used to respond to お元気ですか.

While 習う “to learn” is used mainly for acquiring skills, 学ぶ “to learn/study” is for acquiring knowledge. Many activities require both skills and knowledge, so both 習う and 学ぶ can be used.

習う：　うんてん、絵、お茶 “tea ceremony”、外国語、ギター、テニス、料理
学ぶ：　絵、外国語、しゅうかん、すうがく、文化、文学、読み方

3 できるだけ consists of できる “to be able to” and だけ “as much/as many/as far as”, meaning “as much/as far as one can”.

6 後 in 後三十分 means “remaining”. しゅっぱつまで後三十分です literally means “30 minutes remain until departure”.

文法 (ぶんぽう)

18a	**CLAUSE1 Dictionary フォーム + 前に CLAUSE2**	**"Before C1, C2"**
18b	**CLAUSE1 たフォーム + 後で CLAUSE2**	**"After C1, C2"**
18c	**Dictionary ／ないフォーム + ようにする**	**"I make an effort (not) to do VERB; I make things so that ~"**
18d	**Dictionary ／ Potential ／ないフォーム + ようになる**	**"It's gotten so that ~; It's become (im)possible that ~"**
18e	**Pre- ますフォーム + 始める**	**"begin / start VERB-ing"**
	Pre- ますフォーム + 終わる	**"finish VERB-ing"**
18f	**Transitive and Intransitive Verbs**	

18a CLAUSE1 Dictionary フォーム + 前に CLAUSE2 "Before C1, C2"

Dict

This construction indicates that C2 occurs **before** C1. The predicate of C1 must be in the Dictionary フォーム, regardless of the tense of the main clause C2.

Event Order 2 1

けっこんしきに出る前に、とこ屋に行きます。

Before attending the wedding ceremony, I'm going to the barbershop.

姉が来る前に、部屋をかたづけます。

I'll straighten up the room before my (older) sister comes.

映画館(えいがかん)に行く前に、何か食べましょう。

Let's eat something before we go to the movie theater.

今朝、授業(じゅぎょう)に出る前に、日本語を復習(ふくしゅう)するつもりです。

I plan to review some Japanese before I attend class this morning.

家を出る前に電話しましたが、いませんでしたね。

I tried calling you before I left home, but you weren't at home, were you?

毎晩、寝る前に、はをみがきます。

Every night I brush my teeth before going to bed.

暗くなる前に、家へ帰りましょう。

Let's go home before it gets dark.

Noun + の前に is possible when the noun denotes an activity or event (vis-à-vis a thing).

りょこうの前に、ホテルをよやくします。
I reserve a hotel (room) before traveling.
授業の前に話しましょう。
Let's talk before class.
昨日、かいぎの前に、村山さんとそうだんしました。
I discussed (it) with Murayama-san before the meeting yesterday.
試験の前に、もう一度(いちど)文法を復習しました。
I reviewed grammar one more time before the exam.
晩ごはんの前に、何か飲みますか。
(Lit.) Would you like to drink something before dinner?
Would you like a drink before dinner?
食事の前に、手を洗います。
I wash my hands before meals.

18b　CLAUSE1 たフォーム + 後で CLAUSE2　"After C1, C2"

This construction indicates that C2 occurs after C1. The predicate of C1 must be in the たフォーム, regardless of the tense of C2. で is frequently omitted.

Event Order	1	2
	おふろに入った後（で）、	晩ごはんを食べました。
	After taking a bath, I ate dinner.	

ようじが終(お)わった後（で）、行ってみましょう。
(Lit.) Let's go take a look after our business is (errands are) finished.
Let's go take a look after finishing our business (errands).
今朝、しゅじんが仕事に行った後（で）、母に電話しました。
I called my mother after my husband left for work this morning.
試験を受けた後（で）、先生にそうだんしました。*
After I took an exam, I consulted my teacher.
はをみがいた後（で）、ひげをそります。
(Lit.) After brushing (my) teeth, I shave (my) beard.
I shave after brushing my teeth.
授業が終わった後（で）、こくばんをけして下さい。
Please erase the blackboard when class is over.

* X にそうだんする
to consult X for advice

X とそうだんする
to discuss something with X

Noun + の後で: The noun must denote an activity or event, rather than a thing.

さんぽの後(で)、晩ごはんを食べます。
I'll eat dinner after taking a walk.
授業の後(で)、青木(あおき)さんに会いました。
I met Aoki-san after class.
電話の後(で)、銀行へ行って下さい。
Please go to the bank after (you make) your phone call.
晩ごはんの前におふろに入りたいですか。晩ごはんの後(で)入りたいですか。
Would you like to bathe before or after dinner?

18c Dictionary／ないフォーム + ようにする "I make an effort (not) to do VERB; I make things so that ~"

Dict 

In 第十四課, we studied a construction similar to this one, viz. 「Dictionary／ないフォーム + ことにする」 "I/We decide (not) to do ~", which is used to indicate the subject's decision to perform some act. 「Dictionary／ないフォーム + ようにする」, on the other hand, emphasizes the subject's *effort* to bring about a state of affairs. In both constructions, the verb must be in the Dictionary フォーム or ないフォーム, and the phrase できるだけ "as much as possible" frequently appears in this construction.

A When the verb denotes an intentional act, both ～ことにする and ～ようにする can be used.

できるだけ予習(よしゅう)するようにします。
I'll try (to make an effort) to prepare for the classes as much as I can.
できるだけ予習することにします。
I've decided to prepare for the classes as much as I can.

つぎの宿題は、できるだけ早く出すようにします。
I'll try (to make an effort) to turn in the next homework as early as I possible.
つぎの宿題は、できるだけ早く出すことにします。
I've decided to turn in the next homework as early as I possible.

単語(たんご)をできるだけたくさん覚えるようにしています。
I'm trying to memorize as many words as I can.
単語をできるだけたくさん覚えることにしています。
(Lit.) I decided and have been trying to memorize as many words as I can.
I've been making a point of memorizing as many words as I can.

毎月、ちょきんするようにしています。

I'm trying to save money every month.

毎月、ちょきんすることにしています。

I decided and have been trying to save money every month.

にくを食べないようにしています。

I'm trying not to eat meat.

にくを食べないことにしています。

(Lit.) I decided and have been trying not to eat meat.

I've been making a rule of not eating meat.

できるだけタバコをすわないようにしています。

I'm making a great effort not to smoke (cigarettes).

できるだけタバコをすわないことにしています。

(Lit) I decided and have been trying as much as I can not to smoke (cigarettes).

I'm making a point of smoking as little as possible.

お金がないので、買い物に行かないようにしています。

Since I don't have (much) money, I've been trying to keep myself from going shopping.

お金がないので、買い物に行かないことにしています。

Since I don't have (much) money, I've been making a rule of not going shopping.

B　If the verb denotes a non-intentional act or event, ～ようにする can be used, but ～ことにする cannot.

○　小づつみは、月曜日までにつくようにします。

×　小づつみは、月曜日までにつくことにします。

I'll arrange things so that the parcel will arrive by Monday.

このまどが楽に開くようにして下さい。

Please make this window open smoothly/easily.

寝ぼうしないようにしています。

I'm trying not to oversleep.

ふとらないようにしています。

I'm trying not to gain weight.

ビタミンCをたくさん飲んで、かぜをひかないようにしています。

By taking a lot of vitamin C, I'm making an effort not to catch a cold.

18d Dictionary ／ Potential ／ ないフォーム + ようになる
"It's gotten so that ~; It's become (im)possible that ~"

Dict **Pot** 

Dictionary／ないフォーム＋ようになる is the intransitive version (i.e. no direct object) of Dictionary／ないフォーム＋ようにする and is almost always used in the past tense, i.e. ～ようになった. Furthermore, the verb is frequently in the potential フォーム (cf. 第十三課, **13a**). Whereas ～ことになった／なっている "was／has been decided that X does ~" involves a decision, ～ようになった emphasizes the result itself, no matter how the result was obtained.

(1) 来学期(らいがっき)から、キャンパスでお酒が飲めるようになりました。
It's become possible to drink alcohol on campus starting the next semester.

(2) 来学期から、キャンパスでお酒が飲めることになりました。
It's been decided that we can drink alcohol on campus starting the next semester.

(1) indicates the change of state (i.e. drinking on campus was prohibited, but is now permitted), but how that change came about is unmentioned. (2), on the other hand, indicates that this change was brought about by some authority's permission.

If some change occurs by acquiring a relevant ability (for a person) or condition (for a thing), only ～ようになった can be used. For example, in (3), the speaker could not drink alcohol, but now she can. (It might be the case that alcohol made her sick before, but not any longer.) (4) indicates that the speaker could drink alcohol but was prohibited by, say, her doctor, and that this prohibition has been lifted.

(3) 私はお酒が飲めるようになりました。
I've become able to drink alcohol.

(4) 私はお酒が飲めることになりました。
(Lit.) It became the case that I'm allowed to drink alcohol.
I'm allowed to drink alcohol now.

(5) 日本語の新聞が読めるようになりました。
I've become able to read Japanese newspapers.

(6) 英語の文法が分かるようになりました。
I've become able to understand English grammar.

(7) 私の子供は歩(ある)けるようになりました。
My child has learned to walk.

(8) 何さいの時に、およげるようになりましたか。
(Lit.) At what age did you became able to swim?
How old were you when you learned to swim?

(9) まどが楽に開くようになりました。
(Lit.) It's become possible for the window to open smoothly.
The window opens easily now.

(10) 電気がつくようになりました。
(Lit.) It's become possible for the light to turn on.
The light is working now.

If a certain state of affairs becomes unavailable, nonexistent, or impossible, you can say ～ないようになる, but ～なくなる is by far more natural.

(11) ビルがたったので、子供達はあきちで { あそべないようになりました。 / あそべなくなりました。 }
Because a building has been built there, children can no longer play in the vacant lot.

(12) 父はさいきん、タバコを { すわないようになりました。 / すわなくなりました。 }
(Lit.) Recently, my father came to not smoke cigarettes.
Recently, my father quit smoking.

With 分かる, ～ないようになる is rarely used.

(13) とても漢字が多いので、分からなくなりました。
Because there are so many kanji, I can no longer understand.
Because there are so many kanji, I've become confused.

18e PRE-ますフォーム + 始める "begin / start VERB-ing"
PRE-ますフォーム + 終わる "finish VERB-ing"

ます

始める "to begin" and 終わる "to end" can be combined with another verb to form a compound verb. The first verb in these constructions must be in the Pre-ますフォーム. The resulting compound verbs are somewhat peculiar. While 始める by itself is transitive and 終わる by itself is intransitive, the transitivity of the compound verb is determined by the first verb: if it is intransitive, the entire verb becomes intransitive (e.g. 雨が降り始める, とうちゃく

し終わる); if the first verb is transitive, the entire verb becomes transitive (ごはんを食べ始める, ローンをはらい終わる). 始める is commonly combined with both intransitive and transitive verbs, but 終わる is predominantly combined with transitive verbs.

私の子供は、やっと歩き始めました。 *My child finally started walking.*
63ページから読み始めて下さい。 *Please start reading from p. 63.*
何さいの時にちょきんし始めましたか。 *At what age did you start saving money?*
雨が降り始める前に家へ帰りましょう。 *Let's go home before it starts raining.*
やっとローンをはらい終わりました。 *I've finally finished paying off my loan.*

料理がさめますから、どうぞおさきに*食べ始めて下さい。
The meal will get cold, so please start eating before me.
もう一ぱい飲み終わるまで待って下さい。
(Lit.) Please wait until I finish drinking one more glass.
Please wait until I finish one more drink.
多分、今晩十時ごろ宿題をし終わるでしょう。
I'll probably finish doing my homework at around 10 o'clock tonight.

* おさきに is a polite form of さきに "ahead /before".

Naturally, the first verb denotes an action which spans some period of time. If the subject is plural, however, punctual verbs can appear as the first verb, meaning that some *repetitive* action starts or ends.

学生が教室に来始めました。 *Students started arriving in class.*
おきゃくさまがとうちゃくし始めました。 *Guests began to arrive.*
おきゃくさまがとうちゃくし終わりました。 *(Lit.) The guests finished arriving.*
All the guests have arrived.

18f Transitive and Intransitive Verbs

As explained in 第十課, **10d**, many English verbs permit different types of subject. For example,

(1) I opened the door.
(2) This key opened the door.
(3) The door opened.

In (1) the subject is a human, who can make the door open; in (2) it is a tool that someone can use to open the door; in (3) it is the door itself, which was opened by someone or by a natural force, e.g. wind. Many English verbs can be used either transitively, e.g. (1)-(2), or intransitively, e.g. (3). By contrast, with only a few exceptions, Japanese verbs are either transitive or intransitive, but cannot be both.

Therefore, we must say:

(4) (私は) ドアを開けた。 *I opened the door.*

(5) ドアが開いた。 *The door opened.*

Note that in the transitive sentence (4), ドア is marked with を, whereas in the intransitive (5), it is marked with が (or は). Because 開ける and 開く are similar in meaning, the same 漢字 is used in both verbs. The following table provides some examples of such transitive-intransitive pairs.

Transitive	**Intransitive**	**例文(れいぶん)**
開(あ)ける open	開(あ)く open	あついので、まどを開けて下さい。 *It's hot, so please open the window.* しゅうりしたので、まどが開くようになりました。 *Because I fixed it, the window can open now.*
上(あ)げる raise	上(あ)がる rise go up	しつもんする時は、手を上げて下さい。 *Please raise your hand when you ask questions.* 家に上がる時は、くつをぬいで下さい。 *Please take off your shoes when you enter a house.*
入(い)れる put X into Y	入(はい)る enter	コーヒーに(お)さとうを入れますか。 *Would you like to put sugar into your coffee?* 部屋に入る時は、ノックして下さい。 *Please knock at the door when you enter the room.*
終(お)える finish	終(お)わる finish	宿題を終えてからテレビを見て下さい。 *Feel free to watch TV after you finish your homework.* 日本語の授業は何時に終わりますか。 *What time does the Japanese class end?* The transitive 終える is less frequently used than the intransitive 終わる. Therefore, this sentence can more naturally be said as 宿題が終わってからテレビを見て下さい.
けす turn off erase	きえる turn off	授業が終わった後で、電気をけして下さい。 *Please turn off the lights when class is over.* 十一時になると、電気がきえます。 *The lights turns off at 11 o'clock.*

こわす break	こわれる break	とけいをこわしてしまいました。 *I broke my watch.* とけいがこわれてしまいました。 *My watch broke.*
閉める close	閉まる close	あまりおきゃくさんが来ないので、早く店を閉めるつもりです。 *Not too many customers are coming, so I plan to close the store early.* 銀行は何時に閉まりますか。 *What time does the bank close?*
出す turn in send out	出る attend come out leave	宿題を出して下さい。 *Please turn your homework in.* 日本語のクラスは宿題がたくさん出ます。 *In Japanese class, there are many homework assignments.* 今日は八時ごろ家を出ました。 *I left home at about 8 o'clock today.* 出る in the sense of "leave" marks the location with を, but it is still considered as intransitive because it does not specify a relationship between two entities, but rather a single entity's change of location.
つける turn on	つく turn on	暗いので、電気をつけて下さいませんか。 *Because it's dark, could you please turn on the light?* スイッチを入れましたが、電気はつきませんでした。 *I flipped the switch, but the light didn't turn on.*
始める start begin	始まる start begin	それでは、かいぎを始めましょう。 *Well then, let's begin the meeting.* かいぎは三時に始まりました。 *The meeting began at 3 o'clock.*

練習問題

I. Role play をしましょう。あなたのパートナーはわるい学生です。あなたは先生になって、わるい学生にちゅういしましょう。

例 1 先生 : Xさん、よく授業におくれますね。
学生 : すみません。

先生：　おくれないようにして下さい。

学生：　はい、これからもっと早くおきるようにします。

例2 先生：　Xさん、よくクラスでボーッとしていますね。

学生：　すみません。

先生：　ボーッとしないようにして下さい。

学生：　はい、これからまじめに勉強するようにします。

例1 授業におくれる

例2 クラスでボーッとしている

1. クラスで英語を話している
2. 授業を休む
3. クラスで寝ている
4. クラスで宿題をしている

II. インタビューしましょう。

1. 日本語が上手になりたいですか。何をするようにしていますか。
2. 病気になりたくありませんね。何をしないようにしていますか。

III. ただしいこたえに○を書いて下さい。

1. しゅうりしたので、まどが（開ける・開く）ようになりました。
2. 九時にかいぎを（始まる・始める）ことにしましょう。
3. すみません、CDプレーヤーを（こわして・こわれて）しまいました。
4. 大きいですから、この本をかばんに（入れる・入る）ことはできません。
5. すみません、電気を（きえて・けして）下さいませんか。
6. 銀行が（閉めて・閉まって）いるので、お金がおろせません。
7. いらっしゃい。どうぞ、（上げて・上がって）下さい。
8. コンピューターが（こわした・こわれた）ので、コンピューターショップへ行きました。

IV. 何ができるようになりましたか。文を作って下さい。

1. 大学生になったので、＿＿＿＿＿＿＿＿＿＿＿＿＿＿＿＿ようになりました。
2. 一人で住んでいるので、＿＿＿＿＿＿＿＿＿＿＿＿＿＿＿ようになりました。
3. 日本語のクラスを取りましたから、＿＿＿＿＿＿＿＿＿＿＿ようになりました。

V. あなたはとても古いアパートに住んでいます。それで、もんだいがたくさんあります。下の絵を見て文を作って下さい。

例

テナント　：まどが開きません。

テナント　：おおやさん、まどが開くようにして下さい。
おおや　：はい、まどが開くようにします。

しゅうり屋：まどが開くようにしました。

テナント　：まどが開くようになりました。

1.

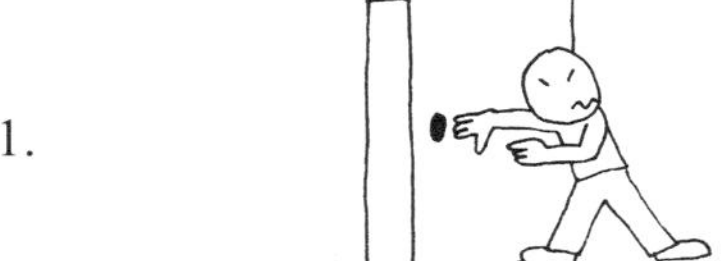

テナント　：＿＿＿＿＿＿＿＿＿＿＿＿＿＿。

テナント　：＿＿＿＿＿＿＿＿＿＿＿＿＿＿。
おおや　：＿＿＿＿＿＿＿＿＿＿＿＿＿＿。

しゅうり屋：＿＿＿＿＿＿＿＿＿＿＿＿＿＿。

テナント　：＿＿＿＿＿＿＿＿＿＿＿＿＿＿。

2.

テナント　：＿＿＿＿＿＿＿＿＿＿＿＿＿＿。

テナント　：＿＿＿＿＿＿＿＿＿＿＿＿＿＿＿＿＿＿。
おおや　：＿＿＿＿＿＿＿＿＿＿＿＿＿＿＿＿＿＿。

しゅうり屋：＿＿＿＿＿＿＿＿＿＿＿＿＿＿＿＿＿＿。

テナント　：＿＿＿＿＿＿＿＿＿＿＿＿＿＿＿＿＿＿。

3. テナント　：＿＿＿＿＿＿＿＿＿＿＿＿＿＿＿＿＿＿。

テナント　：＿＿＿＿＿＿＿＿＿＿＿＿＿＿＿＿＿＿。
おおや　：＿＿＿＿＿＿＿＿＿＿＿＿＿＿＿＿＿＿。

しゅうり屋：＿＿＿＿＿＿＿＿＿＿＿＿＿＿＿＿＿＿。

テナント　：＿＿＿＿＿＿＿＿＿＿＿＿＿＿＿＿＿＿。

VI. 「ようにする」と「ようになる」を使って会話を作って下さい。(You may have to change the verb form.)

例　車がうごきませんでした。それで、しゅうりしに行きました。

私　：この車はうごきません。車がうごくようにして下さい。
店の人：はい、車がうごくようにします。
(しゅうりした後で)
私　：ありがとうございました。車がうごくようになりました。

1. 車のまどがこわれてしまいました。それで、しゅうりしに行きました。

私　　：この車のまどが閉まりません。

____下さい。

店の人：はい、____。

(しゅうりした後で)

私　　：ありがとうございました。________________________________

____。

2. 私のテレビの音(おと)が出ません。それで、電気屋をよびました。

私　　：このテレビの音が出ません。

____下さい。

電気屋：はい、____。

(しゅうりした後で)

私　　：ありがとうございました。

____。

VII. 下の絵を見て下さい。あなたのパートナーは何をさきにしますか。聞いて下さい。そして、ただしいやじるし (arrow) に〇をつけて下さい。

例(れい)　A:　～さんは晩ごはんを食べる前に勉強しますか。食べた後で勉強しますか。

　　B:　私は晩ごはんを食べる前に勉強します。

例

→

(←)

1.

→

←

2.

→

←

3.

4.

VIII. 今週の土曜日にパーティーがあります。けれども、パーティーのプログラムにコーヒーをこぼしてしまったので、スケジュールが分かりません。パートナーにしつもんしましょう。

例　A:　<u>さいとうさんは何時ごろスピーチをし</u>始めますか。
　　B:　<u>五時半ごろスピーチをし</u>始めます。
　　A:　<u>さいとうさんは何時ごろスピーチをし</u>終わりますか。
　　B:　<u>六時ごろスピーチをし</u>終わります。

A

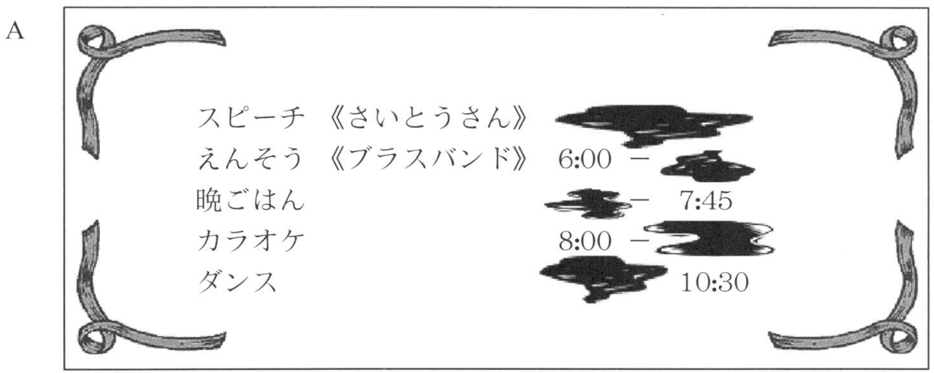

スピーチ	《さいとうさん》			
えんそう	《ブラスバンド》	6:00	−	
晩ごはん			−	7:45
カラオケ		8:00	−	
ダンス				10:30

B

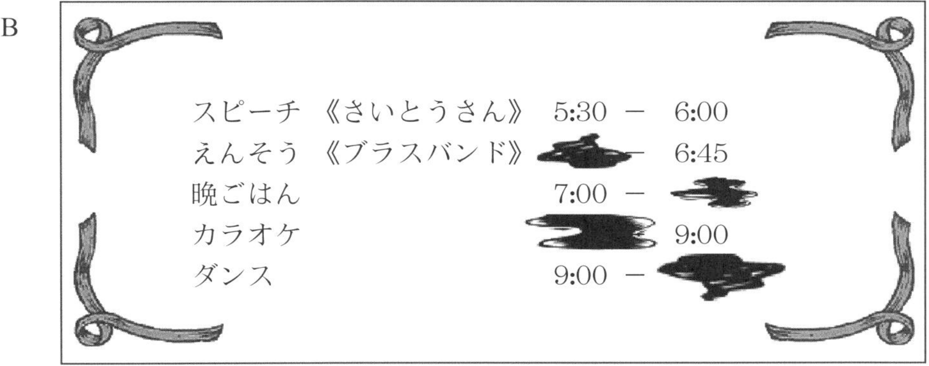

スピーチ	《さいとうさん》	5:30	−	6:00
えんそう	《ブラスバンド》		−	6:45
晩ごはん		7:00	−	
カラオケ				9:00
ダンス		9:00	−	

IX. パートナーにインタビューしましょう。

例(れい) A: Bさんは、何さいの時にじてんしゃに乗り始めましたか。

B: 私は六さいの時にじてんしゃに乗り始めました。

例	じてんしゃに乗る	(六)	さい	～		
1.	コンピューターを使う	(　　)	さい	～		
2.	車をうんてんする	(　　)	さい	～		
3.	(昨日) 勉強する	(　　)	時	～	(　　)	時
4.	(昨日) 晩ごはんを食べる	(　　)	時	～	(　　)	時

X. 読む練習

毎年、アメリカ人の留学生がおおぜい、日本へ行きます。そして、さいきん、ホームステイをする学生が多くなっています。日本人のかぞくといっしょに住むと、日本のしゅうかんが色々学べるからです。

ヒルマンさんは大学生の時、一年間、京都でホームステイをしました。ホストファミリーはすずきさんのかぞくでした。すずきさんの家はとても古くてりっぱでした。ヒルマンさんはとくに、にわが好きでした。きれいな花がたくさんさいていたからです。

すずきさんの家のおばあさんは毎朝五時におきて、二時間、花のせわをしました。ヒルマンさんも毎朝早くおきて、できるだけおばあさんのてつだいをするようにしました。始めはちょっと大変でしたが、だんだんなれました。

ヒルマンさんはおばあさんから京都の古いしゅうかんや文化を学びました。アメリカに帰る日、ヒルマンさんはおばあさんからすてきなプレゼントをもらいました。プレゼントはおばあさんが作ったきものでした。おばあさんからもらったきものは今でもヒルマンさんのたから物です。

◯ ですか。×ですか。

1. (　) おおぜいのアメリカ人の学生が日本で勉強しています。
2. (　) ホームステイをすると、日本のしゅうかんを色々学ぶことができます。
3. (　) ヒルマンさんは一年間京都に住んでいました。
4. (　) すずきさんの家のにわにきれいな花がたくさんさいていました。
5. (　) ヒルマンさんは日本では朝早くおきられませんでした。
6. (　) ヒルマンさんは日本の大学で京都の古いしゅうかんや文化を学びました。
7. (　) ヒルマンさんが帰国してから、おばあさんはヒルマンさんにきものをおくりました。

新しい漢字

～度(ど)	歩(ある)く	急(いそ)ぐ	終(お)える	終(お)わる	今度(こんど)
授業(じゅぎょう)	卒業(そつぎょう)	単語(たんご)	乗(の)る	復習(ふくしゅう)	文化(ぶんか)
文法(ぶんぽう)	予習(よしゅう)	練習(れんしゅう)			

新しい使い方

青木(あおき)	上(あ)げる	後(あと)	入(い)れる	色々(いろいろ)	映画館(えいがかん)
音(おと)	外国語(がいこくご)	帰国(きこく)	閉(し)める	寝(ね)ぼう	始(はじ)まる
始(はじ)め	毎月(まいつき)	学(まな)ぶ	来学期(らいがっき)		

Radicals: 糸(いと)へん・食(しょく)へん

紙, 終, and 練 contain the radical 糸, which is called いとへん. 糸(いと) by itself is a 漢字, meaning "thread". Many 糸へん漢字 are said to be related to "thread/cloth". 紙 was said to be made of 絹(きぬ) "silk" in ancient China.

食 can appear as a radical, as in 飲 and 館, and is called 食(しょく)へん. Although the radical 飠 consists of eight strokes, the 食へん is listed as a nine-stroke radical.

度	丶	亠	广	户	庐	庐	庐	度	度	
ド	*times, degree*									
後	丿	彳	彳	彳	徉	徉	後	後	後	
ゴ・あと・うし(ろ)	*after, back:* 午後 *P.M.*									
歩	丨	卜	止	止	步	步	步	歩		
ある(く)	*to walk*									
急	丿	ク	刍	刍	刍	刍	急	急	急	
いそ(ぐ)	*to hurry*									

Kanji	Reading	Meaning
入	い（れる）・はい（る）	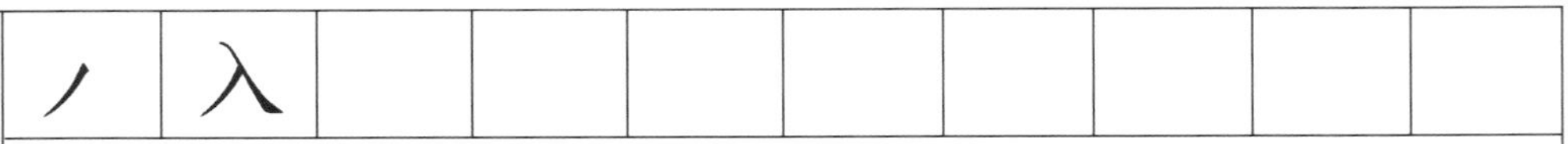 *to enter;* this 漢字 is the mirror image of 人 *person.*
終	お（える）・お（わる）	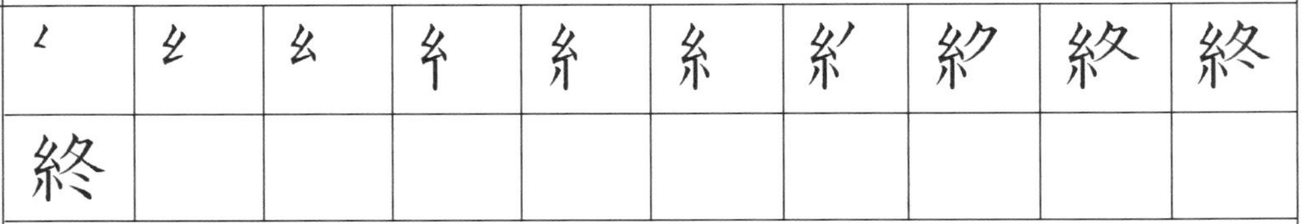 *to end, to finish*
音	オン・おと	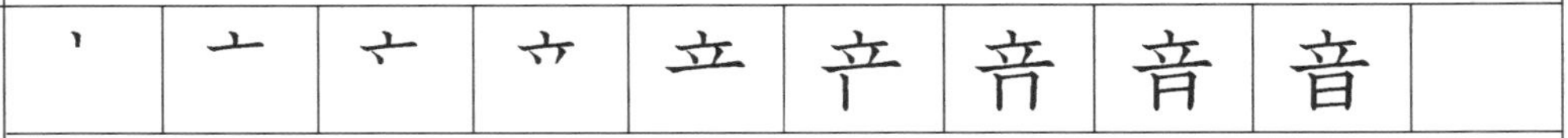 *sound:* 音楽 *music (comfort by sounds)*
帰	キ・かえ（る）	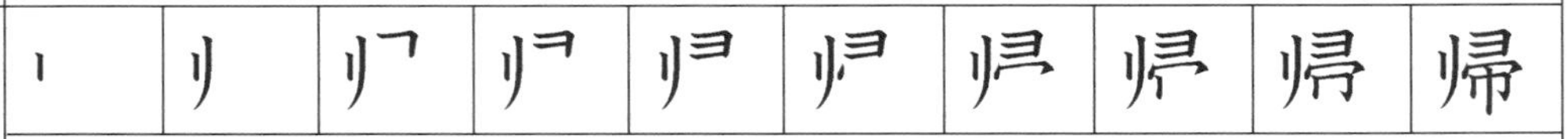 *to go home, to return:* 帰国 *going back to one's home country*
授	ジュ	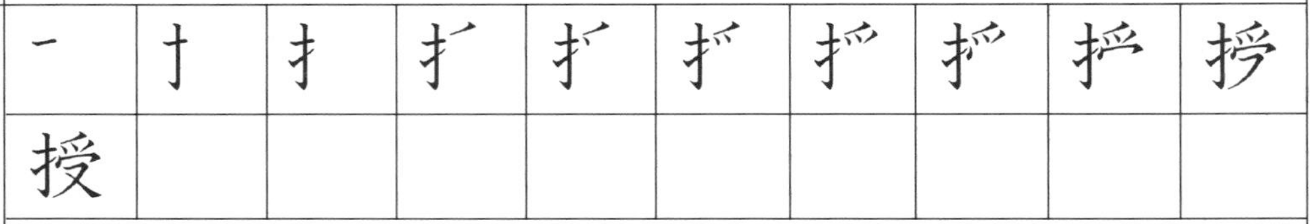 *to give:* 授業 *class*
業	ギョウ	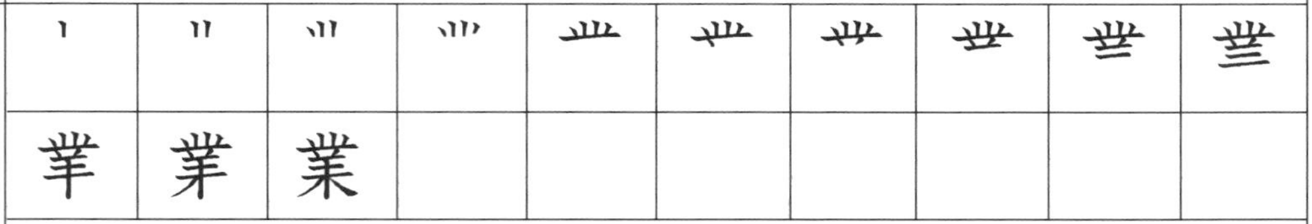 *vocation, studies:* 授業 *class,* 卒業 *graduation*
卒	ソツ	 *soldier:* 卒業 *graduation*
単	タン	 *unit:* 単語 *word (language unit)*
乗	の（る）	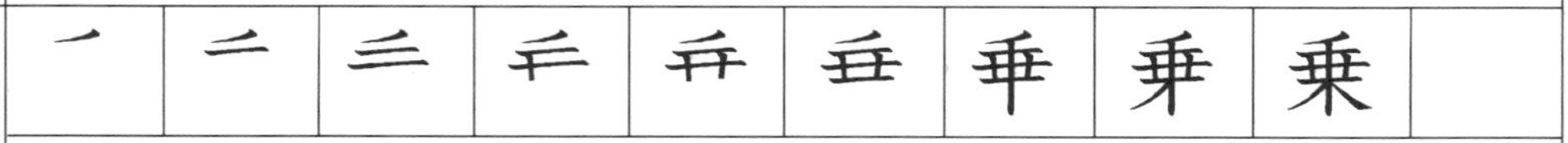 *to ride*

◧ 復	フク	*to return:* 復習 *review*
習	シュウ・なら(う)	*to learn:* 復習 *review,* 練習 *exercise,* 予習 *preparatory study*
◧ 化	カ	*influence, to change:* 文化 *culture*
◧ 法	ホウ・ポウ	*law:* 文法 *grammar*
学	ガク・まな(ぶ)	*study:* 学生 *student (studying person),* 留学生 *foreign student,* 小学校 *elementary school,* 中学校 *junior high school,* 大学 *college, university,* 学校 *school,* 文学 *literature,* 学期 *academic term*
予	ヨ	*in advance:* 予習 *preparatory study*
◧ 練	レン	*to train:* 練習 *exercise*

漢字の復習

I. 読みましょう。

1. 飛行機に乗るのは好きではありません。
2. 図書館へ行きましたが、閉まっていました。
3. キムさんは背が高いです。
4. 週末は、映画館で働いています。
5. 来学期、英文学の授業を取るつもりです。

II. どちらの方がいいですか。単語の読み方を書いてから、ただしいフォームにして、＿＿＿＿＿＿＿＿に入れて下さい。

	単語		使い方
1.	出る	出す	宿題を＿＿＿＿＿＿下さい。 日本語のクラスは宿題がたくさん＿＿＿＿＿＿ます。 今日は午前八時ごろ家を＿＿＿＿＿＿ました。
2.	開く	開ける	しゅうりしたので、まどが＿＿＿＿＿＿ようになりました。 あついので、まどを＿＿＿＿＿＿下さい。
3.	閉まる	閉める	おきゃくさんがあまり来ないので、早く店を＿＿＿＿＿＿つもりです。 銀行は何時に＿＿＿＿＿＿ますか。
4.	入る	入れる	コーヒーにおさとうを＿＿＿＿＿＿ますか。 部屋に＿＿＿＿＿＿時は、ノックして下さい。
5.	始まる	始める	それでは、かいぎを＿＿＿＿＿＿ましょう。 かいぎは三時に＿＿＿＿＿＿ました。
6.	終わる	終える	宿題を＿＿＿＿＿＿てから、テレビを見て下さい。 日本語の授業は何時に＿＿＿＿＿＿ますか。

新しい語彙(ごい)

あきち		*vacant lot*
後(あと)		*remaining*
急(いそ)ぐ	㋒ ⓘ	*to hurry*
今(いま)でも		*still now, even now*

うごく	㋒ ⓘ	*to move*
映画館(えいがかん)		*movie theater*
終(お)える	㋸ ⓣ	*to finish*
おおぜい		*many (people)*

おおや（さん）	*landlord*
おきゃくさま	*guest (respectful)*
おきゃくさん	*guest*
お茶 [ちゃ]	*tea ceremony*
音 [おと]	*sound*
おろす (ウ)(t)	*to withdraw (money)*
終わる [お] (ウ)(i)	*to finish*
かいぎ	*meeting*
外国語 [がいこくご]	*foreign language*
かたづける (ル)(t)	*to straighten (clean) up*
帰国 [きこく]（する）	*returning to one's home country*
きもの	kimono
ゲーム	*game*
けす (ウ)(t)	*to erase*
こくばん	*blackboard*
こぼす (ウ)(t)	*to spill*
こわす (ウ)(t)	*to break*
コンピューターショップ	*computer store*
さめる (ル)(i)	*to get cold*
閉める [し] (ル)(t)	*to close*
しゅうり（する）	*repair*
しゅうり屋 [や]	*repair person*
しゅっぱつ（する）	*departure*
スケジュール	*schedule*

すてき (ナ)	*superb, splendid*
スピーチ（する）	*speech*
せわ（する）	*care*
そうだん（する）	*consultation*
そる (ウ)(t)	*to shave*
それでは	*well then (formal)*
たから物 [もの]	*treasure*
たつ (ウ)(i)	*to be built*
だんだん	*gradually*
ちゅうい（する）	*warning*
ちょきん（する）	*savings*
てつだい	*help, assistance*
テナント	*tenant*
出る [で] (ル)(t)	*to come out, to go out*
電気屋 [でんきや]	*electric appliance shop*
とくに	*especially*
とこ屋 [や]	*barbershop*
なれる (ル)(i)	*to get used to*
ノック（する）	*knock*
始まる [はじ] (ウ)(i)	*to begin*
始め [はじ]	*first, beginning*
ひげ	*beard, mustache*
ビタミン	*vitamin*
ブラスバンド	*brass band*
文化 [ぶんか]	*culture*
ページ	*page*

ボーッとする Ⓘ ⓘ	*to become absent-minded*
ほんとうに	*truly*
毎月(まいつき)	*every month*
学(まな)ぶ ㋒ ⓣ	*to learn, study*
もう(一(いっ)ぱい／一度(いちど))	*(one) more*

よく	*often, frequently*
よやく(する)	*reservation*
来学期(らいがっき)	*next semester*
楽(らく)に	*easily, smoothly*
りっぱ ㋤	*splendid*
ローン	*loan*

名前

青木(あおき)	*Aoki*
ヒルマン	*Hillman*

第十九課 LESSON 19

オフィス・アワー
Office Hours

今、お忙(いそが)しいですか
Are you busy now?

会話

1　石川先生：どうぞ。

Please (come in).

2　ミラー：しつれいします。先生、今、お忙しいですか。

Excuse me. Sensei, are you busy now?

石川先生：あら、ミラーさん。どうぞ。

Oh, Miller-san. Please (come in).

3　石川先生：どうですか。さいきんは忙しいですか。

How are you? Have you been busy recently?

ミラー：はい、もうすぐ中間試験が三つあるんです。

Yes, I've got three midterm exams coming up.

4　石川先生：まあ、それは大変ですね。

Oh, I bet that's a lot of work.

ミラー：日本語のクラスは中間試験がないので、たすかります。

It's nice that there's no midterm exam in Japanese class.

5　ミラー：あのう、先生はおせんべいはお好きですか。

Uh... Sensei, do you like osenbei*?*

6　石川先生：ええ、好きですけれど……。

Yes, I do ...

7　ミラー：これは日本のホストファミリーからのプレゼントなんです。昨日とどいたんですが、たくさんあったので、半分(はんぶん)もって来ました。どうぞめし上(あ)がって下さい。

Well, this is a present from my host family in Japan. It arrived yesterday, and since there was so much, I brought half of it. Please have it.

8　石川先生：まあ、ありがとうございます。えんりょなくいただきます。

Oh, thank you. Thanks a lot.

9　石川先生：ミラーさんは、今でもホストファミリーとれんらくを取っているんですか。

Are you still in contact with your host family?

10 ミラー : ええ、できるだけ手紙を書くようにしています。来週、私のコンピューターに日本語のEメールプログラムをインストールします。

Yes, I try to write to them as often as I can. Next week I'm going to install a Japanese email program on my computer.

11 石川先生 : まあ、それは便利になりますね。

Oh, that'll be convenient.

ミラー : ええ、Eメールで日本語が使えたら、ホストファミリーとれんらくが取りやすくなるので、本当(ほんとう)にたすかります。

Yes, if I can use Japanese over email, it'll become easier to get in touch with my host family. It'll really be helpful.

使い方

2 あら "Oh/Oh my/Why!" is an interjection used by female speakers to express surprise or doubt, e.g. あら、これはだれのかさでしょう "Oh, whose umbrella is this?" あら、本当？ "Why! Really?"

4 まあ is also a female interjection to express surprise or admiration. まあ、おどろいた "What a surprise!" (literally, "I got surprised") まあ、きれい "How beautiful!"

たすかる originally means that the person is rescued or escapes from danger. The verb can be used more casually in the form of「CLAUSE ので、たすかる」to convey that the person can save a great deal of trouble because of what the CLAUSE indicates.

8 えんりょなくいただきます consists of えんりょ "reservation/modesty/diffidence/holding back", ない "be without", and いただく "I receive". In Japanese culture, if you do not practice えんりょ, you will be considered pushy or boorish. Here, Ishikawa-sensei literally says "I'll take it without modesty" because it is considered proper etiquette to show hesitation when one is offered something. When you let someone feel free to do something, you add the honorific prefix ご and say どうぞごえんりょなく "please feel free to do it".

質問(しつもん)がある時には、ごえんりょなくEメールして下さい。

When you have a question, please feel free to send me an email.

9 れんらく is a verbal noun meaning "contact/communication". X とれんらくを取る means "to contact/communicate with X"; X にれんらくする means "to notify X".

文法

19a Verb Honorifics
19b Adjective and Nominal Honorifics
19c CLAUSE1 たフォーム + ら CLAUSE2 = CLAUSE1 たら CLAUSE2 **"After C1, C2; If C1, C2"**

19a Verb Honorifics

Japanese has an elaborate system of *honorific expressions* that impart honor and/or respect. The use of such honorifics is, to a great extent, mandatory. That is, when the use of honorifics is expected by the speech community, failure to do so is considered vulgar or arrogant, not neutral. An appropriate level of honorifics is determined in great part by (i) the social relationship between the interlocutors, (ii) psychological distance that the speaker feels toward a target person, (iii) the situation in which conversation takes place, and (iv) the nature of the topic of conversation.

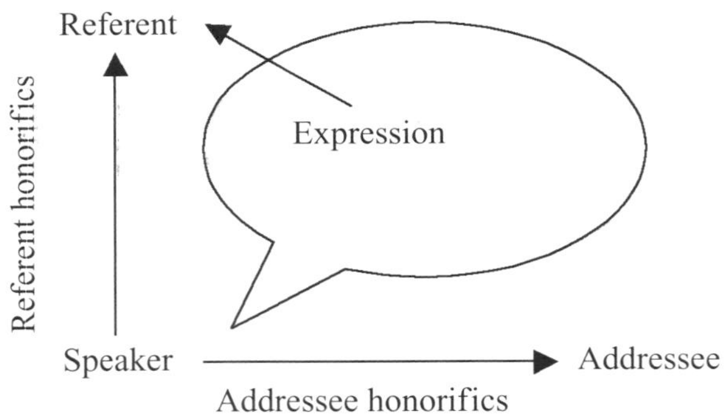

There are two orthogonal dimensions in the Japanese honorific system: *addressee honorifics* and *referent honorifics*. We have already studied addressee honorifics, i.e. the use of polite forms (vis-à-vis plain forms). For example, if you say 雨が降っています, rather than 雨が降っている, you are polite and showing respect to the addressee.

In this lesson, you are going to learn referent honorifics, which are somewhat different from addressee honorifics.

Many sentences contain an expression that refers to a person; the person referred to by such an expression is called the *referent* of the expression. The addressee and the referent can be the same person; e.g. in "Will you come to the meeting?" the referent of "you" is the addressee. In such a case, both addressee and referent honorifics can be used simultaneously.

When the referent of the subject is to be exalted, the most common way is to use (**A**) a special honorific verb (a verb used exclusively in honorific expressions) or (**B**) a derived honorific verb (an ordinary verb which has been made honorific through the use of a special grammatical construction).

A Honorific Verbs: These are special verbs used to show respect to the referent. There are only a handful of such verbs, but they occur very frequently in conversation.

Non Honorific	Honorific	Non Honorific	Honorific
行く	いらっしゃる	だ	でいらっしゃる
来る	いらっしゃる	する	なさる
いる	いらっしゃる	言う	おっしゃる
飲む	めし上がる	知っている	ごぞんじだ
食べる	めし上がる	見る	ごらんになる

いらっしゃる corresponds to "come／go／stay／be"; めし上がる is used for "intake" in general, "drink／eat／smoke (a cigarette)".

As explained in 第五課, **5c**, いらっしゃいます, which is an う -verb, exhibits irregularity due to its historical changes; it was pronounced as いらっしゃ[り]ます, but in Modern Japanese it is pronounced as いらっしゃ[い]ます. The same change is observed in なさ[り]ます → なさ[い]ます and おっしゃ[り]ます → おっしゃ[い]ます.

石川先生は何時ごろオフィスにいらっしゃいますか。

About what time will Ishikawa-sensei come to her office?

石川先生は何時ごろまでオフィスにいらっしゃいますか。

Until what time will Ishikawa-sensei be in her office?

石川先生でいらっしゃいますか。

Are you Ishikawa-sensei?

お元気でいらっしゃいますか。

(Lit.) Are you in good health?

How are you?

じゅうどうをなさいますか。

Do you practice judo?

どうぞお先(さき)にめし上がって下さい。

Please have (eat／drink) some before me.

もう旅館(りょかん)をよやくなさいましたか。

Have you already made a hotel reservation?

村上(むらかみ)先生は毎日ジョギングをしていらっしゃいます。そして、週末ジムで運動(うんどう)していらっしゃいます。

Murakami-sensei jogs every day, and he exercises at the gym on weekends.

村上先生のおくさんは運転(うんてん)なさいません。

Murakami-sensei's wife doesn't drive.

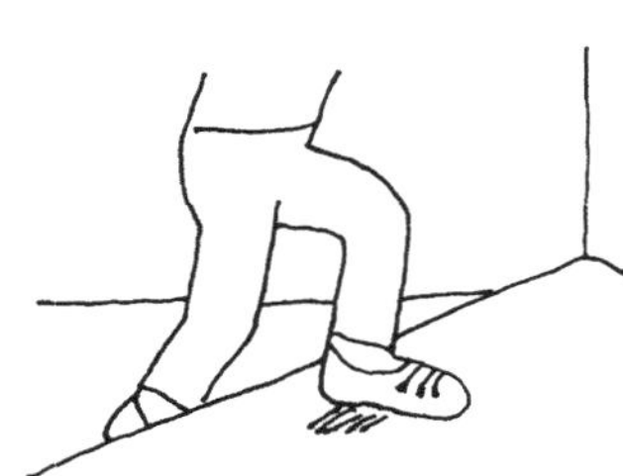

ミラーさんがくつをぬがないで上がったので、秋山さんはびっくりなさいました。
Because Miller-san entered the house without taking his shoes off, Akiyama-san was surprised.
もう一度おっしゃって下さいませんか。
Would you please say it again?

先生はちゅうかがいのおまつりをごらんになったことがありますか。
Sensei, have you seen the Chinatown festival?
この写真(しゃしん)をごらんになりますか。
Would you like to take a look at this photo?

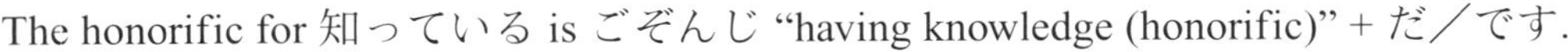
The honorific for 知っている is ごぞんじ "having knowledge (honorific)" + だ／です.

石川先生、千葉(ちば)先生をごぞんじですか。
Ishikawa-sensei, do you know Chiba-sensei?
石川先生は千葉先生をごぞんじでした。
Ishikawa-sensei knew Chiba-sensei.

～ている becomes ～ていらっしゃる.

村上先生は今、電話をしていらっしゃいます。(＝電話をなさっています)
Murakami-sensei is talking on the phone at the moment.
石川先生は今、新聞を読んでいらっしゃいます。(＝お読みになっています)
Ishikawa-sensei is reading the newspaper at the moment.

B　お-Verb になる

This is the most productive process for deriving honorific verbs: add the prefix お to the Pre- ますフォーム, followed by the particle に and the verb なる "become".

Non Honorific	Honorific	Non Honorific	Honorific
急ぐ	お急ぎになる	眠(ねむ)る／寝る／休む	お休みになる
帰る	お帰りになる	話す	お話しになる
書く	お書きになる	出る	お出になる
すわる	おすわりになる	やめる	おやめになる
たつ	おたちになる	よぶ	およびになる
できる	おできになる	よろこぶ	およろこびになる

千葉先生はもうお帰りになりました。
Chiba-sensei has already gone home.
どうぞ、おすわりになって下さい。
Please sit down.
千葉先生はゴルフがおできになります。
Chiba-sensei can play golf.
石川先生はもうお休みになっています。
Ishikawa-sensei has already gone to bed/is sleeping.
千葉先生はさいきん、タバコをおやめになりました。
Chiba-sensei quit smoking recently.
およびになりましたか。
Did you call me?

You can use referent honorifics with or without addressee honorifics. For example, if you talk with 千葉先生, you should use both of them, whereas when you talk with your close friends, you should use only referent honorifics.

石川先生はもうお帰りになりましたか。	To 千葉先生
石川先生はもうお帰りになった？	To your classmate

Has Ishikawa-sensei already gone home?

Never use these honorific verbs when the subject is you or your family member.

× 私は石川先生をごぞんじです。
× 母は新聞をお読みになります。

19b Adjective and Nominal Honorifics

Adjectives that describe a person can form honorifics by adding the prefix お.

A い-Adjectives

忙しい → お忙しい
石川先生はいつもお忙しいです。
Ishikawa-sensei is always busy.

強い → お強い
青木せんぱい*はじゅうどうがお強いです。
Aoki-senpai is good (strong) at judo.

* せんぱい is a person with seniority in a particular area. In a university setting, the sophomores outrank the freshmen, and the juniors outrank the sophomores. The use of the term せんぱい frequently carries the connotation of "mentor". Like せんせい, せんぱい can be used as a title, e.g. 青木せんぱい.

眠(ねむ)い　→　お眠い

お眠いですか。

Are you sleepy?

やさしい　→　おやさしい

石川先生はおやさしい方です。

Ishikawa-sensei is a gentle / kind person.

B　な -Adjectives

きれい　→　おきれい　石川先生はおきれいです。
Ishikawa-sensei is pretty.

元気　→　お元気　山田(やまだ)先生はお元気でした。
Yamada-sensei was cheerful / well.

上手　→　お上手　山田先生はしょどうがお上手です。
Yamada-sensei is good at calligraphy.

ひま　→　おひま　せんぱい、今おひまですか。
(Lit.) Senpai, are you in leisure time now?
Senpai, are you free at the moment?

好き　→　お好き　石川先生は動物(どうぶつ)がお好きです。
Ishikawa-sensei likes animals.

Some な -adjectives take the prefix ご, rather than お.

しんせつ　→　ごしんせつ　山田先生はごしんせつな方です。
Yamada-sensei is a kind person.

ていねい　→　ごていねい　ごていねいに、お電話、ありがとうございました。
(Lit.) Thank you for (giving me) a telephone call courteously.
Thank you for your courteous telephone call.

りっぱ　→　ごりっぱ　山田先生はごりっぱな家に住んでいらっしゃいます。
Yamada-sensei is living in a splendid house.

C Verbal Nouns

Most verbal nouns take the prefix ご.

えんりょ → ごえんりょ　どうぞごえんりょなさらないで下さい。
(Lit.) Please don't hesitate.
Please feel at home.

しんぱい → ごしんぱい　ごしんぱいなさらないで下さい。
Please don't worry (about me).

卒業 → ご卒業　石川先生は日本の大学をご卒業なさいました。
Ishikawa-sensei graduated from a Japanese university.

旅行 → ご旅行　山田先生はヨーロッパへご旅行なさいます。
Yamada-sensei is going to travel to Europe.

勉強 → お勉強　千葉先生は大学で言語学をお勉強なさいました。
Chiba-sensei studied linguistics at college.

Here again, do not use these honorific adjectives to describe yourself or your family members.

19c CLAUSE1 たフォーム + ら CLAUSE2 "After C1, C2; If C1, C2" = CLAUSE1 たら CLAUSE2

This construction is made by adding ら to the たフォーム of a verb, adjective, or です, which is commonly called the たら *construction*. It indicates that C1 is completed before C2; it does not specify whether the sequence is factual (i.e. took place in the past) or conditional/hypothetical.

A When C2 (main clause) is in the past tense, it is natural to interpret the sentence to be factual, not conditional or hypothetical.

(1) 週末、きっさ店に行ったら、田中さんに会いました。
(Lit.) After going to (arriving at) the café (last) weekend, I ran into Tanaka-san.
When I went to the café (last) weekend, I ran into Tanaka-san.

(2) この問題は、先生に聞いたら、かんたんに分かりました。
As for this problem, I understood it easily when/after I asked my teacher.

(3) おさしみを食べたら、おなかがいたくなりました。
When/After I ate sashimi, *I felt pain in my stomach.*

There is one important restriction on this construction when C2 is in the past tense, viz. **C2 cannot express an intentional act**. For example, 会う has two meanings: to meet someone intentionally or to run into someone. In (1), only the latter interpretation is possible. In (2)-(3), かんたんに分かる and おなかがいたくなる are events, not intentional acts.

B **When C2 is in the non-past tense,** the constraint of intentionality does not apply: C2 can express an intentional act, e.g. (4). On the other hand, with a non-past C2, the sentence can be ambiguous between factual and conditional readings.

(4) 子供が眠ったら、電話します。
When / If the kids fall asleep, I'll call you.

(5) ちがったら、言って下さい。
When / If I'm wrong, please tell me.

If the occurrence of C1 is certain, *when* is more appropriate; if the probability of C1 is unknown, *if* is preferred. The sentence can be disambiguated by the use of もし "if".

(6) 家についたら、電話します。
When I get home, I'll call you.

(7) 早く家についたら、電話します。
If I get home early, I'll call you.

(8) もし、お金がたりなかったら、言って下さい。
If you don't have enough money, please tell me.

(9) もし、分からなかったら、質問して下さい。
If you don't understand, please ask me.

C **～たら vs. ～た時 (に):** In 第十三課, we learned that when the たフォーム is used in C1 of 「C1 時 (に) C2」, C1 occurs before C2 is realized / completed. So, ～たら and ～た時 are similar, and in fact they are frequently interchangeable, as in (10).

(10) 週末、きっさ店に { 行ったら / 行った時 } 、田中さんに会いました。
I met Tanaka-san when I went to the café (last) weekend.

However, in (11), ～たら and ～た時 (に) are not equivalent. ～たら strongly suggests a causal relationship, whereas the ～た時 (に) sentence lacks such a connotation. Therefore, (11a) implies that the cause of the stomachache was the *sashimi*, but (11b) indicates that when the speaker felt a stomachache, s/he was incidentally eating *sashimi*. Because of its lack of causal connotation, ～た時 (に) is inappropriate in (12b) and (13b).

(11a) ○ おさしみを食べたら、おなかがいたくなりました。
I ate sashimi *and had a stomachache.*

(11b) ○ おさしみを食べた時(に)、おなかがいたくなりました。
I had a stomachache while I was eating sashimi .
(or) *I had a stomachache when I ate* sashimi .

(12a) ○ ぜいきんをはらったら、お金がなくなってしまいました。
After paying my taxes, I didn't have much money left.
(12b) × ぜいきんをはらった時(に)、お金がなくなってしまいました。

(13a) ○ よく寝たら、元気になりました。
When I slept well, I became refreshed.
(13b) × よく寝た時(に)、元気になりました。

D Another construction similar to「C1 たら C2」is「C1 てから C2」(第十五課). Again, they are sometimes interchangeable. For example, in (14)-(16), either たら or てから can be used without changing the meaning.

(14) しゅうしょく{したら / してから}、日本へ行ってみるつもりです。
After finding a job, I plan to go to Japan (to see what it is like.)

(15) コーヒーを{飲んだら / 飲んでから}、映画を見に行きませんか。
After having some coffee, would you like to go see a movie?

(16) 宿題が{終わったら / 終わってから}、来て下さい。
Please come over after you finish your homework.

However, in (17), たら cannot replace てから because C2 represents an intentional act in the past.

(17a) ○ 家へ帰ってから、宿題をしました。
After I got home, I did my homework.
(17b) × 家へ帰ったら、宿題をしました。
(17c) ○ 家へ帰ったら、宿題をします。
After I get home, I'll do my homework.

E When ～たら is used with an adjective or nominal predicate, the sentence is almost always interpreted as conditional/hypothetical.

(i) い-Adjectives

(18) 暗かったら、電気をつけて下さい。
If it's too dark, please turn on the light.

(19) 外が暗くてこわかったら、いっしょに行きますよ。

If it's too dark and scary, I'll go with you.

(20) おもしろかったら、かして下さい。

If it's interesting, please lend it to me.

(21) 安かったら、買えます。

If it's inexpensive, I can afford to buy it.

(22) もしよかったら*、見せて下さい。

If it's okay, please show it to me.

* Note that the たフォーム of いい is よかった, not いかった.

(23) あまりからくなかったら、食べられます。

If it's not too spicy, I can eat it.

(24) つめたかったら、飲みたいです。

If it's cold, I want to drink it.

(25) もし試験が少なかったら、その授業を取るつもりです。

If there are only a few tests, I'll take the course.

(ii) な -Adjectives

(26) ひまだったら、あそびに来て下さい。

If you are free, please come visit me.

(27) きらいだったら、食べなくてもいいですよ。

If you don't like it, you don't have to eat it.

(28) 大変だったら、したくないです。

If it's a lot of work, I don't want to do it.

(29) もしあまりふくざつじゃなかったら、勉強してみたいです。

If it's not too complicated, I'd like to study it.

(iii) Nominal Predicates

(30) 十時だったら、来られます。

If it's at 10 o'clock, I can come over.

(31) 自転車(じてんしゃ)だったら、三十分いじょうかかります。
If by bicycle, it'll take more than 30 minutes.

(32) もし、その手紙が日本語だったら、読めます。
If the letter is in Japanese, I can read it.

(33) もし、明日いいてんきだったら、いっしょにジョギングに行きませんか。
If the weather's nice tomorrow, would you like to go jogging with me?

練習問題

I.　Honorific Form を使って、文を作って下さい。

例(れい)A 先生はかいぎに行きます。　→　先生はかいぎにいらっしゃいます。
例B 先生は話します。　→　先生はお話しになります。

例A 行く	3. 歌う	7. 書く	11. する	15. 飲む
例B 話す	4. 教える	8. 来る	12. 食べる	16. 乗る
1. 言う	5. 買う	9. 知っている	13. 作る	17. 見る
2. いる	6. 帰る	10. タバコをすう	14. 眠る	18. 読む

II.　文をかんせいして下さい。

1. 学生：先生、コーヒーを＿＿＿＿＿＿＿＿＿＿＿＿か。
先生：そうですか。いただきます。
学生：おかしも＿＿＿＿＿＿＿＿＿＿＿＿か。
先生：いいですね。いただきます。

2. 学生：先生、今日もおそくまで仕事を＿＿＿＿＿＿＿＿＿＿＿＿か。
先生：いいえ、今日はしません。もうやめます。
学生：それじゃ、もう＿＿＿＿＿＿＿＿＿＿＿＿か。
先生：ええ、もう帰ります。

3. 学生：先生、さいとう先生を＿＿＿＿＿＿＿＿＿＿＿＿か。
先生：はい、知っています。
学生：電話ばんごうも＿＿＿＿＿＿＿＿＿＿＿＿か。
先生：いいえ、電話ばんごうは知りません。

4. 学生 ： 先生、今日、二時ごろ、オフィスに＿＿＿＿＿＿＿＿＿＿＿＿＿＿＿＿か。
ちょっと質問があるんです。
先生 ： ええ、いますから、来て下さい。

5. 学生 ： 先生は昨日の晩、七時ごろ何を＿＿＿＿＿＿＿＿＿＿＿＿＿＿＿＿か。
先生 ： 七時ごろですか。ええと、晩ごはんを食べていました。

6. 学生 ： 先生はどんな音楽を＿＿＿＿＿＿＿＿＿＿＿＿＿＿＿＿か。
先生 ： 私はクラシックをよく聞きます。
学生 ： そうですか。私はロックが好きです。

7. 学生 ： 先生、毎朝、何時ごろ大学へ＿＿＿＿＿＿＿＿＿＿＿＿＿＿＿＿か。
先生 ： 七時四十五分ごろ来ます。
学生 ： 八時のクラスを＿＿＿＿＿＿＿＿＿＿＿＿＿＿＿＿か。
先生 ： はい、毎日教えています。

8. 学生 ： 先生は日本の新聞を＿＿＿＿＿＿＿＿＿＿＿＿＿＿＿＿か。
先生 ： はい、毎日インターネットで日本の新聞を読みます。日本のニュースが知りたいですから。
学生 ： 先生は日本の映画もよく＿＿＿＿＿＿＿＿＿＿＿＿＿＿＿＿か。
先生 ： いいえ、映画はあまり見ません。

9. 学生 ： 先生はよく日本料理を＿＿＿＿＿＿＿＿＿＿＿＿＿＿＿＿か。
先生 ： いいえ、忙しいので、あまり作りません。
学生 ： そうですか。でも日本料理をよく＿＿＿＿＿＿＿＿＿＿＿＿＿＿＿＿か。
先生 ： はい、食べます。さいきん、きんじょのスーパーでおすしが買えるようになりましたから。

III. 昨日クラブのせんぱいは何をなさいましたか。絵を見てパートナーに質問して下さい。

例(れい)1 学生A: せんぱいは昨日、午前八時に何をなさいましたか。
学生B: せんぱいは昨日、午前八時に朝ごはんをめしあがりました。

例2 学生B: せんぱいは昨日、午前九時ごろ、何をなさいましたか。
学生A: せんぱいは昨日、午前九時ごろ、買い物をなさいました。

	A	B
8:00 A.M.	?	
9:00 10:00 11:00		?
12:00 P.M.		?
1:00 2:00 3:00		?
4:00	?	
5:00	?	
6:00	?	
7:00		?
8:00 9:00	?	 TV
10:00		?
11:00	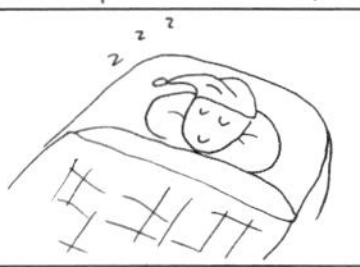	?

IV. パートナーに質問して先生の今週の日曜日のスケジュールをかんせいしましょう。

例(れい) 学生 A: 先生は日曜日に朝ごはんをめし上がってから何をなさいますか。
学生 B: 先生は日曜日に朝ごはんをめし上がってから本をお読みになります。

A 例 →？→ 1. 2. →？→ 3. 4. →？→ 5. 6. →？→ 7. 8.

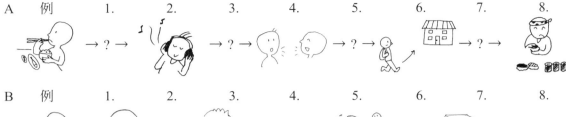

B 例 → 1. →？→ 2. 3. →？→ 4. 5. →？→ 6. 7. →？→ 8.

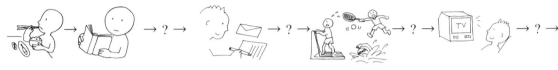

V. 来年の日本語の先生はさいとう先生です。さいとう先生はどんな先生でしょうか。せんぱいに聞いてみましょう。

例 あなた　: さいとう先生は<u>ごしんせつ</u>ですか。
せんぱい: はい、さいとう先生は<u>ごしんせつな</u>先生です。

VI. 質問にこたえて下さい。

1. もしたくさん貯金(ちょきん)があったら、何がしたいですか。

____________________________________。

2. 週末ひまだったら、何をしますか。

____________________________________。

3. もし日本へ行けたら、日本で何がしたいですか。

____________________________________。

4. 卒業したら、何がしたいですか。

____________________________________。

5. もし車が動(うご)かなかったら、どうしますか。

____________________________________。

VII. AとBのはこからてきとうなペアを作って下さい。そして、「〜たら」を使って文を書きましょう。

A	B
1. 友達が作った料理を食べました。	a. 電話して下さい。
2. ショッピングセンターへ行きました。	b. 田中さんに会いました。
3. きょうかしょを読みました。	c. 日本で働きたいです。
4. くうこうにつきます。	d. 文法がよく分かりました。
5. 大学を卒業します。	e. おなかがいたくなりました。

VIII. AとBのはこからてきとうなペアを作って下さい。そして、「〜たら」を使って文を書きましょう。

A	B
1. 車がなおりません。	a. お金をはらわなくてはいけません。
2. 日本人です。	b. 日本の大学で勉強できます。
3. 料理がからいです。	c. ピクニックをしましょう。
4. しょうがくきん*がもらえます。	d. おすしを食べたことがあるでしょう。
5. 明日、てんきがいいです。	e. 食べられません。
6. ラボのコンピューターをこわします。	f. ドライブに行けません。

* Like せんたくき → せんたっき (cf. 第十六課 使い方ノート1), しょうがくきん is normally pronounced as しょうがっきん.

IX. 文をかんせいして下さい。

1. オフィスアワーに行ったら、＿＿＿＿＿＿＿＿＿＿＿＿＿＿＿＿＿＿＿＿。
2. ＿＿＿＿＿＿＿＿＿＿＿＿＿＿＿＿たら（だら）、友達があそびに来ました。
3. ＿＿＿＿＿＿＿＿＿＿＿＿＿＿＿＿たら（だら）、友達に会いました。
4. ＿＿＿＿＿＿＿＿＿＿＿＿＿＿＿＿たら（だら）、病気になりました。
5. ＿＿＿＿＿＿＿＿＿＿＿＿＿＿＿＿たら（だら）、元気になりました。

X.　つぎの文を読んで質問にこたえて下さい。

私の日本語の先生は山田先生です。とてもごしんせつな先生です。山田先生はもう十五年ぐらいアメリカに住んでいらっしゃいます。日本の大学をご卒業なさってからこちらにいらっしゃって、アメリカの大学院で言語学をお勉強なさいました。五年前(ねんまえ)から私達の大学で教えていらっしゃいます。先生は学生といつも日本語でお話しになりますが、英語もとてもお上手です。山田先生のごしゅじんも大学の先生で、物理学(ぶつりがく)を教えていらっしゃいます。

山田先生はとてもお忙しい方です。いつもおそくまでオフィスで仕事をしていらっしゃいます。けれども、学生は質問があったら、いつでも先生に聞きに行けます。

先生は授業中、いつも、分かりやすく文法をごせつめいなさいます。そして、時々じょうだんをおっしゃいます。先生はとてもおやさしいので、学生に人気があります。

この前、オフィスアワーに行って、山田先生と話しました。先生と話すのはとても楽しいです。先生は夏休みに、ごかぞくといっしょにヨーロッパへご旅行なさいます。

1.　山田先生は何を教えていらっしゃいますか。
2.　山田先生はどのぐらいこの人の大学で教えていらっしゃいますか。
3.　山田先生はアメリカの大学院で何をお勉強なさいましたか。
4.　山田先生はけっこんしていらっしゃいますか。
5.　学生は山田先生が好きでしょうか。
6.　山田先生は夏休みに何をなさいますか。

新しい漢字

忙(いそが)しい	動(うご)く	運転(うんてん)	運動(うんどう)	質問(しつもん)	自転車(じてんしゃ)
写真(しゃしん)	田中(たなか)	貯金(ちょきん)	動物(どうぶつ)	眠(ねむ)い	眠(ねむ)る
本当(ほんとう)	問題(もんだい)	山田(やまだ)	旅館(りょかん)	旅行(りょこう)	

新しい使い方

言語学(げんごがく)	先(さき)	少(すく)ない	千葉(ちば)	～年前(ねんまえ)	半分(はんぶん)
物理学(ぶつりがく)	見(み)せる	村上(むらかみ)	めし上(あ)がる		

Radicals: 貝(かい)へん

貝(かい) "shell" appears in 買, 質, and 貯. (Although it also appears in 員, 員 is customarily included in the 口 "mouth" group, rather than the 貝(かい) group; see 第十六課漢字ノート for such conventions.) When 貝 appears in the left side, it is called 貝(かい)へん. 貝 can appear as 足(あし) (bottom part) as well. Most 貝(かい)漢字 are related to money or to commercial transaction (買う "buy", 貯金 "savings") because, it is said, shells were used as money in ancient China. 質 in 質問 is also used in 質屋(しちや) "pawn shop".

忙	いそが(しい)	busy
動	ドウ・うご(く)	to move: 動物 animal, 運動 exercise
運	ウン	fate, to transport: 運転 drive, 運動 exercise
転	テン	to turn: 運転 drive, 自転車 bicycle
言	ゲン・い(う)・こと	to say: 言葉 language, word, 言語学 linguistics
先	セン・さき	preceding: 先生 teacher (preceding person)

Kanji	Reading	Meaning and examples
質	シツ	*substance:* 質問 *question*
問	モン	*question:* 質問 *question,* 問題 *problem*
自	ジ	*self:* 自転車 *bicycle (self turning wheel)*
写	シャ	*to copy:* 写真 *photograph (copying the reality)*
真	シン	*truth, reality:* 写真 *photograph (copying the reality)*
少	すく（ない）・すこ（し）	*a little, few:* 少 contains 小 *small.*
田	た・だ	*rice field:* 田中 *Tanaka,* 山田 *Yamada*
千	せん・ち	*thousand:* 千葉 *Chiba*
葉	ば	*leaf:* 言葉 *language, word,* 千葉 *Chiba*

貯 チョ	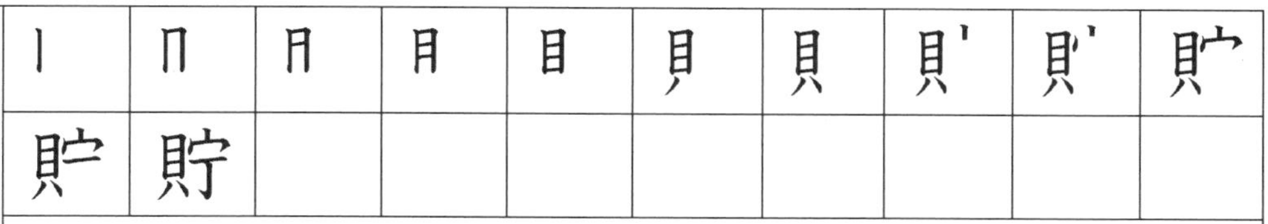 *to save:* 貯金 *savings*
物 ブツ・もの	 *thing:* 買い物 *shopping,* 見物 *sightseeing,* 食べ物 *food,* 動物 *animal,* 物理学 *physics,* 読み物 *something to read*
当 トウ	 *to hit:* 本当 *true*
眠 ねむ（い）・ねむ（る）	 *to sleep*
題 ダイ	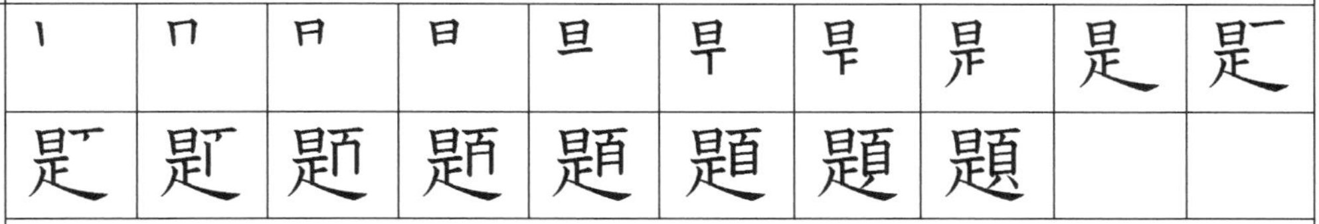 *subject, topic:* 宿題 *homework assignment (subject to do at home),* 問題 *problem*
旅 リョ	 *travel:* 旅行 *travel,* 旅館 *inn*

漢字の復習

I.　読みましょう。

1. 期末試験が終わったら、何がしたいですか。
2. 日本まちの店でお米とお酒を買いました。
3. 飲み物の中で、何が一番好きですか。
4. 教室で歌わないで下さい。
5. 冬休みに会えるのを楽しみにしています。

II. 漢字には色々な読み方があります。つぎの漢字の読み方を書いて下さい。いみが分かりますか。

1.	大	1.	大きい	2.	大変	3.	大好き	4.	大学院生
2.	国	1.	中国	2.	外国人	3.	帰国		
3.	木	1.	木村	2.	木曜日	3.	木の葉	4.	六本木
4.	月	1.	四月	2.	来月	3.	月	4.	月曜日
5.	言	1.	言う	2.	言葉	3.	言語学		
6.	人	1.	日本人	2.	二人	3.	三人	4.	あの人
7.	上	1.	村上	2.	上	3.	上がる	4.	上手
8.	後	1.	後ろ	2.	午後	3.	勉強した後(で)		

新しい語彙(ごい)

Xいじょう	*more than X*
いらっしゃる ㋒ ⓘ	*to come, go (honorific)*
インストール(する)	*installation*
えんりょ(する)	*reservation, hesitation*
おしゃべり(する)	*chat*
おそくまで	*until late*
おっしゃる ㋒ ⓣ	*to say (honorific)*
おどろく ㋒ ⓘ	*to get surprised*
からい ㋑	*hot, spicy, salty*
かんせい(する)	*completion*
きんじょ	*neighborhood*
くわしい ㋑	*detailed*
けっこん(する)	*marriage*
言語学(げんごがく)	*linguistics*
ごぞんじだ	*to know (honorific)*
ごらんになる ㋒ ⓣ	*to see, watch (honorific)*

こわい ㋑	*threatening, scary*
しゅうしょく(する)	*getting a job*
じゅうどう	*judo*
しょうがくきん	*scholarship (money)*
じょうだん	*joke*
ショッピングセンター	*shopping center / mall*
しょどう	*calligraphy*
しんぱい(する)	*anxiety, concern, worry*
少(すく)ない	*very few / little*
ぜいきん	*tax*
せんぱい	*one's senior*
(お)せんべい	*rice cracker*
たすかる ㋒ ⓘ	*to be saved*
たりる ㋸ ⓘ	*to be sufficient*
ちがう ㋒ ⓘ	*wrong, different*
ちゅうかがい	*Chinatown*

つめたい (イ)	*cold*
ていねい (ナ)	*polite, courteous*
てきとう (ナ)	*appropriate*
動物(どうぶつ)	*animal*
とどく (ウ)(i)	*to reach, arrive*
ドライブ(する)	*drive*
なおる (ウ)(i)	*to be repaired*
なくなる (ウ)(i)	*to run out of*
X 年前(ねんまえ)	*X years ago*
ばんごう	*number*
半分(はんぶん)	*half*

びっくりする (I)(i)	*to get surprised*
ふくざつ (ナ)	*complicated*
物理学(ぶつりがく)	*physics*
ペア	*pair*
見(み)せる (ル)(t)	*to show*
めし上(あ)がる (ウ)(t)	*to eat (honorific)*
もし	*if*
もって来(く)る (I)(t)	*to bring (a thing)*
れんらく(する)	*contact*
れんらくを取(と)る	*to contact, communicate*

名前

田中(たなか)	*Tanaka*
千葉(ちば)	*Chiba*

村上(むらかみ)	*Murakami*
山田(やまだ)	*Yamada*

日本の中学生
Japanese Junior High Students

また日本へ行こうと思(おも)います
I'm thinking about going to Japan again

会話

1　山本　：ミラーさん、京都はどうでしたか。

Miller-san, how was Kyoto?

ミラー　：とてもきれいでした。そして、中学生がおおぜいいました。

It was very beautiful. And there were lots of junior high school students.

2　ミラー　：なぜ、あんなに学生が多いんですか。

Why are there so many students (there)?

山本　：ああ、それはきっとしゅうがく旅行ですよ。

Oh, I bet it's (because of) school excursions.

ミラー　：しゅうがく旅行？

School excursions?

3　山本　：学校を卒業する前に、みんなでいっしょに旅行するんです。京都や奈良(なら)はれきしてきな所(ところ)ですから、とても人気があります。

They go on group trips together before graduating from school. Kyoto and Nara are historical places, so they're very popular (as destinations).

4　ミラー　：そうですか。学生達は私に「Hello, hello, this is a pen」と言いました。それで、私は「こんにちは。これはペンです」と答(こた)えました。

Oh really. The students said to me, "Hello, hello, this is a pen." So I answered, "Konnichiwa. Kore wa pen desu."

5　山本　：ハッハッハッ。ミラーさんはおもしろい人ですね。みんなびっくりしたでしょう。

Ha, ha, ha! You're a funny person, Miller-san. They must have been surprised.

ミラー　：ええ。びっくりしていました。そして、私に日本語が分かるかどうか聞きました。「Yes, I do」と答えました。

Yes, they were. Then they asked me whether or not I understood Japanese, and I answered, "Yes, I do."

6　山本　：ハッハッハッ。いじわるですね。それで、ホームステイはどうでしたか。

Ha, ha, ha! That was mean. Well, how was the homestay?

ミラー　：色々しっぱいをしましたが、みなさん本当に親切(しんせつ)でした。

I made all kinds of mistakes, but everyone was really kind.

7 山本 ： それはよかったですね。
Sounds very nice.
ミラー ： ええ。でも、もっと日本語が話せるようになりたいと思います。それに、日本の子供達に英語を教えてみたくなりました。ですから、卒業したら、また日本へ行こうと思います。
Yeah. But I'd like to become more fluent in Japanese. And I'd also like to try teaching English to Japanese children. Therefore I plan to go to Japan again when I graduate.

8 山本 ： そうですか。じゃあ、がんばって卒業まで日本語を勉強しなくてはいけませんね。
Well, then you have to continue studying Japanese hard until your graduation.
ミラー ： ええ、そうしようと思います。そして、日本語が上手になったら、もっと日本の文化も学びたいです。
Yes, I plan to do so. And once my Japanese has improved, I want to study more of Japanese culture.

使い方

2 あんなに here means "so many/much".

As 山本さん explains, in Japanese elementary through senior high schools, students travel together before they graduate. This trip is called しゅうがく旅行.

3 てき in れきしてき is a suffix to transform a noun into a な-adjective. So, れきし "history" + てき means "historical". Other examples are:

けいざい	*economy*	けいざいてき	*economical*
		けいざいてきな車	*economical car*
せいじ	*politics*	せいじてき	*political*
		せいじてきなイベント	*political event*
せんもん	*specialty*	せんもんてき	*professional*
		せんもんてきなせつめい	*professional explanation*
文化	*culture*	文化てき	*cultural*
		文化てきなちがい	*cultural difference*
日本人てきなかんがえ方		*a Japanese way of thinking*	

8 Below are the connective expressions that we have studied so far. They normally appear sentence-initially and connect the sentence to the preceding one.

そして	*and then*
それから	*and after that* (Similar to そして, but sequentiality of the two events is emphasized more. そして and それから can occur sentence-medially as well.)
それで	*therefore, so that*
それでは	*well then, if that's the case, given that*
じゃ (あ), それじゃ (あ)	*Casual forms of* それでは.
それに	*besides, moreover, in addition to that*
ですから	*so*
けれども	*but*
でも	Casual form of けれども

文法

20a　Direct and Indirect Quotations
20b　Indirect Questions
20c　Plain フォーム + と思う　　"I think that ~"
20d　Verb Conjugation: Volitional フォーム
20e　Volitional フォーム + と思う　　"I think I'm going to do ~"

20a　Direct and Indirect Quotations

Plain

In both direct and indirect quotations, と is used as a quotation marker. The main verb is normally 言う, 話す, or 答える. In direct quotes, a set of symbols「　」(called かぎ or かぎかっこ) delimits the quotation; in indirect quotes, かぎ are not used. Whereas direct quotes use actual patterns of speech, indirect quotes must include only **plain forms of the predicate**.

> The use of the punctuation symbol '。' (called 句点(くてん) or 丸(まる)) is optional in a direct quotation.

ソンさんは「中国語が読めます」と言いました。
Son-san said "I can read Chinese."
ソンさんは、中国語が読めると言いました。
Son-san said that she could read Chinese.

ミラーさんは「石川先生はオフィスにいらっしゃいます」と言いました。

Miller-san said "Ishikawa-sensei is in her office."

ミラーさんは、石川先生はオフィスにいらっしゃると言いました。

Miller-san said that Ishikawa-sensei was in her office.

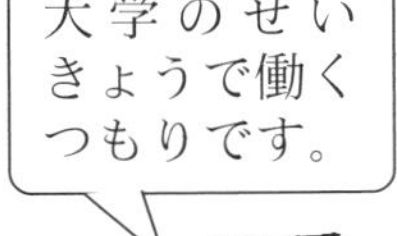

山本さんは「大学のせいきょうで働くつもりです」と言いました。

Yamamoto-san said "I plan to work at the Student Union Store."

山本さんは、大学のせいきょうで働くつもりだと言いました。

Yamamoto-san said that he planned to work at the Student Union Store.

小山さんは「大事(だいじ)な用事(ようじ)があるので早く帰らなくてはいけません」と言いました。

Koyama-san said "I have to go home early because I have an important matter (to attend to)."

小山さんは、大事な用事があるので早く帰らなくてはいけないと言いました。

Koyama-san said that she had to go home early because she had an important matter (to attend to).

ミラーさんは「秋山さんの家でしっぱいしてしまって、はずかしかったです」と言いました。

Miller-san said "I made a mistake at Akiyama-san's house, and I felt embarrassed."

ミラーさんは、秋山さんの家でしっぱいしてしまって、はずかしかったと言いました。

Miller-san said that he made a mistake at Akiyama-san's house and felt embarrassed.

In indirect quotes, some adjustments with time expressions may be needed, but unlike in English, tense cannot be adjusted.

青木さんは「作文を書きたくありません」と言いました。

Aoki-san said "I don't want to write essays."

青木さんは、作文を書きたくないと言いました。

(Lit.) Aoki-san said that he doesn't want to write essays.

Aoki-san said that he didn't want to write essays.

Consider the following sentence:

東山さんは「明日は授業に出ません」と言いました。

Higashiyama-san said "I'm not going to attend class tomorrow."

If this utterance is reported on the same day,

東山さんは、明日は授業に出ないと言いました。
(Lit.) Higashiyama-san said she's not going to attend class tomorrow.
Higashiyama-san said she wasn't going to attend class tomorrow.

If this utterance is reported on the next day,

東山さんは、今日は授業に出ないと言いました。
(Lit.) Higashiyama-san said she's not going to attend class today.
Higashiyama-san said she wasn't going to attend class today.

If it is reported on some other day,

東山さんは、つぎの日は授業に出ないと言いました。
(Lit.) Higashiyama-san said she's not going to attend class the next day.
Higashiyama-san said she wasn't going to attend class the next day.

Additionally, some adjustments in honorific expressions may be necessary.

安川さんは「二月に両親(りょうしん)が来ます」と言いました。
Yasukawa-san said "My parents are coming in February."
安川さんは、二月にご両親がいらっしゃると言いました。
Yasukawa-san said her parents would come in February.
(or) *Yasukawa-san said her parents are coming in February.*

Normally, the subject of a subordinate clause is marked with が, rather than は, but quoted clauses are different from normal subordinate clauses in that if the subject is marked with は in a direct-quote sentence, it is also marked with は in the corresponding indirect quote.

ソンさんは「山本さんの車は赤いです」と言いました。
Son-san said, "Yamamoto-san's car is red."
ソンさんは、山本さんの車は赤いと言いました。
Son-san said that Yamamoto-san's car was/is red.

小山さんは「このしょうせつはつまらなかったです」と言いました。
Koyama-san said, "This novel was boring."
小山さんは、このしょうせつはつまらなかったと言いました。
Koyama-san said this novel was boring.

早川さんは「図書館はジムの後ろのたてものです」と言いました。
Hayakawa-san said, "The library is the building behind the gym."
早川さんは、図書館はジムの後ろのたてものだと言いました。
Hayakawa-san said that the library was / is the building behind the gym.

山本さんは「ワトソンさんはテニスが上手です」と言いました。
Yamamoto-san said, "Watson-san is good at tennis."
山本さんは、ワトソンさんはテニスが上手だと言いました。
Yamamoto-san said that Watson-san was / is good at tennis.

The first-person pronoun 私 appearing in a direct quote cannot be used in its corresponding indirect quote. Typically, if the subjects of the main clause and quoted clause are identical, the latter normally remains unmentioned.

木村さんは「先週、私は病気でした」と言いました。
Kimura-san said "I was sick last week."
木村さんは、先週、病気だったと言いました。
Kimura-san said she was sick last week.

If 私 is used in an indirect quote, it will refer to the speaker, rather than the person who said the quoted clause. If some confusion is likely to occur, 自分(じぶん), rather than 私, is used to refer to the person whose speech is quoted.

木村さんは、私は先週病気だったと言いました。
Kimura-san said that I (= speaker) was sick last week.
木村さんは、先週、自分は病気だったと言いました。
Kimura-san said she (= Kimura-san) was sick last week.

田中さんは「私のアパートは大学に近(ちか)いです」と言いました。
Tanaka-san said "My apartment is close to the university."
田中さんは、自分のアパートは大学に近いと言いました。
Tanaka-san said that his (Lit. self's) apartment is close to the university.

～と言っている Like English "said" vs. "says / has said", ～と言った "said" simply reports a past speech event. If the content of the utterance is directly relevant to the current discourse, ～と言っている (literally "X is saying") is used and indicates "X says / has said that ~".

ミラーさんもさそいましょう。
Let's invite Miller-san too.

○ ええ、でも、ミラーさんはさいきん忙しいと言っていますよ。
Yes, but he says he's been busy recently.

× ええ、でも、ミラーさんはさいきん忙しいと言いましたよ。
Yes, but he said he'd been busy recently.

20b Indirect Questions

When you quote a question, you can cite the question as a direct quote, or make it into an *indirect question*. If the question is directly quoted, the construction is the same as direct quotation with the main verb of 聞く, rather than a verb of speaking.

Yes / No Questions

ミラーさんはソンさんに「コンピューターを使いますか」と聞きました。

Miller-san asked Son-san, "Are you going to use the computer?"

An indirect question is the reporting of a question without using the exact words of the speaker. Like indirect quotations, only plain forms of the predicate can appear in indirect questions. Thus, 使います becomes 使う. If an indirect question is a Yes-No question, かどうか, rather than mere か, is used at the end of the indirect question. かどうかと is also possible, but less common than merely かどうか.

ミラーさんはソンさんに、コンピューターを使うかどうか（と）聞きました。
Miller-san asked Son-san whether she would use the computer.
ソンさんはミラーさんに「はい、コンピューターを使います」と答えました。
Son-san answered Miller-san, "Yes, I'm going to use the computer."
ソンさんはミラーさんに、コンピューターを使うと答えました。
Son-san answered Miller-san that she would use the computer.

Note that はい or いいえ is omitted in answers in the form of indirect quotation.

ミラーさんはまゆみさんに「日本人はベランダでバーベキューをしますか」と聞きました。
Miller-san asked Mayumi-san, "Do Japanese people (like to) have barbecues (out) on their balconies?"
ミラーさんはまゆみさんに、日本人はベランダでバーベキューをするかどうか（と）聞きました。
Miller-san asked Mayumi-san whether Japanese people (like to) have barbecues (out) on their balconies.

まゆみさんはミラーさんに「いいえ、日本人はベランダでバーベキューはしません」と答えました。

Mayumi-san answered Miller-san, "No, we don't have barbecues (out) on our balconies."

まゆみさんはミラーさんに、日本人はベランダでバーベキューはしないと答えました。

Mayumi-san answered Miller-san that Japanese people don't have barbecues (out) on their balconies.

小山さんはミラーさんに「木村さんの住所(じゅうしょ)を知っていますか」と聞きました。

Koyama-san asked Miller-san, "Do you know Kimura-san's address?"

小山さんはミラーさんに、木村さんの住所を知っているかどうか（と）聞きました。

Koyama-san asked Miller-san if he knew Kimura-san's address.

ソンさんは私に「切手(きって)をはりましたか」と聞きました。

Son-san asked me, "Did you attach a stamp?"

ソンさんは私に、切手をはったかどうか（と）聞きました。

Son-san asked me whether I'd attached a stamp.

小山さんは私に「教科書(きょうかしょ)を読まないで授業へ行ったことがありますか」と聞きました。

Koyama-san asked me, "Have you ever gone to class without reading the textbook?"

小山さんは私に、教科書を読まないで授業へ行ったことがあるかどうか（と）聞きました。

Koyama-san asked me whether I'd ever gone to class without reading the textbook.

As indicated by **Ø** in the following examples, です must be omitted in indirect questions.

ラウールさんはソンさんに「漢字を覚えるのはむずかしいですか」と聞きました。

Raoul-san asked Son-san, "Is it difficult to memorize kanji?"

ラウールさんはソンさんに、漢字を覚えるのはむずかしい **Ø** かどうか（と）聞きました。

Raoul-san asked Son-san whether or not memorizing kanji was difficult.

田中さんは木村さんに「新しいアパートは静かですか」と聞きました。

Tanaka-san asked Kimura-san, "Is your new apartment quiet?"

田中さんは木村さんに、新しいアパートは静か **Ø** かどうか（と）聞きました。

Tanaka-san asked Kimura-san whether or not Kimura-san's new apartment was quiet.

ソンさんはミラーさんに「山本さんは日本から来た留学生ですか」と聞きました。

Son-san asked Miller-san, "Is Yamamoto-san a foreign student from Japan?"

ソンさんはミラーさんに、山本さんは日本から来た留学生 **Ø** かどうか（と）聞きました。

Son-san asked Miller-san whether or not Yamamoto-san was a foreign student from Japan.

石川先生はソンさんに「来年も日本語を取るつもりですか」とお聞きになりました。
Ishikawa-sensei asked Son-san, "Do you plan to take Japanese again next year?"
石川先生はソンさんに、来年も日本語を取るつもり **Ø** かどうか（と）お聞きになりました。
Ishikawa-sensei asked Son-san whether she planned to take Japanese again next year.

WH Question If an indirect question is a WH question, just か（と）, not かどうか（と）, is used. The use of と is more common in indirect WH questions than indirect Yes-No questions.

山田さんは私に「いつから日本語を勉強していますか」と聞きました。
(Lit.) Yamada-san asked me, "Since when have you been studying Japanese?"
Yamada-san asked me, "When did you begin studying Japanese?"
山田さんは私に、いつから日本語を勉強しているか（と）聞きました。
(Lit.) Yamada-san asked me since when I'd been studying Japanese.
Yamada-san asked me when I began studying Japanese.
私は「一年前からです」と答えました。
I answered, "Since a year ago."
私は、一年前からだと答えました。
(Lit.) I answered that it is since a year ago.
I answered that (I'd been studying Japanese) for a year.

木村さんはソンさんに「何が食べたいですか」と聞きました。
Kimura-san asked Son-san, "What do you want to eat?"
木村さんはソンさんに、何が食べたいか（と）聞きました。
Kimura-san asked Son-san what she wanted to eat.

ソンさんは「かにが食べたいです」と答えました。
Son-san answered, "I want to eat crab."
ソンさんは、かにが食べたいと答えました。
Son-san answered that she wanted to eat crab.

ミラーさんは山本さんに「この漢字はどういう意味ですか*」と聞きました。
Miller-san asked Yamamoto-san, "What does this kanji mean?"

薬

ミラーさんは山本さんに、この漢字はどういう意味か（と）聞きました。
Miller-san asked Yamamoto-san what this kanji means / meant.
山本さんは「それは medicine という意味です**」と答えました。
Yamamoto-san answered, "It means 'medicine'."

*X はどういう意味ですか
What does X mean?

**X は Y という意味です
X means Y

This construction literally means "X has the meaning that says Y".

山本さんは、それは medicine という意味だと答えました。
Yamamoto-san answered that it means / meant "medicine".

コールさんはキムさんに「しょうらい何になりたいですか」と聞きました。
Cole-san asked Kim-san, "What would you like to be in the future?"
コールさんはキムさんに、しょうらい何になりたいか (と) 聞きました。
Cole-san asked Kim-san what he would like to be in the future.
キムさんは「べんごしかかいけいしになりたいです」と答えました。
Kim-san answered, "I'd like to be a lawyer or an accountant."
キムさんは、べんごしかかいけいしになりたいと答えました。
Kim-san answered that he'd like to be a lawyer or an accountant.

Indirect questions can occur with verbs other than 聞く, e.g. 覚える, 知る, 分かる, わすれる. と is not used with these verbs.

ミラーさんは今日、授業に出ますか。
Is Miller-san going to attend class today?
さあ、出るかどうか分かりません。
Well, I don't know whether he will or not.

山本さんは何時ごろ来るか知っていますか。
Do you know what time Yamamoto-san is coming?
すみません。(何時ごろ来るか) 知りません。
Sorry, I don't know.

ミラーさんは日本語を勉強して何をするつもりか知っていますか。
Do you know what Miller-san intends to do by learning Japanese?
(or) *Do you know what Miller-san plans to do with Japanese he's learning?*
ミラーさんは日本の文化をけんきゅうしたいと言っています。
He says he wants to do research on Japanese culture.

石川先生、ソンさんは中国語が話せるかどうかごぞんじですか。
Ishikawa-sensei, do you know whether Son-san can speak Chinese?
さあ、ソンさんは日本語を話しますが、中国語を話すかどうか知りません。
Well, Son-san speaks Japanese, but I don't know if she speaks Chinese.

今週の宿題を出しましたか。
Have you turned in this week's homework?

さあ、出したかどうか覚えていません。
Hmmm... I don't remember whether I turned it in or not.

ソンさんは、明日学校に来ると言いましたか。
Did Son-san say she would come to school tomorrow?
さあ、言ったかどうかわすれました。
Hmmm... I forgot whether she said (she would or not).

その病院は近いですか。
Is the hospital near here?
さあ、近いかどうか分かりません。
Hmmm... I don't know whether it's close or not.

ソンさんは今日、授業に来ませんでしたね。病気ですか。
Son-san didn't come to class today. Is she sick?
さあ、病気かどうか知りません。
Hmmm... I don't know if she's sick.

20c Plain フォーム + と思う "I think that ~"

The quotation marker と appears in this construction. Like indirect quotes and indirect questions, the predicate of the embedded clause must be in a plain form.

In declarative sentences, the subject of the main clause (the person who thinks) is always the first person, i.e. the speaker; the subject is therefore normally not mentioned. In (1) below, 石川先生, marked with は, is the subject of the embedded predicate いらっしゃる, but not the subject of the main-clause predicate 思う. The complete sentence, though unnatural, is provided in (2).

(1) 石川先生はオフィスにいらっしゃると思います。
I think (that) Ishikawa-sensei is in her office.

(2) 私は、石川先生はオフィスにいらっしゃると思います。
I think (that) Ishikawa-sensei is in her office.

Other examples:

(3) ソンさんは今、図書館で宿題をしていると思います。
I think Son-san is doing her homework in the library now.

(4) 駅(えき)は遠(とお)いと思います。

I think the train station is far away.

(5) ブラウンさんはまじめだと思います。

I think Brown-san is serious-minded.

(6) チャンさんは中国人だと思います。

I think Chan-san is Chinese.

In questions, the subject is understood to be the second person (i.e. the addressee).

(7) その仕事は大変だと思いますか。

Do you think that task is a lot of work?

(8) こうえんは何時に始まると思いますか。

What time do you think the lecture will begin?

(9) あのきっさ店は高いと思いますか。

Do you think that café is expensive?

(10) ソンさんは村山さんを知っていると思いますか。

Do you think Son-san knows Murayama-san?

(11) あの人は外国人だと思いますか。

Do you think that person over there is a foreigner?

(12) キムさんはどんな人だと思いますか。

What kind of person do you think Kim-san is?

The embedded clause can contain a negative form, e.g. (13). It is also possible to change 思います to 思いません, e.g. (14). (13) is somewhat stronger than (14) in asserting that the book is not difficult.

(13) この本はむずかしくないと思います。

I think this book is not difficult.

(14) この本はむずかしいと(は)思いません。

I don't think this book is difficult.

Agreement Seeking Questions

Like English "Don't you think ...,"「〜と思いませんか」is frequently used to elicit the addressee's agreement.

(15) 日本語のクラスは宿題が少ないと思いませんか。
Don't you think there are too few homework assignments in Japanese class?
そうですね。もっとたくさんしたいですね。
I agree. We want to do more.

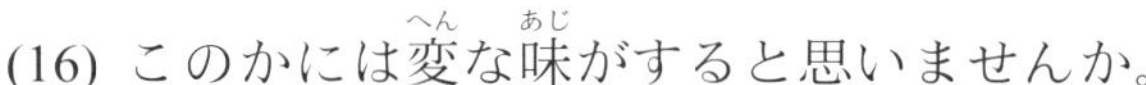

(16) このかには変(へん)な味(あじ)がすると思いませんか。
Don't you think this crab tastes strange?
そうですね。ちょっとすっぱいですね。
Yes, it's a little sour.

In such agreement seeking questions, the usage of *Yes* and *No* differs from regular questions. In 第六課, **6h**, we learned that *Yes-No* and はい - いいえ behave oppositely when the question is negative. For example:

(17) 昨日は出かけませんでしたか。	*Didn't you go out yesterday?*
はい、出かけませんでした。	*(Lit.) [Yes], I didn't go out.*
いいえ、出かけました。	*(Lit.) [No], I did go out.*

This is because Japanese はい and いいえ respond to the question (whether the speaker's negative assumption is true or false), whereas English *Yes* and *No* correspond to the content of the answer (whether the answer is affirmative or negative). However, this rule applies only when the question is used for seeking information like (17). When an interrogative sentence is used for making a suggestion, recommendation, invitation, eliciting agreement, etc., はい or いいえ is selected according to the intention of the speaker, rather than the negative form of the utterance. If the addressee agrees, はい is selected; when s/he does not, いいえ is selected. Compare the following:

(18) そのレストランは高くありませんか。 (Information seeking)
Isn't that restaurant expensive?
[はい]、高くありません。 (Negative)
Yes (your assumption is correct), it's not expensive.
[いいえ]、高いです。 (Affirmative)
No (your assumption is incorrect), it's expensive.

(19) そのレストランは高いと思いませんか。 (Agreement seeking)
Don't you think that restaurant is expensive?
はい、高いと思います。 (Affirmative)
Yes (I agree with you), I think it's expensive.
いいえ、高いとは思いません。 (Negative)
No (I don't agree with you), I don't think it's expensive.

(20) ソンさんは日本語が上手だと思いませんか。 (Agreement seeking)
Don't you think Son-san is fluent in Japanese?
はい、そう思います。 (Affirmative)
Yes (I agree with you), I think so.
そうですかあ。うーん……。 (Hedging)
You think so? Umm...

In the information-seeking question (18), はい occurs with a negative sentence, whereas in the agreement-seeking questions (19)-(20), はい occurs with an affirmative sentence. When the speaker wishes to avoid a blatant disagreement, e.g. (20), some hedging expression should be employed.

Hedging Another important function of the ～と思う construction is to soften the locution. For instance, the following two sentences convey the same meaning, but the one with 思う is less assertive. English speakers also utilize the verb *think* in this way, but 思う is more frequently used in Japanese.

(21) もっと日本語が上手に話せるようになりたいです。
もっと日本語が上手に話せるようになりたいと思います。
I want to become able to speak Japanese better.

(22) 今週中にとどけられます。
I can deliver (it) this week.
今週中にとどけられると思います。
I think I can deliver (it) this week.

(23) 夏休みに日本へ行きたくありませんか。
Don't you want to go to Japan during summer vacation?
夏休みに日本へ行きたいと思いませんか。
(Lit.) Don't you think you want to go to Japan during summer vacation?

(24) 今月はせつやくしなくてはいけないと思います。
I think I have to save money this month.

(25) 今週末（こんしゅうまつ）はひまだと思います。
I think I'll have time this weekend.

～と思っている Unlike ～と思う, ～と思っている can be used with a 3rd-person subject.

(26) パクさんは、中国語の方が日本語よりむずかしいと思っています。
Pak-san thinks that Chinese is more difficult than Japanese.

(27) 木村さんは、カリフォルニアは住みやすい所だと思っています。
(Lit.) Kimura-san thinks that California is a place that is easy to live in.
Kimura-san thinks it's easy to live in California.

(28) チャンさんは、大学のりょうはもんげんがあると思っていました。
Chan-san thought that the university dormitories had curfew.

20d Verb Conjugation: Volitional フォーム

As the name suggests, the *volitional* フォーム indicates the speaker's volition or will to do something. Naturally, therefore, only those verbs that denote intentional actions can appear in this construction. Volitional forms are derived by the following rules:

A　う Verbs: Drop the final *u* of the Dictionary フォーム and add *ō*.

わ	ら	や	ま	は	な	た	さ	か	あ
	り		み	ひ	に	ち	し	き	い
	る	ゆ	む	ふ	ぬ	つ	す	く	う
	れ		め	へ	ね	て	せ	け	え
を	ろ	よ	も	ほ	の	と	そ	こ	お

a–u → a– ō
あ~~う~~（会~~う~~）→ あおう（会おう）
kak–u → kak– ō
か~~く~~（書~~く~~）→ かこう（書こう）

言う → 言おう	使う → 使おう	習う → 習おう	急ぐ → 急ごう
聞く → 聞こう	働く → 働こう	返す → 返そう	待つ → 待とう
しぬ → しのう	学ぶ → 学ぼう	よぶ → よぼう	住む → 住もう
休む → 休もう	読む → 読もう	帰る → 帰ろう	取る → 取ろう
がんばる → がんばろう			

B　る Verbs: Drop the final *ru* of the Dictionary フォーム and add *yō*.

おきる → おきよう	かりる → かりよう	見る → 見よう
開ける → 開けよう	覚える → 覚えよう	しらべる → しらべよう
食べる → 食べよう	始める → 始めよう	かたづける → かたづけよう

C　Irregular Verbs

来る　→　来よう
する　→　しよう

20e　Volitional フォーム + と思う　"I think I'm going to do ~"

Vol

「Volitional フォーム + と思う」means that the speaker is thinking about doing something.

(1) 私は来年、日本へ行こうと思います。
I'm thinking of going to Japan next year.

(2) 明日、図書館で勉強しようと思います。
I think I'll study in the library tomorrow.

「Volitional フォーム＋と思う」is similar to ～つもりです "to intend to do ~" (cf. 第五課), but the speaker's determination is less emphasized in the former. Like ～つもりです, the subject of this construction is only the 1st or 2nd person. Do not use「Volitional フォーム＋と思う」with a 3rd-person subject.

When you plan not to do something, the use of 「Volitional フォーム＋と（は）思わない」is possible, but not very common. In such a case, use「Negative フォーム＋ないつもりだ」(cf. 第六課) or「Dictionary フォーム + つもりはない」.

(3) 来年も日本へ行くつもりですか。
Do you plan to go to Japan again next year?
いいえ、行こうとは思いません。
No, I don't think I will go.
いいえ、行かないつもりです。
No, I don't plan to go.
いいえ、行くつもりはありません。
No, I don't have plans to go.

～(よ)うと思っている

Like「Plain フォーム + と思っている」, you can use「Volitional フォーム + と思っている」with a 3rd-person subject; however, to describe another person's intention is considered a presumptuous act in Japanese society. So limit this construction to only people you are familiar with.

(4)　山田さんは、週末、映画を見ようと思っています。
Yamada-san is thinking about going to see a movie this weekend.

(5)　ラウールさんは期末しけんが終わった後で、パーティをしようと思っています。
Raoul-san is thinking about having a party when the final exam is over.

(6)　田中さんはおすしを作ろうと思っていましたが、おすがなかったので作れませんでした。
Tanaka-san was thinking about making sushi, *but because there was no vinegar, she couldn't make them.*

練習問題

I.　絵を見て direct quotation と indirect quotation の文を作って下さい。

例(れい)　ソンさんは「月曜日は授業を休みます」と言いました。
ソンさんは、月曜日は授業を休むと言いました。

例
月曜日は授業を休みます。
1.
ミラーさんのアパートは静かじゃありません。
ソンさん
2.
冬休みに日本へ帰らないつもりです。
3.
週末、友達と日本まちへ行きたいです。
山本さん
4.
夏に両親が日本から来ます。
5.
私は今週、元気になりました。
小山さん
6.
さいきん日本のしょうせつを読んでいます。
7.
先月読んだしょうせつはおもしろくありませんでした。
ミラーさん
8.
ミラーさんが日本でとった写真を見ました。
石川先生

II. 絵を見て、direct quotation と indirect question の文を作って下さい。

例 小山さんは山本さんに「せいきょうの仕事はどうでしたか」と聞きました。
小山さんは山本さんにせいきょうの仕事はどうだったか（と）聞きました。

III. Indirect quotation と indirect question を使って、文を作って下さい。

1.
私はジムで運動をします。ソンさんは何をしますか。

ミラーさんは、＿＿＿＿＿＿＿＿＿＿＿＿＿＿＿＿
＿＿＿＿＿＿＿＿＿＿＿＿＿＿＿＿と言いました。
そして、＿＿＿＿＿＿＿＿＿＿＿＿＿＿＿＿＿＿
＿＿＿＿＿＿＿＿＿＿＿＿＿＿＿（と）聞きました。

2. ミラーさんは、＿＿＿＿＿＿＿＿＿＿＿＿＿＿＿＿＿＿＿＿＿＿＿＿＿＿＿(と)聞きました。
ソンさんは、＿＿＿＿＿＿＿＿＿＿＿＿＿＿＿＿＿＿＿＿＿＿＿＿＿＿＿と答えました。

3. ミラーさんは、＿＿＿＿＿＿＿＿＿＿＿＿＿＿＿＿＿＿＿＿＿＿＿＿＿＿＿。
ソンさんは、＿＿＿＿＿＿＿＿＿＿＿＿＿＿＿＿＿＿＿＿＿＿＿＿＿＿＿。

4. ソンさんが、＿＿＿＿＿＿＿＿＿＿＿＿＿＿＿＿＿＿＿＿＿。それで小山さんは、＿＿＿＿＿＿＿＿＿＿＿＿＿＿＿＿＿＿＿＿＿＿＿＿＿＿＿。

IV.　「～か」か「～かどうか」を使って、答(こた)えを書いて下さい。

1. モーツァルトは何年に生(う)まれましたか。
さあ、＿＿＿＿＿＿＿＿＿＿＿＿＿＿＿＿＿＿＿＿＿＿＿＿＿＿＿知りません。

2. この大学には日本語の学生が何人いますか。
さあ、＿＿＿＿＿＿＿＿＿＿＿＿＿＿＿＿＿＿＿＿＿＿＿＿＿＿＿分かりません。

3. 明日、雨が降りますか。
さあ、＿＿＿＿＿＿＿＿＿＿＿＿＿＿＿＿＿＿＿＿＿＿＿＿＿＿＿分かりません。

4. 先週の宿題はむずかしかったですか。
さあ、＿＿＿＿＿＿＿＿＿＿＿＿＿＿＿＿＿＿＿＿＿＿＿＿＿＿＿覚えていません。

V.　ミラーさんは六本木のこうばんでおまわりさんに聞きました。
Indirect Question を使って、言って下さい。

例　ミラー：東京タワーはどこにありますか。
ミラーさんは六本木のこうばんでおまわりさんに東京タワーはどこにあるか（と）聞きました。

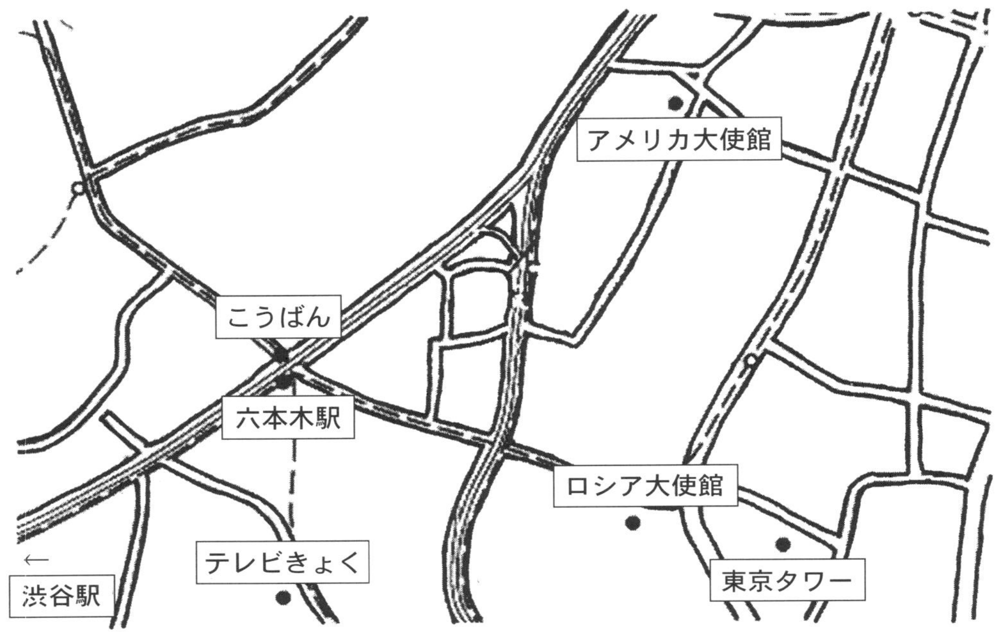

1. アメリカ大使館はどこですか。
2. 六本木で一番古いクラブを知っていますか。
3. 六本木から渋谷までバスとちかてつとでは、どちらの方が便利ですか。
4. この近くに映画館がありますか。
5. テレビきょくが見学できますか。

VI.　パートナーに聞きましょう。

1. 日本語のクラスはどうですか。
2. ソンさんはどんな人だと思いますか。
3. ミラーさんはどんな人だと思いますか。
4. 日本語が上手になったら、何ができると思いますか。
5. 何をしたら、漢字が覚えられると思いますか。
6. このコースは漢字が多いと思いませんか。
7. このクラスは楽しいと思いませんか。
8. 日本語の先生はみんな元気だと思いませんか。

VII.　ビンゴの時間です。クラスメートに聞きましょう。

例　Q:　週末、映画を見ようと思っていますか。

A:　はい、見ようと思っています。

(or) いいえ、見ないつもりです。

VIII. 読みましょう。

富士山(ふじさん)は日本で一番高い山(やま)です。富士山の近(ちか)くには高い山がないので、てんきがいい時には東京からも富士山を見ることができます。私は富士山はとてもきれいな山だと思います。

富士山は火山(かざん)です。むかし、ふんかしました（ふんかする "erupt"）が、今はふんかしていません。夏には、おおぜいの人が富士山にのぼります。のぼるのはかんたんではありません。けれども、子供ものぼれます。富士山は高いので、夜になると、とても寒くなりますが、午後はとてもあつくて大変です。

富士山のきたにはきれいなみずうみが五つあります。そこでキャンプしたり、ハイキングしたり、ボートに乗ったりすることができます。私は五月の休みの日に、みずうみの近くへキャンプしに行こうと思っています。まだ少し寒いでしょうが、花がきれいだと思います。山田さんがキャンプをしたいと言っていたので、いっしょに行くつもりです。キャンプは用意(ようい)が大変ですが、とても楽しいと思います。

ただしい答えには〇、まちがっている答えには×を書いて下さい。

1.　(　　) 富士山の近くには高い山がありません。
2.　(　　) 東京から富士山を見ることはできません。
3.　(　　) この人は富士山はきれいだと思っています。
4.　(　　) 富士山にのぼるのは大変なので、子供達はのぼれません。
5.　(　　) 富士山は高いので、夜は寒いです。
6.　(　　) この人は五月に友達とキャンプしに行こうと思っています。

新しい漢字

味(あじ)	意味(いみ)	駅(えき)	思(おも)う	切手(きって)	教科書(きょうかしょ)
答(こた)え	答(こた)える	住所(じゅうしょ)	親切(しんせつ)	近(ちか)い	近(ちか)く
遠(とお)い	所(ところ)	用意(ようい)	用事(ようじ)	両親(りょうしん)	

新しい使い方

生(う)まれる	火山(かざん)	見学(けんがく)	今週末(こんしゅうまつ)	自分(じぶん)	大事(だいじ)
大使館(たいしかん)	出(で)かける	変(へん)	山(やま)		

Radicals: 心(こころ)

心(こころ) "heart" is another common radical. Like 貝(かい) (cf. 第十九課), 心 appears either as a へん (left side) or 足(あし) (bottom part). As a へん, it is called 立心(りっしん)べん "standing heart hen-radical", whose shape is 忄. 立心べん consists of three strokes, as opposed to 心, which consists of four strokes. However, as explained in 第十六課 "Weird Conventions," 立心べん is conventionally listed as a four-stroke radical in 漢字 dictionaries. So far, we have learned one 立心べん漢字, 忙 (第十九課). When this radical appears as an 足, it is called 下心(したごころ). We have learned 急, 思, and 意 (although 意 is normally categorized as an 音 group 漢字.)

漢字	1	2	3	4	5	6	7	8	9	10
味 ミ・あじ	丨	冂	口	口一	口二	叶	味	味		
	taste: 意味 *meaning*									
意 イ	丶	亠	亠	亣	立	产	音	音	音	音
	意	意	意							
	will: 意味 *meaning*									
生 セイ・う(まれる)	丿	𠂉	牛	牛	生					
	life: 学生 *student (studying person),* 高校生 *high school student,* 先生 *teacher (preceding person),* 大学院生 *graduate student,* 留学生 *foreign student*									
駅 えき	丨	𠂆	冂	円	用	馬	馬	馬	馬	馬
	馬	馬	駅	駅						
	station									
思 おも(う)	丨	冂	冂	田	田	田	思	思	思	
	to think									
山 サン・ザン・やま	丨	山	山							
	mountain: 火山 *volcano,* 小山 *Koyama,* 富士山 *Mt. Fuji,* 村山 *Murayama,* 山田 *Yamada,* 山本 *Yamamoto*									

Kanji	Reading	Meaning
切	セツ・きっ	*to cut:* 切手 *postal stamp,* 親切 *kind*
科	カ	*course, branch:* 教科書 *textbook*
答	こた (え)・こた (える)	*to answer*
分	フン・プン・ブン・わ (かる)	*to divide:* 一分（いっぷん）*one minute,* 二分（にふん）*two minutes,* 自分 *oneself,* 分かる *to understand*
住	ジュウ・す (む)	*to live:* 住所 *address*
所	ショ・ところ	*place:* 住所 *address*
親	シン	*parent:* 親切 *kind,* 両親 *parents (both parents)*
使	シ・つか (う)	*to use:* 大使館 *embassy,* 使い方 *way to use*
近	ちか (い・く)	*close to:* 近く *vicinity*

漢字										
遠 とお(い)	一	十	土	土	吉	吉	声	声	袁	袁
	袁	遠	遠							
	far from									
用 ヨウ	丿	冂	月	月	用					
	work, function: 用意 *preparation,* 用事 *errand, business*									
両 リョウ	一	丆	丙	币	両	両				
	both: 両親 *parents (both parents)*									

漢字の復習

I.　読みましょう。

1. 週末に中間試験の勉強をしなくてはいけません。
2. 電車に乗って、京都見物をしました。
3. あそこで音楽を聞きながら新聞を読んでいる人の名前を知っていますか。
4. 頭がとてもいたかったので、病院に行きました。
5. 村山さんの部屋は広くて明るいです。

II.　山田さんは色々な所へいきました。どんなじゅんばんで行きましたか。山田さんが書いた文を読んで [　] に書いて下さい。

山田さんが行った所						
家	映画館	銀行	大使館	図書館	友達の家	病院

昨日は忙しかったです。図書館で勉強したり、映画を見に行ったりしました。

朝、図書館へ勉強しに行く前に病院へ行きました。頭がいたかったんです。病院へ行ってから、銀行へ行って貯金しました。それから、図書館へ行って、勉強しました。三時間ぐらい勉強した後で、家へ帰りました。家でひるごはんを食べようと思ったんです。でも、家に帰ってかばんを開けると、辞書がありませんでした。図書館に辞書をわすれてしまったんです。それで、図書館へ辞書を取りに行きました。図書館を出る時にとけいを見ると、午後一時半でした。それで、ひるごはんを食べないで、図書館から友達の家へ行きました。午後、友達と映画を見るつもりでした。でも、とてもつかれてしまったので、友達に映画は見ないと言って、家へ帰りました。

家へ帰ってから、ちょっとひるねをしたら、元気になりました。それから、大使館へパスポートをもらいに行きました。大使館の近くから友達に電話すると、友達は今から映画を見に行くつもりだと言いました。それで、私も映画館へ行って、いっしょに映画を見ることにしました。映画館で会うことにしました。大使館から映画館まで二十分ぐらいかかりました。

映画を見て、家へ帰ったら、とてもおなかがすいていました。

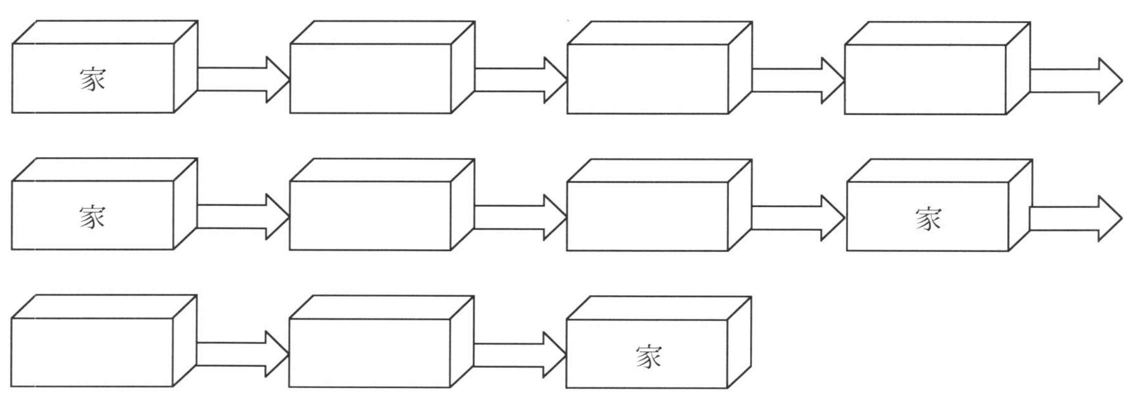

新しい語彙(ごい)

味(あじ)	*taste*
あんなに	*so many, so much*
イベント	*event*
生(う)まれる　(ル)(i)	*to be born*
おまわりさん	*police(wo)man*
思(おも)う　(ウ)(t)	*to think*
かいけいし	*accountant*
火山(かざん)	*volcano*
かに	*crab*
かんがえ方(かた)	*way of thinking*
きた	*north*

きっと	*surely*
キャンプ(する)	*camping*
クラブ	*club, disco*
見学(けんがく)(する)	*study tour*
けんきゅう(する)	*research*
けいざい	*economy*
けいざいてき　(ナ)	*economical*
こうえん(する)	*lecture*
こうばん	*police box*
今週末(こんしゅうまつ)	*this weekend*
さそう　(ウ)(t)	*to invite*

しっぱい（する）	*mistake*
自分（じぶん）	*oneself*
しゅうがく旅行（りょこう）	*school excursion*
住所（じゅうしょ）	*address*
しょうらい	*in the future*
すっぱい ㋑	*sour*
せいじ	*politics*
せいじてき ㋤	*political*
せつやく（する）	*saving, thrift*
せんもんてき ㋤	*professional*
それに	*besides, moreover, in addition to that*
大事（だいじ） ㋤	*important*
大使館（たいしかん）	*embassy*
たてもの	*building*
ちがい	*difference*
テレビきょく	*TV station*
どういう	*what kind of*
とどける ㋸ ⓣ	*to deliver*
日本人（にほんじん）てき ㋤	*Japanese*
のぼる ㋒ ⓘ	*to climb*
バーベキュー	*barbecue*
ハイキング	*hiking*
はずかしい ㋑	*ashamed, embarrassed*
文化（ぶんか）てき ㋤	*cultural*
ベランダ	*balcony*
変（へん） ㋤	*strange*
べんごし	*lawyer*
ボート	*boat*
みずうみ	*lake*
むかし	*old days*
山（やま）	*mountain*
用意（ようい）（する）	*preparation*
れきし	*history*
れきしてき ㋤	*historical*

名前

しぶや（渋谷）	*Shibuya*
東京（とうきょう）タワー	*Tokyo Tower*
モーツアルト	*Mozart*

第二十一課 LESSON 21

病気
Illness

この薬(くすり)を飲めば、すぐに熱(ねつ)が下(さ)がります
If you take this medicine, your fever will go down immediately

会話

1 ソン ： ただいま、小山さん。さっきケーキ屋へ行ったんですが、チーズケーキがとてもおいしそうだったので、二つ買って来ました。いっしょに食べませんか。

Hi, I'm home, Koyama-san. I went to a bakery a little while ago, and their cheesecakes looked so delicious, so I bought (and brought) two. Would you like to have some together?

2 ソン ： あら、小山さん、どうしたんですか。顔色(かおいろ)がわるいですね。

Oh, Koyama-san, what happened? You look pale.

小山 ： ええ、ちょっと気分(きぶん)がわるいんです。今日、上着(うわぎ)を着(き)て行かなかったので、かぜをひいたんだと思います。

Yes, I feel a little ill. Because I went out without my jacket, I think I caught a cold.

3 ソン ： 熱がありそうですね。はかってみましょう。たいおんけいをもって来ます。

You look like you have a fever. Let's check your temperature. I'll bring a thermometer.

小山 ： ちょっとしかないと思います。だいじょうぶです。

I think I have only a slight (fever). I'll be all right.

4 ソン ： わあ、１０２度もありますよ。今すぐ、お医者(いしゃ)さんに行きましょう。

Wow, it's (as high as) 102 degrees! Let's go right now and see a doctor.

5 小山 ： いえ、だいじょうぶです。少し休めば、元気になると思います。心配(しんぱい)しないで下さい。

No, I'm all right. If I rest a little while, I think I'll be fine. Please don't worry.

6 ソン ： そうですか。じゃあ、今日はゆっくり休んで下さい。あ、そうだ。いい薬があります。

Are you sure? Well then, please rest well today. — Oh, that's right. I have some good medicine.

7 ソン ： これを飲めば、すぐに熱が下がりますよ。

If you take this, your fever will go down immediately.

小山 ： ありがとうございます。飲んでみます。

Thank you. I'll try it.

8 ソン ： もし、明日までに熱が下がらなければ、いっしょに病院へ行きましょう。

If your fever hasn't gone down by tomorrow, let's go to the hospital together.

9 小山 ： はい、おねがいします。

Yes, thank you.

使い方

1 As explained in 第七課, **7h**, the conjunctive particle が does not always indicate an opposing relationship between the conjoined clauses. Here, the first clause supplies a background or setting for the subsequent clauses.

2 顔色 = 顔(かお)の色

気分 is a general term for referring to psychological states: feelings, moods, sentiments, etc. 気分がわるい literally means "(my) feeling is bad".

Because かぜをひいたんだと思います is an explanation by 小山さん for why she feels ill, the use of ん (the informal version of の) sounds more natural than just かぜをひいたと思います, cf. 第六課, **6g**.

4 The Celsius (Centigrade) scale is utilized in Japan. 32ºF = 0ºC, 102ºF = 38.9ºC. To convert Fahrenheit to Celsius, subtract 32 and multiply by 5/9.

6 あ、そうだ is an interjection indicating that the speaker has suddenly remembered or thought of something.

文法

21a	**Verb Conjugation: ばフォーム**	
21b	**CLAUSE1 ば CLAUSE2**	**"If C1, C2"**
21c	**～そうだ**	**"It looks (like) ~"**
21d	**てフォーム + 行く／来る／帰る**	**"do ~ and go/come/go back"**
21e	**NOUN (Quantity) + も**	**"as many/as much as NOUN"**
21f	**NOUN + しか + Negative**	**"only NOUN"**
21g	**Parts of the Body**	
21h	**Expressions of Illness**	

21a Verb Conjugation: ばフォーム

In this lesson, we are going to study a new verb conjugation called the *conditional form*, or the ばフォーム because it appears almost exclusively with the conjunctive particle ば. You can derive the ばフォーム by using the following rules:

A　う Verbs

Stem + e + ば　　行けば、出せば、話せば、読めば

If the last consonant of the stem is *w*, it is deleted as in other conjugation forms, except the Negative フォーム.

Conjugation	Negative	Pre- ます	Dictionary	Conditional	Volitional
Final Vowel	あ	い	う	え	お
	会わ - ない 洗わ - ない 言わ - ない	会い - ます 洗い - ます 言い - ます	会う 洗う 言う	会え - ば 洗え - ば 言え - ば	会おう 洗おう 言おう

B　る Verbs

Stem + れば　　教えれば、答えれば、食べれば、寝れば、いれば、着れば、見れば

C　Irregular Verbs

来る　→　来(く)れば
する　→　すれば

D　い -Adjectives

Stem + ければ　　赤ければ、忙しければ、多ければ、暗ければ、寒ければ、近ければ

E　な -Adjectives

Stem + であれば　　元気であれば、静かであれば、親切であれば、有名であれば

F　Nominals

Noun + であれば　　雨であれば、音楽であれば、学生であれば、午後であれば

21b　CLAUSE1 ば CLAUSE2　　"If C1, C2"

This construction can be used with or without もし "if".

A　Verbs

今日、時間があれば、ひるねをします。
If I have time today, I'll take a nap.
試験に受(う)かれば*、日本へ行けます。
If I pass the exam, I can go to Japan.

なれれば、だいじょうぶですよ。
(Lit.) If you get used to it, it'll be all right.
Once you get used to it, it'll be all right.
もしお金が足(た)りなければ、両親にかります。
If I'm short of money, I'll borrow from my parents.
かぜをひいた時は、外へ出なければ、早くなおりますよ。
When you have a cold, you'll recover quickly if you don't go out.

> * X {が/は} 試験に受かる
> *X passes the exam.*
>
> Do not confuse this construction with 「X は試験を受ける」 "X takes the exam".

明日のパーティーに行きますか。
Are you going to the party tomorrow?
そうですねえ。もし田中さんが行けば、私も行きますが……。
Let's see. If Tanaka-san goes, I guess I'll go too …

When the C1 verb denotes an action or event, C2 cannot be a command, request, suggestion, etc. In such a case, the ～たら construction should be used instead.

○　中村さんが来れば、にぎやかになります。
　　If Nakamura-san comes, things will get lively.
×　中村さんが来れば、電話して下さい。
○　中村さんが来たら、電話して下さい。
　　If Nakamura-san comes, please call me.

○　授業が早く終われば、映画を見に行けます。
　　If the class ends early, I can go see a movie.
×　授業が早く終われば、映画を見に行きませんか。
○　授業が早く終わったら、映画を見に行きませんか。
　　If the class ends early, shall we go see a movie?

If the C1 verb is stative, this restriction does not apply.

> 日本のことわざ
> Japanese Proverb
>
> 犬(いぬ)も歩けば、ぼうに当(あ)たる。
> *Even a dog, if it walks around, will clash with a stick/pole.*
>
> 
>
> This proverb originally meant, "if you butt in, you'll get what's coming to you." However, most people today use it to mean, "When you walk outside, you could possibly meet with an unexpected fortune."

分からなければ、いつでもえんりょなく聞きに来て下さい。
If you don't understand (something), please feel free to come and ask me any time.
もし石川先生がオフィスにいらっしゃれば、質問しましょう。
If Ishikawa-sensei is in her office, let's ask her the question.

B　い-Adjectives

Because all adjectives are stative, we do not need to consider the above restriction.

安ければ買えますが、高ければ買えません。
If it's inexpensive, I can buy it, but if it's expensive, I can't.
もし遠ければ、タクシーで行きましょう。
If it's far, let's take a taxi (Lit. go by taxi).

午前十時はどうですか。もしおそければ、もう少し早くしましょうか。
How about 10 A.M.? If that's too late, shall we make it a little earlier?
もし寒ければ、ヒーターをつけて下さい。
If it's too cold, please (feel free to) turn on the heater.

C　な-Adjectives

「な-adjective + であれば」 is rarely used in informal conversations; the なら construction (to be introduced in 第二十六課) is used instead.

もしきらいであれば（＝きらいなら）、食べなくてもいいですよ。
If you don't like it, it's okay not to eat it.
もしおひまであれば（＝ひまなら）、あそびにいらっしゃいませんか。
If you aren't busy, would you like to come visit me? (very polite)

D　Nominal Predicates

Like な-adjectives, the なら construction is used in informal conversations, rather than「Nominal + であれば」.

楽な仕事であれば（＝仕事なら）、ひき受(う)けます。
If it's an easy job, I'll take it.
来週の水曜日であれば（＝水曜日なら）、しゅっせきできます。
If it's next Wednesday, I can attend (it).

NEGATION:

Because the negative ない is an adjective, ～なければ is the negative version of the ば construction.

分からなければ、ウェブでしらべます。
If I don't understand it, I'll look it up on the Web.
高くなければ買えます。
If it's not expensive, I can buy it.

そのアパートがうるさくなければ、来月からかりるつもりです。

If that apartment isn't (too) noisy, I plan to rent it starting (Lit. from) next month.

アパートが静かじゃなければ、かりないつもりです。

If the apartment isn't quiet, I won't rent it.

学生じゃなければ、このプログラムで留学できません。

If you are not a student, you can't go study abroad through this program.

21c ～そうだ "It looks (like) ~"

This construction represents the speaker's subjective judgment of a situation (e.g. estimate, forecast) based on appearances or intuition rather than on objective information.

A Verbs: Use the Pre- ますフォーム.

ます

雨が降りそうです。

It looks like it's going to rain.

明日は晴れそうです。

It looks like we'll have clear skies tomorrow.

もうすぐ、かいぎが始まりそうです。

It seems that the meeting will start soon.

そのじしょはやくにたちそうですね。

That dictionary looks useful.

小山さんは赤い顔をしています。* 熱がありそうです。

Koyama-san has a red face (her face is flushed). She seems to have a fever.

あのかびんはたおれそう**ですから、なおして下さい。

That vase looks like it's going to fall, so please put it straight.

この宿題は長いので、ずいぶん時間がかかりそうです。

Because this homework assignment is long, it looks like it'll take a very long time.

* する(normally used as している) with a certain phrase means "to have", e.g. 赤い顔をしている "to have a flushed face (due to a fever or embarrassment)".

小山さんはまるい顔をしています。

Koyama-san has a round face.

山本さんはしかくい顔をしています。

Yamamoto-san has a square face.

歩きながら歌わないで下さい。みんな変な顔をして見ていますよ。

Please don't sing while walking. Everyone is looking at (us) with strange (puzzled) faces.

** While たおれる, 下がる, and おちる can all be translated as "to fall", they are not interchangeable. たおれる is used when something that is normally standing falls down, e.g. 木がたおれる. 下がる is used when something moves down (smoothly), e.g. 熱が下がる. おちる is used when something drops, e.g. 本が（つくえから）おちる.

B　い-Adjectives: Use only the stem.

しんかんせんはとてもはやそうですね。*
The Shinkansen (bullet trains) look very fast, don't they?

つぎの試験はむずかしそうです。
It looks like the next quiz is going to be difficult.

そのはこはおもそうです。
That box looks heavy.

かなしそうですね。どうしたんですか。
You look sad. What happened?

ケーキがとてもおいしそうだったので、一つちゅうもんしました。
Because the cake looked so delicious, I ordered one.

小山さん、うれしそう** ですね。何かいいことがありましたか。
Koyama-san, you look happy. Did something good happen?

> * This はやい "fast" is written as 速い, not as 早い "early".
>
> ** As explained in 第十二課 regarding ほしい／ほしがっている and ～たい／～たがっている, Japanese is very strict about accessibility of information. Because you do not have direct access to others' mental states, when you use うれしい to describe other people, you need to add an expression like そうです to indicate that it is your conjecture. Thus, a sentence like ソンさんはうれしいです is unacceptable.

For いい, use よさそう; いさそう does not exist.

そのコンピューターはよさそうですね。	*That looks like a good computer.*
ソンさんは、頭がよさそうですね。	*Son-san seems smart, doesn't she?*

C　な-Adjectives: Use only the stem.

このじしょは便利そうですね。	*This dictionary looks convenient.*
ミラーさんはいつも元気そうです。	*Miller-san always looks energetic / healthy.*

> Nominal predicates cannot be used in this construction when it is in the affirmative, but they can be used when the clause is negated (see section (d)).

NEGATION:

(a)　**With verbs,** use ～そう（に）もない.

ミラーさんは、その問題が分かりそうにもありません。
It looks like Miller-san doesn't understand the problem.

今夜(こんや)は雨が降りそうもありません。
It doesn't look like it'll rain tonight.

明日のパーティーには、あまり人が来そうにもありません。
As for tomorrow's party, not many people are likely to come.

(b) **With い-adjectives, use ～そうじゃない, ～そうではない, or ～くなさそう.**

次の試験はむずかしそうじゃありません。
The next quiz doesn't look difficult.
次の試験はむずかしくなさそうです。
It looks like the next quiz isn't difficult.

あの店の食べ物はおいしそうではありません。
The food at that shop doesn't look tasty.
あの店の食べ物はおいしくなさそうです。
The food at that shop looks un-tasty.

ソンさんはさいきん、忙しそうじゃありません。
Son-san doesn't look busy recently.
ソンさんはさいきん、忙しくなさそうです。
It appears Son-san is not busy recently.

(c) **With な-adjectives,** use ～そう {じゃ / では} ない or ～ {じゃ / では} なさそう.

キムさんは、さかなが好きそうじゃありません。
Kim-san doesn't appear to like fish.
キムさんは、さかなが好きじゃなさそうです。
It appears that Kim-san doesn't like fish.

ソンさんは元気そうではありません。
Son-san doesn't look cheerful.
ソンさんは元気じゃなさそうです。
It looks like Son-san isn't cheerful.

新しく来た学生はあまりまじめそうじゃありません。
The newly-enrolled student doesn't appear to be serious (about his/her work).
新しく来た学生はあまりまじめではなさそうです。
It appears the newly-enrolled student isn't serious (about his/her work).

(d) **With nominal predicates,** only ～ {じゃ / では} なさそう can be used.

あの人は学生ではなさそうです。 *That person doesn't look like a student.*
ソンさんは病気じゃなさそうです。 *It looks like Son-san isn't ill.*

Note that affirmative そう sentences with a nominal predicate like あの人は学生そうです are ungrammatical.

21d てフォーム + 行く／来る／帰る "do ~ and go/come/go back"

て This construction does not have a direct equivalent in English, but is very frequently used in Japanese. Although the second verb (行く／来る／帰る) is more commonly written in ひらがな, we use 漢字 in this textbook. The meaning of this construction differs slightly according to the nature of the てフォーム verb.

A Do something and then go/come/go back.

ケーキを買って来ました。

I bought a cake and came (home).

行って来ます。

I'll go out and then come back. (A fixed expression you say when you leave home, work, etc.)

薬屋(くすりや)でかぜ薬(くすり)*を買って来て下さいませんか。

Could you buy some cold medicine at the drug store (and come back)?

> * kaze + kusuri
> → kaze-gusuri
> by sequential voicing,
> cf. 第十一課, **11f**.

スーパーでかにを買って帰りました。

I bought crabs at a supermarket and went home.

かならず、教科書を読んで来て下さい。

(Lit.) Please be sure to read the textbook and then come (to class).

Please be sure to have read the textbook when you come (to the next class).

B Go/Come/Go back in the condition resulting from doing something.

お金をもって来ましたか。(もつ "hold" + 来る "come")

Did you bring money?

友達をつれて行ってもいいですか。

(つれる "to bring/take along (a person or animal)" + 行く "go")

Is it okay to bring (Lit. take) my friend?

ソンさんをつれて来ますから、ちょっと待っていて下さい。

I'll bring Son-san, so please wait (Lit. be waiting) a moment.

上着を着て行かなかったので、かぜをひいてしまいました。

Because I went out without my jacket, I caught a cold.

21e NOUN (Quantity) + も "as many/as much as NOUN"

When「Quantity + も」appears in an affirmative sentence, it means "as many/as much as", connoting that the quantity is more than the speaker's expectation. This contrasts with しか (see **21f**).

十ドルぐらいだと思っていましたが、五十ドルもかかりました。

I thought it would cost about $10, but it (actually) cost (as much as) $50.

明日出す作文は、十ページも書かなくてはいけません。

For the composition assignment due tomorrow, I have to write 10 whole pages!

飛行機がおくれたので、くうこうで三時間も待ちました。

Because the plane was delayed, I waited at the airport 3 whole hours!

このプロジェクトはすぐできると思いましたが、二週間もかかってしまいました。

I thought this project could be done quickly, but it took as long as 2 entire weeks!

21f NOUN + しか + Negative "only NOUN"

しか appears only in negative clauses, where it means "(not) more than". Like English *only*, 「しか + Negative」frequently implies that the state of affairs does not meet the speaker's expectations. While が and を do not co-occur with しか, other particles (e.g. に, で, と, まで, etc.) must be used with しか.

(1) ○ 両親は来ませんでした。妹しか来ませんでした。
× 両親は来ませんでした。妹[が]しか来ませんでした。
My parents didn't come. Only my sister came.

(2) ○ 授業では、日本語しか話しません。
× 授業では、日本語[を]しか話しません。
In class, we speak only Japanese.

(3) ○ 今日はコーヒーしか飲んでいないから、とてもおなかがすいています。
× 今日はコーヒー[を]しか飲んでいないから、とてもおなかがすいています。
Because I've had nothing but coffee today, I'm very hungry.

(4) 石川先生[に]しか会えませんでした。
I couldn't meet with anyone but Ishikawa-sensei.

(5) バー[で]しか日本語を話しません。
(Lit.) I don't speak Japanese anywhere but in bars.
I speak Japanese only in bars.

(6) 田中さん[と]しかテニスをしません。
(Lit.) I don't play tennis with anyone but Tanaka-san.
I play tennis only with Tanaka-san.

(7) がんばりましたが、六ページ[まで]しか読めませんでした。
(Lit.) I did my best, but I couldn't read more than up to page 6.
I did my best, but I couldn't read beyond page 6.

21g　Parts of the Body

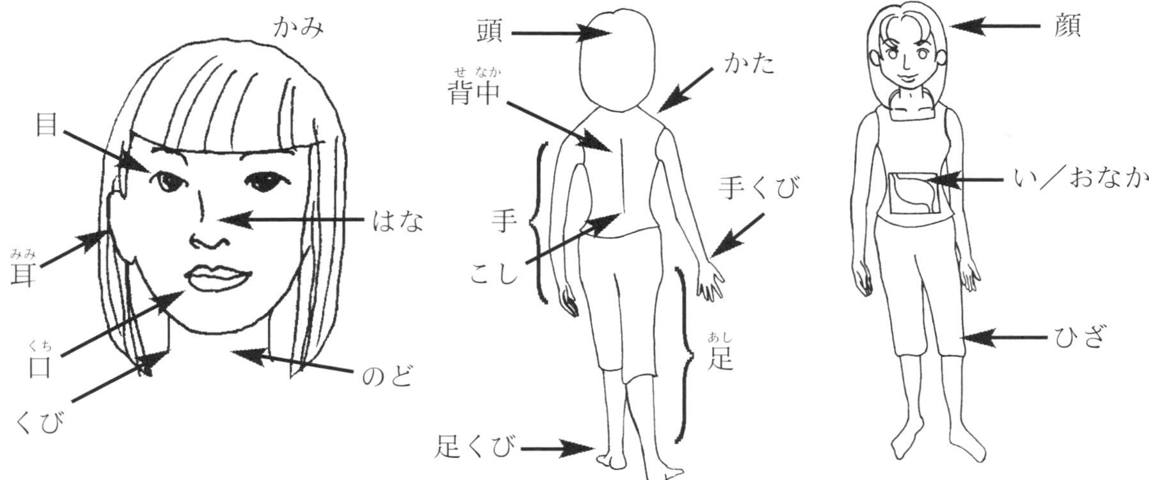

21h　Expressions of Illness

かぜをひきました。	*I've got a cold.*
気分／気もちがわるいです。	*I feel sick.*
	I feel nauseated.
熱があります。	*I have a fever.*
くしゃみが出ます。	*I'm sneezing.*
せきが出ます。	*I have a cough.*
はなが出ます。	*I have a runny nose.*
足がかゆいです。	*My leg itches.*
どこが痛いんですか。	*Where does it hurt?*
頭が痛いです。	*I have a headache.*
はが痛いです。	*I have a toothache.*
耳が痛いです。	*My ear hurts.*
のどが痛いです。	*I have a sore throat.*
かたが痛いです。	*I have stiff shoulders.*
いが痛いです。	*I have a stomachache.*
おなかが痛いです。	*I have a stomachache / cramps.*
背中が痛いです。	*I have a backache.*
ここが痛いです。	*I have a pain here.*
お大事に。	*(Lit.) Treat it (your health) as something of high importance. Take care of yourself. (said to someone who is ill)*

日本のことわざ

Japanese Proverb

かべに耳あり、しょうじに目あり。

The walls have ears; the shōji *(paper doors) have eyes.*

あり comes from あります.

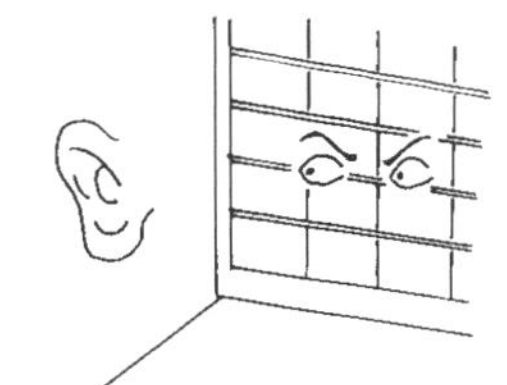

Secret conversations are easily overheard/observed.

練習問題

I. ばフォームを練習しましょう。

1.	あそぶ	11.	かりる	21.	ただしい	31.	病気だ
2.	当たる	12.	暗い	22.	使う	32.	ふくざつだ
3.	あつい	13.	来る	23.	着(つ)く	33.	待つ
4.	いい・よい	14.	下がる	24.	てきとうだ	34.	休みだ
5.	急ぐ	15.	さそう	25.	とくいだ	35.	有名だ
6.	入れる	16.	親切だ	26.	なおる	36.	読む
7.	受かる	17.	すっぱい	27.	のぼる	37.	楽だ
8.	およぐ	18.	する	28.	はかる	38.	りっぱだ
9.	買う	19.	大変だ	29.	はずかしい	39.	わかい
10.	帰る	20.	出す	30.	晴れる	40.	わるい

II. AとBのはこからてきとうなペアを作って下さい。そして、「ば」を使って文を書きましょう。

A

1. 今日、忙しいです。
2. 例(れい)をよく読みます。
3. 毎日運動します。
4. 今日、宿題がありません。
5. 気分がわるいです。
6. お金をかります。
7. ブラウンさんがリーダーです。
8. ソンさんが今晩のパーティーに行きます。

B

a. 新しい車が買えます。
b. 明日来て下さい。
c. いっしょにあそびに行けます。
d. 病院へ行きましょう。
e. 私も行きます。
f. もっと元気になります。
g. この問題はやり方がすぐ分かります。
h. このプロジェクトは早くできるでしょう。

III. AとBの会話を作って下さい。

1. A: 日本語の試験でいいてんが取れません。
   B: ＿＿＿＿＿＿＿＿＿＿＿＿＿＿ば、いいてんが取れますよ。

2. A: 今晩パーティーをします。来ませんか。
   B: ＿＿＿＿＿＿＿＿＿＿＿＿＿＿ば、行きます。

3. A: 新しいコンピューターを買いますか。
   B: はい、＿＿＿＿＿＿＿＿＿＿＿＿＿＿ば、買おうと思います。

4. A:　私はいつも寝ぼうします。今日も日本語のクラスにおくれてしまいました。
   B:　________________ば、寝ぼうしませんよ。

IV.　パートナーにインタビューしましょう。

例　Q:　どうすれば、たくさん貯金ができますか。
　　A:　お金をあまり使わなければ、貯金ができます。

1. ________________ば、単語が覚えられます。
2. ________________ば、日本人の友達ができます。
3. ________________ば、いい大学院に入れます。
4. ________________ば、病気がなおります。

V.　文を作ってみましょう。

1. 毎日早くおきれば、________________。
2. よく勉強すれば、________________。
3. 宿題が大変じゃなければ、________________。
4. ________________ば、いいかいしゃにしゅうしょくできるでしょう。
5. ________________ば、大学がもっときれいになります。
6. ________________ば、いい友達になれます。
7. ________________ば、そのアパートをかりるつもりです。

VI.　下の絵を見て下さい。そして、「～そうだ」を使って言ってみましょう。

例　おちそうです。

例	1.	2.

VII.　下の絵を見て質問の答えを書いて下さい。

1.　Q:　この車ははやそうですか。

　　A: ＿＿＿＿＿＿＿＿＿＿＿＿＿＿＿＿＿＿。

2.　Q:　ブラウンさんはひまそうですか。

　　A: ＿＿＿＿＿＿＿＿＿＿＿＿＿＿＿＿＿＿。

3.　Q:　雨が降りそうですか。

　　A: ＿＿＿＿＿＿＿＿＿＿＿＿＿＿＿＿＿＿。

4.　Q:　三時までに、この宿題ができそうですか。

　　A: ＿＿＿＿＿＿＿＿＿＿＿＿＿＿＿＿＿＿。

VIII.　絵を見て文を作ってください。

例（れい）　リンさんは友達の家へ犬を（ つれて行きます ）。

1.　さいとう先生は毎日大学へ大きいかばんを（　　　　　　）。

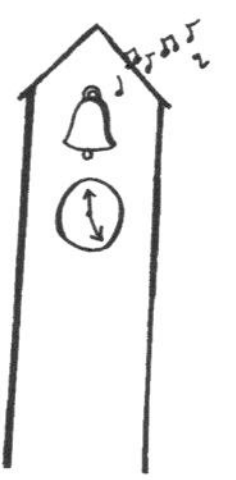

2.　昨日、木村さんの家へ行く時に、花を（　　　　　　）。

木村さんの家

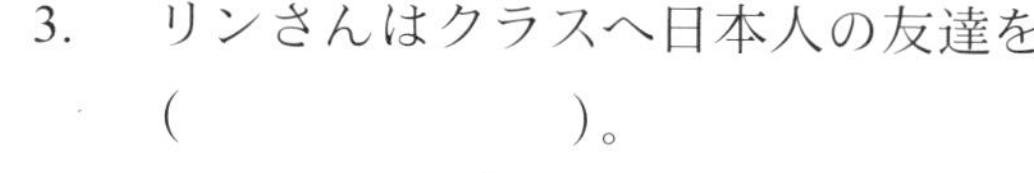

3.　リンさんはクラスへ日本人の友達を（　　　　　　）。

4.　今晩、家へワンさんが来ることになっています。それで、家へ帰る時に、ケーキ屋へ行って、ケーキを（　　　　　　）つもりです。

IX.　下のはこの中から一番いい言葉をえらんで下さい。そして、フォームをかえて、（　　）の中に書いて下さい。

例　家へ帰る時に、スーパーでお茶を買います。そして、帰ります。
→　スーパーでお茶を（買って帰ります）。

つれて行く、もって来る、買って行く、買って帰る、もって帰る、読んで来る

1.　田中さんの家でパーティーがあります。パーティーへ行く時に、飲み物を買います。それから、行きます。
→　パーティーに飲み物を（　　　　　　　　　　）。

2.　日本語の授業で毎日、教科書を使います。日本語のクラスの学生は、家で教科書を（　　　　　　　　　　）ことになっています。そして、クラスへ教科書を（　　　　　　　　　　）ことになっています。

3.　今週の週末、ダウンタウンのびじゅつ館で日本画(にほんが)のてんらん会(かい)があります。私は日本画が大好きですから、見に行くつもりです。妹も行きたがっています。それで、びじゅつ館へ妹を（　　　　　　　　　　）つもりです。

4.　来週の月曜日にろんぶんを出さなくてはいけません。それで、私は図書館でたくさん本をかりました。本はとてもおもいです。でも、週末に家で読まなくてはいけないので、今日、家へかりた本を（　　　　　　　　　　）。

X.　文の ＿＿＿＿＿ に「も」か「しか」を書いて下さい。

1. リンさんはいつも七時間ぐらい寝ます。でも、昨日はプロジェクトのしめきりだったので、おととい三時間 ＿＿＿＿＿ 寝られませんでした。でも、昨日、プロジェクトをていしゅつしてしまったので、十時間 ＿＿＿＿＿ 寝ました。

リンさんが寝る時間	
いつも	七時間
おととい	三時間
昨日	十時間

2. リンさんの家から大学まで、バスで三十分ぐらいかかります。でも、昨日はどうろがとてもこんでいたので、一時間 ＿＿＿＿＿ かかりました。今日はどうろがすいていたので、二十分 ＿＿＿＿＿ かかりませんでした。

大学までの時間	
いつも	三十分
昨日	一時間
今日	二十分

3. 私のアパートはきたないです。でも、私は大学院生ですから、毎日とても忙しいです。それで、一か月に一度 ＿＿＿＿＿ そうじできないんです。

4. とてもおいしかったので、ケーキを三つ ＿＿＿＿＿ 食べてしまいました。

XI.　英語の意味はどれですか。A か B を（　）に書いて下さい。

1. （　）この本を二十ページも読みました。
   （　）この本を二十ページしか読めませんでした。
   A. *I read 20 pages, which was less than I expected (planned).*
   B. *I read 20 pages, which was more than I expected (planned).*

2. （　）ゆうべ両親と電話で一時間も話しました。
   （　）ゆうべ両親と電話で一時間しか話しませんでした。
   A. *Last night I talked with my parents on the phone for an hour, which was more than I usually do / expected.*
   B. *Last night I talked with my parents on the phone for an hour, which was less than I usually do / expected.*

XII.　絵を見て答えましょう。

例(れい)　医者　：どうしましたか。
　　あなた：頭が痛いんです。

XIII.　読んで下さい。そして、質問に答えて下さい。

私はラムです。今、大学四年生で、今年の五月に大学を卒業することになっています。せんもんは生物学(せいぶつがく)です。しょうらい、医者になりたいので、卒業したら医科(いか)大学院へ行きたいと思っています。それで、毎日いっしょうけんめいに勉強しています。

さいきん、とても忙しくて、毎日四時間ぐらいしか寝られません。ですから、あまり元気じゃありません。たとえば、時々クラスで頭が痛くなったり、気分がわるくなったりします。でも、家へ帰る前にジムでちょっと運動すれば、よくなります。

医科大学院に入るために、さ来週の土曜日に試験を受けなくてはいけません。試験まで後二週間しかありません。医科大学院に入るのはとてもむずかしそうですから、心配です。でも、試験が終わればゆっくりすることができます。とにかく、試験の日までがんばらなくてはいけません。

1.　ラムさんはしょうらい、何になりたいと思っていますか。
2.　ラムさんはどうして毎日いっしょうけんめいに勉強しているんですか。
3.　ラムさんは毎日たくさん寝ることができますか。
4.　頭が痛くなったり気分がわるくなったりした時に、ラムさんはどうすればよくなりますか。
5.　試験まで、まだたくさん時間がありますか。
6.　医科大学院に入るのはやさしそうですか。

新しい漢字

足（あし）	医科大学院（いかだいがくいん）	医者（いしゃ）	痛い（いたい）	犬（いぬ）	上着（うわぎ）
顔（かお）	顔色（かおいろ）	かぜ薬（ぐすり）	着る（きる）	薬（くすり）	薬屋（くすりや）
口（くち）	心配（しんぱい）	足りる（たりる）	着く（つく）	熱（ねつ）	耳（みみ）

新しい使い方

当たる（あたる）	受かる（うかる）	気分（きぶん）	今夜（こんや）	下がる（さがる）	生物学（せいぶつがく）
背中（せなか）	てんらん会（かい）	日本画（にほんが）	ひき受ける（ひきうける）		

Radicals: 病（やまい）だれ

The radical 疒 appearing in 病 and 痛 is called 病（やまい）だれ, where 病 means 病気. As the name suggests, most 漢字 with this radical are related to illness.

漢字	読み	意味
足	あし・た（りる）	foot, leg, to be sufficient: 足くび ankle
当	トウ・あ（たる）	appropriate, to hit upon: 本当 really
医	イ	medicine: 医者 medical doctor
者	シャ	person; 医者 medical doctor
痛	いた（い）	pain

犬	いぬ	*dog*
上	ジョウ・あ(がる)・うえ・うわ	*top, up:* 上がる *move up,* 上げる *move something up,* 上着 *coat,* 上手 *skillful*
着	き(る)・ぎ・つ(く)	*to wear, to arrive:* 上着 *coat*
顔	かお	*face:* 顔色 *complexion*
薬	くすり・ぐすり	*medicine drug:* かぜ薬 *cold medicine,* 薬屋 *drug store*
口	くち	*mouth*
夜	ヤ・よ・よる	*night:* 今夜 *tonight,* 夜中 *middle of the night*
下	した・くだ(さい)・さ(がる)	*below, under, down:* 下さい *please give downward,* 下がる *move down,* 下げる *move something down,* 下手 *bad at*
心	シン	*heart:* 心配 *anxiety, concern (distributing one's heart)*

配	一					西	酉			配
パイ	*to distribute:* 心配 *anxiety, concern (distributing one's heart)*									
熱	一	十	土					坴		
ねつ					熱					
	heat, fever									
耳	一					耳				
みみ	*ear:* 聞く *hear, listen* has a 耳 in it. (The ear as a gate?)									

漢字の復習

I.　読みましょう。

1. むずかしい単語はたくさん書くと、覚えられます。
2. 卒業したら、外国旅行をするつもりです。
3. 田中さんのお姉さんは大学院で東アジアの文化を学んでいます。
4. 子供が寝たら、仕事を始めます。
5. 文法を全部復習しました。

II.　知っている言葉を使って新しい言葉を作りましょう。たとえば、「かぜ」と「薬」を使うと、「かぜ薬」です。＿＿＿＿＿の言葉を使って新しい言葉を作って下さい。そして、（　　）にひらがなで書いて下さい

例(れい)　かぜをひいたら、［かぜ薬］（かぜぐすり）を飲みます。いが痛い時は、［い薬］（いぐすり）を飲みます。目が痛い時には、［目薬］（めぐすり）を使います。

1. 今日の朝は［今朝］（　　　　）です。今日の夜は［　　　］（　　　　）です。
2. セーターの上に［上着］（　　　　）を着ます。セーターの下に［　　　］（　　　　）を着ます。
3. ［洗濯機］（　　　　）で洗濯をします。［　　　機］（　　　　）でそうじをします。［　　　機］（　　　　）でコピーをします。
4. 一週間が終わる時は、［週末］（　　　　）です。一か月が終わる時は、［　　　末］（　　　　）です。一年が終わる時は、［　　　末］（　　　　）です。

新しい語彙(ごい)

X ど	*X degree*
足(あし)くび	*ankle*
当(あ)たる ㋒ ⓘ	*to hit*
い	*stomach*
医科大学院(いかだいがくいん)	*medical school*
いっしょうけんめい(に)	*with all one's might*
受(う)かる ㋒ ⓘ	*to pass / succeed at (exam, class, etc)*
上着(うわぎ)	*jacket*
顔色(かおいろ)	*face color, complexion*
かぜ薬(ぐすり)	*cold medicine*
かた	*shoulder*
かならず	*be sure to do ~*
かびん	*vase*
かべ	*wall*
かゆい ㋑	*itchy*
気分(きぶん)	*feeling*
くしゃみ(する)	*sneeze*
くび	*neck*
こし	*waist, hips*
こむ ㋒ ⓘ	*to get crowded*
今夜(こんや)	*this evening*
下(さ)がる ㋒ ⓘ	*to come down, fall*
しかくい ㋑	*square*
しゅっせき(する)	*attendance*
しょうじ	shoji *screen*
せき	*cough*
背中(せなか)	*back (body)*
たいおんけい	*thermometer*
たおれる ㋸ ⓘ	*to fall over*
たとえば	*for example*
チーズケーキ	*cheesecake*
ちゅうもん(する)	*order*
つれて行(い)く ㋒ ⓣ	*to take along (a person or animal)*
ていしゅつ(する)	*submission*
手(て)くび	*wrist*
(はなが)出(で)る ㋸ ⓘ	*to have a runny nose*
てんらん会(かい)	*exhibition*
どうろ	*street*
とにかく	*anyway*
なおす ㋒ ⓣ	*to fix, repair, cure, put straight, correct*
なおる ㋒ ⓘ	*to recover, be fixed*
日本画(にほんが)	*Japanese painting*
熱(ねつ)	*fever*
バー	*bar*
はかる ㋒ ⓣ	*to measure*
ひき受(う)ける ㋸ ⓣ	*to undertake*

ひざ	*knee*
プロジェクト	*project*
ぼう	*stick, pole*
まるい ㋑	*round*
もって行(い)く ㋒ ⓣ	*to take along (a thing)*
やり方(かた)	*way of doing ~*
ゆっくり	*leisurely*
ゆっくりする Ⓘ ⓘ	*to relax*
リーダー	*leader*
ろんぶん	*thesis, article*

名前

ウェブ	*Web*
中村(なかむら)	*Nakamura*

コンサート
The Concert

日本のたいこのコンサートがあるそうです
I heard there's going to be a Japanese drum concert

5
じゃあ、私は見たことがあります。とてもはくりょくがあって、いいコンサートでしたよ。

6
そうですか。今年も去年と同じぐらいよければいいんですが……。

7
ところで、ユニバーシティー・ホールはどうですか。私は三年もこの大学で勉強しているのに、ユニバーシティー・ホールへ行ったことがありません。いいコンサートホールですか。

8
ダウンタウンのシンフォニー・ホールほどはよくありませんが、いいホールだと思います。いいコンサートをたくさんやっています。そして、シンフォニー・ホールほど高くありません。
9
そうですか。じゃあ、今すぐに、コンサートの切符を買いに行きます。
いいせきが買えるといいですね。

会話

1　ミラー：ソンさん、何を見ているんですか。

Son-san, what are you looking at?

ソン：ユニバーシティー・ホールのパンフレットです。

The University Hall pamphlet.

2　ミラー：そうですか。いいコンサートがありますか。

Oh. Are there any good concerts?

ソン：ええ、このパンフレットによると、日本のたいこのコンサートがあるそうです。それで、行ってみようと思っています。

Yes, according to the pamphlet, there's a Japanese drum concert, so I'm thinking about going.

3　ミラー：そうですか。いつですか。

Really? When is it?

ソン：五月です。最後（さいご）のクラスが終わってからですけれど、期末試験の前かも知れません。

In May. It's after the last day of classes, but it might be before finals.

4　ミラー：そうですか。そのたいこのグループは去年も来たグループですか。

I see. Is that taiko *group the same as the one that came last year?*

ソン：はい、同（おな）じグループだそうです。

Yes, it says it's the same group.

5　ミラー：じゃあ、私は見たことがあります。とてもはくりょくがあって、いいコンサートでしたよ。

Well then, I've seen them. They were very powerful, and it was a good concert.

6　ソン：そうですか。今年も去年と同じぐらいよければいいんですが……。

Was it? I hope this year's (performance) is as good as last year's.

7　ソン：ところで、ユニバーシティー・ホールはどうですか。私は三年もこの大学で勉強しているのに、ユニバーシティー・ホールへ行ったことがありません。いいコンサートホールですか。

By the way, how is University Hall? Although I've been studying at this university (as many as) three years, I've never been there. Is it a good concert hall?

8 ミラー：ダウンタウンのシンフォニー・ホールほどはよくありませんが、いいホールだと思います。いいコンサートをたくさんやっています。そして、シンフォニー・ホールほど高くありません。

It's not as good as Symphony Hall downtown, but I think it's a good hall. It hosts a lot of good concerts. And it's not as expensive as Symphony Hall.

9 ソン：そうですか。じゃあ、今すぐに、コンサートの切符(きっぷ)を買いに行きます。

Really? Well then, I'll go buy a concert ticket right now.

ミラー：いいせきが買えるといいですね。

I hope you can get (buy) a good seat.

使い方

2 While various たいこ drums have been used in Japan for well over 2,000 years in the religious ceremonies and folk festivals, the modern art form of たいこ drumming, involving athletic group performances, has a relatively short history beginning in the 1950's. It has enjoyed growing worldwide popularity ever since the 1960's.

4 Historically, 同じ behaved as both an い-adjective and a な-adjective. In Modern Japanese, it is an irregular adjective. Like い-adjectives, 同じ can modify a noun without な (e.g. 同じグループ); like な-adjectives, the negative form is 同じではない／同じじゃない, **not** 同じ[く]ない.

8 いいコンサートをたくさんやっています literally means "It is doing a lot of good concerts".

9 いいせきが買えるといいですね literally means "It will be nice if you can buy a good seat".

文法

22a	**CLAUSE1 のに CLAUSE2**	**"Although / Even though C1, C2"**
22b	**CLAUSE + そうだ**	**"I heard that ~; It is said that ~"**
22c	**Plain フォーム + かも知れない**	**"It possibly / may / might be ~"**
22d	**X と同じぐらい ADJECTIVE**	**"as ADJECTIVE as X"**
	X ほど (は) ADJECTIVE -neg	**"not as ADJECTIVE as X"**

22a CLAUSE1 のに CLAUSE2 "Although / Even though C1, C2"

Like English *although* sentences, this construction conveys the idea that the speaker feels C2 is contrary to, or is not fully consonant with, C1. Therefore, ～のに contrasts with ～ので "because". The predicate of C1 must be in a Plain フォーム.

A **Verbs:** Plain フォーム + のに

あまり食べないのに、ドンドン*ふとります。

Even though I'm not eating much, I'm gaining weight very fast.

雨が降っているのに、遠山(とおやま)さんはかさをさしていません。

Even though it's raining, Toyama-san isn't putting up her umbrella.

> * ドンドン／どんどん is a sound-symbolic word to represent that something progresses rapidly. Sound-symbolic words are explained in 第二十五課.

かぞくがはんたいしたのに、ホームズさんは日本へ留学することにしました。

Although his family opposed (the idea), Holmes-san has decided to go to Japan to study abroad.

さっき新しいボールペンを買ったのに、もうなくしてしまいました。

Although I bought a new ballpoint pen (only) a little while ago, I've already lost it.

一生(いっしょう)けんめい練習したのに、大切(たいせつ)なしあいにまけてしまいました。

Although we practiced as hard as we could, we (still) lost an important game.

たくさん眠ったのに、まだ眠いです。

Although I slept a lot, I'm still sleepy.

急いだのに、間(ま)にあいませんでした。

Even though I hurried, I couldn't make it in time.

ぜんぜん勉強しなかったのに、まんてんをもらいました。

Although I didn't study at all, I got a perfect score.

がんばったのに、試験におちてしまいました。

Although I did my best, I failed the exam.

> 日本のことわざ
> Japanese Proverb
>
> まけるがかち
> *Losing is winning.*
>
> かち comes from かちます.
>
> Makes sense? Well, sometimes in life, the best gain is obtainable by losing.

B **い-Adjectives:** Plain フォーム + のに

この車は、新しいのに、すぐこしょうします。

Although this car is new, it breaks down quickly.

この答えは正(ただ)しいのに、ばつでした。

Even though this answer is correct, I received a batsu *(X mark).*

このクラスは朝とても早いのに、だれもちこくしません。
Although this class is very early in the morning, no one comes late.
トラックがほしかったのに、買えませんでした。
Although I wanted a truck, I couldn't (afford to) buy one.
寒くないのに、遠山さんはオーバーを着ています。
Although it isn't cold, Toyama-san is wearing an overcoat.

C　な-Adjectives: Use ～なのに (non-past) and ～だったのに (past). Note that in most constructions, the plain non-past form of な-adjectives and nominal predicates is だ, but in ～のに, you need to use な.

あのアパートは、駅から遠くてふべんなのに、とても高いです。
Even though that apartment is far from the train station and inconvenient, it's very expensive.
昨日のテストはかんたんだったのに、あまりよくできませんでした。
Even though yesterday's test was easy, I couldn't do very well.
キムさんは、日本酒(にほんしゅ)が好きなのに、飲まないようにしています。
Although Kim-san likes sake, he's trying not to drink.
ホームズさんは木村さんが大好きなのに、言えません。
Although Holmes-san likes Kimura-san very much, he can't say it.
ジョーンズさんは絵をかくのが好きじゃないのに、とても上手です。
Although Jones-san doesn't like to draw, she's very good at it.

D　Nominal Predicates: Same as な -adjectives.

山下さんは、仕事中なのに、おしゃべりしています。
Although he's in the middle of work, Yamashita-san is chatting (with his colleagues).
まゆみさんといちろうさんは兄弟なのに、あまりにていません。*
Although Mayumi-san and Ichiro-san are siblings, they don't look much alike.
遠山さんは、病気なのに、仕事を休みません。
Even though Toyama-san is sick, she doesn't take any days off from work.
オフィスアワーなのに、だれも来ません。
Although office hours are (being held) now, nobody is coming.
今日は休みじゃないのに、ウォンさんは家にいます。
Today isn't a holiday, but (nonetheless) Wong-san is at home.

* になる means "to become similar". To describe a current state of affairs, にている "to resemble" must be used.

The ～のに construction is similar to ～が (cf. 第七課, **7h**) and ～けれど／～けど (cf. 第十三課 Usage Notes). For example, the following are all quite similar in meaning.

週末なのに、みんな勉強しています。
Although it's a weekend, everyone is studying.
週末ですが、みんな勉強しています。
It's a weekend, but everyone is studying.
週末ですけれど、みんな勉強しています。
It's a weekend, but everyone is studying.

There are some important differences, however. With ～のに, C2 cannot be a request, suggestion, or any volitional expression, whereas with ～が and ～けれど, it can be.

Request:
○ (このげんこうは) 長いです {が / けれど}、タイプして下さい。
× (このげんこうは) 長いのに、タイプして下さい。
This draft is long, but please type it.

Suggestion:
○ (あのレストランは) ちょっと高いです {が / けれど}、行ってみませんか。
× (あのレストランは) ちょっと高いのに、行ってみませんか。
That restaurant is a little expensive, but would you like to try it?

Desire:
○ 明日は試験です {が / けれど}、映画を見に行きたいです。
× 明日は試験なのに、映画を見に行きたいです。
There's an exam tomorrow, but I want to go see a movie.

Intention:
○ お金がありません {が / けれど}、ステレオを買うつもりです。
× お金がないのに、ステレオを買うつもりです。
I don't have the money, but I intend to buy a stereo.

○ 水着(みずぎ)を買いました {が / けれど}、色がはでなので、返そうと思います。
× 水着を買ったのに、色がはでなので、返そうと思います。
I bought a bathing suit, but because its colors are too bright (loud), I think I'm going to return it.

22b CLAUSE + そうだ "I heard that ~; It is said that ~"

In 第二十一課, **21c**, we studied the「pre- ますフォーム + そうだ」construction, which expresses the speaker's conjecture based mainly on appearances: "It seems that …". In this lesson, we are learning the so-called *hear-say* そうだ *construction*. This pattern is used to report what the speaker heard or read. The predicate of the CLAUSE must be in a plain form. X によると "according to X" frequently co-occurs with this construction. In English, "I heard …" is often used to convey something rumored; the Japanese phrase does not have the same connotation.

A Verbs

新聞の天気(てんき)よほうによると、夕方(ゆうがた)、雨が降るそうです。

According to the newspaper weather forecast, it's going to rain in the evening.

遠山さんは夕食(ゆうしょく)までに帰るそうです。

I was told that Toyama-san would come home by dinner (time).

ミラーさんは昨日、授業を休んだそうです。

I hear Miller-san didn't come to class yesterday.

ラボのコンピューターがこわれたそうです。

I heard that the computers in the lab broke down.

山下さんは最近(さいきん)、自転車に乗る練習をしているそうです。

I hear Yamashita-san has been practicing riding a bicycle recently.

ラジオによると、どうろは今、こんでいるそうです。

(Lit.) According to the radio, the streets are crowded now.

The radio says there's heavy traffic now.

小山さんは、来週、試験を受けないそうです。

I heard that Koyama-san isn't going to take the test next week.

B い-Adjectives

つぎのテストは難(むずか)しいそうです。

They say the next quiz will be difficult.

あの洗濯機はとても使いやすいそうです。

I heard that that washing machine is very easy to use.

ミラーさんによると、東京はあまり寒くなかったそうです。

According to Miller-san, it wasn't very cold in Tokyo.

ミラーさんは日本で色々しっぱいして、はずかしかったそうです。

I heard that Miller-san made all kinds of mistakes in Japan and was frequently embarrassed.

日本は今年、雨が少ないそうです。

I heard that Japan has little rain this year.

冬、富士山(ふじさん)にのぼるのはあぶないそうです。

I heard that it's dangerous to climb Mt. Fuji in winter.

C な-Adjectives

まだ乗ったことはありませんが､しんかんせんはとても便利だそうです。

I haven't ridden on it yet, but I hear the Shinkansen *bullet train is very convenient.*

石川先生の文法の説明(せつめい)はとてもていねいだそうです。

I heard that Ishikawa-sensei's grammar explanations are very thorough.

さいとう先生はむかし*、ゴルフがお上手だったそうです。

I hear that Saito-sensei used to be good at golf in the old days.

このおてらは、あまり有名じゃないそうです。

I hear that this temple isn't very famous.

> * むかし means "ancient times / long ago / the old days", but people tend to use it to refer to the recent past. For example, you may hear a junior high school student saying, むかしはもっとよく覚えられました "In むかし, I could remember better".

D Nominal Predicates

ソンさんによると、ミラーさんの専門(せんもん)はコンピューター・サイエンスだそうです。

According to Son-san, Miller-san's major is computer science.

よていひょうによると、こうえんは三時からだそうです。

According to the schedule, the lecture starts at (Lit. is from) 3 o'clock.

さいとう先生はむかし、小学校の先生だったそうです。

I heard that Saito-sensei used to be an elementary school teacher.

遠山さんはむかし、勉強しない子供だったそうです。

(Lit.) I heard that in the past, Toyama-san was an unstudious child.

I heard that Toyama-san didn't study much when she was a child.

ジョーンズさんは、日本に住んでいた時は、英語の先生だったそうです。

I heard that Jones-san was an English teacher when she was living in Japan.

テレビのニュースによると、日本は今とてもいいきせつだそうです。

According to the news on TV, it's a very nice season in Japan now.

ウィルソンさんは英国人(えいこくじん)じゃないそうです。

I heard that Wilson-san isn't British.

22c　PLAIN フォーム + かも知れない　“It possibly / may / might be ~”

〜かも知れない “it possibly / may / might be” expresses uncertainty on the part of the speaker. The plain form of a verb, adjective, or nominal predicate can be used in this construction, which consists of:

Plain フォーム	+	か	+	も	+	知れない
		Q		also		can't know

Literally, it means “I can't know whether ~”.

A　Verbs

今晩、友達が来るかも知れません。
A friend of mine might come this evening.
ミラーさんは来年も日本語を取るかも知れません。
Miller-san might take Japanese again next year.
明日は天気がよくなるかも知れません。
The weather might be better tomorrow.
木村さんは試験におちたかも知れません。受かったかも知れません。
Kimura-san might have failed the exam. Or she might have passed it.
ソンさんはかぞくに電話しないかも知れません。
Son-san might not call her family.
この説明は難しいので、だれも分からなかったかも知れません。
Because this explanation is difficult, it's possible nobody understood it.
そらにほしが出ているので、明日は晴れるかも知れません。
Because stars are out in the sky (tonight), it may be clear tomorrow.

B　い-Adjectives

こうえんは短(みじか)いかも知れません。
The lecture may be short.
このペンは書きやすいかも知れません。
This pen might be easy to write with.
この小説(しょうせつ)は有名ですが、おもしろくないかも知れません。
This novel is famous, but it may not be interesting.
石川先生の車は高かったかも知れません。
Ishikawa-sensei's car may have been expensive.

C　な -Adjectives

With a な -adjective or nominal predicate, the non-past tense of the copula だ is not used in this construction.

その仕事は楽かも知れません。
That task might be easy.
しゅうしょく試験はだめだったかも知れません。
I may have failed my employment exam.
パーティーはにぎやかじゃなかったかも知れません。
The party may not have been lively.

D　Nominal Predicates

ブラウンさんは英国人かも知れません。
Brown-san might be British.
山本さんの専門は物理学かも知れません。化学(かがく)かも知れません。
Yamamoto-san's major might be physics. Or maybe it's chemistry.
三十年前、このへんは駅だったかも知れません。
Thirty years ago, this area was perhaps a train station.
あの日は雨だったかも知れません。
There may have been rain on that day.
もんげんは十時じゃないかも知れません。
Perhaps the curfew isn't 10 o'clock.

22d　X と同じぐらい ADJECTIVE　"as ADJECTIVE as X"
X ほど (は) ADJECTIVE -neg　"not as ADJECTIVE as X"

今日は昨日と同じぐらい寒いです。
Today is as cold as yesterday.
グアムはハワイと同じぐらい暑(あつ)いそうです。
I hear that Guam is as hot as Hawaii.
ミラーさんはソンさんと同じぐらいまじめです。
Miller-san is as diligent as Son-san.
京都は奈良(なら)と同じぐらいきれいです。
Kyoto is as beautiful as Nara.

アフリカは中東(ちゅうとう)と同じぐらいおもしろい所です。
Africa is as interesting as the Middle East.
Africa and the Middle East are equally interesting places (regions).

Normally,「Xと同じぐらい～」is used only in affirmative sentences. The negative counterpart, "X is not as ~ as Y" is expressed by the use of「XはYほど（は）～くありません／じゃありません」.

× 今日は昨日と同じぐらい寒くありません。
○ 今日は昨日ほど（は）寒くありません。
Today is not as cold as yesterday.

× キムさんはソンさんと同じぐらいまじめじゃありません。
○ キムさんはソンさんほど（は）まじめじゃありません。
Kim-san is not as diligent as Son-san.

サンフランシスコはロサンゼルスほど（は）あぶなくないそうです。
I heard that San Francisco is not as dangerous as Los Angeles.
金沢(かなざわ)は京都ほど有名ではありませんが、れきしてきなまちです。
Kanazawa is not as famous as Kyoto, but it is (nevertheless) a historical town (too).

練習問題

I. 文を作りましょう。

1. 山下さんはやくそくしたのに、＿＿＿＿＿＿＿＿＿＿＿＿＿＿＿＿＿＿。
2. すずきさんは大学が休みなのに、＿＿＿＿＿＿＿＿＿＿＿＿＿＿＿＿＿＿。
3. 明日試験があるのに、＿＿＿＿＿＿＿＿＿＿＿＿＿＿＿＿＿＿。
4. 山田さんは昨日、かなり熱があったのに、＿＿＿＿＿＿＿＿＿＿＿＿＿＿＿＿＿＿。
5. スミスさんはさとうさんが大好きなのに、＿＿＿＿＿＿＿＿＿＿＿＿＿＿＿＿＿＿。
6. ＿＿＿＿＿＿＿＿＿＿＿＿＿＿＿＿＿＿のに、授業におくれてしまいました。
7. ＿＿＿＿＿＿＿＿＿＿＿＿＿＿＿＿＿＿のに、眠いです。
8. ＿＿＿＿＿＿＿＿＿＿＿＿＿＿＿＿＿＿のに、まだつかれています。
9. ＿＿＿＿＿＿＿＿＿＿＿＿＿＿＿＿＿＿のに、みんな勉強しています。
10. ＿＿＿＿＿＿＿＿＿＿＿＿＿＿＿＿＿＿のに、東山さんはオーバーを着ています。

II.　「ので」か「のに」を使って文を作って下さい。

1.

＿＿＿＿＿＿＿＿＿＿＿＿＿＿＿＿＿＿＿＿＿＿＿＿＿＿＿＿＿。

2.　先週

＿＿＿＿＿＿＿＿＿＿＿＿＿＿＿＿＿＿＿＿＿＿＿＿＿＿＿＿＿。

3.　先学期

＿＿＿＿＿＿＿＿＿＿＿＿＿＿＿＿＿＿＿＿＿＿＿＿＿＿＿＿＿。

4.　夕（ゆう）べ

＿＿＿＿＿＿＿＿＿＿＿＿＿＿＿＿＿＿＿＿＿＿＿＿＿＿＿＿＿。

5.

＿＿＿＿＿＿＿＿＿＿＿＿＿＿＿＿＿＿＿＿＿＿＿＿＿＿＿＿＿。

III.　絵を見て文を作って下さい。

例

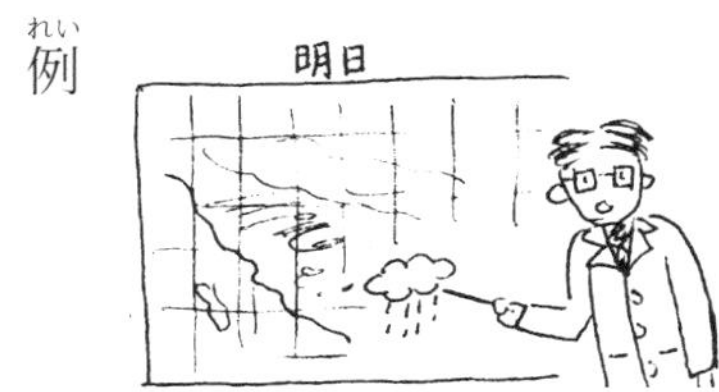

天気よほうによると明日は雨だそうです。

1.

(明日、だいとうりょうが日本に行きます。)

____

______________________________。

2.

(昨日、大学のバスケットボールのチームがかちました。)

____

______________________________。

3.

(今朝七時ごろこうつうじこがありました。)

____

______________________________。

4.

____

______________________________。

5.

____

______________________________。

IV.　「～かも知れない」を使って文を作って下さい。

例　A:　明日は晴れるでしょうか。

　　B:　今日も晴れましたから、明日もいい天気かも知れません。

　　A:　そうですね。

1.　A:　今度の日本語の試験は難しいでしょうか。

　　B:　__________________________________から、

　　__________________________________かも知れません。

2.　A:　あのコンピューターは使いやすいでしょうか。

　　B:　__________________________________から、

　　__________________________________かも知れません。

3.　A:　来学期、いいアパートが見つかるでしょうか。

　　B:　__________________________________から、

　　__________________________________かも知れません。

4.　A:　X さんはしゅうしょく試験に受かったでしょうか。

　　B:　__________________________________から、

　　__________________________________かも知れません。

V.　文を作りましょう。

1.　オーストラリアは (　　　　　　) ほど__________________________。

2.　私のまちは (　　　　　　) ほど__________________________。

3.　(　　　　　　) のクラスは日本語のクラスほど__________________________。

4.　(　　　　　　) はグランドキャニオンほど __________________________。

5.　私の大学は (　　　　　　) と同じぐらいいい大学です。

VI.　パートナーと話しましょう。

例　A:　B さんはどこから来ましたか。

　　B:　私ですか。__________________ から来ました。

　　A:　そうですか。__________________ はどうですか。

　　B:　そうですね。ニューヨークと同じぐらい楽しい所です。でも、ニューヨークほどにぎやかじゃありません。

　　A:　そうですか。

VII.　読みましょう。

アメリカの大学生はたくさん勉強しなくてはいけないので大変です。新聞によると、日本の大学の授業はアメリカの大学の授業ほど難しくないそうです。

ソンさんとミラーさんはアメリカの大学生です。いっしょに日本語のクラスを取っています。ソンさんは今、心理学(しんりがく)のろんぶんを読んでいます。もう二回(かい)も読んだのに、まだよく分かりません。それで、もう一回読んでいます。ソンさんは、心理学のクラスは日本語のクラスほど難しくないと思っています。日本語のクラスほど宿題や試験が多くないからです。でも、心理学のクラスはろんぶんをたくさん読まなくてはいけないので、時間がかかります。

ミラーさんの専門はコンピューター・サイエンスです。コンピューターのクラスは日本語のクラスと同じぐらい大変です。コンピューターのクラスは、試験はあまりありませんが、プロジェクトをたくさんしなくてはいけないからです。時々、てつやしてがんばらなくてはいけません。ミラーさんは、今週末もてつやしなくてはいけないかも知れないと言っています。

質問に答えて下さい。

1. アメリカの大学の授業は日本の大学の授業と同じぐらい難しいですか。
2. ソンさんとミラーさんはいっしょに何を勉強していますか。
3. ソンさんとミラーさんはまじめな学生でしょうか。
4. ソンさんは、心理学のクラスと日本語のクラスとではどちらの方が難しいと思っていますか。どうしてですか。
5. ミラーさんは、コンピューター・サイエンスのクラスと日本語のクラスとではどちらの方が大変だと思っていますか。どうしてですか。

新しい漢字

暑(あつ)い	同(おな)じ	～回(かい)	切符(きっぷ)	最近(さいきん)	最後(さいご)
小説(しょうせつ)	説明(せつめい)	専門(せんもん)	正(ただ)しい	天気(てんき)	短(みじか)い
難(むずか)しい	夕方(ゆうがた)	夕食(ゆうしょく)	夕(ゆう)べ		

新しい使い方

一生(いっしょう)けんめい		英国人(えいこくじん)	化学(かがく)	心理学(しんりがく)	大切(たいせつ)
中東(ちゅうとう)	遠山(とおやま)	日本酒(にほんしゅ)	間(ま)にあう	水着(みずぎ)	見(み)つかる

Radicals: 竹(たけ)かんむり・円(えん)がまえ

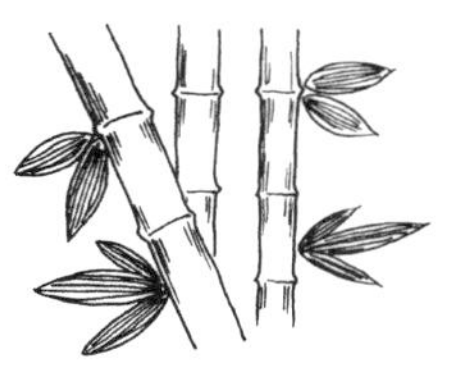

The かんむり "crown" radical ⺮, appearing in 第, 符, and 答, is called 竹(たけ)かんむり, which is derived from the 漢字「竹(たけ)」"bamboo". The meanings of this radical are not apparent from the 漢字 we have studied so far; other 漢字 belonging to this radical group are: 箱(はこ) "box", 箸(はし) "chopsticks" (typically made from bamboo sticks), 筆(ふで) "brush" (bamboo is used to make the body of brushes).

The かまえ "enclosure" radical 冂, appearing in 円 and 同, is called 円(えん)がまえ or 同(どう)がまえ. This radical does not designate particular meanings.

暑 あつ(い)	丨 冂 日 日 旦 早 旦 {暑 partial forms} 暑 暑
	hot (weather)
生 ショウ・セイ・う(まれる)	ノ 𠂉 牛 牛 生
	life: 一生けんめい *as hard as one can,* 学生 *student (studying person),* 高校生 *high school student,* 生物学 *biology,* 先生 *teacher (preceding person),* 大学院生 *graduate student,* 留学生 *foreign student*
同 おな(じ)	丨 冂 冂 同 同 同
	same
回 カイ	丨 冂 冂 冋 回 回
	~ time(s): 一回 *once,* 二回 *twice,* 三回 *three times*
切 セツ・きっ	一 七 切 切
	to cut: 切手 *postage stamp,* 切符 *ticket,* 親切 *kind,* 大切 *important*
符 プ	ノ 𠂉 ⺈ ⺮ ⺮ ⺮ ⺮ 符 符 符 符
	sign, mark: 切符 *ticket*

最	サイ	*most, maximum:* 最近 *recently,* 最後 *last, ultimate*
近	キン・ちか（い）	*near:* 最近 *recently*
小	ショウ・こ・ちい（さい）	*small:* 小づつみ *parcel,* 小山さん *Koyama-san,* 小学校 *elementary school,* 小説 *novel*
説	セツ	*opinion:* 小説 *novel,* 説明 *explanation*
明	メイ・あか（るい）	*shining, clearness,* 明日（あした）*tomorrow,* 説明 *explanation*
専	セン	*mainly, solely:* 専門 *specialty*
門	モン	*gate:* 専門 *specialty*
正	ただ（しい）	*correct;* the strokes of this character are used to count things, i.e. it is used like:
天	テン	*sky, heaven:* 天気 *weather*
酒	シュ・さけ	*liquor:* 日本酒 *Japanese sake*

短 みじか(い)	ノ				矢					
		短								
	short									
難 むずか (しい)	一	十	艹							
								難		
	difficult									
夕 ゆう	ノ	ク	夕							
	evening: 夕方 *evening,* 夕食 *evening meal,* 夕べ *yesterday evening/last night*									
方 ホウ・ かた・が	丶	亠		方						
	direction, way: 夕方 *evening*									

漢字の復習

I.　読みましょう。

1. アメリカ大使館を見学することができますか。
2. 急がなくてはいけなかったので、駅からタクシーに乗りました。
3. 食事の前には、かならず、手を洗いましょう。
4. 中学校の時は、作文を書くのが大好きでした。
5. お母さんはお元気ですか。

II.　つぎの漢字のグループは同じ部首(ぶしゅ) (radical) が足りません。どんな部首ですか。

1. 主　吏　木　更
2. ラ　云　王
3. 市　未　台　子
4. 軍　周　反　斤
5. 音　亡　田

6. 化　楽　央

7. 月　音　寺　央　青

8. 火　斗　刂　ム

9. 交　寸　幾

10. 会　氏　冬　東

新しい語彙（ごい）

あぶない ㋑	*dangerous*
英国人（えいこくじん）	*British (person)*
オーバー	*overcoat*
同（おな）じ	*same (irregular adj.)*
化学（かがく）	*chemistry*
(～に) かつ ㋒ ⓘ	*to win (a game)*
かなり	*fairly*
きせつ	*season*
げんこう	*draft*
こうつうじこ	*traffic accident*
こしょう (する)	*breakdown*
コンサート	*concert*
最後（さいご）	*final, last*
さす ㋒ ⓣ	*to put up (an umbrella)*
さっき	*a little while ago*
しあい	*match, game*
しゅうしょく試験（しけん）	*employment exam*
シンフォニー	*symphony*

心理学（しんりがく）	*psychology*
せき	*seat*
そら	*sky*
たいこ	*Japanese drum*
大切（たいせつ） ㋤	*important*
だいとうりょう	*president of a country*
タイプ (する)	*typing*
ちこく (する)	*being late for something*
ていねい ㋤	*through, careful, meticulous*
てつや (する)	*staying up all night*
(ほしが) 出（で）る ㋸ ⓘ	*to come out (stars)*
天気（てんき）よほう	*weather forecast*
トラック	*truck*
ドンドン	*rapidly*
日本酒（にほんしゅ）	*Japanese sake*
ニュース	*news*
にる ㋸ ⓘ	*to resemble*

はくりょくがある	*powerful*
ばつ	*batsu (X mark)*
はで ㋤	*flamboyant*
はんたい（する）	*opposition*
パンフレット	*pamphlet*
へん	*vicinity*
ホール	*hall*
ほし	*star*
（～に）まける ㋸ ⓘ	*to lose (a game)*
まち	*town*
間(ま)にあう ㋒ ⓘ	*to make it in time*
まんてん	*perfect score*
水着(みずぎ)	*bathing suit, swimsuit*
見(み)つかる ㋒ ⓘ	*to be found*
やくそく（する）	*promise*
夕方(ゆうがた)	*evening*
夕食(ゆうしょく)	*dinner*
ユニバーシティー	*university*
よていひょう	*schedule*

名前

オーストラリア	*Australia*
かなざわ（金沢）	*Kanazawa*
グアム	*Guam*
グランドキャニオン	*Grand Canyon*
中東(ちゅうとう)	*Middle East*
遠山(とおやま)	*Toyama*

おくり物
Gifts

小山さんは日本語の辞書(じしょ)をあげるそうです
I heard Koyama-san is going to give him a Japanese dictionary

1
山本さん、来週の土曜日はミラーさんのたんじょう日です。
そうですか。じゃあ、たんじょう日のパーティーをした方がいいですね。
2
ええ、私の家でしようと思います。山本さんもぜひ来て下さい。
はい、もちろん行きますよ。ところで、ソンさんは、もうプレゼントをきめましたか。
3
ええ、私はアニメのビデオをあげようと思います。
それはいいですね。ミラーさんはアニメが好きですから、きっとよろこびますね。
4
小山さんは日本語の辞書をあげるそうです。
5
じゃあ、私は何をあげたらいいでしょうか。
そうですねえ。ミラーさんは音楽も好きですから、CDをあげたらどうでしょう。
6
そう言えば、私はこの間、友達に日本の音楽のCDをもらったんですが、その話をしたら、ミラーさんも聞きたいと言っていました。じゃあ、私はJポップのCDにします。
7
わあ、Jポップですか。いいですね。小山さんも私もJポップが大好きです。CDがあったら、パーティーでみんなでいっしょに歌えますね。
そうですね。練習して、いつかいっしょにカラオケへ行きましょう。

会話

1　ソン　：山本さん、来週の土曜日はミラーさんのたんじょう日です。

Yamamoto-san, next Saturday is Miller-san's birthday.

山本　：そうですか。じゃあ、たんじょう日のパーティーをした方がいいですね。

Oh really? Then we should have a birthday party.

2　ソン　：ええ、私の家でしようと思います。山本さんもぜひ来て下さい。

Yes, I'm planning on having it at my house. And I certainly hope you'll be able to join us.

山本　：はい、もちろん行きますよ。ところで、ソンさんは、もうプレゼントをきめましたか。

Sure, of course I will. By the way, have you decided on a gift?

3　ソン　：ええ、私はアニメのビデオをあげようと思います。

Yeah, I think I'll give him an anime video.

山本　：それはいいですね。ミラーさんはアニメが好きですから、きっとよろこびますね。

That'll be good. Miller-san likes anime, so he'll definitely be happy.

4　ソン　：小山さんは日本語の辞書をあげるそうです。

I heard that Koyama-san's going to give him a Japanese dictionary.

5　山本　：じゃあ、私は何をあげたらいいでしょうか。

Well then, I wonder what I should give him.

ソン　：そうですねえ。ミラーさんは音楽も好きですから、CDをあげたらどうでしょう。

Let's see… He likes music too, so how about a CD?

6　山本　：そう言えば、私はこの間(あいだ)、友達に日本の音楽のCDをもらったんですが、その話をしたら、ミラーさんも聞きたいと言っていました。じゃあ、私はJポップのCDにします。

Now that you mention it, I got a Japanese music CD from a friend the other day. When I mentioned it to Miller-san, he said he wanted to listen to it too. So I'll give him a J-pop CD.

7 ソン : わあ、Jポップですか。いいですね。小山さんも私もJポップが大好きです。CDがあったら、パーティーでみんなでいっしょに歌えますね。

Wow, J-pop? That'll be great. Koyama-san and I love J-pop too. If we have a CD, we can all sing together at the party.

山本 : そうですね。練習して、いつかいっしょにカラオケへ行きましょう。

That's true. Let's practice and go do karaoke *together someday.*

使い方

5 〜たらいいでしょうか is a gentler/less forceful version of 〜たらいいですか, to be studied in **23d**.

〜たらどうでしょう and 〜たらどうでしょうか are gentler/less forceful versions of 〜たらどうですか, also to be learned in **23d**.

6 そう言えば literally means "if (you) say so". It is used when you introduce a new topic which is related to the previous utterance in the conversation. You can also translate this phrase as "That reminds me …".

7 Jポップ is an abbreviation of ジャパニーズポップソング "Japanese pop music".

いつか	*someday/sometime*				
いつ	*when*	だれ	*who*	何	*what*
いつも	*always*	だれも	*anyone**	何(なに)も	*anything**
いつか	*sometime*	だれか	*someone*	何(なに)か	*something*

*だれも and 何も mean "anyone" and "anything", respectively, and because they are generally used in negative sentences, they actually convey the idea of "no one" and "nothing".

カラオケ consists of から "empty" and an abbreviation of オーケストラ "orchestra". The カラオケ music is usually produced in a version similar to the original recording, and with the music the lyrics are panned on a TV screen. The singer supplies the lead vocals following the lyrics on the screen.

文法

23a Verbs of Giving and Receiving
23b たフォーム + 方がいい — **"It'd be better if X did ~; X had better do ~"**
23c ないフォーム + 方がいい — **"It'd be better not to do ~; X had better not to do ~"**
23d たフォーム + らいいですか — **"What/how should I do ~?"**
たフォーム + らどうですか — **"How about VERB-ing?; Why not try VERB-ing?"**

23a Verbs of Giving and Receiving

Unlike in English, verbs of *giving* and *receiving* form a special class in Japanese grammar. There are three groups of verbs: the **アゲル** verbs (上(あ)げる, やる, さし上げる)*, **クレル** verbs (くれる, 下(くだ)さる), and **モラウ** verbs (もらう, いただく). (下さる is the same verb as 下さい, which has been used throughout this textbook, and we have also already studied もらう in 第十一課.) With the **アゲル** and **クレル** verbs, the *giver* is selected to be the subject, and the *receiver* is marked with the particle に; with the **モラウ** verbs, the *receiver* is the subject, and the *giver* is marked with either に or から. Thus, the **アゲル** and **クレル** verbs can be translated as "give", and the **モラウ** verbs as "receive".**

* The majority of people today write 上げる in ひらがな (i.e.あげる), rather than with 漢字. However, many people still use 漢字 for さし上げる because its original meaning, "to raise", is still clearly noticeable. さし上げる is an honorific verb.

** In this textbook, **アゲル**, **クレル**, and **モラウ** are used to represent these three groups of donatory verbs. Individual verbs are written in the normal font.

The selection of an appropriate verb of giving or receiving depends on (i) the direction of transfer with respect to the in-group/out-group distinction, and (ii) the relative status of the giver and the receiver. If you violate the rules regarding (i), the sentence will be ungrammatical and thus unacceptable; if you violate the rules regarding (ii), the sentence itself will be acceptable, but your judgment of the relative status of the people involved may be rejected as inappropriate.

Let's look at the diagrams on the opposite page. You are in the center of the universe. Surrounding you are in-group members; that is, your family members and close friends. The rest of the universe makes up the out-group.

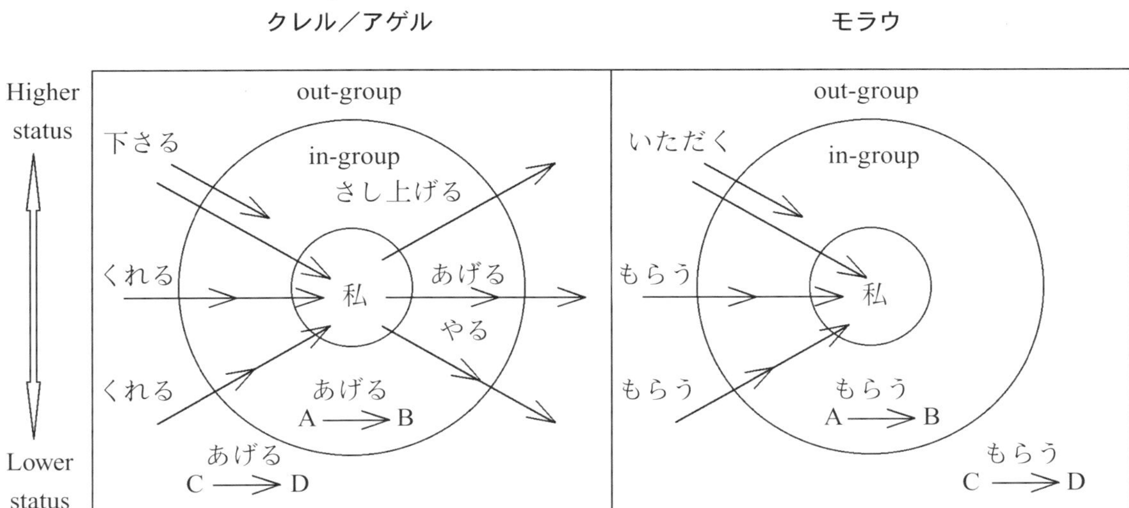

These diagrams show that:

A **アゲル** verbs cannot be used for inward transfer.

OK : 私 ⇨ In-group
私 ⇨ Out-group
In-group ⇨ Out-group
In-group ⇨ In-group
Out-group ⇨ Out-group
Bad : In-group ⇨ 私
Out-group ⇨ 私
Out-group ⇨ In-group

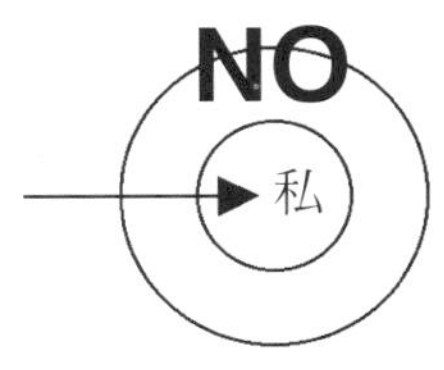

In principle, when the receiver is higher in status* than the giver, さし上げる is used; when they are of equal status, 上げる／あげる is used. As 上 implies, these verbs originally meant to "move something upward". This is the reason why you cannot be the receiver with an **アゲル** verb, e.g. ×友達は私に辞書を上げました; if you were, you would place yourself higher than the giver.

やる is used when the receiver is "inferior" to the giver. The question, then, is what or who is conventionally considered inferior. A safe assumption is that animals and plants are inferior to humans (you may not agree with this idea, though). Therefore, when you feed an animal or water a plant, you can use やる. Many people feel uncomfortable with やる and avoid it entirely.

* Relative status of the giver and the receiver is highly conventionalized; that is, it is socioculturally determined and you do not have total freedom to decide on it. In every culture, certain people are regarded as higher in status. The criteria may be age, body size or shape, gender, lineage, occupation, wealth, wisdom, etc. Furthermore, there are normally different hierarchies within a single culture, and you have the right not to observe prevailing hierarchies.

GIVERS {は / が}	RECEIVER に	{さし上げる / あげる / やる}

私は石川先生に写真をさし上げました。

I gave a photo to Ishikawa-sensei.

毎日、犬にえさをやらなくてはいけません。

(Lit.) I have to give food to the dog every day.

I have to feed the dog every day.

うえ木に水をやって下さい。

(Lit.) Please give water to the plants.

Please water the plants.

私は高田(たかだ)さんにまんがの本を二冊(さつ)あげました。

I gave Takada-san two comic books.

小山さんはソンさんにみかんを五個(こ)あげました。

Koyama-san gave Son-san five mandarin oranges.

私は弟に自転車を {あげよう / やろう} と思っています。

I'm thinking of giving my brother a bicycle.

父は会社(かいしゃ)のじょうしにお中元(ちゅうげん)**をさし上げました。

My father gave ochūgen *to his company superiors.*

** 日本では、七月と十二月に会社のじょうしやおせわになった人達におくり物をします。七月のおくり物は「お中元」と言います。「中元」は「一年のまん中」という意味です。七月は lunar calendar のまん中の月だからです。そして、十二月のおくり物は「おせいぼ」と言います。「せいぼ」は「一年の終わり」という意味です。

B　**クレル** verbs can be used only for inward transfer.

OK : In-group ⇨ 私
　　Out-group ⇨ 私
　　Out-group ⇨ In-group
　　In-group ⇨ In-group*

Bad : 私 ⇨ In-group
　　私 ⇨ Out-group
　　In-group ⇨ Out-group

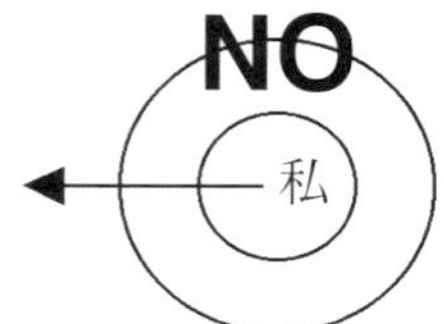

*Within the in-group (which is flexibly defined according to the situation), you may feel someone is closer than others to you. In such a case, you can use **クレル** verbs when the receiver is closer than the giver is to you, e.g., when the receiver is a younger sibling and the giver is a friend.

GIVER {は / が}	RECEIVER に you or in-group	{下さる / くれる}

さいとう先生は妹にけしゴム**を下さいました。

Saito-sensei gave my sister an eraser.

母は（私に）時計(とけい)をくれました。

My mother gave me a watch.

そふは（私に）何もくれませんでした。

My grandfather didn't give me anything.

** けしゴム consists of けす "to erase" and ゴム "gum/rubber".

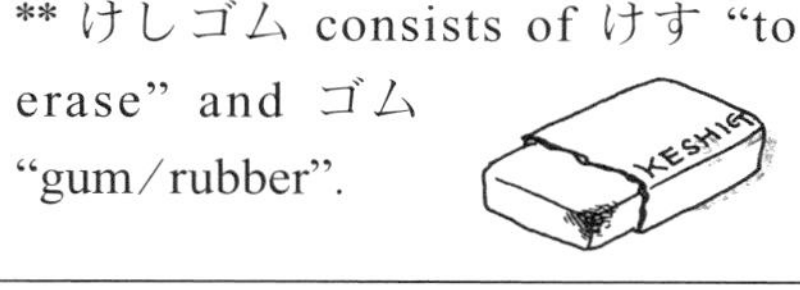

When the receiver is 私, it is normally omitted.

C　**モラウ** verbs cannot be used for outward transfer.

OK : In-group ⇨ 私
Out-group ⇨ 私
Out-group ⇨ In-group
In-group ⇨ In-group
Out-group ⇨ Out-group

Bad : 私 ⇨ In-group
私 ⇨ Out-group
In-group ⇨ Out-group

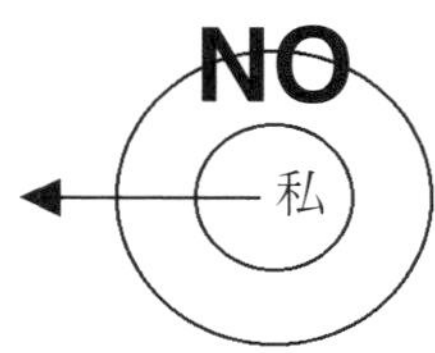

RECEIVER {は / が}	GIVER {に / から}	{いただく / もらう}

○　妹はさいとう先生にボールペンをいただきました。

My sister received a ballpoint pen from Saito-sensei.

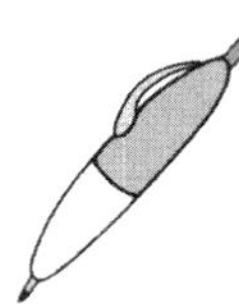

○　さいとう先生は（私の）妹にボールペンを下さいました。

Saito-sensei gave my sister a ballpoint pen.

×　さいとう先生は（私の）妹にボールペンをもらいました。

Saito-sensei received a ballpoint pen from my sister.

○　昨日は私のたんじょう日だったので、おばからこうすいをもらいました。

Because it was my birthday yesterday, I received (a bottle of) perfume from my aunt.

○　昨日は私のたんじょう日だったので、おばが（私に）こうすいをくれました。

Because it was my birthday yesterday, my aunt gave me perfume.

× 昨日はおばのたんじょう日だったので、おばは私にこうすいをもらいました。

Because it was her birthday yesterday, my aunt received perfume from me.

○ ミラーさんは山本さんからCDを三枚もらったそうです。

I heard that Miller-san got three CDs from Yamamoto-san.

○ 山本さんはミラーさんにCDを三枚あげたそうです。

I heard that Yamamoto-san gave Miller-san three CDs.

「山本さんはミラーさんにCDを三枚くれたそうです」is inappropriate unless you consider Miller-san to be in your close circle (with the transfer thus being inward).

23b　たフォーム + 方がいい　"It'd be better if X did ~; X had better do ~"

This pattern is related to the comparison construction (第九課, **9c**), in which the Dictionary フォーム precedes 方, e.g.:

スポーツをするより映画を見る方が好きです。

I like watching movies more than playing sports.

When ～た方がいい is used to make a suggestion, it is normally followed by some hedging expression to ease its strong assertiveness.

この作文は、文法のまちがいが多いですから、書きなおした方がいいと思います。

Because there are many grammatical errors in this essay, I think you should rewrite it.

人にお金を貸す時は、相手のこと*をよく調べた方がいいですよ。

If you're going to lend someone money, you'd better check him / her out thoroughly.

手紙をもらった時は、すぐに返事を出した方がいいですよ。

When you receive a letter, you ought to send a reply right away.

意見があったら、今言った方がいいですよ。

If you have an opinion, you'd better express it now.

漢字が分からないので、困っています。

I'm in trouble because I don't understand kanji.

それじゃ、漢字のコースを取った方がいいですよ。

In that case, (I think) you should take a kanji course.

先生に相談した方がいいと思います。

I think you'd better consult your teacher.

* 相手のこと literally means "things of / about the other party". Here you can just as well say 相手をよく調べた方がいい, but this use of こと is very common in conversation:

カーターさんは遠山さんのことが好きだそうです。

I heard that Carter-san likes Toyama-san.

最近、かなりふとってしまいました。
I've gained a lot of weight recently.
少し運動をした方がいいと思いますよ。
I think you'd better get a little exercise.

せきがとまらないんです。
(Lit.) The coughs don't stop.
I can't stop coughing.
タバコをやめた方がいいかも知れませんね。
Perhaps you'd better quit smoking (cigarettes).

23c　ないフォーム + 方がいい　　"It'd be better not to do ~; X had better not to do ~"

In order to make a prohibitory suggestion, you need to use ないフォーム + 方がいい.

あぶないですから、夜、一人で歩かない方がいいですよ。
Because it's dangerous, you'd better not walk alone at night.
後で大変ですから、あまりたくさんお金を借りない方がいいですよ。
Since it would be tough (to deal with) afterwards, you'd better not borrow too much money.
かぜをひいた時には、お酒は飲まない方がいいと思います。
I think it's better not to drink sake when you have a cold.
おかださんは赤ちゃんがいるので、夜は電話しない方がいいかも知れません。
Because Okada-san has a baby, it might be better not to call her at night.

23d　たフォーム + らいいですか　　"What / How should I do ~?"
たフォーム + らどうですか　　"How about VERB-ing?; Why not try VERB-ing?"

「たフォーム + らいいですか」 is used to solicit advice. If you do not wish to force your opinions, you may want to use ～たらどうですか rather than ～た方がいいです "you'd better do ~" or ～たらいいです "you should do ~".

目がとてもつかれています。どうしたらいいでしょうか。
My eyes are really tired. I wonder what I should do (about it)?
目がつかれた時には、ひやしたらいいですよ。
You should cool (put a cold cloth on) your eyes when they're tired.
目薬をさしたらどうですか。
(Lit.) How about putting eye medicine (in your eyes)?
How about trying some eye drops?

卒業しきには何を着て行ったらいいですか。

What should I wear for the graduation ceremony?

スーツを着て行ったらどうですか。

How about wearing a suit?

デジタルカメラを買う時には、何に気をつけたらいいですか。

What should I pay attention to when I buy a digital camera?

コンピューターにつなげやすい物を買った方がいいですよ。

It's best to buy one that's easy to connect to your computer.

事故(じこ)の時は、どうしたらいいですか。

What should I do if (Lit. when) I have an accident?

けいさつをよばなくてはいけません。

You have to call the police.

練習問題

I.　絵を見て文を書いて下さい。

例(れい)　田中さんは木村さんに花をあげました。
木村さんは田中さんに花をもらいました。

1.　木村さんは ______________________________ に
______________________________ をあげました。
さとうさんは ____________________________ に
____________________________ をもらいました。

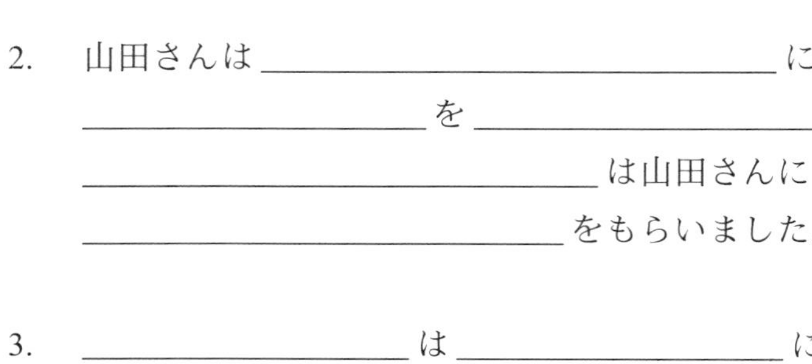

2.　山田さんは ______________________________ に
____________________ を ____________________。
______________________________ は山田さんに
____________________________ をもらいました。

3.　____________________ は ____________________ に
______________________________ をあげました。
____________________ は ____________________ に
____________________ を ____________________。

4. ＿＿＿＿＿＿＿＿ は ＿＿＿＿＿＿＿＿ に
＿＿＿＿＿＿＿＿ をやりました／あげました。

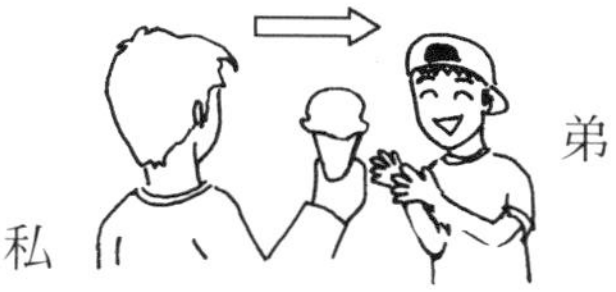

私　弟

5. ＿＿＿＿＿＿＿＿ は ＿＿＿＿＿＿＿＿ に
＿＿＿＿＿＿＿＿ を ＿＿＿＿＿＿＿＿。

私

6. ＿＿＿＿＿＿＿＿ は ＿＿＿＿＿＿＿＿ に
＿＿＿＿＿＿＿＿ をくれました。
＿＿＿＿＿＿＿＿ は ＿＿＿＿＿＿＿＿ に
＿＿＿＿＿＿＿＿ をもらいました。

高田　私　chocolate

7. ＿＿＿＿＿＿＿＿ は ＿＿＿＿＿＿＿＿ に
＿＿＿＿＿＿＿＿ を ＿＿＿＿＿＿＿＿。
＿＿＿＿＿＿＿＿ は ＿＿＿＿＿＿＿＿ に
＿＿＿＿＿＿＿＿ をもらいました。

私　チョー

8. ＿＿＿＿＿＿＿＿ は ＿＿＿＿＿＿＿＿ に
＿＿＿＿＿＿＿＿ を ＿＿＿＿＿＿＿＿。
＿＿＿＿＿＿＿＿ は ＿＿＿＿＿＿＿＿ に
＿＿＿＿＿＿＿＿ を ＿＿＿＿＿＿＿＿。

山田　私

9. ＿＿＿＿＿＿＿＿ は ＿＿＿＿＿＿＿＿ に
＿＿＿＿＿＿＿＿ を ＿＿＿＿＿＿＿＿。
＿＿＿＿＿＿＿＿ は ＿＿＿＿＿＿＿＿ に
＿＿＿＿＿＿＿＿ を ＿＿＿＿＿＿＿＿。

父　私

10. ＿＿＿＿＿＿＿＿ は ＿＿＿＿＿＿＿＿ に
＿＿＿＿＿＿＿＿ を ＿＿＿＿＿＿＿＿。
＿＿＿＿＿＿＿＿ は ＿＿＿＿＿＿＿＿ に
＿＿＿＿＿＿＿＿ を ＿＿＿＿＿＿＿＿。

母　私達

11. ______________________ は ______________________ に
______________________ を ______________________。
______________________ は ______________________ に
______________________ を ______________________。

山田 私の妹

12. ______________________ は ______________________ に
______________________ を下さいました。
______________________ は ______________________ に
______________________ を ______________________。

私
さいとう先生

13. ______________________ は ______________________ に
チョコレートを ______________________。
______________________ は ______________________ に
______________________ を ______________________。

私達
父の友達

14. ______________________ は ______________________ に
ハンドアウトを ______________________。
______________________ は ______________________ に
______________________ を ______________________。

日本語の先生
私達

15. ______________________ は妹に
______________________ を ______________________。
______________________ は母の友達に
______________________ を ______________________。

私の妹
母の友達

16. ______________________ は先生に
______________________ を ______________________。

私達
先生

17. 姉は ______________________ に
______________________ を ______________________。

会社の
じょうし
私の姉

II.　みなさんはいつ、だれに、何をあげましたか。いつ、だれに、何をもらいましたか。クラスメートと話しましょう。

例　友達がけっこんした時に、私はかびんをあげました。
たんじょう日に、私は母にブーツをもらいました。

III.　田中さんは色々な問題があります。いいアドバイスをして下さい。

例

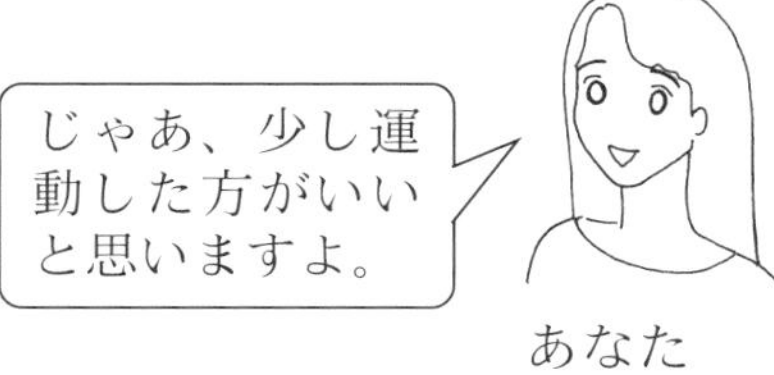

1.　田中　：＿＿＿＿＿＿＿＿＿＿＿＿＿＿＿＿＿＿＿＿
＿＿＿＿＿＿＿＿＿＿＿＿＿＿＿＿＿＿＿＿。
あなた：＿＿＿＿＿＿＿＿＿＿＿＿＿＿＿＿＿＿＿＿
＿＿＿＿＿＿＿＿＿＿方がいいと思いますよ。

2.　田中　：＿＿＿＿＿＿＿＿＿＿＿＿＿＿＿＿＿＿＿＿
＿＿＿＿＿＿＿＿＿＿＿＿＿＿＿＿＿＿＿＿。
あなた：＿＿＿＿＿＿＿＿＿＿＿＿＿＿＿＿＿＿＿＿
＿＿＿＿＿＿＿＿＿＿方がいいと思いますよ。

3.　田中　：＿＿＿＿＿＿＿＿＿＿＿＿＿＿＿＿＿＿＿＿
＿＿＿＿＿＿＿＿＿＿＿＿＿＿＿＿＿＿＿＿。
あなた：＿＿＿＿＿＿＿＿＿＿＿＿＿＿＿＿＿＿＿＿
＿＿＿＿＿＿＿＿＿＿方がいいと思いますよ。

IV.　会話を作って下さい。

例　A:　このへんは夜、安全ですか。
B:　いいえ、あぶないですから、一人で歩かない方がいいですよ。

1.　A:　このジュースを飲んでもいいですか。
B:　いいえ、そのジュースは古いですから、＿＿＿＿＿＿＿＿＿＿方がいいですよ。

2.　A:　私はタバコが好きなので、毎日十五本ぐらいすっています。
B:　それはよくありませんねえ。＿＿＿＿＿＿＿＿＿＿＿＿方がいいですよ。

3. A: このMP3プレーヤーを買おうと思っています。

B: このプレーヤーはよくありませんから、＿＿＿＿＿＿＿＿＿＿方がいいですよ。

4. A: 駅の近くにあるレストランで食べてみるつもりです。

B: あのレストランはまずくて高いですから、あそこで＿＿＿＿＿＿＿＿＿＿方がいいですよ。

V. 会話を作って下さい。

例(れい) A: 来週は木村さんのたんじょう日です。何をあげたらいいでしょうか。

B: そうですねえ。コンピューターゲームをあげたらどうですか。

A: じゃあ、コンピューターゲームをあげることにします。

1. A: 明日、日本語の試験があるんですが、漢字が覚えられません。

＿＿＿＿＿＿＿＿＿＿＿＿＿＿＿＿＿＿＿＿いいでしょうか。

B: そうですねえ。＿＿＿＿＿＿＿＿＿＿＿＿＿＿＿＿＿＿＿＿どうですか。

A: じゃあ、＿＿＿＿＿＿＿＿＿＿＿＿＿＿＿＿＿＿＿＿ことにします。

2. A: 春休みに友達が日本からあそびに来ます。

いっしょにどこへ＿＿＿＿＿＿＿＿＿＿＿＿＿＿＿＿＿＿＿＿いいでしょうか。

B: そうですねえ。＿＿＿＿＿＿＿＿＿＿＿＿＿＿＿＿＿＿＿＿どうですか。

A: じゃあ、＿＿＿＿＿＿＿＿＿＿＿＿＿＿＿＿＿＿＿＿ことにします。

3. A: 来週みんなでパーティーをするつもりです。

どんな料理を＿＿＿＿＿＿＿＿＿＿＿＿＿＿＿＿＿＿＿＿いいでしょうか。

B: そうですねえ。＿＿＿＿＿＿＿＿＿＿＿＿＿＿＿＿＿＿＿＿どうですか。

A: じゃあ、＿＿＿＿＿＿＿＿＿＿＿＿＿＿＿＿＿＿＿＿ことにします。

4. A: カラオケパーティーで歌を歌わなくてはいけません。

どんな歌を＿＿＿＿＿＿＿＿＿＿＿＿＿＿＿＿＿＿＿＿いいでしょうか。

B: そうですねえ。＿＿＿＿＿＿＿＿＿＿＿＿＿＿＿＿＿＿＿＿どうですか。

A: じゃあ、＿＿＿＿＿＿＿＿＿＿＿＿＿＿＿＿＿＿＿＿ことにします。

VI.　下の文は日本でホームステイをしたカーターさんの作文です。読んで質問に答えて下さい。

日本人はよくプレゼントをあげたりもらったりする。まず、お正月(しょうがつ)に子供達は大人からお年(とし)だまをもらうことになっている。お年だまはお金で、小さくてきれいなふうとうに入っている。ホストファミリーの七さいの正子(まさこ)ちゃん*もおばあさんにお年だまをもらった。ふうとうを開けると、五千円も入っていた。

二月にはバレンタインデーがある。日本では女の人が男の人にチョコレートをあげることになっている。それで、私はデパートでハートのかたちのチョコレートを買って、大学のクラスメートのよしださんにプレゼントした。でも、よしださんはほかの人からチョコレートを五個ももらったので、私はちょっとがっかりした。

三月には卒業する人にプレゼントをあげたり、四月には入学(にゅうがく)する人や入社(にゅうしゃ)する人にプレゼントをあげたりする。ホストファミリーの両親はしんせきの子供が高校に入ったので、すてきなペンをあげた。

七月と十二月には、会社のじょうしやおせわになった人におくり物をする**。七月のおくり物は「お中元」と言う。そして、十二月のおくり物は「おせいぼ」と言う。私もホストファミリーにお中元とおせいぼをあげた。お中元は、お母さんが好きなクッキーにした。おせいぼは、お父さんが好きなウィスキーにした。お中元やおせいぼのきせつには、デパートはとてもこんでいて大変だった。

たんじょう日やクリスマスや母の日や父の日などにもプレゼントをあげる。私もたんじょう日にたくさんプレゼントをもらってうれしかった。

それから、旅行した時に、かぞくや友達におみやげを買って帰る。むかし、旅行するのが難しかった時に、旅行に行く人にお金をあげて（「おせんべつ」と言うそうだ）、めずらしいおみやげをもらった。そのしゅうかんが今もつづいている。私がアメリカから来た時、大学のＴシャツやアメリカのチョコレートやビーフジャーキーなどをホストファミリーにあげたら、みんなとてもよろこんだ。

* ちゃん, instead of さん, is normally used with a name of a child to show affection. Its function is similar to *-y* as in Andy (Andrew), Cathy (Catherine), Danny (Daniel), Jenny (Jennifer), Teddy (Theodore), Terry (Teresa), etc.

** おくり物をする "give someone something as a gift"

1. 子供達はお正月に何をもらいますか。
2. 日本ではバレンタインデーに、だれが何をもらいますか。
3. カーターさんはバレンタインデーにどうしてがっかりしたんですか。
4. 三月にはだれにプレゼントをあげますか。
5. おせわになった人に七月にあげるおくり物は何と言いますか。
6. おせわになった人に十二月にあげるおくり物は何と言いますか。
7. 旅行した時に何を買って帰りますか。

新しい漢字

相手(あいて)	会社(かいしゃ)	貸(か)す	借(か)りる	～個(こ)	困(こま)る
～冊(さつ)	事故(じこ)	辞書(じしょ)	調(しら)べる	相談(そうだん)	時計(とけい)
入社(にゅうしゃ)	～枚(まい)				

新しい使い方

赤(あか)ちゃん	後(あと)で	安全(あんぜん)	意見(いけん)	お正月(しょうがつ)	お中元(ちゅうげん)
お年(とし)だま	終(お)わり	下(くだ)さる	この間(あいだ)	高田(たかだ)	入学(にゅうがく)
正子(まさこ)	目薬(めぐすり)				

Radicals: 人(ひと)やね・人足(ひとあし)

The かんむり "crown" radical 𠆢 in 今, 会, and 全 is derived from 人(ひと) and called 人(ひと)やね (やね "roof"). 金 and 食 contain the same shape, but conventionally they are themselves radicals and do not belong to this radical group.

The 足(あし) radical 儿 in 兄, 先, and 元 is called 人足(ひとあし). The same lines appear in 見, but 見 itself is considered a radical and is not categorized in this group.

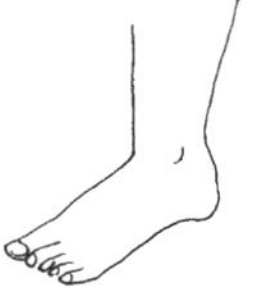

Most 漢字 with these radicals are vaguely related to the notion of 人.

相	一	十	才	木	朩	机	相	相	相	
ソウ・あい	*aspect, phase, each other:* 相手 *partner, opponent,* 相談 *consultation*									
後	ノ	ク	彳	彳	彳	彳	彳	後	後	
ゴ・あと・うし(ろ)	*after, back:* 午後 *P.M.*									
正	一	丅	下	正	正					
ショウ・ただ(しい)・まさ	*correct:* お正月 *(1st month of) new year,* 正子 *Masako*									
終	く	幺	幺	糸	糸	糸	糹	紁	終	終
	終									
お(える)・お(わり)・お(わる)	*to end, to finish:* 終わり *end*									
社	丶	ラ	ネ	ネ	ネ一	社	社			
シャ	*shrine, association:* 会社 *company,* 入社 *entering a company (as an employee)*									
貸	ノ	イ	仁	代	代	代	貸	貸	貸	貸
	貸	貸								
か(す)	*to lend*									
借	ノ	イ	仁	什	仕	件	借	借	借	借
か(りる)	*to borrow*									
個	ノ	イ	仆	们	们	個	個	個	個	個
コ	*individual:* 一個 *one (thing)*									

Kanji	Reading	Meaning
間	カン・あいだ	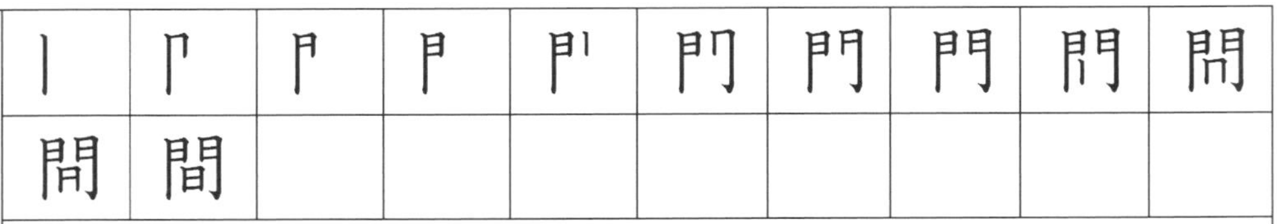 *interval, between:* 時間 *time,* 〜時間 〜 *hours,* 〜週間 〜 *weeks,* 中間 *midterm,* この間 *a little while ago*
困	こま(る)	 *to be in trouble*
冊	サツ	 *book volume:* 一冊 *one (bound thing)*
故	コ	 *reason, cause:* 事故 *accident*
辞	ジ	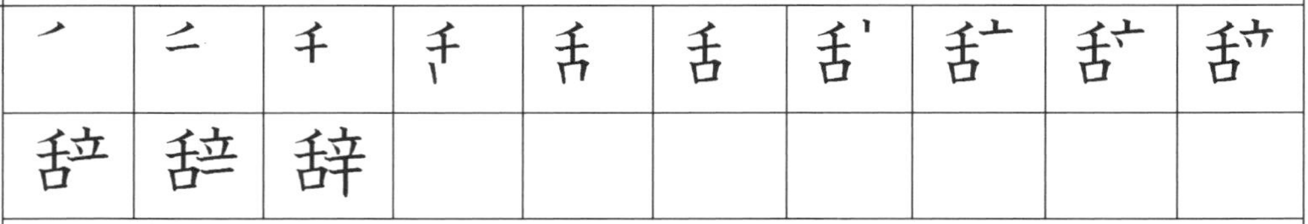 *word, term:* 辞書 *dictionary*
調	しら(べる)	 *to investigate*
談	ダン	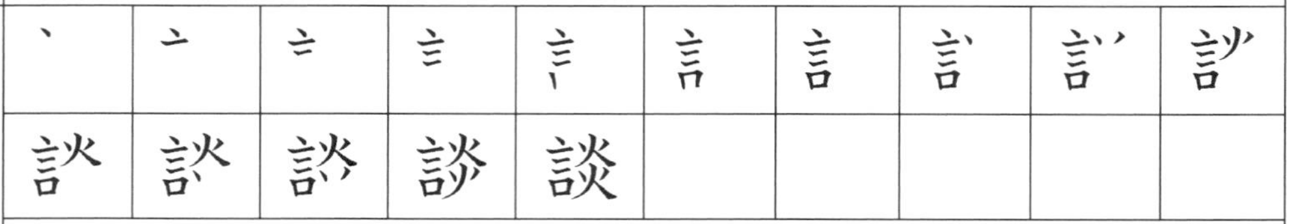 *conversation:* 相談 *consultation*
時	ジ・とき・と	 *time:* 時間 *time,* 〜時間 〜 *hours,* 時々 *sometimes,* 時計 *watch, clock*

計	丶	亠	亠	言	言	言	言	言一	計	
ケイ	*to measure:* 時計 *watch, clock*									
入	ノ	入								
ニュウ・いれ（る）・はい（る）	*to enter:* 入学 *entering a school (as a student),* 入社 *entering a company (as an employee).* This 漢字 is a mirror image of 人 person.									
枚	一	十	才	木	木'	木ᅩ	杓	枚		
マイ	*counter for thin flat things*									

漢字の復習

I.　読みましょう。

1. この薬は強いので、飲んだ時は運転してはいけません。
2. 言語学の試験の問題はとても難しかったので、半分しか答えられませんでした。
3. あの店は、店員が親切なので、人気があります。
4. 昨日、眠れなかったので、今日は気分がよくありません。
5. 動物の中では、犬が一番好きです。

II.　つぎの漢字の読み方は全部「かん」です。どの「かん」を使いますか。□ に書いて下さい。

漢　間　館

映画□　中□試験　五週□　図書□　□字

III.　つぎの漢字の読み方は全部「き」です。どの「き」を使いますか。□ に書いて下さい。

木　気　機　期　帰

人□　洗濯□　□村　□末　□国

元□　飛行□　病□　今学□

IV. つぎの漢字の読み方は全部「しん」です。どの「しん」を使いますか。□ に書いて下さい。

親 新 心 真

写□　□切　□聞　両□　□配

V. つぎの漢字の読み方は全部「じ」です。どの「じ」を使いますか。□ に書いて下さい。

事 字 時 辞 自

□書　□分　食□　四□　漢□

VI. つぎの漢字の読み方は全部「しゃ」です。どの「しゃ」を使いますか。□ に書いて下さい。

車 者 社 写

電□　会□　□真　医□　入□

VII. つぎの漢字の読み方は全部「ぶん」です。どの「ぶん」を使いますか。□ に書いて下さい。

分 文 聞

□法　多□　英□学　□化　新□

VIII. どちらの「り」ですか。□ に書いて下さい。

理 利

物□学　便□　料□　心□学

新しい語彙(ごい)

Jポップ	*Japanese pop music*
MP 3 プレーヤー	*MP3 player*
相手(あいて)	*partner, opponent*
赤(あか)ちゃん	*baby*
あげる (ル)(t)	*to give*
後(あと)で	*afterwards, later*
アドバイス(する)	*advice*
アニメ	*animated cartoon*
安全(あんぜん) (ナ)	*safe*
意見(いけん)	*opinion*
いつか	*someday, sometime*
うえ木(き)	*garden plant, tree*
えさ	*feed, pet food*
お年(とし)だま	*new year's gift money*
終(お)わり	*end*
書(か)きなおす (ウ)(t)	*to rewrite, revise*
かたち	*shape*
がっかりする (I)(i)	*to be disappointed*
きめる (ル)(t)	*to decide*
気(き)をつける (ル)(i)	*to pay attention to*
下(くだ)さる (ウ)(t)	*to give*
くれる (ル)(t)	*to give*
けいさつ	*police*
けしゴム	*eraser*
こうすい	*perfume*
さしあげる (ル)(t)	*to give*
(目薬(めぐすり)を)さす (ウ)(t)	*to apply (eye drops)*
事故(じこ)	*accident*
じょうし	*one's superior*
しんせき	*relatives*
(お)せいぼ	*year-end present*
(お)せんべつ	*good-bye present*
卒業(そつぎょう)しき	*graduation ceremony*
父(ちち)の日(ひ)	*Father's Day*
Xちゃん	*suffix for a child's name*
(お)中元(ちゅうげん)	*midyear present*
つづく (ウ)(i)	*to continue*
つなげる (ル)(t)	*to connect*
デジタルカメラ	*digital camera*
とまる (ウ)(i)	*to stop*
入学(にゅうがく)(する)	*entering a school*
入社(にゅうしゃ)(する)	*entering a company*
ハート	*heart*
母(はは)の日(ひ)	*Mother's Day*
バレンタインデー	*Valentine's Day*
ビーフジャーキー	*beef jerky*
ひやす (ウ)(t)	*to cool (transitive)*
ブーツ	*boots*
まちがい	*mistake*

まんが	*comic strip*
みかん	*mandarin orange*
目薬 (めぐすり)	*eye drops*

めずらしい ㋑	*rare*
やる ㋒ ⓣ	*to give*

名前

高田 (たかだ)	*Takada*

正子 (まさこ)	*Masako*

第二十四課 LESSON 24

たんじょう日のパーティー
A Birthday Party

小山さんにのりまきを作ってもらいました
I got Koyama-san to make *norimaki* for us

会話

1 ソン : 小山さん、のりまきはどうですか。

Koyama-san, how are the norimaki?

小山 : もうできましたよ。それから、おせんべいとクッキーもテーブルの上に出してあります。

They're ready. And the osenbei *and cookies are already (put) on the table.*

2 ソン : 飲み物はどうですか。

What about drinks?

小山 : だいじょうぶですよ。今朝、ジュースとコーラとシャンペンをれいぞうこに入れておきましたから。

They're taken care of, too. I put the juice, cola, and champagne in the refrigerator ahead of time this morning.

ソン : じゃあ、もうじゅんびは全部終わりましたね。

In that case, we're all done with the preparations.

3 ソン : あっ、来ましたよ。

Ah, here they are!

4 ソン : ミラーさん、山本さん。いらっしゃい。

Miller-san, Yamamoto-san, welcome!

5 小山 : ミラーさん、おたんじょう日おめでとうございます。

Happy birthday, Miller-san!

ミラー : どうもありがとうございます。

Thank you very much.

6 山本 : わあ、おいしそうですね。

Wow, this looks delicious!

ソン : ええ、ミラーさんはのりまきが好きですから、小山さんに作ってもらいました。

Yes, Miller-san likes norimaki, *so I got Koyama-san to make them for us.*

7 ミラー : ありがとうございます。ごうかですねえ。これは何ですか。プリンですか。

Thank you so much! This is really gorgeous! What's this? Is this pudding?

小山 : それは、茶(ちゃ)わんむしです。どうぞ食べてみて下さい。

That's chawan-mushi. *Please try it.*

8　ミラー　：これも小山さんが作ってくれたんですか。
Did Koyama-san make it too?
ソン　：ええ、そうです。
Yes, she did.

9　ミラー　：大変だったでしょう。どうもありがとうございます。
It must have been a lot of work! Thanks a lot!
小山　：いいえ、どういたしまして。じゃあ、パーティーを始めましょうか。
You're welcome. Well, shall we begin the party?

使い方

5　おめでとう (casual) and おめでとうございます (formal) are used to convey congratulatory remarks. Unlike in English, this phrase can be used for many occasions:

新年(しんねん)おめでとうございます。	*Happy New Year!*
おたんじょう日おめでとうございます。	*Happy Birthday!*
(ご) 入学おめでとうございます。	*Congratulations for entering school!*
(ご) 卒業おめでとうございます。	*Congratulations on your graduation!*
(ご) しゅうしょくおめでとうございます。	*Congratulations on your new job!*

7　The word 茶わんむし consists of 茶わん "rice bowl, teacup" and the verb むし（ます）"to steam". It is a savory egg custard. Because it is very soft, 茶わんむし is eaten with a teaspoon.

文法

24a	**てフォーム + クレル**	**"X does a favor for me (or my in-group)"**
	てフォーム + モラウ	**"I (or my in-group) receive a favor from Y"**
	てフォーム + アゲル	**"X does a favor for Z"**
24b	**NOUN のために**	**"for NOUN"**
24c	**てフォーム + おく**	**"do ~ in advance"**
24d	**てフォーム + ある**	**"~ has been done; ~ was done and kept that way"**

24a てフォーム + クレル "X does a favor for me (or my in-group)"
てフォーム + モラウ "I (or my in-group) receive a favor from Y"
てフォーム + アゲル "X does a favor for Z"

て The verbs of giving and receiving are used not only for describing a transfer of tangible objects, but also for marking the beneficiary of some favorable action. In English, it is possible to say "My mother bought me a new monitor." But the Japanese equivalent 母は私に新しいモニターを買いました does not sound natural at all. You need to express your evaluation (i.e. appreciation) of such an event. In this case, you need to say either (1) or (2):

(1) 母は（私に）新しいモニターを買ってくれました。
(Lit.) My mother gave me the favor of buying a new monitor.
My mother bought me a new monitor.

(2) 私は母に新しいモニターを買ってもらいました。
(Lit.) I received from my mother the favor of buying a new monitor.
I got a new monitor bought for me by my mother.

The rules for the selection of an actual verb of giving or receiving are exactly the same as what was described in 第二十三課 for physical (tangible) transfers.

てフォーム + **クレル**

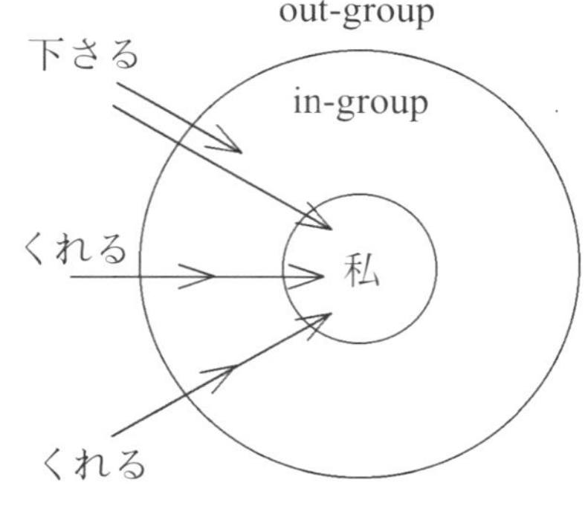

石川先生は私達に辞書の使い方を教えて下さいました。
Ishikawa-sensei taught us how to use a dictionary.
私は明日、授業に行けません。石川先生にそう* 伝えて下さいませんか。**
I can't go to class tomorrow. Would you tell Ishikawa-sensei (so), please?

> * そう can represent a phrase, like English "so".
> そう言う *to say so*
> そう思う *to think so*
>
> ** The ～て下さいませんか construction, cf. 第八課, **8b**, is a variation of ～て下さる.

山本さんはJポップを歌ってくれました。
Yamamoto-san sang J-pop songs for us.
弟はホチキスを買ってきてくれました。
My brother bought (and brought) a stapler for me.
小山さんは茶わんむしの作り方を教えてくれました。
Koyama-san taught me how to make chawan-mushi.
山本さんは私の家にスピーカーを運んでくれました。
Yamamoto-san (kindly) moved the speakers to my house.

木村さんは姉に日本のまんがの本をたくさん貸してくれました。

Kimura-san lent my sister lots of Japanese comic books.

ソンさんは（私に）ミラーさんを紹介してくれました。

Son-san introduced Miller-san to me.

安田さんはことをえんそうしてくれました。

Yasuda-san played the koto *for us.*

ミラーさんは私のコンピューターにEメールのソフトをインストールしてくれました。

Miller-san installed email software on my computer for me.

てフォーム＋**モラウ**

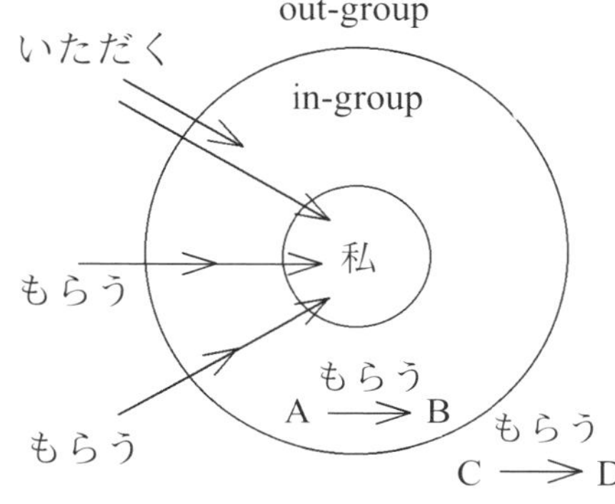

私は石川先生に文法をくわしく説明していただきました。

Ishikawa-sensei explained the grammar to me thoroughly.

私はいつも、石川先生に作文のげんこうをなおしていただきます。

(Lit.) I always get (the favor of having) my composition drafts corrected by Ishikawa-sensei.

Ishikawa-sensei always corrects my composition drafts for me.

さいとう先生にすいせんじょうを書いていただきました。

Saito-sensei wrote a recommendation letter for me.

ミラーさんにおそくまで開いているきっさ店を教えてもらいました。*

Miller-san told me of a café that is open until late.

私は友達にアパートをさがしてもらいました。

A friend of mine looked for an apartment for me.

日本の会社にしゅうしょくしたいので、友達にりれきしょを日本語にやくしてもらいます。**

I want to get a job in a Japanese company, so I'm going to get my friend to translate my résumé into Japanese for me.

> * 教える can mean "to tell / inform".
>
> ** X を Y にやくす to translate X into Y

おなかがとても痛かったので、ルームメートに病院へつれて行ってもらいました。

Because I had a serious stomachache, I had my roommate take me to the hospital.

お酒を飲んでしまったので、友達に運転してもらいました。

Because I ended up drinking alcohol, I got my friend to drive (my car).

ソンさんは小山さんに着物を貸してもらいました。

Son-san got Koyama-san to lend (her) a kimono.

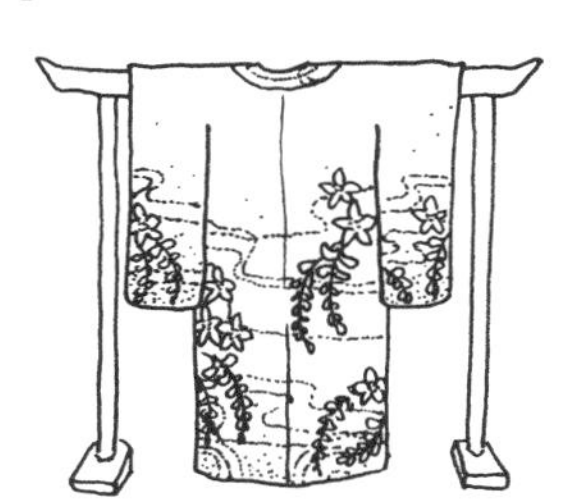

ソンさんにひっこしを手伝ってもらいました。

I got (the favor of having) Son-san help me move (to a new place).

てフォーム + **アゲル**

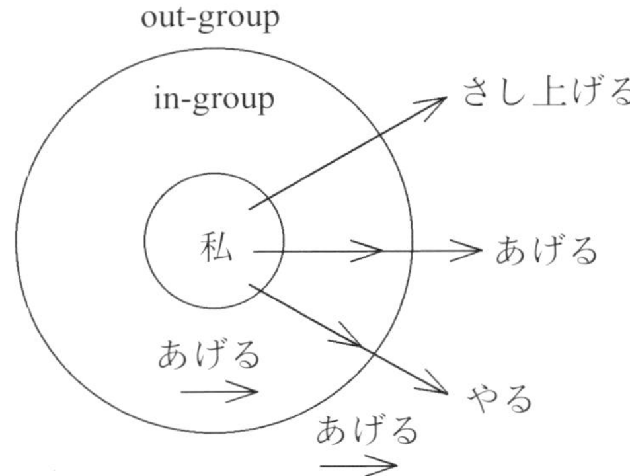

ソンさんはさいとう先生にクッキーをやいてさし上げました。

Son-san baked Saito-sensei some cookies.

私はミラーさんに日本語の文法を説明してあげました。

I explained some Japanese grammar to Miller-san.

小山さんは弟さんにパジャマをぬってあげました。

Koyama-san sewed her brother (a pair of) pajamas.

私は妹にセーターをあんであげました。

I knitted my sister a sweater.

ソンさんはキムさんに冷(つめ)たいレモネードを作ってあげました。

Son-san made Kim-san some cold lemonade.

リンさんは犬をさんぽにつれて行ってやりました。

Lin-san took her dog for a walk.

小山さんは気(き)持(も)ちが悪(わる)そうだったので、私は水を持(も)って来てあげました。

Because Koyama-san looked sick, I brought her some water.

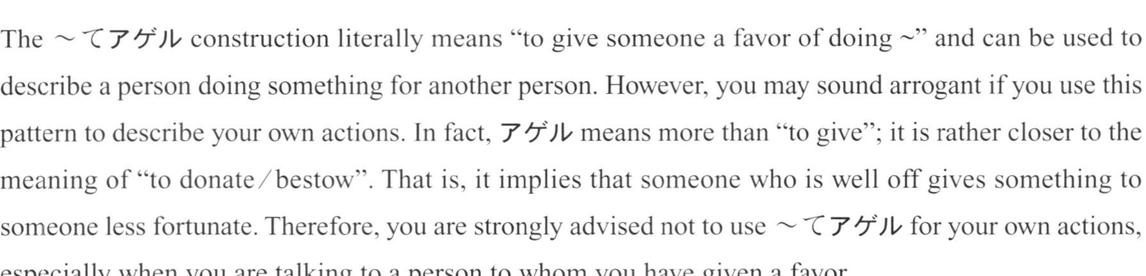

The ～て**アゲル** construction literally means "to give someone a favor of doing ~" and can be used to describe a person doing something for another person. However, you may sound arrogant if you use this pattern to describe your own actions. In fact, **アゲル** means more than "to give"; it is rather closer to the meaning of "to donate / bestow". That is, it implies that someone who is well off gives something to someone less fortunate. Therefore, you are strongly advised not to use ～て**アゲル** for your own actions, especially when you are talking to a person to whom you have given a favor.

24b　NOUN のために　　"for NOUN"

The に -marked nouns in the ～て**クレル** and ～て**アゲル** constructions are called the *beneficiaries* because they designate the ones who receive benefit. There are two ways to be a beneficiary: one is by virtue of receiving something (*recipient beneficiary*), and the other by virtue of having someone do something on one's behalf (*deputative beneficiary*). In ～て**クレル** and ～て**アゲル**, only the former can appear with に; the latter must be expressed with ～のために.

A Recipient Beneficiary

○ 私は友達に手(て)ぶくろをあんであげました。

I knitted my friend a pair of gloves. (The friend received the gloves.)

○ ミラーさんは私の子供に本を読んでくれました。

Miller-san read my child a book. (My child heard/received the story.)

○ ソンさんは近所(きんじょ)の薬屋へ行って、小山さんにかぜ薬を買って来てあげました。

Son-san went to the neighborhood drugstore and bought (and brought) Koyama-san some cold medicine. (Koyama-san received it.)

○ 山本さんは私に食事をおごって* くれました。

Yamamoto-san bought me a meal. (I ate the meal.)

○ 小山さんはミラーさんにお茶を入れてあげました。

Koyama-san made/poured Miller-san (a cup of) tea. (Miller-san received the tea.)

○ 山本さんはソンさんにJポップを歌ってあげました。

Yamamoto-san sang Son-san J-pop songs. (Son-san heard/received the songs.)

○ 私は電車の中でおばあさんに** せきをゆずって*** あげました。

I gave up my seat in the train to an old woman. (The old woman received the right to sit in the seat.)

* Xに Yをおごる
to treat X to Y
to buy Y (food) for X
This is a casual verb; a more formal version is: Xに Yをごちそうする.

ミラーさんのお母さんは私にターキーをごちそうして下さいました。
Miller-san's mother treated me to a turkey dinner.

While ごちそうする can be used when you *prepare* a meal by yourself or when you take someone out to meal, おごる can be used only for the latter.

** おばあさん *old woman*
Other kinship terms can also be used to mean:

おじいさん	*old man*
おばさん	*middle-aged woman*
おじさん	*middle-aged man*

*** XにYをゆずる *to hand over/give up/give way to/spare/abdicate*

Here, you cannot use あげる alone because you do not possess the seat.

B Deputative Beneficiary

× ミラーさんは私にドアを開けてくれました。

○ ミラーさんは私のためにドアを開けてくれました。

Miller-san opened the door for me.

× ソンさんは私に銀行へ行ってくれました。

○ ソンさんは私のために銀行へ行ってくれました。

Son-san went to the bank for me.

× ミラーさんは ソンさんに コンピューターをなおしてあげました。
○ ミラーさんは ソンさんのために コンピューターをなおしてあげました。
Miller-san repaired the computer for Son-san.

× 小山さんは ソンさんに 部屋をそうじしてあげました。
○ 小山さんは ソンさんのために 部屋をそうじしてあげました。
Koyama-san cleaned the room for Son-san.

In some cases, both ～に and ～のために are possible, but the interpretation of the sentence may be different depending on which choice is used.

山田さんは私に手紙を書いてくれました。
Yamada-san wrote me a letter.
(I received the letter.)
山田さんは私のために手紙を書いてくれました。
Yamada-san wrote a letter for me.
(I may or may not be the receiver, but I was benefited from Yamada-san's writing the letter.)

スミスさんは青木さんに夕食を作ってあげました。
Smith-san made dinner for Aoki-san. (Aoki-san ate the dinner.)
スミスさんは青木さんのために夕食を作ってあげました。
Smith-san made a dinner for Aoki-san. (Aoki-san may or may not be the recipient, e.g. Aoki-san was supposed to prepare a dinner for her brother, but because she could not do so, Smith-san made it on behalf of Aoki-san.)

Omitting the beneficiary sounds more natural when it is easily inferable from the context.

24c てフォーム + おく "do ~ in advance"

This construction is used to express a situation in which an action is performed ahead of time in preparation for, or in anticipation of, some future event. Compare (1) and (2):

(1) ドアを開けました。 *(I) opened the door.*
(2) ドアを開けておきました。 *(I) have opened the door (in advance).*

In both cases, the speaker opened the door. (1) indicates only that the speaker opened the door sometime in the past, and whether it is still open is unknown. By contrast, (2) implies that the door is open now, and that the speaker opened it in preparation for some event, e.g. guests are arriving soon.

今晩、友達が遊びに来ますから、シャンペンを冷やしておきましょう。
Friends are coming over this evening, so let's chill some champagne (in advance).
来月のパーティーはマリーナのレストランでするので、みんなに地図を送っておきます。
Next month's party will be held at a restaurant on the marina, so I'll send everyone a map (in advance).
パーティーでスピーチをしていただきたいんですが、考えておいて下さいませんか。
We would like you to give a speech at the party. Could you think about it (and prepare something) in advance?
旅行に行くので、銀行からお金をおろしておきました。
Because I'm going on a trip, I've withdrawn some money from the bank.
来週、しゅうしょく試験のめんせつがあるので、ワイシャツにアイロンをかけておきます。
I have a job interview next week, so I'm ironing a dress shirt (ahead of time).

This construction can accommodate intransitive verbs as well.

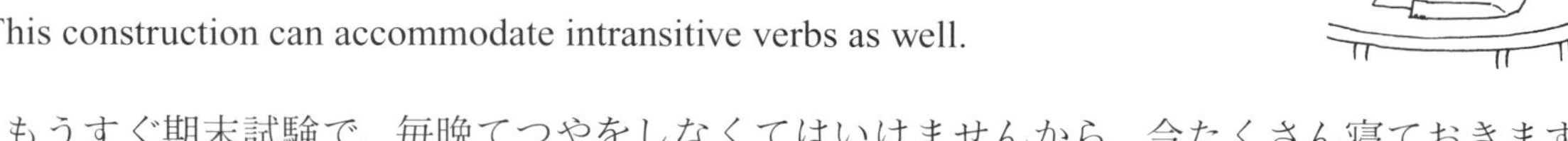

もうすぐ期末試験で、毎晩てつやをしなくてはいけませんから、今たくさん寝ておきます。
Final exams are soon and I'll have to pull an all-nighter every night, so I'm sleeping a lot now (hoping that I can save up some energy).

24d　てフォーム + ある　"~ has been done; ~ was done and kept that way"

て The てフォーム + ある construction is used to describe a current state of affairs that was brought about **purposefully** by some known or unknown person(s). This construction focuses on the resultant state of a past action rather than the action itself or the person who performed it. Compare (1)-(2) and (3)-(4):

(1) ソンさんはドア[を]開けました。
Son-san opened the door.

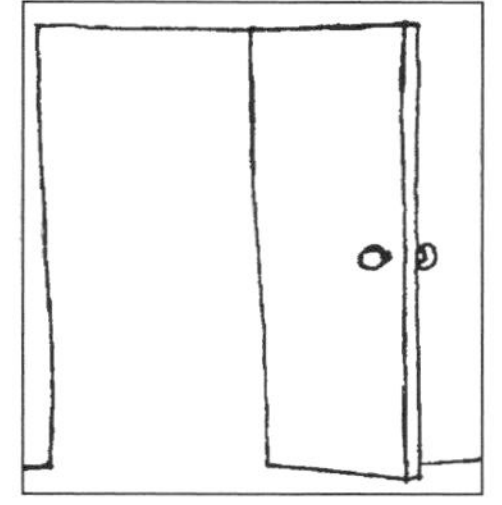

(2) ドア[が]開けてあります。
The door has been opened.

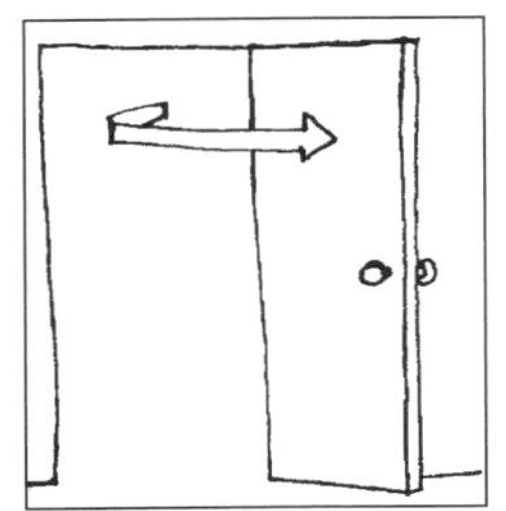

(3) ドア[が]開きました。

The door opened.

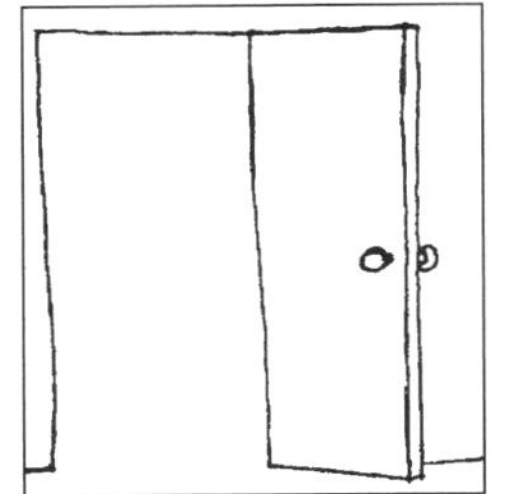

(4) ドア[が]開いています。

The door is in a state of being open.

First, the verb 開く in (3)-(4) is intransitive, and thus ドア (the subject) is marked with が, whereas 開ける in (1) is transitive, so ドア (the direct object) is marked with を. Although 開ける is transitive, its derived verb 開けてある in (2) is intransitive. Therefore, ドア must be marked with が in (2). That is, the direct object of the verb becomes the subject of the corresponding 〜てある construction.

Second, the use of the transitive 開ける requires a subject (normally a person), overtly or covertly. In (5) below, the subject is not mentioned, but it is understood to be the speaker or someone who has already been introduced into the conversation. If the identity of the subject person is irrelevant or unknown, だれか "someone" is used to fill the subject slot, as shown in (6). By contrast, because the derived verb 開けてある is intransitive, the person who opened the door cannot be a subject in (2).

(5) [　　　]ドアを開けました。 *(I) opened the door.*

(6) [だれか]がドアを開けました。 *Someone opened the door.*

Third, let us compare (2) and (4). In (2), although the person who opened the door is not mentioned, the existence of such a person is strongly implied. That is, it is understood that the door was opened purposefully by someone, and it remains open at the time of the utterance. In (4), by contrast, the existence of an intentional agent is not implied at all; the door could have been opened by a natural force, e.g. wind.

〜てある is similar to 〜ておく in that both express that some action was performed in preparation for a subsequent event. However, these constructions focus on different aspects. Compare (7) and (8), both of which can depict the same situation.

(7) チーズとクラッカーをテーブルの上に出して[おきました]。

I've put some cheese and crackers on the table (in advance).

(8)　チーズとクラッカーがテーブルの上に出してあります。
The cheese and crackers have (already) been put on the table.

Because ～ておく emphasizes the actions and the intentions of the person who performed it, the tense of a ～ておく sentence corresponds to the time of the action, viz. the past in (7). ～てある, on the other hand, focuses on the resultant state rather than the action, so the tense of (8) is in the non-past, although the action itself apparently took place in the past.

As further illustration, consider the following situation:

今晩、山田さんの家でパーティーがあるので、じゅんびを手伝いに行きます。何をしなくてはいけないでしょうか。山田さんに聞いてみましょう。
There's a party at Yamada-san's house tonight, so I'm going to go help him prepare for it. What needs to be done? Let's ask Yamada-san.

あなた　：何をしましょうか。部屋はそうじしてありますか。
What shall I do? Has the room been cleaned?

山田さん：はい、昨日そうじしておきました。
Yes, I cleaned it yesterday.

あなた　：コーラはれいぞうこに入れてありますか。
Is the cola in the refrigerator?

山田さん：はい、さっき入れておきました。
Yes, I put it in a little while ago.

あなた　：料理はしてありますか。まだしてありませんか。
Is the food ready? Or still not done?

山田さん：やさいはもう切(き)ってあります。肉(にく)と魚(さかな)は、みんなが来てからやきます。

The vegetables are already cut. We'll broil the meat and fish after everyone has arrived.

あなた　：クラッカーとチーズは買ってありますか。ケーキはどうですか。
Have crackers and cheese been bought? What about a cake?

山田さん：クラッカーとチーズは買っておきましたが、ケーキは安田さんが持って来てくれることになっています。
I bought crackers and cheese, but Yasuda-san is supposed to bring a cake.

あなた　：じゃあ、何を手伝ったらいいでしょうか。
Then, what shall I do for you?

練習問題

I.　山田さんとスミスさんと私は友達です。スミスさんがお金がない時に、何をしてあげましたか。山田さんが元気じゃない時に、何をしてあげましたか。絵を見て文を作りましょう。

例　Q:　スミスさんが病気の時に、何をしてあげましたか。

A:　私はスミスさんにスープを作ってあげました。

山田さんはスミスさんにノートを貸してあげました。

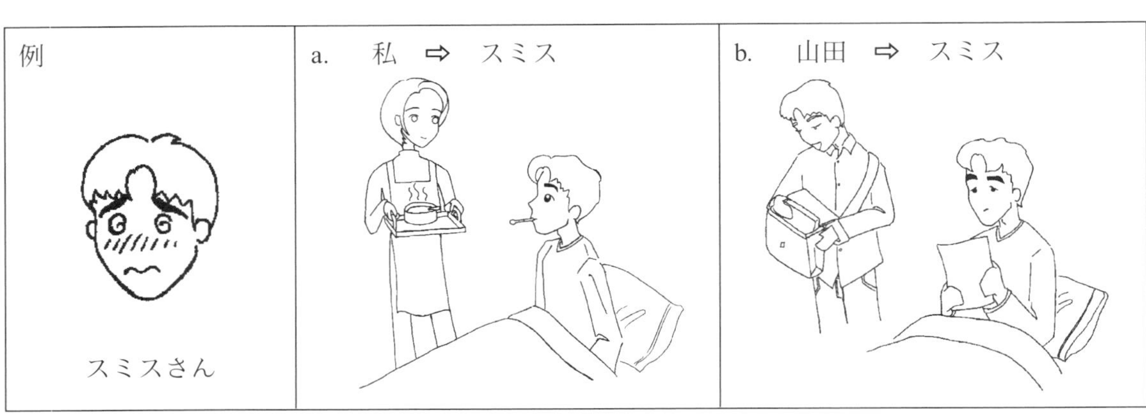

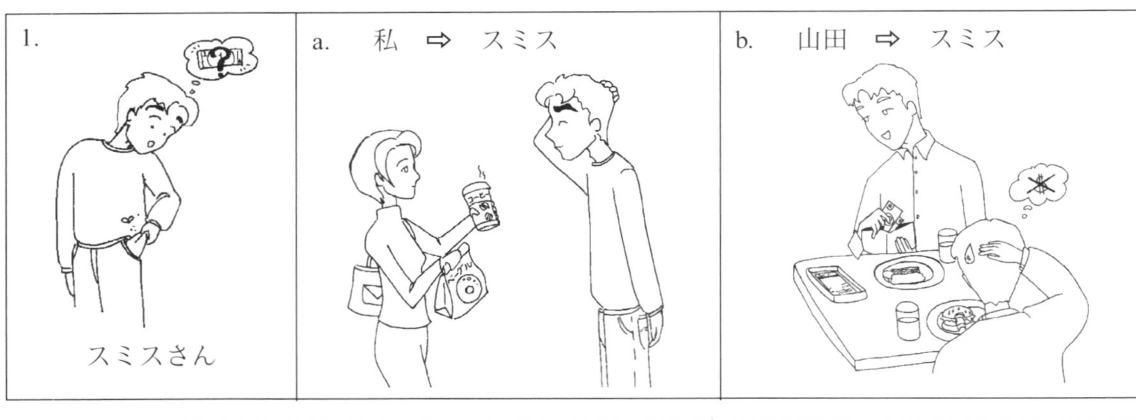

II. 安田さん、ワトソンさん、ブラウンさんは学生です。三人は先生に何をしてさし上げましたか。絵を見て文を作りましょう。

例 Q: 昨日、ワトソンさんは先生に何をしてさし上げましたか。

A: (昨日、ワトソンさんは) 先生にお茶を入れてさし上げました。

III. あなたが病気の時に、友達は何をしてくれますか。絵を見て文を作りましょう。

例 Q: 友達はあなたが病気の時に、何をしてくれますか。

A: 友達は (私に) 薬を買って来てくれます。

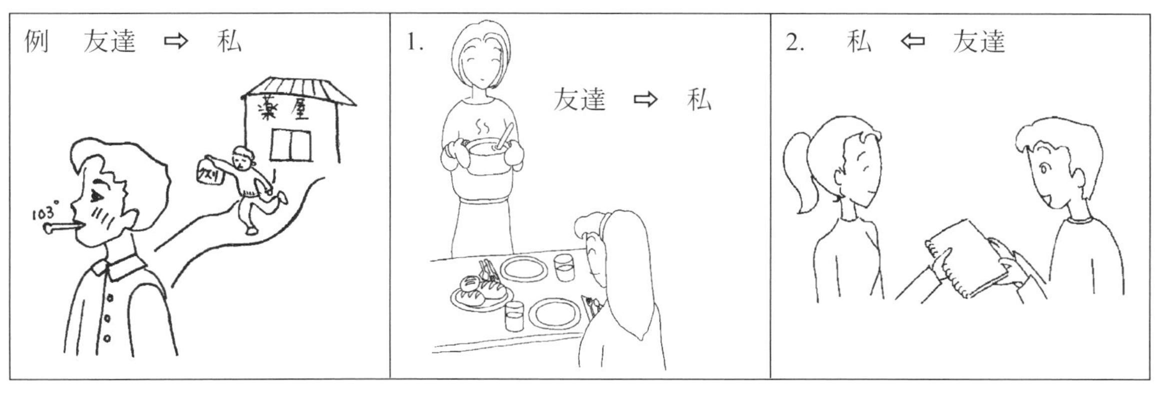

IV.　先生はいつも何をして下さいますか。絵を見て文を作りましょう。

例(れい)　Q:　先生は (学生に) 何をして下さいますか。

　　A:　先生は日本語の辞書を貸して下さいます。

V.　学生は先生に何をしていただきますか。練習問題 IVの絵を見て文を作ってみましょう。

例　Q:　先生に何をしていただきますか。

　　A:　(私は先生に) 日本語の辞書を貸していただきます。

VI.　「～てもらう」を使って、文を作ってみましょう。

例　私は友達にゲームのし方を教えてもらいました。

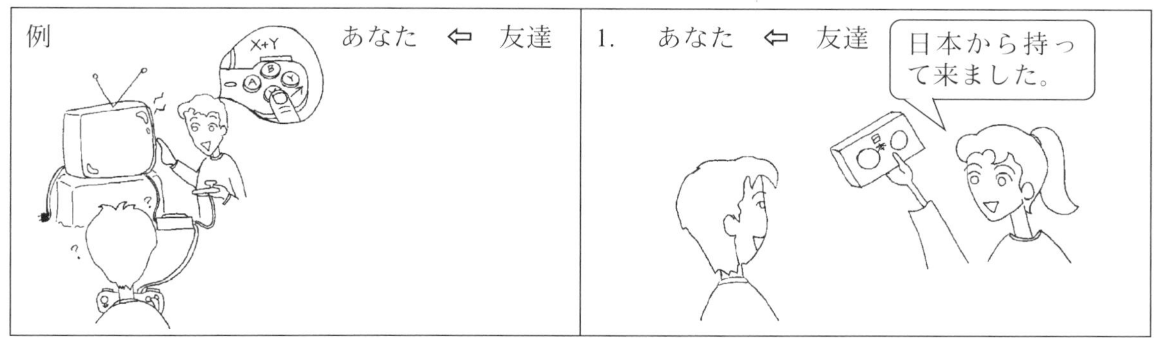

VII.　下の絵を見て文を書いてみましょう。

1.　私は ＿＿＿＿＿＿＿＿＿＿＿＿＿＿＿＿＿＿＿＿＿＿＿＿＿＿＿＿。

2.　山田さんは＿＿＿＿＿＿＿＿＿＿＿＿＿＿＿＿＿＿＿＿＿＿＿＿＿＿。

　　田中さんは＿＿＿＿＿＿＿＿＿＿＿＿＿＿＿＿＿＿＿＿＿＿＿＿＿＿。

3.　私は＿＿＿＿＿＿＿＿＿＿＿＿＿＿＿＿＿＿＿＿＿＿＿＿＿＿＿＿。

　　先生は＿＿＿＿＿＿＿＿＿＿＿＿＿＿＿＿＿＿＿＿＿＿＿＿＿＿＿。

4. チェンさんは＿＿＿＿＿＿＿＿＿＿＿＿＿＿＿＿＿＿＿＿。
   私は＿＿＿＿＿＿＿＿＿＿＿＿＿＿＿＿＿＿＿＿＿＿。

5. すずきさんは＿＿＿＿＿＿＿＿＿＿＿＿＿＿＿＿＿＿＿＿。
   ユーさんは＿＿＿＿＿＿＿＿＿＿＿＿＿＿＿＿＿＿＿＿＿。

6. 私は＿＿＿＿＿＿＿＿＿＿＿＿＿＿＿＿＿＿＿＿＿＿。

7. フォンさんは＿＿＿＿＿＿＿＿＿＿＿＿＿＿＿＿＿＿＿＿。

8. フォンさんは＿＿＿＿＿＿＿＿＿＿＿＿＿＿＿＿＿＿＿＿。

9. 私は＿＿＿＿＿＿＿＿＿＿＿＿＿＿＿＿＿＿＿＿＿＿。

VIII. Intransitive Verb と Transitive Verb の復習をしましょう。Verb を書いてみましょう。

	Intransitive Verb	Transitive Verb		Intransitive Verb	Transitive Verb
1.	開く		6.		出す
2.		閉める	7.	こわれる	
3.		(電気を) つける	8.		なおす
4.	(電気が) きえる		9.		始める
5.	入る		10.	終わる	

IX.　朝、開店(かいてん)する前に、店長(てんちょう)と店員が話しています。絵を見て会話をかんせいして下さい。

例(れい)　店長　：かぎは開けてありますか。

店員　：はい、開けてあります。

(or) いいえ。まだです。かぎを開けておきます。

1.　店長　：営業中(えいぎょうちゅう) (open) のサインは外に ________ か。

店員　：________。

2.　店長　：ヒーターは ________ か。

店員　：________

________。

3.　店長　：店の電気は ________ か。

店員　：________

________。

4.　店長　：お金はレジに ________ か。

店員　：________

________。

X.　夕方、閉店(へいてん)する前に、店長と店員が話しています。会話をかんせいして下さい。

例　店長　：かぎはかけてありますか。

店員　：はい、かけてあります。

(or) いいえ。まだです。かぎをかけておきます。

1.　店長　：店はそうじしてありますか。

店員　：________。

2.　店長　：ヒーターは ________ か。

店員　：________。

3.　店長　：店の電気は ________ か。

店員　：________。

4.　店長　：営業中(えいぎょうちゅう) (open) のサインは中に ________ か。

店員　：________。

XI.　友達とパーティーをすることになったので、じゅんびをしなくてはいけません。どんなじゅんびをしておきますか。絵を見て言ってみましょう。

例　田中　：私は招待じょうを送っておきますが、だれを招待しましょうか。

XII.　パーティーは来週の週末です。じゅんびがしてあるかどうか心配ですね。友達にじゅんびがしてあるかどうか聞いてみたら、まだぜんぜんしていないそうです。友達は何と言いましたか。練習問題 XI の絵を見ながら考えましょう。

例　あなた：田中さん、招待じょうは送ってありますか。
　　田中　：すみません。まだ送ってありません。今日、送っておきます。

XIII.　明日はパーティーの日です。パーティーのじゅんびはどうですか。じゅんびがしてあるかどうか聞いたら、だいじょうぶでした。友達は何と言いましたか。練習問題 XI の絵を見ながら考えましょう。

例　あなた：田中さん、もう招待じょうは送ってありますか。
　　田中　：はい、送ってあります。月曜日に送っておきましたから、安心して下さい。

XIV. 夏目さんのご両親からたんてい (private detective) に電話がありました。夏目さんが先週からいません。アパートにもオフィスにもいません。それで、たんていが夏目さんのアパートを調べています。たんていは調べながらメモしています。何を書いていますか。「～てある」を使って、文を作りましょう。

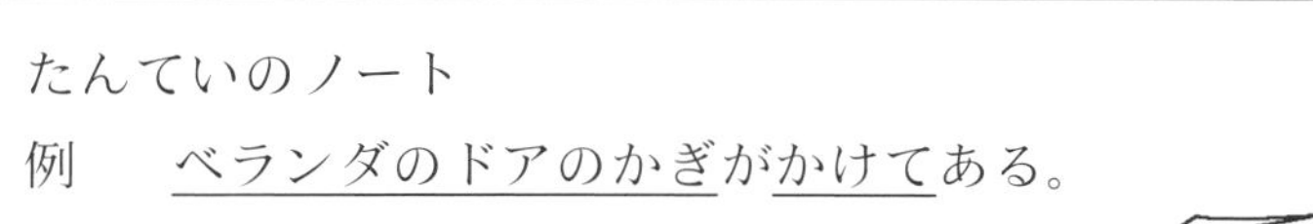

たんていのノート
例　ベランダのドアのかぎがかけてある。

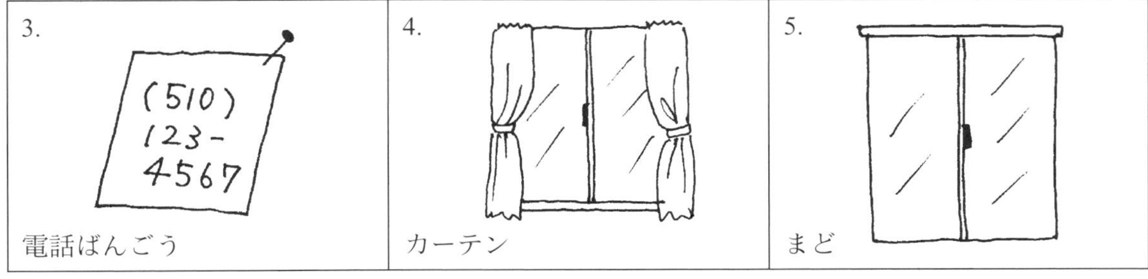

XV.　読む練習

私は今年の五月に大学を卒業します。今、仕事をさがしていますが、いい会社をえらぶのはとても難しいです。ですから、冬休みに、父に色々な会社の説明をしてもらいました。それから、友達のお父さんに色々な会社の人を紹介していただきました。

一月ごろからしゅうしょく試験を受けたり、めんせつに行ったりしています。めんせつの前に、図書館で会社のことを調べてじゅんびをしておきます。でも、最近のことはよく分かりませんから、その会社を知っている人に相談して教えてもらいます。それから、めんせつの時に色々な質問に答えなくてはいけないので、会社でしたいことをくわしく書いておきます。

先週、サンフランシスコにある大きい日本の会社のめんせつを受けました。部屋に入ると、男の人が一人と女の人が一人すわっていました。つくえの上の紙には、質問が三つ書いてありました。それで、その質問に答えました。女の人は「大学の勉強の中で何が一番楽しかったですか」と聞きました。私は「日本語が一番楽しかったです」と答えました。男の人は「この会社で何ができると思いますか」と聞きました。私は自分の考(かんが)えを話しました。

めんせつのけっかは、来週か、さ来週に手紙で教えてくれるそうです。さいようしてくれるかどうか分かりませんが、めんせつは上手にできたと思います。

正しい答えには○、まちがっている答えには×を書いて下さい。

1.　(　　) この人は去年大学を卒業しました。
2.　(　　) この人は友達のお父さんに色々な会社の人を紹介していただきました。
3.　(　　) この人は去年の秋にしゅうしょく試験を受け始めました。
4.　(　　) よく分からないので、この人はめんせつのじゅんびはしません。
5.　(　　) この人はしゅうしょくするために、先週、めんせつを受けました。
6.　(　　) この人はめんせつの時、質問に答えられませんでした。
7.　(　　) めんせつが終わった時、すぐにけっかが分かりました。

新しい漢字

遊(あそ)ぶ	送(おく)る	考(かんが)え	考(かんが)える	気持(きも)ち	魚(さかな)
紹介(しょうかい)	招待(しょうたい)	地図(ちず)	伝(つた)える	冷(つめ)たい	手伝(てつだ)う
肉(にく)	冷(ひ)やす	持(も)つ	悪(わる)い		

新しい使い方

安心(あんしん)	開店(かいてん)	着物(きもの)	切(き)る	近所(きんじょ)	新年(しんねん)
茶(ちゃ)わん	手(て)ぶくろ	店長(てんちょう)	運(はこ)ぶ	閉店(へいてん)	安田(やすだ)

Radicals: 手(て)へん・にすい

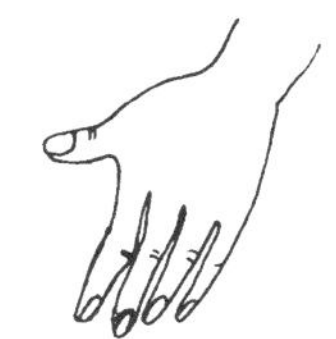

The radical 扌 is derived from 手 and called 手(て)へん. Although the 手へん is written with three strokes, 手 consists of four strokes. Therefore, it is traditionally categorized as a four-stroke radical. So far, we have learned three 手へん漢字: 授, 持 and 招.

In 第十六課 we learned the 氵（さんずい） radical. The radical 冫 appearing in 冷 is called にすい because there are two strokes rather than three. Like the さんずい漢字, some にすい漢字 are also related to the notion of water.

Kanji	Reading	Meaning
遊	あそ(ぶ)	*to play*
送	おく(る)	*to send*
開	カイ・あ(く) あ(ける)	*to open:* 開店 *opening a store*
考	かんが(え)・かんが(える)	*to think:* 考え *thought*
持	も(つ)	*to hold:* 気持ち *feeling*

切	セツ・きっ・き (る)	*to cut:* 切手 *postage stamp,* 親切 *kind*
近	キン・ちか (い)	*to be close to:* 近所 *neighborhood*
所	ショ・ジョ・ところ	*place:* 住所 *address,* 近所 *neighborhood*
魚	さかな	*fish*
紹	ショウ	*help:* 紹介 *introduction*
介	カイ	*to be in between:* 紹介 *introduction*
招	ショウ	*to invite:* 招待 *invitation*
待	タイ・ま (つ)	*to wait:* 招待 *invitation*
地	チ	*ground:* 地図 *map*
図	ズ・ト	*to plan, a diagram:* 地図 *map,* 図書館 *library (a mansion to keep texts)*

Kanji	Reading	Meaning
伝	つた（える）・（て）つだ（う）	*to communicate, to go along:* 手伝う *to help*
手	て	*hand:* 上手（じょうず）*good at,* 下手（へた）*bad at,* 手紙 *letter,* 手ぶくろ *gloves*
長	チョウ・なが（い）	*long, chief:* 店長 *shop or branch manager*
冷	つめ（たい）・ひ（やす）	*cold*
肉	にく	*meat*
閉	ヘイ・し（まる）・し（める）	*to close:* 閉店 *closing a store*
運	ウン・はこ（ぶ）	*fate, to transport:* 運転 *drive,* 運動 *exercise*
悪	わる（い）	*bad*

漢字の復習

I.　読みましょう。

1. ふうとうに住所を書いて、切手をはっておいて下さい。
2. 夕方五時ごろ旅館に着きました。
3. この漢字の意味を説明して下さいませんか。
4. 心配しますから、このことは両親には言わないで下さい。
5. 男の人が一人と女の人が二人、外で待っています。

II.　スミスさんはアメリカ人の留学生で、もうすぐ帰国します。それで、高田さんと田中さんはプレゼントをあげることにしました。二人はカタログ (catalogue) を見ながら相談しています。何をあげることにしましたか。

高田:　どれをあげたらいいでしょうか。

田中:　そうですね。この日本画はきれいですね。

高田:　ええ、でも、この間、スミスさんは絵の先生が日本画をかいてくれたと言っていました。

田中:　そうですか。じゃあ、ほかの物の方がいいですね。この時計はどうですか。かたちがおもしろいですよ。

高田:　ああ、それは、スミスさんとデパートへ行った時に見ました。スミスさんも好きだと言っていました。

田中:　あ、この小説もいいかも知れません。日本に住んでいるアメリカ人の話だそうですよ。

高田:　へえ、おもしろそうですね。でも、漢字が多いですから辞書をひきながら読むのは大変だと思います。

田中:　そうですね。あ、この手ぶくろはきれいで、あたたかそうですね。

高田:　でも、今はもう春ですから、手ぶくろはちょっと……

田中:　そうですか。あ、日本料理の本がありますよ。スミスさんは日本料理を作ってみたいと言っていましたから、この本はどうですか。

高田:　いいですね。この本があれば、アメリカに帰ってから、ご家族に日本料理を作ってあげることができますね。

田中:　時計と料理の本とではどちらの方がいいですか。

高田:　難しいですね。時計と料理の本は同じぐらいいいおくり物だと思います。

田中:　でも、____________________をあげたら、時間を見る時にいつも私達のことを考えてくれるかも知れませんよ。

高田:　そうですね。じゃあ、____________________をあげることにしましょう。

田中:　そうしましょう。きっと、よろこびますよ。

新しい語彙(ごい)

アイロン	iron
あむ ㋒ⓣ	*to knit*
あんしん（する）	*relief*
いらっしゃい	*welcome (casual)*
（お茶(ちゃ)を）入(い)れる ㋸ⓣ	*to make tea*
えらぶ ㋒ⓣ	*to choose, select*
おごる ㋒ⓣ	*to treat someone to something*
おじいさん	*old man*
教(おし)える ㋸ⓣ	*to tell, inform*
おじさん	*middle-aged man*
おばあさん	*old woman*
おばさん	*middle-aged woman*
おめでとう（ございます）	*congratulations*
カーテン	*curtain, drapes*
開店(かいてん)（する）	*the opening of a store*
（アイロンを）かける ㋸ⓣ	*to iron*
（かぎを）かける ㋸ⓣ	*to lock (with a key)*
考(かんが)え	*thought*
切(き)る ㋒ⓣ	*to cut, chop*
クラッカー	*cracker*

けっか	*result*
ごうか ㋤	*deluxe, luxurious, gorgeous*
ごちそうする Ⓘⓣ	*to treat someone to something (formal)*
こと	koto *(Japanese musical instrument)*
さいよう（する）	*employment*
サイン	*signboard, sign*
サラダ	*salad*
シャンペン	*champagne*
じゅんび（する）	*preparation*
招待(しょうたい)（する）	*invitation*
招待(しょうたい)じょう	*invitation letter*
新年(しんねん)	*new year*
すいせんじょう	*recommendation letter*
スープ	*soup*
スピーカー	*speaker*
そう	*so*
ソフト	*software*
ターキー	*turkey*
出(だ)す	*to serve, put out*
チーズ	*cheese*
茶(ちゃ)わん	*rice bowl*
茶(ちゃ)わんむし	*thick custard soup*

伝える（つたえる） ㋸ ⓣ	*to tell, inform*
手伝う（てつだう） ㋒ ⓣ	*to help, assist*
手ぶくろ（てぶくろ）	*gloves*
店長（てんちょう）	*shop/branch manager*
ぬう ㋒ ⓣ	*to sew*
運ぶ（はこぶ） ㋒ ⓣ	*to carry, transport*
パジャマ	*pajamas*
パスタ	*pasta*
ひっこし（する）	*moving a household*
プリン	*pudding*
閉店（へいてん）（する）	*closing a store*

ホチキス	*stapler*
マリーナ	*marina*
むす ㋒ ⓣ	*to steam*
メモ（する）	*memo*
めんせつ（する）	*interview*
モニター	*monitor*
やく ㋒ ⓣ	*to bake, broil*
やくす ㋒ ⓣ	*to translate*
ゆずる ㋒ ⓣ	*to give up, hand over*
りれきしょ	*résumé*
レモネード	*lemonade*

名前

フォン	*Fong*
安田（やすだ）	*Yasuda*

ユー	*Yu*

しかられる
Being Scolded

買い物をしすぎたので、母にしかられました
Because I did too much shopping, I got scolded by my mother

7
じゃあ、今月は買い物はできませんね。
ええ、そうなんです。
8
じゃ、私は今からデパートへ行かなくてはいけないので、また後で。
ええっ、ソンさん、まだ買い物をするつもりですか。

会話

1 ソン：ミラーさん、うれしそうですね。何かいいことがありましたか。

Miller-san, you look happy. Did something good happen?

ミラー：ええ、先週の試験がよくできたので、先生にほめられました。

Yes, I did very well on last week's quiz, so I got praised by the teacher.

2 ソン：それはよかったですね。

That's great.

ミラー：ええ、うれしいです。ソンさんはあまり元気がありませんね。どうしたんですか。

Yeah, I'm very happy. You don't seem too cheerful, Son-san. What's the matter?

3 ソン：先月買い物をしすぎたので、母にしかられたんです。

I did too much shopping last month, so I got scolded by my mother.

ミラー：へえ。何を買ったんですか。

Oh, what did you buy?

4 ソン：ブラウスを五枚と、スカートを三枚と、CDを十枚、まんがの本を三冊、それから、ええと……。

Five blouses and three skirts and ten CDs and three comic books, and uh...

5 ミラー：わあ、本当にたくさん買いましたねえ。

Wow, you really bought a lot!

6 ソン：ストレスがたまると、買い物をしたくなるんです。それで、母のクレジットカードを使ったので、しかられてしまいました。

When I get stressed (Lit. when stress builds up), I get an urge to go shopping. And so, I used my mother's credit card and ended up getting scolded.

7 ミラー ：じゃあ、今月は買い物はできませんね。
Well then, you can't do any shopping this month, can you?
ソン ：ええ、そうなんです。
No, I really can't.

8 ソン ：じゃ、私は今からデパートへ行かなくてはいけないので、また後で。
Well, I have to go to a department store now, so see you later.
ミラー ：ええっ、ソンさん、まだ買い物をするつもりですか。
What? Are you still thinking of going shopping?

9 ソン ：いえ、ちがいますよ。このブラウスが大きすぎるので、返しに行くんです。
Oh, no. It's not what you think. This blouse is too big, so I'm going there to return it.
ミラー ：あ、そうですか。じゃあ、行ってらっしゃい。
Oh, I get it. Okay, see you later.

使い方

1 何かいいこと literally means "some good thing". Like in English, this expression requires a special word order; e.g. *something good* (NOUN + ADJ), not *good something* (ADJ + NOUN).

何かおもしろいこと	*something interesting*
何か食べたいもの	*something (you) want to eat*
だれか会いたい人	*someone (you) want to meet*
だれか知っている人	*someone (you) know or someone who knows it*
どこか行きたい所	*somewhere (you) want to go*

2 元気 can be used as either a な -adjective or a noun.

元気じゃありません。	*Not cheerful/not high-spirited.*	(な -adjective)
元気がありません。	*Lacking high spirits.*	(Noun)

4 ええ(と) is an interjection equivalent to English "Uh…"

8 今から (literally "from now") here means "right now, immediately".

また後で (literally "again later") means "see you later".

9 ちがう is a verb meaning "to be different" or "to be wrong". (We sometimes consider people or things that are different to be wrong.) Here, Son is saying that Miller's assumption that she is going to go shopping is incorrect/different from her actual plans.

文法

25a	**Verb Conjugation: Passive フォーム**	
25b	**Simple (Direct) Passive Construction**	
25c	**Adversity (Indirect) Passive Construction**	
25d	**Pre- ますフォーム + すぎる**	**"to do ~ excessively"**
25e	**ADJECTIVE + すぎる**	**"too ADJECTIVE"**
25f	**DURATION に X**	**"X per DURATION"**

25a Verb Conjugation: Passive フォーム

In this lesson, we are going to study a new verb conjugation called the *Passive* フォーム. You can derive the Passive フォーム by applying the following rules:

A う **Verbs:** Stem + a + れる

聞く	kik-u	kik-a-reru	聞かれる
なくす	nakus-u	nakus-a-reru	なくされる
待つ	mats-u	mat-a-reru	待たれる
よぶ	yob-u	yob-a-reru	よばれる
読む	yom-u	yom-a-reru	読まれる
さわる	sawar-u	sawar-a-reru	さわられる

Like the Negativeフォーム, the consonant *w* appears in the Passiveフォーム if the Dictionaryフォーム ends in う, without a preceding consonant, eg.:

使う	tsuka-u	tsukaw-a-reru	使われる

The following table shows verb conjugations of such verbs:

Final Vowel	あ	い	う	え	お
Conjugation	**Negative**	**Pre- ます**	**Dictionary**	**Conditional**	**Volitional**
	洗わ - ない	洗い - ます	洗う	洗え - ば	洗おう
	言わ - ない	言い - ます	言う	言え - ば	言おう
	買わ - ない	買い - ます	買う	買え - ば	買おう

Conjugation	Passive
	洗わ - れる
	言わ - れる
	買わ - れる

B　る Verbs: Stem + られる (identical to the Potential フォーム)

教える	oshie-ru	oshie-rareru	教えられる
とどける	todoke-ru	todoke-rareru	とどけられる
調べる	shirabe-ru	shirabe-rareru	調べられる
やめる	yame-ru	yame-rareru	やめられる
わすれる	wasure-ru	wasure-rareru	わすれられる
着る	ki-ru	ki-rareru	着られる
見る	mi-ru	mi-rareru	見られる
借りる	kari-ru	kari-rareru	借りられる

C　Irregular Verbs

来る　→　来(こ)られる
する　→　される

25b　Simple (Direct) Passive Construction

Pass There are two kinds of passive constructions in Japanese: the *simple (or direct) passive* and the *adversity (or indirect) passive*. The simple passive is similar to that of English: the direct or indirect object of the active sentence appears as the subject of the passive counterpart.

A　Direct Object Becomes Subject

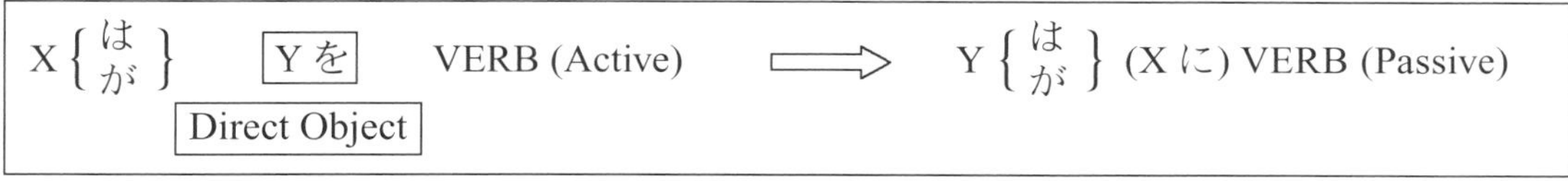

石川先生は ミラーさんを ほめました。　*Ishikawa-sensei praised Miller-san.*

ミラーさんは 石川先生にほめられました。　*Miller-san was praised by Ishikawa-sensei.*

大事なかいぎにおくれたので、社長(しゃちょう)は前田(まえだ)さんをしかりました。
Because he was late to an important meeting, the company president reprimanded Maeda-san.
大事なかいぎにおくれたので、前田さんは社長にしかられました。
Because he was late to an important meeting, Maeda-san was reprimanded by the company president.

たくさんの人がこの本を読んでいます。

Many people are reading this book.

この本はたくさんの人に読まれています。

This book is being read by many people.

ねこはトラックにひかれました。

The cat was run over by a truck.

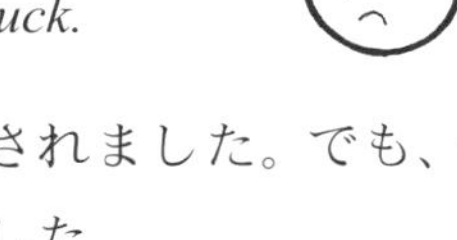

前田さんに音楽会(おんがくかい)に招待されました。でも、忙しかったのでことわりました。

I got invited to a music concert by Maeda-san. But I was busy, so I declined (his offer).

> 日本のことわざ
>
> Japanese Proverb
>
> 出るくいはうたれる。
>
> *A protruding stake gets hammered down.*
>
> くい　*stake, post*
>
> うつ　*to hit, knock*
>
> Stand out from the crowd and you just invite trouble for yourself.

クラスで寝てしまって、クラスメートにおこされました。それで、みんなに笑(わら)われました。*

When I fell asleep in class, I got woken up by a classmate. Then, I got laughed at by everyone.

Although the subject of the active sentence can appear, with に, in the passive counterpart, it is frequently suppressed when unnecessary or irrelevant.

来週、試験の成績(せいせき)がはり出(だ)されます。

The exam grades will be posted next week.

英語はせかい中(じゅう)で話されています。

English is spoken all over the world.

せかい中で自然(しぜん)がはかいされています。

Nature is being destroyed all over the world.

この小説の作者(さくしゃ)はよく知られています。

The author of this novel is well known.

『源氏物語(げんじものがたり)』** はいつごろ書かれたんですか。

When (Lit. About when) was The Tale of Genji *written?*

さあ、よく知りませんが、千年ぐらい前でしょう。

Well, I don't know exactly when, but probably it was about 1,000 years ago.

> * 笑う can be used either intransitively (laugh) or transitively (laugh at).
>
> ソンさんはよく笑います。
>
> *Son-san laughs a lot.*
>
> みんなソンさんを笑いました。
>
> *Everyone laughed at Son-san.*
>
> **物語 consists of 物(もの) "thing" and 語(かた)る "to talk" (かたり becomes がたり by sequential voicing, cf. 第十一課, **11f**).
>
> Can you guess what these are?
>
> イソップ物語　　カンタベリー物語
>
> 千夜一夜(せんやいちや)物語　　二都(にと)物語

B Indirect Object Becomes Subject

X {は / が} [Y に] Z を VERB (Active) ⟹ Y {は / が} (X に) Z を VERB (Passive)
[Indirect Object]

村上さんは[山本さんに]スピーチをたのみました。 *Murakami-san asked Yamamoto-san for a speech.*

[山本さんは]村上さんにスピーチをたのまれました。 *Yamamoto-san was asked by Murakami-san for a speech.*

「スピーチをお願(ねが)いします」と言って、村上さんは山本さんにマイクをわたしました。
Murakami-san said to Yamamoto-san, "Please say a few words (Lit. make a speech)" and handed him the microphone.
山本さんは村上さんにマイクをわたされました。
Yamamoto-san was handed the microphone by Murakami-san.

クラスメートが私にいやな仕事をたのみました。
My classmate asked me to do an annoying task.
クラスメートにいやな仕事をたのまれました。
I was asked by a classmate to do an annoying task.

先生は私に文法が弱(よわ)いと言いました。
My teacher told me that I'm bad at grammar (Lit. weak in grammar).
私は先生に文法が弱いと言われました。
I was told by my teacher that I'm bad at grammar (Lit. weak in grammar).

25c Adversity (Indirect) Passive Construction

The second type of passive is frequently called the *adversity* (or *indirect*) *passive* because its typical use is to describe unfortunate events. There are two subtypes of adversity passives: one with a transitive verb, and the other with an intransitive verb.

A Transitive Verbs

We have seen that in the simple (direct) passive construction, the direct object remains as the direct object when *the indirect object of the corresponding active sentence becomes the subject*. In adversity passive sentences, the direct object of the active sentence remains as such, but *the subject of the passive (the Z in the following diagram) is the person who is affected by the event*. Such a person does not appear in the active counterpart, or may be present as a possessive noun, e.g. [ミラーさんの] 自転車.

X {は／が} (Zの) Yを Tr.VERB (Active) ⟹ Z {は／が} (Xに) Yを Tr.VERB (Passive)

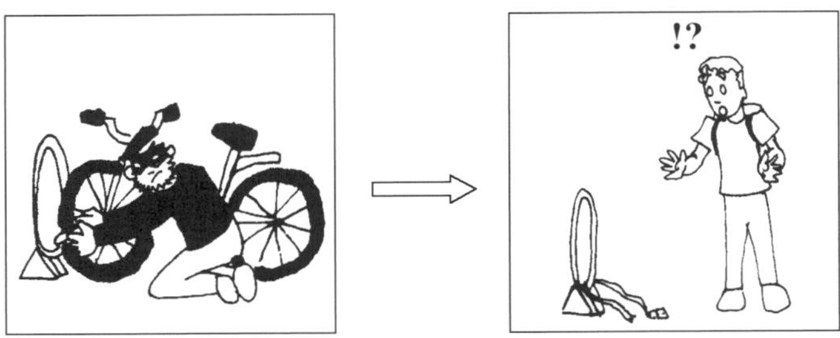

どろぼうが ミラーさんの 自転車を ぬすみました。 *A thief stole Miller-san's bicycle.*

ミラーさんは どろぼうに 自転車を ぬすまれました。

(Lit.) Miller-san was adversely affected by a thief's stealing his bicycle.

Miller-san had his bicycle stolen.

You can also make the simple passive version of the sentence:

ミラーさんの自転車は どろぼうにぬすまれました。

Miller-san's bicycle was stolen by a thief.

However, this sentence reports the incident as a mere fact; it does not convey the speaker's sympathy for ミラーさん's suffering. For this reason, simple passives are less commonly used in these situations than adversity passives.

妹が私のラブレターを読みました。

My sister read my love letter.

私は、妹にラブレターを読まれました。

I had (the misfortune of) my love letter getting read by my sister.

ルームメートは、(私が) 買っておいた日本酒を全部飲んでしまいました。

My roommate drank up all the sake that I'd bought (for some special purpose).

(私は) ルームメートに買っておいた日本酒を全部飲まれてしまいました。

I (unfortunately) had all the sake that I'd bought (for a special purpose) drunk by my roommate.

地下鉄(ちかてつ)の中でハイヒールをはいた女の人に足をふまれて、目から火(ひ)が出ました。

My foot got stepped on in the subway by a woman wearing high-heeled shoes, and sparks came out of my eyes.

山田さんに時計を貸したら、こわされてしまいました。
When I lent my watch to Yamada-san, it got broken (by him).
(私は) くうこうでにもつを調べられました。
My baggage got inspected at the airport.
(私は) クラスメートに悪口(わるぐち)を言われました。*
(Lit.) I had bad things said about me by a classmate.
My classmate spoke ill of me.
夜中にこうえんで花火(はなび)をしていたら、近所の人にけいさつをよばれてしまいました。
When we were playing with fireworks in the park in the middle of the night, a neighbor called the police on us.
使いたいと思った辞書を借(か)り出(だ)されてしまいました。**
(Lit.) I was adversely affected by someone's borrowing (checking out) the dictionary that I wanted to use.
友達に宿題を見せてあげたら、(宿題を) うつされました。
When I (kindly) showed my homework to a friend, she wound up copying it.
ソンさんは知らない人にかたをたたかれました。
Son-san got patted on the shoulder by a stranger.

* XがYにZの悪口を言う
X says to Y bad things about Z

** 出す can be attached to another verb to make a compound verb and indicate the direction "out".

はり出す	*paste out (= "post")*
借(か)り出(だ)す	*to check out*
貸し出す	*to lend out*

B Intransitive Verbs

In this rather unique construction, the intransitive verb enacted by some active subject X (marked with に in the passive sentence) has an adverse effect on the passive subject Z. In English, this subtlety is sometimes expressed through the use of an "adversity *on* phrase".

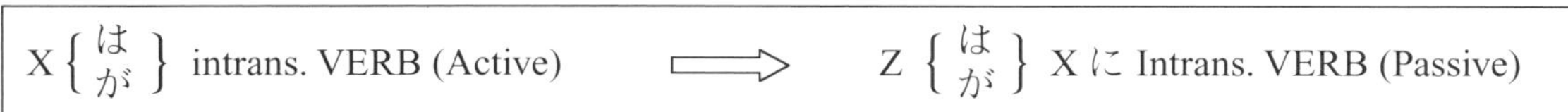

前田さんの お父さんが 死にました。　*Maeda-san's father died.*
⇩ ⇩
前田さんは お父さんに 死なれました。
(Lit.) Maeda-san was adversely affected by his father's death.
Maeda-san's father died on him.

昨日、雨に降られて、かぜをひいてしまいました。
It rained on me yesterday, and I got a cold.
スキットのはっぴょうの日、パートナーに休まれて困りました。
(Lit.) I was troubled by my partner's absence on the day for our skit presentation.
The day of our skit presentation, my partner skipped on me and it was a problem.

夕べ、友達に来られて、宿題ができませんでした。

Last night, I was visited by a friend and couldn't do my homework.

夕べは、一晩中赤ちゃんに泣かれて、全然(ぜんぜん)眠れませんでした。ですから、今日は昼寝(ひるね)をしようと思います。

The baby cried all last night, and I couldn't sleep at all. So, I think I'll take a nap today.

映画館で背が高い人に前にすわられたので、よく見えませんでした。*

Because I got sat in front of by a tall person in the movie theater, I couldn't see (the movie) well.

* 見える is a special intransitive verb. Xが見えます literally means "X is visible/in sight", although it can more naturally be translated as "I/We can see X". 見える can also be used in 目が見える, which means that one's eyes are functional (i.e. one is not blind). 見える should not be confused with 見られる, which is the Potential フォーム of 見る. While 忙しいので、映画が見られません "Because I'm busy, I can't see the movie" is natural, 忙しいので、映画が見えません "Because I'm busy, the movie isn't visible" is anomalous because being busy has nothing to do with one's vision.

Adversity Passive vs. ～てもらう

The adversity passive contrasts with the ～てもらう construction. If you are grateful for someone's action, use ～てもらう; if you are annoyed by his/her action, use the adversity passive.

友達に手伝ってもらいました。

I got help from my friend (and I'm grateful for it).

友達に手伝われました。

My friend lent me a hand (although I didn't want him / her to do so).

母にTシャツを洗ってもらいました。

I got my mother to wash my T-shirt (and I'm grateful for it).

母にTシャツを洗われました。

My mother (went and) washed my T-shirt (although I didn't want her to do so).

The sense of adversity becomes even more prominent if you add ～てしまう.

山田さんに私の電話ばんごうを覚えてもらいました。

I had Yamada-san remember my telephone number (for my own sake).

山田さんに私の電話ばんごうを覚えられてしまいました。

I (unfortunately) got my telephone number memorized by Yamada-san.

25d　Pre-ますフォーム + すぎる　"to do ~ excessively"

ます

Note that "excessively" necessarily carries a negative connotation.

だいじょうぶですよ。あなたは心配しすぎますよ。

It'll be all right. You worry too much.

すみません。言いすぎました。

Sorry, I've said too much.

先生に遊びすぎると* 注意(ちゅうい)されました。

> * This と is the quotation marker; it does not mean "when/if".

I was warned by the teacher that I play around too much (i.e. instead of studying).

先週のパーティーでうっかり飲みすぎてしまいました。

I carelessly drank too much at the party last week.

村上先生は働きすぎて、病気になってしまいました。

Murakami-sensei worked too much and got sick.

このおすしを食べてくれませんか。注文(ちゅうもん)しすぎてしまったんです。

Could you eat this sushi *for me? I ordered too much.*

そのスパイは知りすぎたので、ころされてしまいました。

Because that spy knew too much, he was killed.

最近目が悪くなって、困っています。

I'm having a lot of trouble lately because my eyes are getting bad.

勉強しすぎるからですよ。少し休んだ方がいいですよ。

That's because you're studying too much. You'd better rest a little.

25e　ADJECTIVE + すぎる　"too ADJECTIVE"

A　い-Adjectives: Stem + すぎる

そのアパートは安くてとてもいいんですが、駅から遠すぎます。

That apartment is inexpensive and nice, but it's too far from the train station.

暑すぎたら、言って下さい。ヒーターをけしますから。

If it's too hot, please tell me. I'll turn off the heater.

リーダーをきめなくてはいけません。

We have to decide on a leader.

前田さんはどうですか。
How about Maeda-san?
ちょっと、わかすぎませんか。
Umm… Isn't he a little too young?

こうぎはどうでしたか。
How was the lecture?
教室が広すぎて、よく聞こえませんでした。*
The classroom was too big, and I couldn't hear (the lecturer) well.

> * Like 見える, 聞こえる is a special intransitive verb, meaning "(something) is audible/I can hear (something)". 聞こえる can also be used in (X は) 耳が聞こえる, meaning that one's ears are functional (i.e. one is not deaf).

B　な -Adjectives: Stem + すぎる

田中さんはまじめすぎて、おもしろくありません。
Tanaka-san is excessively serious, and not interesting.
すみません、その話はせいじてきすぎて、私はよく分かりません。
Sorry, but that discussion is too political, and I can't follow it well.
その計画(けいかく)はきけんすぎると思いませんか。
Don't you think that plan is too risky?
今度の試験はかんたんすぎましたね。次(つぎ)はもっと難しくしましょう。
This exam was too easy, wasn't it? Let's make the next one more challenging.
そのようふくはちょっと、はですぎると思いますが……。
I think that outfit is a little too flamboyant …

25f　DURATION に X　"X per DURATION"

今、ダイエット中なので、一日に一回しか食べません。
Because I'm on a diet now, I eat only once a day.
一週間に一回ジムで泳(およ)ぎます。
I swim once a week at the gym.
日本語の授業は一週間に五時間です。
(Our) Japanese class meets five hours a week.
一ヶ月に三～四本映画を見ます。(三～四本 is read as さんよんほん.)
(or) 一ヶ月に三本か四本映画を見ます。
I see three or four movies a month.
一年に一～二回両親に会います。(一～二回 is read as いちにかい.)
(or) 一年に一回か二回両親に会います。
I see my parents once or twice a year.

練習問題

I.　Passive フォームを練習しましょう。

1. ほめる	4. すわる	7. 笑う	10. 来る	13. ふむ	16. 招待する
2. しかる	5. 食べる	8. 見る	11. よぶ	14. さわる	17. ぬすむ
3. たつ	6. 降る	9. 言う	12. 書く	15. なくす	18. 開ける

II.　Passive フォームを使って話をかんせいしましょう。

1. あたたかい春の日です。むしがたくさん飛(と)んでいます。みんなとても楽しそうです。

2. 天気がいいので、寝ぼうしたかえるもおきて、家から出てきました。

3. 「ああ、いい天気だな。本当に気持ちがいいな。でも、おなかがすいてしまったなあ。何かおいしい食べ物はないかな。」

4. よく見ると、くさの中で小さいむしがたくさん遊んでいました。

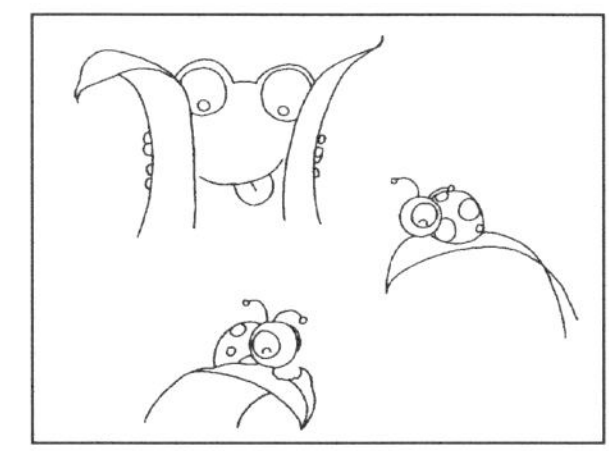

5. かえるはおなかがすいていました。それで、かえるはむしをゴクンと飲みました。
むしは ＿＿＿＿＿＿＿＿＿＿ に ＿＿＿＿＿＿＿＿＿＿。

6.　かえるはむしを食べ終わると、だんだん眠くなりました。そして、グッスリ寝てしまいました。

7.　すると、ずっと寝ていたヘビがおきて、食べ物をさがしに来ました。

8.　ヘビは昼寝をしているかえるを見ると、「ハハーン、おいしそうだな。ばかなかえるが寝ているぞ。今年始めての昼(ひる)ごはん、いただきます。」と言いました。

9.　そして、寝ているかえるをペロっと食べました。

________________ は ________________ に

____________________________________。

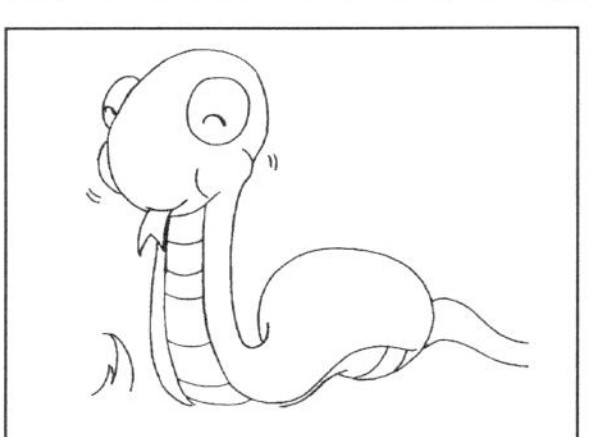

SOUND-SYMBOLIC WORDS

Onomatopoeic and other sound-symbolic words form a notable class of vocabulary in Japanese. Many of them involve repetition, and many others are accompanied by と.

グッスリ（と）眠る	*to sleep deeply/soundly*		
ゴクンと飲む	*to swallow something in one gulp*		
ドンドン VERB	*to progress rapidly*		
	ドンドンふとる	*to gain weight rapidly* (cf. 第二十二課)	
ペロっと食べる	*to eat up rapidly*		
ペラペラ話す	*to speak fluently*		

III.　絵を見て文をかんせいしましょう。

例(れい)　先生はスミスさんをほめました。
スミスさんは先生にほめられました。

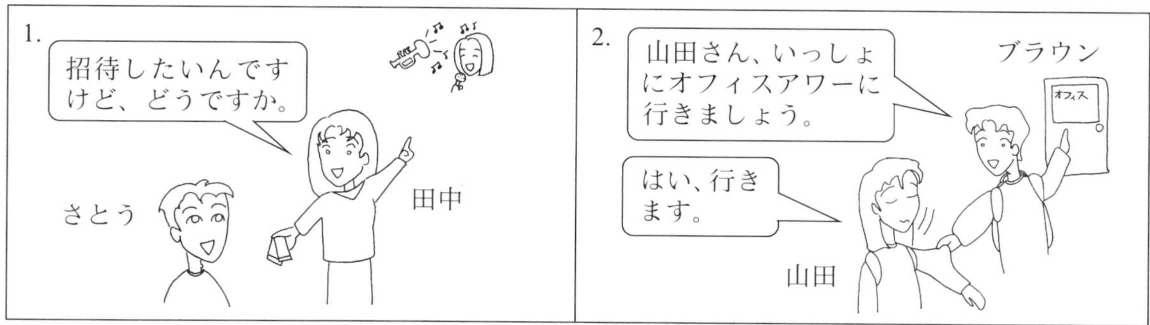

1. 田中さんはさとうさんを音楽会に招待しました。
   さとうさんは＿＿＿＿＿＿＿＿＿＿＿＿＿＿＿＿＿＿＿＿。

2. ブラウンさんは＿＿＿＿＿＿＿＿＿＿＿＿＿＿＿＿＿＿＿＿。
   山田さんは＿＿＿＿＿＿＿＿＿＿＿＿＿＿＿＿＿＿＿＿。

3. お父さんは＿＿＿＿＿＿＿＿＿＿＿＿＿＿＿＿＿＿＿＿。
   男(おとこ)の子(こ)は＿＿＿＿＿＿＿＿＿＿＿＿＿＿＿＿＿＿＿＿。

4. リーさんとシュミットさんは山田さんをパーティーにさそいました。
   山田さんは＿＿＿＿＿＿＿＿＿＿＿＿＿＿＿＿＿＿＿＿。

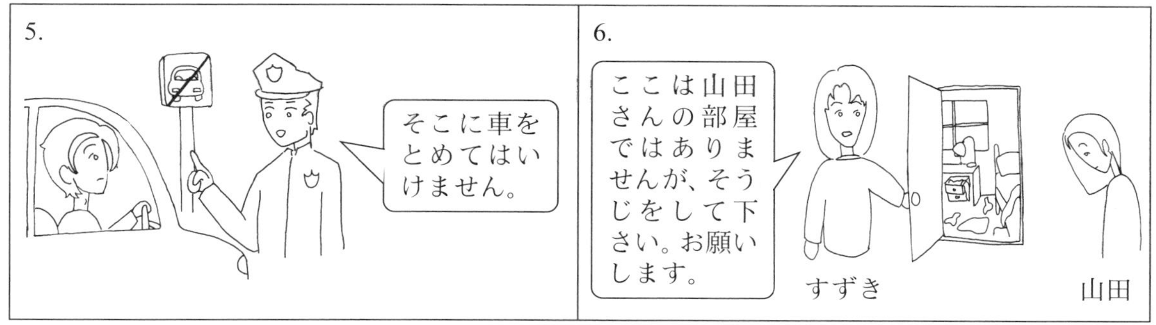

5. おまわりさんは男の人に「そこに車をとめてはいけません」と注意しました。
   男の人は＿＿＿＿＿＿＿＿＿＿＿＿＿＿＿＿＿＿＿＿。

6. すずきさんは山田さんに部屋のそうじをたのみました。
   山田さんは＿＿＿＿＿＿＿＿＿＿＿＿＿＿＿＿＿＿＿＿。

IV.　ビンゴです。クラスメートに聞いてみましょう。クラスでこんなこと*をされたことはありませんか。

例(れい)　Q:　先生にほめられたことがありますか。

A:　はい、先生にほめられたことがあります。

(or) いいえ、先生にほめられたことはありません。

例　先生 ＿＿＿＿＿＿さん	1.　試験 ＿＿＿＿＿＿さん	2. ＿＿＿＿＿＿さん
3.　クラスメート ＿＿＿＿＿＿さん	4.　先生 ＿＿＿＿＿＿さん	5.　宿題 ＿＿＿＿＿＿さん
6.　うるさい ＿＿＿＿＿＿さん	7. ＿＿＿＿＿＿さん	8.　先生　どうぞ……。 ＿＿＿＿＿＿さん

* こんなこと literally means "this kind / type of thing". It is frequently, but not necessarily, used to refer to an undesirable event.

V.　絵を見て文をかんせいしましょう。

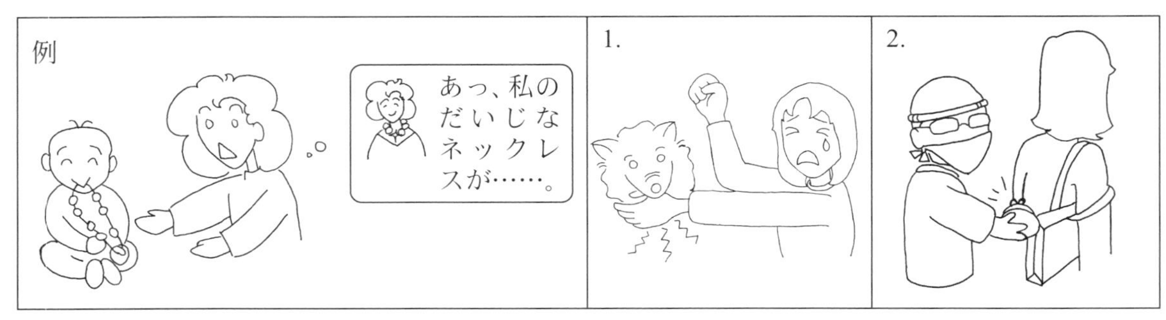

例　子供はお母さんのネックレスをこわしました。
　　お母さんは子供にネックレスをこわされました。

1. 犬は＿＿＿＿＿＿＿＿＿＿＿＿＿＿＿＿＿＿＿＿。
　女(おんな)の子(こ)は＿＿＿＿＿＿＿＿＿＿＿＿＿＿＿＿＿＿。

2. すりは＿＿＿＿＿＿＿＿＿＿＿＿＿＿＿＿＿＿＿＿。
　女の人は＿＿＿＿＿＿＿＿＿＿＿＿＿＿＿＿＿＿＿。

3. シュミットさんのルームメートは＿＿＿＿＿＿＿＿＿＿＿＿。
　シュミットさんは＿＿＿＿＿＿＿＿＿＿＿＿＿＿＿＿＿。

4. ねこは＿＿＿＿＿＿＿＿＿＿＿＿＿＿＿＿＿＿＿＿。
　すずきさんは＿＿＿＿＿＿＿＿＿＿＿＿＿＿＿＿＿＿。

5. 弟は＿＿＿＿＿＿＿＿＿＿＿＿＿＿＿＿＿＿＿＿＿。
　私は＿＿＿＿＿＿＿＿＿＿＿＿＿＿＿＿＿＿＿＿＿。

6. 友達は＿＿＿＿＿＿＿＿＿＿＿＿＿＿＿＿＿＿＿＿。
　私は＿＿＿＿＿＿＿＿＿＿＿＿＿＿＿＿＿＿＿＿＿。

7. 雨が＿＿＿＿＿＿＿＿＿＿＿＿＿＿＿＿＿＿＿＿＿。
　すずきさんは＿＿＿＿＿＿＿＿＿＿＿＿＿＿＿＿＿＿。

8. 背が高い男の人は＿＿＿＿＿＿＿＿＿＿＿＿＿＿＿＿。
　とみたさんは＿＿＿＿＿＿＿＿＿＿＿＿＿＿＿＿＿＿。

VI.　スミスさんは昨日、大変でした。絵を見て話を作って下さい。

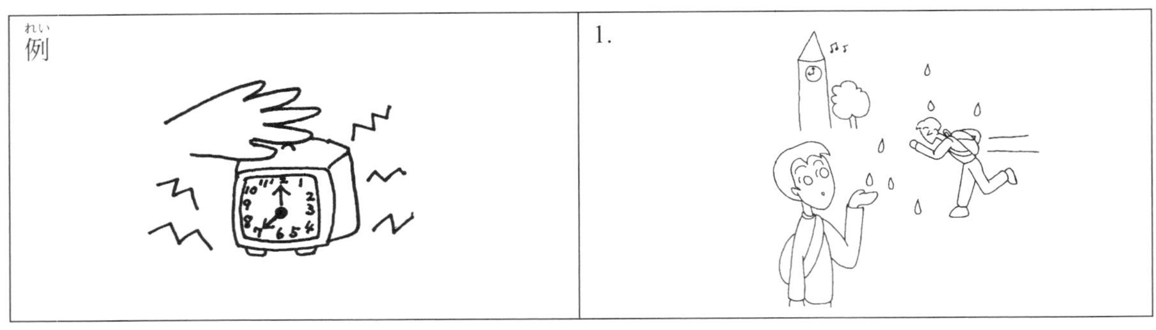

例　昨日の朝、ルームメートにめざまし時計をとめられました。それで、ちこくしてしまいました。

1.　大学へ行く時、＿＿＿＿＿＿＿＿＿＿＿＿＿＿＿＿＿＿＿＿＿＿＿＿
　　それで、かぜをひいてしまいました。

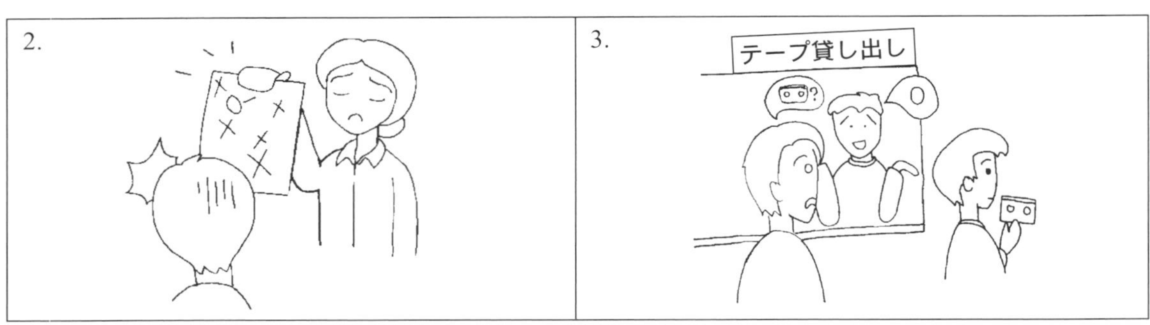

2.　成績が悪くて、＿＿＿＿＿＿＿＿＿＿＿＿＿＿＿＿＿＿＿＿＿＿＿＿
　　それで、勉強がいやになってしまいました。

3.　聞き取りのテープを借りに行きましたが、＿＿＿＿＿＿＿＿＿＿＿＿＿＿
　　それで、宿題をすることができませんでした。

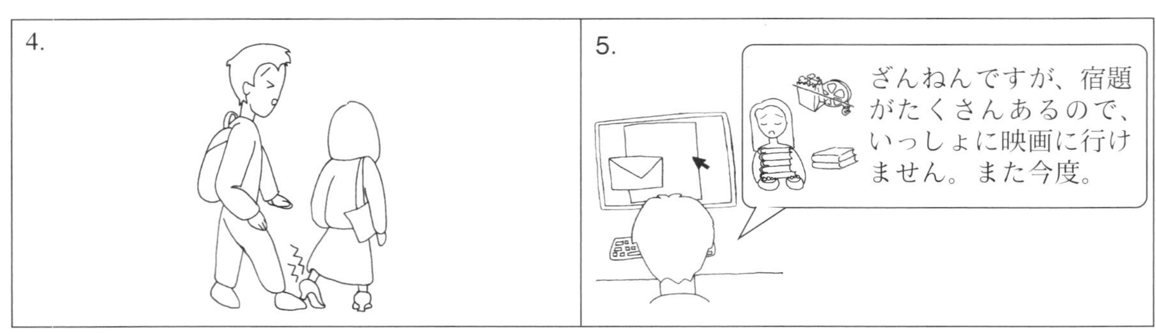

ざんねんですが、宿題
がたくさんあるので、
いっしょに映画に行け
ません。また今度。

4. 家へ帰る時、バスの中で ________________________
痛くて、目から火が出ました。

5. シンさんを映画にさそいましたが、E メールでシンさんに ________________________
________________________ 泣きたくなりました。

VII. どうしましたか。聞きましょう。

例　山田:　田中さん、どうしたんですか。
　　田中:　頭が痛いんです。
　　山田:　何かしたんですか。
　　田中:　昨日、ビールを飲みすぎたんです。

田中
昨日

1. 田中　おなかが痛い。	2. 山田　足が痛い。	3. 田中　つかれた。
 昼ごはん		

4. 山田　目がつかれた。	5. 田中　気持ちが悪い。	6. 山田　こしが痛い。
 コンピューター		

VIII.　パートナーに聞きましょう。

例　A:　Bさんはお酒を飲みすぎると、どうなりますか。

　　B:　そうですね。お酒を飲みすぎると、顔が赤くなります。

例

1.

2.

3.

4.

IX.　困っている人がいます。どうしたのか聞いてみましょう。絵を見て、会話を作りましょう。

例　A:　どうしたんですか。

　　B:　このスカートがはけないんです。

　　A:　どうしてですか。

　　B:　ちょっと小さすぎるんです。

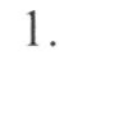

1.

2.

3.

4.

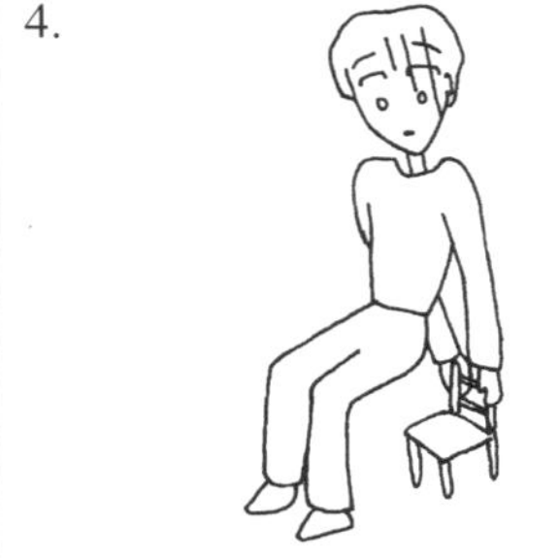

5.

6.

X.　読む練習（ソンさんの作文）

私達の大学は１８６８年3月２３日にそうりつされました。始めは、となりのまちにキャンパスがありましたが、１８７３年にここにひっこししました。その時、学生は全部で１９１人でしたが、今は、三万人ぐらいが勉強しています。その中で、八千五百人いじょうは大学院生です。そして、けんきゅうもさかんです。留学生も多いです。

この大学には学生のグループが５００いじょうあります。そして、いつも色々なかつどうをしています。その中の一つは大学の新聞で、「デイリー・キャンパス・ニュース」とよばれています。

この新聞は、１８７１年に始めてはっこうされましたが、今も学生が作っています。この新聞はただで、大学やこのまちのニュースなどが書かれています。学期中(がっきちゅう)は、月曜日から金曜日まで毎日はっこうされます。夏休みは、一週間に二度です。学生はもちろん読みますが、大学の近くに住んでいる人達も読んでいます。

ほかのかつどうを知りたかったら、昼ごろカフェテリアの前に行ってみて下さい。色々なグループのテーブルがあって、とてもにぎやかです。

正しい答えには○、まちがっている答えには×を書いて下さい。

1.　(　　) ソンさんの大学は１８７３年につくられました。
2.　(　　) ソンさんの大学は、さいしょは小さかったですが、今はとても大きいです。
3.　(　　) ソンさんが勉強しているキャンパスは大学院生の方が学部生(がくぶせい)より多いです。
4.　(　　) ソンさんの大学の学生は勉強とけんきゅうしかしません。
5.　(　　) この大学の新聞の名前は「デイリー・キャンパス・ニュース」です。
6.　(　　)「デイリー・キャンパス・ニュース」は１８７１年からはっこうされています。
7.　(　　)「デイリー・キャンパス・ニュース」は先生達が作っている新聞です。
8.　(　　) 今は春学期です。今日は木曜日ですから、新しい「デイリー・キャンパス・ニュース」を読むことができます。
9.　(　　)「デイリー・キャンパス・ニュース」は大学の新聞ですから、学生しか読みません。
10.　(　　) 昼ごろカフェテリアの前に行くと、色々な学生のかつどうが見られます。

新しい漢字

お願い (ねが)	泳ぐ (およ)	作者 (さくしゃ)	自然 (しぜん)	死ぬ (し)	成績 (せいせき)
全然 (ぜんぜん)	地下鉄 (ちかてつ)	注意 (ちゅうい)	注文 (ちゅうもん)	次 (つぎ)	泣く (な)
昼 (ひる)	昼寝 (ひるね)	弱い (よわ)	笑う (わら)		

新しい使い方

音楽会 (おんがくかい)	男の子 (おとこのこ)	女の子 (おんなのこ)	学部生 (がくぶせい)	貸し出す (かしだす)	学期 (がっき) 借り (か)
出す (だ)	計画 (けいかく)	社長 (しゃちょう)	せかい中 (じゅう)	飛ぶ (と)	花火 (はなび)
はり出す (だ)	火 (ひ)	前田 (まえだ)	めざまし時計 (どけい)		物語 (ものがたり)
悪口 (わるぐち)					

Radicals: 金(かね)へん・れっか

金 is a radical called 金(かね)へん. It appears in 銀 "silver" and 鉄 "iron". The 金へん漢字 are related to the notion of metal.

The 足 radical 灬 is called れっか or れんが "fire in a row", or 四(よ)つ点(てん) "four dots". We have learned two れっか漢字: 然 and 熱. Although 魚 also has this shape, it is not included in the

願	一	厂	厂	厂	斤	盾	盾	厚	原	原
ねが（い）	原	原	原	原	願	願	願	願	願	
	to wish									
泳	丶	丶	氵	氵	汀	汈	泳	泳		
およ（ぐ）	*to swim*									
画	一	丆	丙	而	面	画	画	画		
ガ・カク	*picture, plan:* 映画 *movie,* 計画 *plan,* 日本画 *Japanese paintings*									

自	シ・ジ	*self:* 自然 *nature,* 自転車 *bicycle (self turning wheel),* 自分 *self*
然	ゼン	*proper:* 自然 *nature,* 全然 *(not) at all*
死	し（ぬ）	*death*
成	セイ	*to become:* 成績 *grade*
績	セキ	*unreeling:* 成績 *grade*
下	カ・した・くだ（さい）	*below, under, down:* 下さい *please give downward,* 下手（へた）*bad at,* 下がる（さがる）*to go down,* 下げる（さげる）*to lower,* 地下鉄 *subway*
鉄	てつ	*iron:* 地下鉄 *subway*
注	チュウ	*to pour:* 注意 *warning,* 注文 *order*
文	ブン・モン	*sentence, text:* 英文学 *English literature,* 日本文学 *Japanese literature,* 文化 *culture,* 文法 *grammar,* 注文 *order*

次	つぎ	*next*
飛	ヒ・と（ぶ）	*to fly:* 飛行機 *airplane (flying machine)*
泣	な（く）	*to cry*
昼	ひる	*noon, daytime:* 昼ごはん *lunch,* 昼寝 *nap*
語	ゴ・がたり	*word, language:* 日本語 *Japanese,* 英語 *English,* 物語 *tale*
弱	よわ（い）	*weak*
笑	わら（う）	*to laugh*

group because 魚 by itself is a radical.

漢字の復習

I.　読みましょう。

1. 兄の専門は生物学です。
2. 石川先生のお兄さんは新宿に住んでいらっしゃるそうです。
3. 毎朝、花に水をやって下さい。
4. 雪が降ると、事故が多くなるので、困ります。
5. 熱があって、頭が痛かったんですが、お医者さんに薬をもらって飲んだら、すぐ楽になりました。

II.　□ の中に漢字を書いて下さい。単語が四つできます。どんな単語になりますか。
→ indicates the direction to read.

(例)(れい) 人気（にんき）　　気分（きぶん）　　病気（びょうき）　　気持ち（きもち）

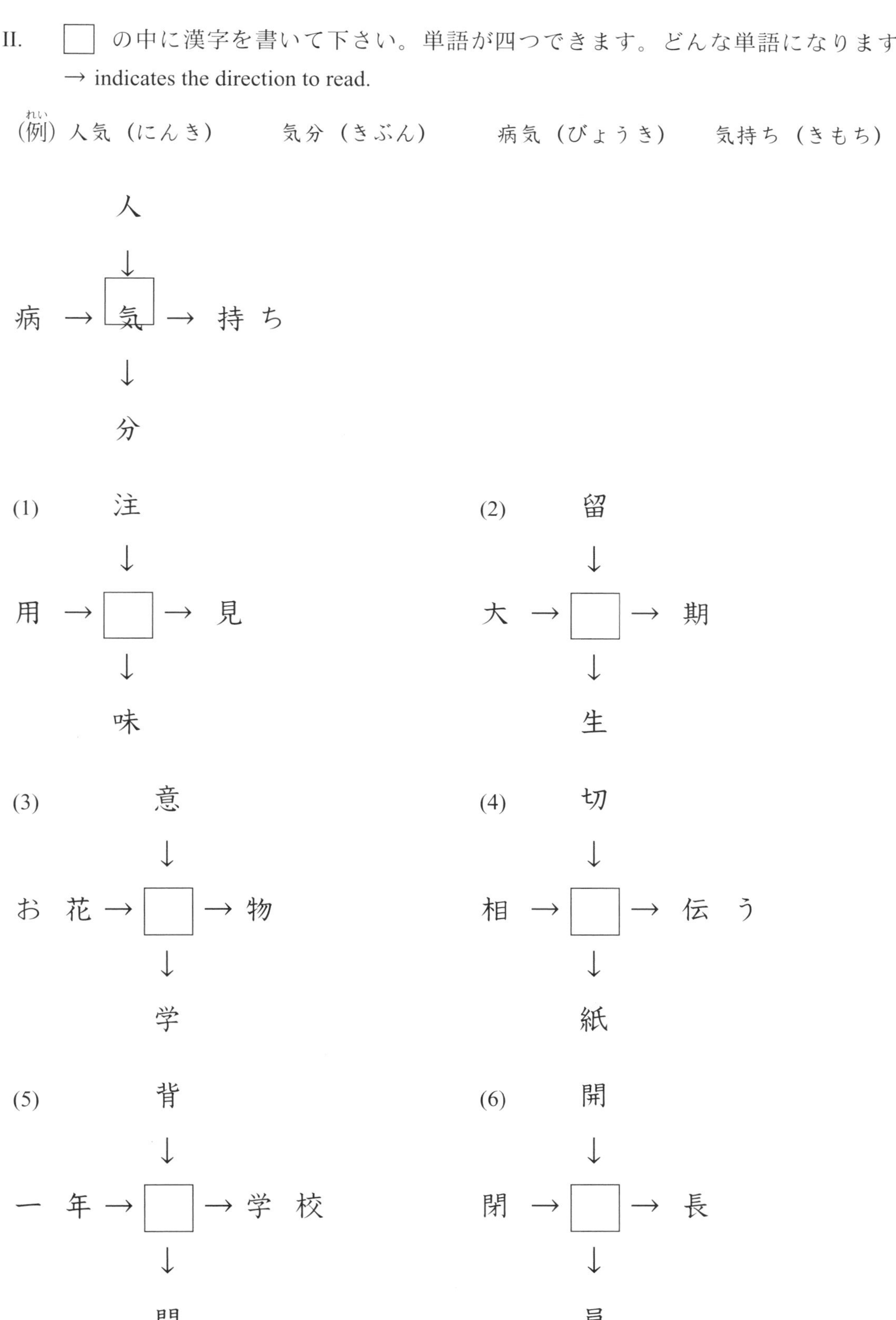

新しい語彙(ごい)

いや	(ナ)	*annoying, unpleasant*
うつす	(ウ)(t)	*to copy*
エネルギー		*energy*
おこす	(ウ)(t)	*to wake (someone) up*
男(おとこ)の子(こ)		*boy*
音楽会(おんがくかい)		*music concert*
女(おんな)の子(こ)		*girl*
かえる		*frog*
学部生(がくぶせい)		*undergraduate*
貸(か)し出(だ)す	(ウ)(t)	*to lend out*
学期(がっき)		*semester, academic term*
かつどう（する）		*activity*
かむ	(ウ)(t)	*to bite*
借(か)り出(だ)す	(ウ)(t)	*to check out (e.g. a book)*
きけん	(ナ)	*dangerous*
聞(き)こえる	(ル)(i)	*to be audible*
くさ		*grass*
グッスリ		*deep sleep (sound symbolic)*
クレジットカード		*credit card*
計画(けいかく)（する）		*plan*
元気(げんき)		*high spirits, good health*
ゴクンと		*swallowing (sound symbolic)*
ことわる	(ウ)(t)	*to decline (an offer)*
ころす	(ウ)(t)	*to kill*
さいふ		*purse, wallet*
さかん	(ナ)	*flourishing*
作者(さくしゃ)		*author*
しかる	(ウ)(t)	*to scold*
自然(しぜん)		*nature*
社長(しゃちょう)		*company president*
ストレス		*stress*
スパイ		*spy*
すり		*pickpocket*
すると		*then*
せかい中(じゅう)		*all over the world*
そうりつ（する）		*establishment, founding*
ただ		*free of charge*
たたく	(ウ)(t)	*to pat*
たのむ	(ウ)(t)	*to ask, request*
たまる	(ウ)(i)	*to accumulate*
貯金(ちょきん)ばこ		*piggy bank*
飛(と)ぶ	(ウ)(i)	*to fly*
とめる	(ル)(t)	*to stop*
どろぼう		*thief*
泣(な)く	(ウ)(i)	*to cry*
にもつ		*baggage*
ぬすむ	(ウ)(t)	*to steal*
ばか	(ナ)	*stupid*

はかい（する）	*destruction*
はっこう（する）	*publication, printing (newspapers, magazines, etc.)*
はっぴょう（する）	*presentation*
花火（はなび）	*fireworks*
はり出（だ）す　ⓤ ⓣ	*to post*
火（ひ）	*spark, fire*
ひく　ⓤ ⓣ	*to run over*
昼（ひる）	*noon*
ふむ　ⓤ ⓣ	*to step on*
へび	*snake*
ペラペラ	*fluently (sound symbolic)*
ペロっと	*rapid eating (sound symbolic)*
ほめる　ⓡ ⓣ	*to praise*
マイク	*microphone*
見（み）える　ⓡ ⓘ	*to be visible*
むし	*insect*
めざまし時計（どけい）	*alarm clock*
よごす　ⓤ ⓣ	*to stain, soil*
弱（よわ）い　ⓘ	*weak*
ラブレター	*love letter*
わたす　ⓤ ⓣ	*to hand over*
笑（わら）う　ⓤ ⓘ ⓣ	*to smile, laugh, laugh at*
悪口（わるぐち）	*slander, (Lit.) bad mouth*

(Circled markers as printed: ⓤ = ㋒ (ウ), ⓡ = ル, ⓘ (after 弱い) = ㋑ (イ), ⓘ = i, ⓣ = t.)

名前

げんじものがたり（源氏物語）	*The Tale of Genji*
サンディエゴ	*San Diego*
前田（まえだ）	*Maeda*

親を心配させる
Making Parents Worry

むりやり勉強させることはできません
We can't force him to study

1
小山さん、元気がありませんね。どうしたんですか。
じつは、両親から手紙が来たんですけど……。
2
どなたかご病気ですか。
いえ、病気じゃないんですが、弟がちょっと……。
3
どうしましたか。
4
大学
弟は来年、大学受験なのに、全然勉強しないそうです。
5
そうですか。それで、ご両親が心配なさっているんですね。
6
ええ、そうなんです。ビデオゲームやウェブで一日中遊んでばかりいるそうです。弟はコンピューターが大好きなんです。
7
そうですか。そんなにコンピューターが好きなら、コンピューターの専門学校へ行かせたらどうですか。
ええ、でも、両親は弟を大学へ行かせたがっているんです。
8
弟は注意されると、はんこうします。それに、子供じゃありませんから、つくえの前にすわらせて、むりやり勉強させることはできません。
9
たしかにそうですね。難しいですね。それに、日本の大学受験はとてもきびしいそうですね。
大学

会話

1　ソン　：小山さん、元気がありませんね。どうしたんですか。

Koyama-san, you look depressed. What's the matter?

小山　：じつは、両親から手紙が来たんですけど……。

Actually, I got a letter from my parents …

2　ソン　：どなたかご病気ですか。

Is someone sick?

小山　：いえ、病気じゃないんですが、弟がちょっと……。

No, no one is sick, but my brother's been kind of …

3　ソン　：どうしましたか。

What's wrong?

4　小山　：弟は来年、大学受験(じゅけん)なのに、全然勉強しないそうです。

Even though he'll be taking college entrance exams next year, but they say he isn't studying at all.

5　ソン　：そうですか。それで、ご両親が心配なさっているんですね。

Oh really? Then your parents must be worried about him.

6　小山　：ええ、そうなんです。ビデオゲームやウェブで一日中遊んでばかりいるそうです。弟はコンピューターが大好きなんです。

Yes, they are. Apparently he does nothing but play video games and surf the Web all day. He really adores computers.

7　ソン　：そうですか。そんなにコンピューターが好きなら、コンピューターの専門学校(せんもんがっこう)へ行かせたらどうですか。

Does he? If he likes computers that much, why not let him go to a computer school?

小山 : ええ、でも、両親は弟を大学へ行かせたがっているんです。
Yes (that might be good), but my parents want him to go to college.

8 小山 : 弟は注意されると、はんこうします。それに、子供じゃありませんから、つくえの前にすわらせて、むりやり勉強させることはできません。
If he gets warned, my brother just rebels. Besides, he's not a child, so we can't make him sit at his desk and study against his will.

9 ソン : たしかにそうですね。難しいですね。それに、日本の大学受験はとてもきびしいそうですね。
That's certainly true. How difficult! And I hear that Japanese college entrance exams are really severe.

10 小山 : 今はむかしほど大変ではありませんが、全然勉強しなければ、落(お)ちてしまいます。
They're not as difficult as they used to be, but you'll fail if you don't study at all.

ソン : そうですか。もう弟さんと話しましたか。
I see. Have you already talked with your brother?

11 小山 : いいえ、まだ話していません。でも、心配ですから、今晩、家に電話してみます。
No, I haven't. But I'm worried, so I'm going to call home tonight.

ソン : 小山さんはとてもやさしいお姉さんですね。
You're such a kind sister, Koyama-san.

使い方

2 ご病気 is the honorific form of 病気, so you cannot use it for yourself or your family members.

いえ is a shortened form of いいえ.

4 受験 is a Sino-Japanese word for 試[験]を[受]ける "to take an (entrance) examination". (It is not used for regular test-taking in a course.) Like in English, in Chinese the direct object is placed after the verb, so 験 appears **after** 受. There are several kinds of entrance examinations in Japan, e.g. 中学受験, 高校受験, 大学受験.

7 専門学校 "vocational school" consists of 専門 "specialization, specialty" and 学校 "school".

文法

26a	Verb Conjugation: Causative フォーム	
26b	Causative Construction	
26c	CLAUSE1 なら CLAUSE2	"If (you say/think that) C1, then C2"
26d	てフォーム + ばかりいる	"do nothing but VERB"
26e	NOUN ばかり VERB	"VERB nothing but NOUN"
26f	まだ + てフォーム + いない	"have not done ~ yet"

26a　Verb Conjugation: Causative フォーム

In this lesson, we are going to study another verb conjugation, the *Causative* フォーム. It can be derived by applying the following rules:

A　**う Verbs:** Stem + a + せる

行かせる、急がせる、返させる、
持たせる、死なせる、運ばせる、
休ませる、送らせる

Like the Negative フォーム and Passive フォーム, the consonant *w* appears if the Dictionary フォーム ends in う, without a preceding consonant.

Final Vowel	あ	い	う	え	お
Conjugation	**Negative**	**Pre- ます**	**Dictionary**	**Conditional**	**Volitional**
	会わ - ない	会い - ます	会う	会え - ば	会おう
	歌わ - ない	歌い - ます	歌う	歌え - ば	歌おう
	使わ - ない	使い - ます	使う	使え - ば	使おう
Conjugation	**Passive**				
	会わ - れる				
	歌わ - れる				
	使わ - れる				
Conjugation	**Causative**				
	会わ - せる				
	歌わ - せる				
	使わ - せる				

B **る Verbs:** Stem + させる

着させる、(シャワーを) あびさせる、
見させる、借りさせる、
考えさせる、受けさせる、上げさせる、
調べさせる、閉めさせる、なれさせる

C **Irregular Verbs**

来る → 来(こ)させる
する → させる

26b Causative Construction

The *causative construction* conveys the meaning that someone (*causer*) makes someone else (*causee*) do something. The means by which the causer brings about this situation is unspecified; it could be by brute force or gentle persuasion. It could also be the case that the causee wants to do something, and the causer merely allows the causee to do it (i.e. lets the causee do something).

A **Intransitive Verbs**

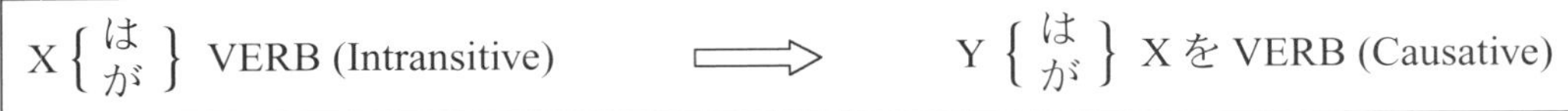

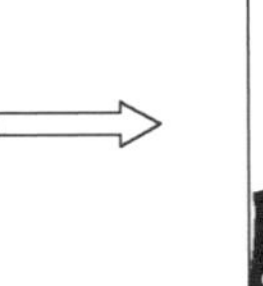

ソンさんは 笑いました。 — *Son-san laughed.*

ミラーさんは ソンさんを 笑わせました。 — *Miller-san made Son-san laugh.*

子供は 学校に行きました。 — *The child went to school.*

お母さんは 子供を 学校に行かせました。 — *The mother made her child go to school.*

私は子供の時、よく病気になって、家族を心配させました。

I became sick frequently when I was a child and made my family worry.

赤ちゃんを泣かせないで下さい。

Please don't make the baby cry.

子供の時、姉はいつも私の物を取って、私を泣かせました。

When I was a child, my older sister always took my things away and made me cry.

入学試験に落ちて、両親をがっかりさせてしまいました。

I failed the entrance examination and caused my parents to be disappointed.

親をよろこばせたいので、一生けんめい勉強しています。

I want to please my parents (Lit. make my parents pleased), so I'm studying very hard.

五月に卒業するよていです。早くしゅうしょくして、親を安心させたいと思います。

I plan to graduate this May. I want to get a job quickly and make my parents feel at ease.

こうえんで子供達を遊ばせて下さい。それから、プールで泳がせて下さい。

Please let the children play in the park, and then please let them swim in the pool.

子供が悪いことをした時には、あやまらせます。

When my children do something bad, I make them apologize.

おどろかせないで下さい。

Please don't startle me. (Lit. Please don't cause me to be startled.)

口の中に物が入っている時は、笑わせないで下さい。

Please don't make me laugh when I have something in my mouth

(Lit.) when something is in my mouth.

B　Transitive Verbs

X {は / が} Y を VERB (Transitive)	⟹	Z {は / が} X に Y を VERB (Causative)

[学生は]作文を書きます。　*Students write compositions.*

先生は[学生に]作文を書かせます。　*The teacher makes the students write compositions.*

子供達にやさいをたくさん食べさせています。

I've been making my children eat a lot of vegetables.

こわされると困るので、ほかの人にコンピューターは使わせません。

I'd be in trouble if my computer got broken, so I don't let other people use it.

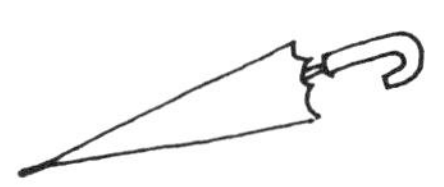

今朝、雨が降りそうだったので、むすこにかさを持って行かせました。

It looked like it would rain this morning, so I had my son take an umbrella.

駅の前の店にどろぼうが入りました。どろぼうは店員にきんこを開けさせたそうです。

A robber broke into the store in front of the station. They say he made the clerk open the safe.

部長(ぶちょう)は毎朝、私にお茶を入れさせます。お茶を入れるのは私の仕事じゃありません。これはセクハラ* です。

My manager makes me prepare tea for him every morning. Making tea is not my job. This is sexual harassment.

日本語の先生方(がた)** は、最初(さいしょ)はとてもやさしくて親切でしたが、今はとてもきびしいです。そして、授業は忙しくて大変です。一日は二十四時間しかありません。ですから、いつも寝不足(ねぶそく)です。私は病気になってしまうかも知れません。

My Japanese teachers were very gentle and kind at first, but now they're very strict. What's more, class is hectic and difficult. There are only 24 hours in a day, so I never get enough sleep. I think I might get sick.

* As explained in 第二課, **2h**, the sound structure of Japanese requires that each consonant (except an [n]) be followed by a vowel. Loan words from English can therefore become very long. For example, the five-syllable phrase *sexual harassment* becomes a ten-mora phrase in Japanese, セクシャル・ハラスメント (see Lesson 1, **1f** for the concept of *mora*). Frequently, therefore, loan words are abbreviated, often by taking the initial two moras from each word.

アメリカン・フットボール → アメフト
カー・ナビゲーション → カーナビ
デジタル・カメラ → デジカメ
ワード・プロセッサー → ワープロ
パーソナル・コンピューター → パソコン
ネットスケープ → ネスケ
コンビニエンス・ストア → コンビニ

** 方 is another plural marker and is politer than 達, e.g. お客様方(きゃくさまがた).

*** 一つ一つの X "each X (thing)"
一人一人(ひとりひとり)の X "each X (person)"

先生は学生に毎週新しい漢字を十三覚えさせます。

The teachers make their students memorize 13 new kanji every week.

先生は学生に一つ一つ(ひとひと)の*** 漢字を百回書かせます。

The teachers make their students write each kanji 100 times.

先生は学生に毎週新しい単語を五十いじょう覚えさせます。

The teachers make their students memorize more than 50 new words every week.

先生は学生に毎日二時間も予習と復習をさせます。

The teachers make their students prepare (for the next class) and review (previous material) as many as two hours every day.

先生は学生に毎週宿題を出させます。

The teachers make their students submit an assignment every week.

先生は学生に毎週試験を受けさせます。

The teachers make their students take a quiz every week.

先生は学生に教室でスキットをはっぴょうさせます。

The teachers make their students present a skit in class.

先生は学生に長い作文を書かせたり、難しいテープを聞かせたりします。

The teachers make their students write long compositions and listen to difficult tapes, among other things.

私達は時々不安になります。でも、先生は「だいじょうぶですよ。がんばりましょう。」と言って、私達をはげまして下さいます。私達は本当に日本語が上手になりました。ですから、来年もまた、日本語のコースを取ろうと思います。

We sometimes feel uneasy. But the teachers encourage us by saying, "It'll be alright. Let's keep at it." We've become really good at Japanese. So I think I'm going to take a Japanese course again next year.

私のガールフレンドの話を聞いて下さい。どう思いますか。結婚しない方がいいですか。アドバイスして下さい。

Please listen to this story about my girlfriend. What do you think? Would it be better if I didn't marry her? Please give me advice.

買物の時、買った物を全部私に持たせます。

When we go shopping, she makes me carry everything she bought.

デートの時、いつも私にお金をはらわせます。

When we go out on date, she always makes me pay.

パーティーに行くと、いつもお酒をたくさん飲んで、私に運転させます。

When we go to parties, she always drinks a lot and makes me drive.

かのじょの家で食べた時は、いつも私におさらを洗わせます。

When I eat at her house, she always makes me wash the dishes.

私に部屋のそうじもさせます。

She makes me clean her room, too.

そして、私に宿題をさせます。

And she makes me do her homework.

授業をサボる時*、いつも私に宿題を出させます。

When she cuts classes, she always makes me turn in her homework.

そして、私に言いわけを考えさせます。

And she makes me think of an excuse (for her).

* The verb サボる is derived from the word "sabotage", so its stem is normally written in カタカナ.

26c CLAUSE1 なら CLAUSE2 "If (you say / think that) C1, then C2"

Plain

Sometimes, we use newly acquired information as the basis for an action or statement whose applicability is contingent on the validity of the information. For example:

小山: 弟はコンピューターが好きなんです。
My brother likes computers.

ソン: コンピューターが好きなら、コンピューターの専門学校へ行かせたらどうですか。
If he likes computers, why don't they (your parents) make / let him go to a computer school?

Here, ソンさん's advice is applicable if 小山さん's preceding statement is true; i.e. her brother indeed likes computers. In this construction, the predicate of CLAUSE1 must be in a Plain フォーム (for verbs and い-adjectives) or the stem of な-adjectives. This construction is frequently used with ～方がいい and ～たらどうですか (cf. 第二十三課).

Son : *My eyesight has been getting worse recently, so I'm thinking about buying a bigger monitor.*

Miller : *If you're buying a monitor, the University Computer Store is having a sale now.*

Son : *Koyama-san, what's the matter?*

Koyama : *I've got a cold and a little bit of a fever.*

Son : *If you have a fever, you'd better go see a doctor.*

何になさいますか。
茶わんむしをお願いします。
すみませんが、茶わんむしは終わってしまいました。
茶わんむしがないなら、ゆどうふにします。

Waiter : *May I take your order (Lit. What would you like to have)?*

Miller : *I'll have* chawan-mushi.

Waiter : *Sorry, but we are out of* chawan-mushi.

Miller : *If you don't have* chawan-mushi, *I'll have* yu-dōfu.

Miller : *It's gotten a little cold, hasn't it?*

Watanabe : *If you're cold, shall I turn on the heater?*

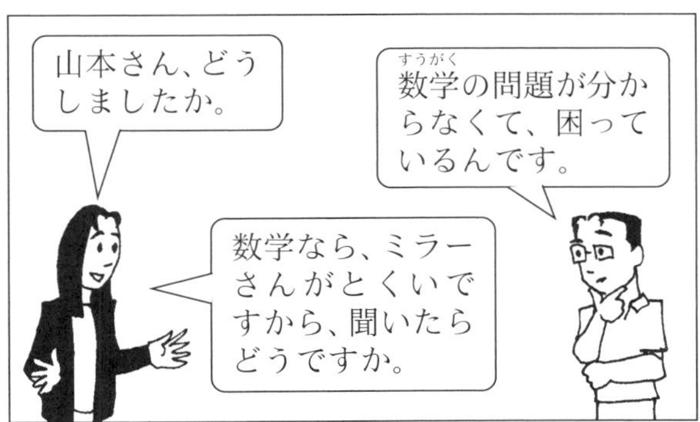

Son : *Yamamoto-san, what's the matter?*

Yamamoto : *I'm in trouble because I don't understand a math problem.*

Son : *If it's math, Miller-san is good at it, so why don't you ask him?*

A　　Verbs

ゆうびんきょくへ行くなら、８０セント切手を２０枚買って来て下さい。

If you're going to the post office, please buy (and bring) twenty 80-cent stamps.

食べないなら、私が食べてもいいですか。

If you aren't going to eat it, may I eat it?

バークレーに行くなら、ソンさんにキャンパスを案内(あんない)してもらったらどうですか。

If you go to Berkeley, how about asking Son-san to give you a campus tour?

おうぼするつもりなら、五月三日までにおうぼ用紙(ようし)を出して下さい。

If you intend to apply, please turn in the application form by May 3.

スピーチコンテストにさんかするなら、金曜日までにげんこうを書いて下さい。

If you participate in the speech contest, please write a draft by Friday.

のりまきが食べたいなら、小山さんに作ってもらったらどうですか。

If you want to eat norimaki, *why don't you ask / get Koyama-san to make some?*

日本語が読めるなら、しゅうしょくするのはかんたんでしょう。

If you can read Japanese, it must be easy to get a job.

たフォーム + なら is possible, but the use of ～たのなら is more common.

ラップトップをぬすまれたのなら、けいさつに行った方がいいですよ。

If your laptop was stolen, you'd better go to the police.

おうぼ用紙をもらわなかったのなら、すぐに先生のオフィスへ行った方がいいですよ。

If you didn't receive an application form, you'd better go to your teacher's office immediately.

B　　い -Adjectives

このCDがほしいなら、日本まちで買えますよ。

If you want this CD, you can buy it in Japantown.

このふくがよくないなら、私は着て行くふくがありません。

If this piece of clothing isn't good, I don't have anything else to wear (when I go there).

C　　な -Adjectives

If a な -adjective is in the non-past affirmative form, add なら without だ. Otherwise, use a Plain フォーム.

こうつうが不便(ふべん)なら、ひっこしした方がいいですね。

If transportation (commuting) is inconvenient, you'd better move (to a better place).

しあわせ { で(は)ないなら / じゃないなら }、りこんした方がいいかも知れません。

If you aren't happy, it might be better to get divorced.

Like with verbs, い-adjective たフォーム + なら and な-adjective + だったなら are possible, but the use of ～たのなら is more common.

そんなに楽しかったのなら、また行きましょうね。

If it was that enjoyable (If you enjoyed it that much), let's go there again.

だめだったのなら、来年また受験します。

If it was no good (If I failed), I'll take the entrance exam again next year.

D　Nominal Predicates

If a nominal predicate is in the non-past affirmative form, add なら without だ. Otherwise, use a Plain フォーム.

日曜日なら家にいます。
If it's on Sunday, I'll be at home.
寝不足なら、もう帰ってもいいですよ。
If you haven't slept enough, you can go home now.
病気じゃないなら、ちゃんと仕事をして下さい。
If you aren't sick, please work properly (i.e. do not become lax).
その時子供だったのなら、覚えていないかも知れませんね。
If you were a child then, you might not remember it.

26d　てフォーム + ばかりいる　"do nothing but VERB"

This construction is used to emphasize/exaggerate a monotonous activity.

むすめはコンピューターで遊んでばかりいます。
My daughter does nothing but play on her computer.
兄はガールフレンドにふられて、泣いてばかりいます。
My older brother was dumped by his girlfriend and does nothing but cry.
本田(ほんだ)さんはさっきから笑ってばかりいます。何がおもしろいんでしょうか。
Since a little while ago, Honda-san has been doing nothing but laugh. What's so funny?
川本(かわもと)さんは最近、授業中に寝てばかりいます。
Kawamoto-san has been doing nothing but sleep in class recently.

26e　NOUN ばかり VERB　"VERB nothing but NOUN"

This construction is similar to **26d**. When there is a noun in the phrase, you can mark it with ばかり instead of marking the verb. When the noun is the direct object, を must be omitted; otherwise, ばかり is added after the particle. As you can see in the following, sometimes **26d** and **26e** have slightly different meanings, but at other times they are basically synonymous.

Direct Object

家田さんはまんがを読んでばかりいます。

Ieda-san does nothing but read comic books.

家田さんはまんがばかり読んでいます。

Ieda-san reads nothing but comic books.

あの人はもんくを言ってばかりいるので、みんなにきらわれています。

That person does nothing but complain, so he's hated by everyone.

あの人はもんくばかり言っているので、みんなにきらわれています。

That person says nothing but complaints, so he's hated by everyone.

Indirect Object

家田さんは友達に電話をしてばかりいます。

Ieda-san does nothing but call his friends.

家田さんは友達にばかり電話をしています。

Ieda-san calls nobody but his friends.

Goal

川本さんはバーへ行ってばかりいます。

Kawamoto-san does nothing but go to bars.

川本さんはバーへばかり行っています。

Kawamoto-san goes nowhere but bars.

Means

家田さんはコンピューターで遊んでばかりいます。

Ieda-san does nothing but play on his computer.

家田さんはコンピューターでばかり遊んでいます。

Ieda-san plays nothing but computer (games).

Verbal Nouns

本田さんふうふはけんかしてばかりいます。

本田さんふうふはけんかばかりしています。

Mr. and Mrs. Honda do nothing but quarrel.

ソンさんは先月買い物してばかりいました。

ソンさんは先月買い物ばかりしました。

Son-san did nothing but shop last month.

外食* { してばかりいる / ばかりしている } と、からだに悪い**ですから、時々は自分で料理をした方がいいですよ。

It's bad for your health if you always eat out, so you'd better cook for yourself sometimes.

> *外食 = 外で食べること
> **X に悪い　*bad for X*
>
> あまい物は、はに悪い。
> *Sweets are bad for your teeth.*
>
> 暗い所で本を読むのは、目に悪いですよ。
> *Reading books in dark places is bad for your eyes.*

私達ふうふの話を聞いて下さい。ひどいと思いませんか。しゅじんとりこんした方がいいでしょうか。

Please listen to our (married couple) story. Don't you think it's terrible? Should I divorce my husband?

しゅじんは毎日会社から帰って来ると、テレビばかり見ています。

Everyday when my husband comes home from work, he does nothing but watch TV.

かれは夜、お酒ばかり飲んでいます。

At night, he does nothing but drink alcohol.

週末は一日中寝てばかりいます。

On weekends, he does nothing but sleep all day.

寝ていない時は、ビデオゲームばかりしています。

When he's not sleeping, he does nothing but play video games.

私が「たまには旅行しましょう」と言うと、反対(はんたい)ばかりします。

If I say "Let's travel once in a while," he always objects.

去年のクリスマスには、自分の物ばかり買いました。

Last Christmas, he bought things only for himself.

26f　まだ + てフォーム + いない　"have not done ~ yet"

もう　**まだ**

When もう appears in an affirmative sentence, it means "already" (cf. 第五課).

もう、昼ごはんを食べましたか。	*Have you already eaten lunch?*
はい、もう食べました。	*Yes, I already have.*

In 第五課, when the answer was negative, いいえ、まだです "No, not yet" was used. In this lesson we are going to study more uses of まだ.

A まだ in Affirmative Sentences

When まだ appears in an affirmative sentence, it means "still" (cf. 第八課). This まだ can be used with all types of predicates.

妹はまだ高校生です。	*My sister is still a high school student.*
兄はまだニューヨークにいます。	*My older brother is still in New York.*
まだ走れます。	*I can still run.*
このラップトップはまだ高いですが、もうすぐ安くなりますよ。	*This laptop is still expensive, but it'll soon get cheaper.*

When まだ is used with an action verb — rather than an adjective, nominal predicate, or stative verb (e.g. いる／ある) — you need to use the 〜ている construction.

まだ勉強しているんですか。	*Are you still studying?*

B まだ in Negative Sentences

When まだ appears in a negative sentence, it means "(not) yet".

まだ日本語の新聞は読めません。	*I can't read Japanese newspapers yet.*

C もう Questions and まだ Answers

むすこさんはもう大学生ですか。	*Is your son already a college student?*
いいえ、まだ高校生です。	*No, he's still a high school student.*

When the answer to a もう question with an action verb is negative, you need to use 〜ていない, rather than 〜なかった.

	もう、昼ごはんを食べましたか。	*Have you already eaten lunch?*
○	いいえ、まだ食べていません。	*No, I haven't eaten lunch yet.*
×	いいえ、まだ食べませんでした。	

Compare the following exchanges:

(1)	昨日、宿題を出しましたか。	*Did you turn in your homework yesterday?*
(2)	はい、出しました。	*Yes, I did (turn it in).*
(3)	いいえ、出しませんでした。	*No, I didn't (turn it in).*
(4)	もう宿題を出しましたか。	*Have you already turned in your homework?*
(5)	はい、もう出しました。	*Yes, I have (turned it in) already.*
(6)	いいえ、まだ出していません。	*No, I haven't (turned it in) yet.*

In (1)-(3), what is at issue is whether the addressee turned in his/her homework yesterday. Therefore, if the answer is negative, the simple past tense is used, as shown in (3), to indicate that the event of submitting the homework did not take place yesterday. In (4)-(6), by contrast, the use of もう indicates that the focus is whether the homework has already been turned in, i.e. the current state of the homework. Thus, when the answer is negative, you need to use the negative of ～ている, as shown in (6), rather than the simple past. When the answer is affirmative, either the simple past, e.g. (5), or ～ています/～てあります can be used: はい、もう出しています/出してあります.

練習問題

I. Causativeフォームを作りましょう。

1. 行く	6. やめる	11. 困る	16. 歌う
2. 来る	7. 休む	12. 話す	17. おごる
3. する	8. さんかする	13. おこる	18. 急ぐ
4. いる	9. よろこぶ	14. 遊ぶ	19. 運ぶ
5. 手伝う	10. 待つ	15. 見る	20. 書く

II. 絵を見て、Causativeフォームを使った文を作りましょう。

例(れい) お父さんは<u>むすめに仕事を手伝わせました</u>。

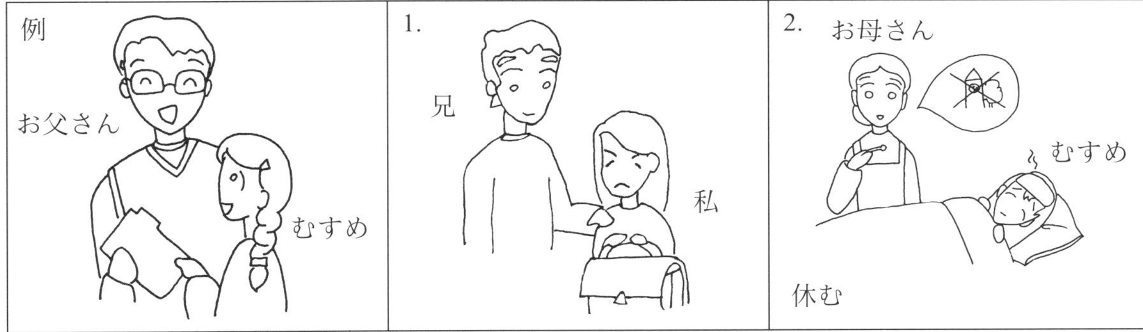

1. 兄は____________________。

2. お母さんは____________________。

3.　先生はクラスで＿＿＿＿＿＿＿＿＿＿＿＿＿＿＿＿＿＿＿＿＿＿＿＿。

4.　先生は＿＿＿＿＿＿＿＿＿＿＿＿＿＿＿＿＿＿＿＿＿＿＿＿＿＿＿。

5.　先生は＿＿＿＿＿＿＿＿＿＿＿＿＿＿＿＿＿＿＿＿＿＿＿＿＿＿＿。

III.　下の絵を見て下さい。はこの中の Verb を Causative フォームにして文をかんせいしましょう。

心配する	おこる	よろこぶ	泣く	笑う	困る	おどろく

例(れい)　子供はケーキが食べたいと言いながら泣いて、お母さんを困らせました。

1.　えんどうさんはJポップを聞いていました。でも、音をとても大きくしたので、ルームメートを
＿＿＿＿＿＿＿＿＿＿＿＿＿＿＿＿＿＿＿＿＿＿＿＿
しまいました。

2.　お父さんはいつもおみやげを買って帰ります。でも、今日は何も買って帰らないで、子供を
＿＿＿＿＿＿＿＿＿＿＿＿＿＿＿＿＿＿＿＿＿＿＿＿。

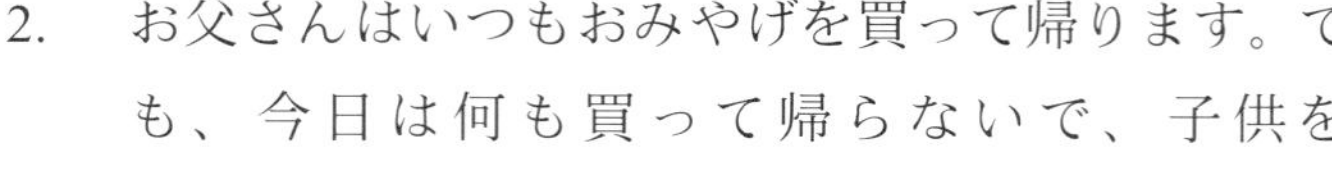

3.　本田さんは試験でまんてんを取って、ご両親を
＿＿＿＿＿＿＿＿＿＿＿＿＿＿＿＿＿＿＿＿＿＿＿＿。

4.　川本さんはボーイフレンドと出かけました。そして、夜中の十二時になったのに、家に電話しないで、ご両親を＿＿＿＿＿＿＿＿＿＿＿＿＿＿＿＿。

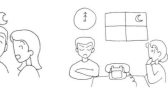

5. 本田さんは、後ろからそっと川本さんのかたをたたいて、(川本さんを) ______________________
______________________。

6. 川本さんはじょうだんを言って、よく友達を
____
______________________。

IV. 次の会話をかんせいして下さい。

1. 客　：コンピューターがほしいんですが……。
店員：このコンピューターはどうですか。今セール中ですから、安くなっていますよ。
客　：そうですか。______________________なら、買いましょう。

2. 川本：もうこの本を読みましたか。とてもおもしろいですよ。
本田：そうですか。______________________なら、私も読んでみます。

3. 川本：パーティーをするんですが、来ませんか。カラオケをするんです。
本田：そうですか。私は歌うのが大好きですから、______________________なら、もちろん行きます。

4. 本田：川本さん、今晩忙しいですか。
川本：いいえ、ひまですよ。
本田：そうですか。______________________なら、いっしょに映画を見に行きませんか。
川本：いいですねえ。行きましょう。

V. ワンさんにアドバイスしましょう。

例　本田：ワンさん、どうしたんですか。
ワン：明日の朝、六時におきなくてはいけないんです。
本田：そうですか。それは大変ですね。六時におきなくてはいけないなら、今晩早く寝た方がいいですよ。
(or) 今晩夜(よ)ふかしをしない方がいいですよ。

1. ワン：本田さん、昨日新しいパソコンを買ったんですが、使い方がよく分からないんです。
本田：そうですか。______________________なら、
______________________どうですか。

2. 本田：ワンさん、どうしたんですか。
   ワン：先生から借りたCDプレーヤーをこわしてしまったんです。
   本田：そうですか。＿＿＿＿＿＿＿＿＿＿＿＿＿＿＿＿＿＿＿＿＿＿＿＿なら、
   ＿＿＿＿＿＿＿＿＿＿＿＿＿＿＿＿＿＿＿＿＿＿＿＿方がいいですよ。

3. ワン：本田さん、来年日本へ行きたいと思っているんですが、どうしたらいいでしょう。
   本田：＿＿＿＿＿＿＿＿＿＿＿＿＿＿＿＿＿＿＿＿＿＿＿＿なら、
   ＿＿＿＿＿＿＿＿＿＿＿＿＿＿＿＿＿＿＿＿＿＿＿＿どうですか。

4. 本田：どうしたんですか。顔色が悪いですね。
   ワン：ええ、ちょっとかぜをひいてしまって、熱があるんです。
   本田：それは大変ですね。＿＿＿＿＿＿＿＿＿＿＿＿＿＿＿＿＿＿＿＿＿＿＿＿なら、
   ＿＿＿＿＿＿＿＿＿＿＿＿＿＿＿＿＿＿＿＿＿＿＿＿方がいいですよ。

5. 本田：ワンさん、日本語の勉強はどうですか。
   ワン：とても楽しいです。でも、漢字が覚えられなくて困っているんです。
   本田：そうですか。＿＿＿＿＿＿＿＿＿＿＿＿＿＿＿＿＿＿＿＿＿＿＿＿なら、
   ＿＿＿＿＿＿＿＿＿＿＿＿＿＿＿＿＿＿＿＿＿＿＿＿どうでしょうか。

VI. 次の文を読んで下さい。そして、「ばかり」を使って質問に答えて下さい。

えんどうさんと本田さんとワンさんはルームメートです。えんどうさんは音楽を聞くのが好きです。でも、クラシックやジャズは聞きません。いつも家へ帰ってからJポップを聞いています。そして、週末は朝から晩まで何もしないで寝ています。

本田さんは大学院生で、いつも勉強しています。そして、忙しくて時間がないので、料理をしません。毎日外食しています。

ワンさんはクラスが終わった後で、図書館で勉強してから家へ帰ります。ですから、家では勉強しません。そして、夜はずっと、まんがを読んでいます。

1. えんどうさんは音楽を聞きますか。どんな音楽を聞きますか。
2. えんどうさんは週末に出かけますか。何をしますか。
3. 本田さんはどんな大学院生ですか。
4. 本田さんは家でごはんを食べますか。
5. ワンさんは時々家で勉強しますか。
6. ワンさんは家へ帰ってから勉強しますか。夜は何をしますか。

VII.　(　　　　)の中に「もう」か「まだ」を書いて下さい。

1.　ワン　：(　　　　)宿題をしましたか。
　　本田　：いいえ、(　　　　)していません。
2.　ワン　：(　　　　)この本を読みましたか。
　　本田　：はい、(　　　　)読んでしまいました。
3.　ワン　：外は(　　　　)明るいですか。
　　本田　：いいえ、(　　　　)暗くなりましたよ。早く家へ帰りましょう。
4.　ワン　：妹さんは(　　　　)大学生ですか。
　　本田　：いいえ、(　　　　)高校生です。

VIII.「もう」か「まだ」を使って、次の質問の答えを書いて下さい。

1.　もう日本語が上手に話せますか。
2.　もう第二十六課の漢字を練習しましたか。
3.　もう第二十六課の文法を勉強しましたか。
4.　もう期末試験のじゅんびを始めましたか。

IX.　次の文を読んで、質問に答えて下さい。

最近、日本の子供達は遊びに行かないそうです。学校から帰って来ると、すぐに習い事やじゅくに行かなくてはいけないからです。今、小学生がじゅくに行くのは当然で、じゅくに行く子供の方がじゅくに行かない子供よりずっと多いそうです。ちょっと成績が悪くなると、先生に「じゅくに行っていますか」と聞かれるそうです。そして、「行っていないなら、行った方がいいですよ」と言われるそうです。

習い事は、親がきめます。今、人気がある習い事は、習字、ピアノ、バレエ、水泳、英会話などで、習い事を三つか四つしている子供が多いそうです。ですから、子供達は学校から帰ると、習い事ばかりしています。

むかしも親は子供に習い事をさせました。けれども、習い事をする子供は今ほど多くありませんでした。人気があった習い事は、習字、ピアノ、そろばんなどで、子供達は一週間に一度か二度しか習い事に行きませんでした。習い事がない日には、子供達は学校から帰ると、すぐに友達と近くのあき地やこうえんで遊びました。そして、時々おそく家へ帰って、親を心配させました。

みなさんは、毎日習い事やじゅくに行かなくてはいけない子供達はかわいそうだと思うかも知れません。けれども、子供達はじゅくや習い事を楽しんでいるそうです。じゅくや習い事へ行けば、友達といっしょにいられるからです。今は、友達といっしょに、じゅくで勉強したり習い事をしたりするのが子供達の遊びだそうです。

1. 最近、日本の子供達は、学校から帰った後で何をしますか。
2. 最近、人気がある習い事は何ですか。
3. むかしの子供達も習い事をしましたか。どんな習い事をしましたか。
4. むかしの日本の子供達は、学校から帰った後で何をしましたか。
5. あなたが子供だった時、じゅくや習い事に行きましたか。
6. あなたが子供だった時、学校から帰った後で何をして遊びましたか。
7. 今の子供達の遊び方と、むかしの子供達の遊び方は同じですか。ちがいますか。ちがうなら、どうちがいますか。

新しい漢字

案内（あんない）	お客様（きゃくさま）	落（お）ちる	家族（かぞく）	結婚（けっこん）	最初（さいしょ）
数学（すうがく）	寝不足（ねぶそく）	反対（はんたい）	不安（ふあん）	不便（ふべん）	

新しい使い方

あき地（ち）	言（い）いわけ	家田（いえだ）	英会話（えいかいわ）	親（おや）	外食（がいしょく）
川本（かわもと）	習字（しゅうじ）	受験（じゅけん）	水泳（すいえい）	先生方（がた）	専門学校（せんもんがっこう）
当然（とうぜん）	習（なら）い事（ごと）	部長（ぶちょう）	本田（ほんだ）	用紙（ようし）	夜（よ）ふかし

Radicals: 方（ほう）へん・ぼくづくり

The 漢字「方」can also appear as a radical, 方 , as in 旅・族, and is called 方（ほう）へん or 方（かた）へん. You may recognize its original meaning of "direction" in those 漢字.

The つくり radical 攵 in 故・教・数 is called ぼくづくり or のぶん (because it looks like 文（ぶん）, but the first stroke looks like カタカナ「ノ」). 枚 also has this radical, but it is conventionally categorized under the 木へん radical. The ぼくづくり originally meant a "wooden whip", but in Modern Japanese does not have clear associations with either the meaning or the pronunciation of the 漢字.

案	`	` `	宀	宀	安	安	宰	案	案	案
アン	*idea:* 案内 *guide*									

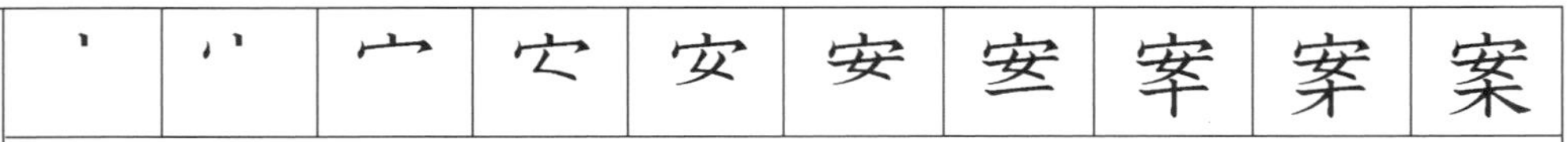

Kanji	Reading	Meaning
内	ナイ	*inside:* 案内 *guide*
家	カ・いえ・うち	*house, home:* 家田 *Ieda,* 家族 *family*
紙	シ・かみ・がみ	*paper:* 手紙 *letter,* 用紙 *form*
客	キャク	*guest:* お客様 *guest*
様	さま	*style, appearance, honorific form of* 〜さん*:* お客様 *guest*
落	お(ちる)	*to fall*
親	シン・おや	*parent:* 親切 *kind,* 両親 *parents (both parents)*
泳	エイ・およ(ぐ)	*to swim:* 水泳 *swimming*
族	ゾク	*tribe:* 家族 *family*

Kanji	Reading	Meaning
結	ケツ	*to tie:* 結婚 *marriage*
婚	コン	*marriage:* 結婚 *marriage*
初	ショ	*beginning:* 最初 *first*
受	ジュ・う(ける)	*to receive:* 受験 *taking an exam*
数	スウ	*number:* 数学 *mathematics*
方	ホウ・かた・がた	*direction, way:* 先生方 *teachers,* 使い方 *usage*
反	ハン	*opposite:* 反対 *opposition*
対	タイ	*to face, opposite, a pair:* 反対 *opposition*
不	フ・ブ	*not:* 寝不足 *not having enough sleep,* 不安 *uneasy,* 不便 *inconvenient*
足	ソク・あし・た(りる)	*foot, leg, be sufficient:* 寝不足 *not having enough sleep*

漢字の復習

I.　読みましょう。

1. 日本画のてんらん会の切符があるんですが、いっしょに行きませんか。
2. 村上さんは今週、会社を休んでいます。多分病気だと思います。
3. 毎週、週末はジムで運動することにしています。
4. お正月に着物を着てみたいです。
5. 最近、聞き取りの練習はとても難しくなりました。

II.　下の単語はまだ勉強していませんが、漢字はもう勉強しました。どんな意味でしょうか。考えてみましょう。

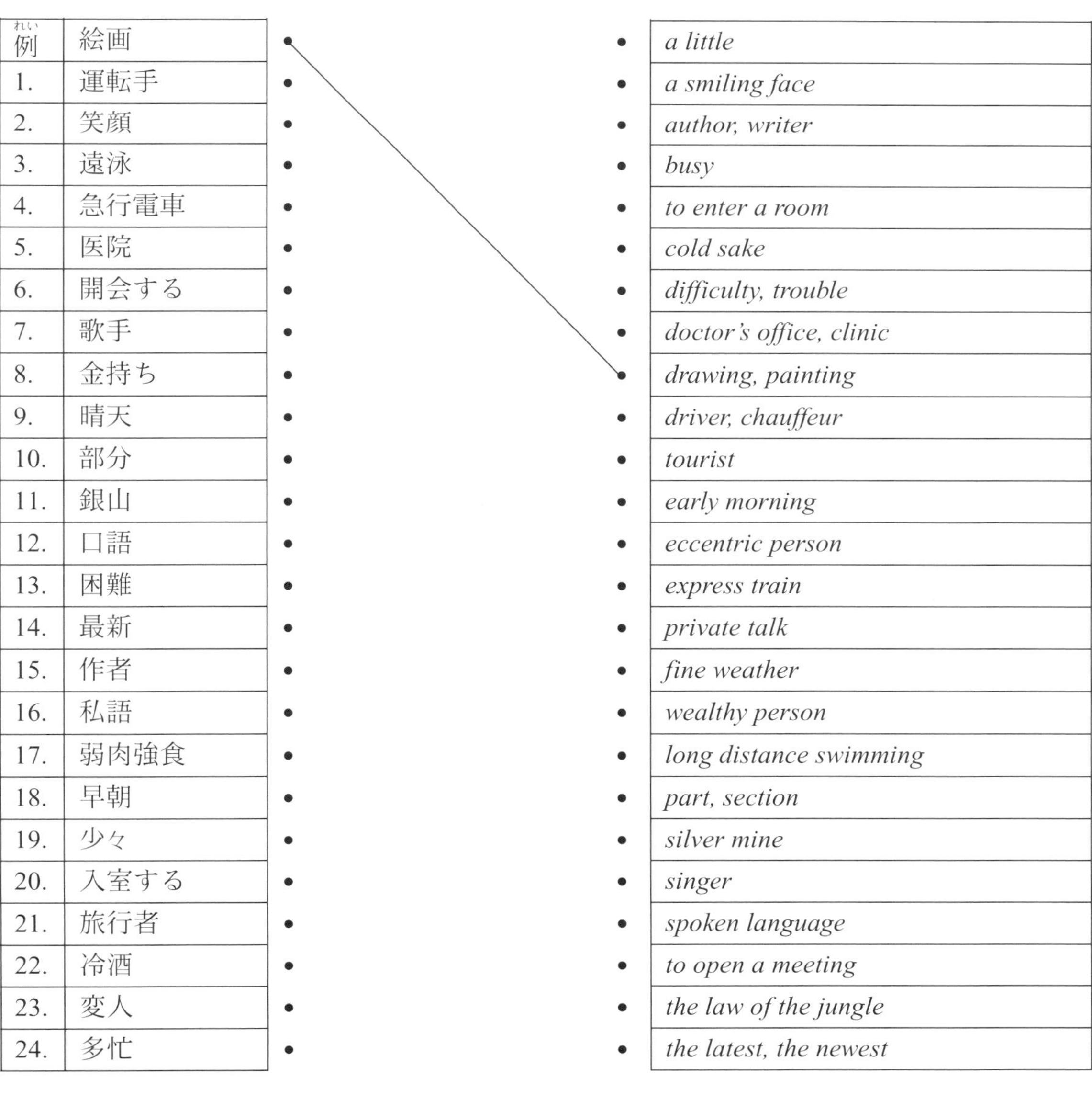

例	絵画	•	• a little
1.	運転手	•	• a smiling face
2.	笑顔	•	• author, writer
3.	遠泳	•	• busy
4.	急行電車	•	• to enter a room
5.	医院	•	• cold sake
6.	開会する	•	• difficulty, trouble
7.	歌手	•	• doctor's office, clinic
8.	金持ち	•	• drawing, painting (example)
9.	晴天	•	• driver, chauffeur
10.	部分	•	• tourist
11.	銀山	•	• early morning
12.	口語	•	• eccentric person
13.	困難	•	• express train
14.	最新	•	• private talk
15.	作者	•	• fine weather
16.	私語	•	• wealthy person
17.	弱肉強食	•	• long distance swimming
18.	早朝	•	• part, section
19.	少々	•	• silver mine
20.	入室する	•	• singer
21.	旅行者	•	• spoken language
22.	冷酒	•	• to open a meeting
23.	変人	•	• the law of the jungle
24.	多忙	•	• the latest, the newest

新しい語彙(ごい)

遊(あそ)び	*play*
あやまる (ウ)(t)(i)	*to apologize*
案内(あんない)(する)	*guide*
言(い)いわけ	*excuse*
いえ	*no*
英会話(えいかいわ)	*English conversation*
おうぼ(する)	*application*
おもしろい (イ)	*funny, amusing*
親(おや)	*parent(s)*
ガールフレンド	*girlfriend*
外食(がいしょく)(する)	*eating out*
〜方(がた)	*(polite plural indicator for people)*
かのじょ	*she*
からだ	*body*
かれ	*he*
かわいそう (ナ)	*pitiable, pitiful*
きびしい (イ)	*severe, strict*
きらう (ウ)(t)	*to hate*
きんこ	*a safe*
こうつう	*transportation*
サボる (ウ)(t)	*to cut classes*
さんか(する)	*participation*
しあわせ (ナ)	*happy*
習字(しゅうじ)	*calligraphy*
じゅく	*cramming school*
受験(じゅけん)(する)	*taking an exam*
水泳(すいえい)(する)	*swimming*
ずっと	*much more*
セクハラ	*sexual harassment*
専門学校(せんもんがっこう)	*vocational school*
そっと	*quietly, softly*
それなのに	*nevertheless*
そろばん	*abacus*
そんなに	*that much*
楽(たの)しむ (ウ)(t)	*to enjoy*
たまに	*once in a while*
ちゃんと	*properly*
デート	*date*
当然(とうぜん)	*a matter of course*
取(と)る (ウ)(t)	*to take something away*
習(なら)い事(ごと)	*lesson, practice, class*
寝不足(ねぶそく)	*not having enough sleep*
はげます (ウ)(t)	*to encourage*
パソコン	*personal computer*
バレエ	*ballet*
はんこう(する)	*rebellion, defiance*
ビデオゲーム	*video game*
ひどい (イ)	*terrible*
不安(ふあん) (ナ)	*uneasy*

ふうふ	*married couple*
部長（ぶちょう）	*department head*
ふる ㋒ ⓣ	*to jilt, dump (a significant other)*
ボーイフレンド	*boyfriend*
むすこ（さん）	*son*
むすめ（さん）	*daughter*
むりやり	*forcefully, against one's will*
物（もの）	*thing*
もんく	*complaint*
もんくを言（い）う	*to complain*
ゆどうふ	*tofu in hot broth*
用紙（ようし）	*form*
よてい	*plan*
夜（よ）ふかし（する）	*staying up late at night*
りこん（する）	*divorce*
ワープロ	*word processor*

名前

家田（いえだ）	*Ieda*
川本（かわもと）	*Kawamoto*
本田（ほんだ）	*Honda*

第二十七課 LESSON 27

復習
Review

I.　こわくてかわいそうな赤ちゃん

II.　さわってもいいですか

次のことを考えましょう。

1.　変な言葉がありませんか。
2.　なぜ、変ですか。
3.　正しい言い方は何ですか。

III.　おもしろい先生

* おれい "gratitude", おれいをする "to show gratitude".

次のことを考えましょう。

1.　この先生はおもしろいと思いますか。
2.　この後どうなったと思いますか。ストーリーを考えてみましょう。
3.　みなさんはおもしろい先生を知っていますか。話しましょう。

IV.　き（っ）て下さい

小山さん、ケーキはテーブルの上に出しておきました。次は何をしましょうか。

ああ、どうもありがとう。じゃあ、ちょっと来て下さい。

はい、分かりました。

ソンさん、早く来て下さい。おすしも作りたいですから、手伝って下さい。

何をしているんですか。

ちょっと、待って下さい。まだケーキを切っているんです。

1. ソンさんは、ケーキをテーブルの上においた後で、小山さんに何と言いましたか。
2. 小山さんはソンさんに何と答えましたか。
3. ソンさんは小山さんの所に行きましたか。
4. ソンさんは何をしていましたか。
5. 小山さんはどうしてびっくりしましたか。

V.　バレンタインデー

1. 日本では、バレンタインデーに何をしますか。知っていることを話しましょう。
2. ミラーさんは小山さんに何をもらいましたか。
3. どうしてミラーさんは山本さんに相談しようと思ったんですか。
4. ミラーさんは山本さんに相談しましたか。
5. 山本さんと話した後で、何が分かりましたか。

VI. おこらないで下さい

1. キムさんは、おかんじょうを見て、何と言いましたか。
2. ソンさんは、「私がおごります」と言いました。どうしてそう言ったと思いますか。
3. 「おごる」はどういう意味ですか。
4. 「おこる」はどういう意味ですか。

VII. お花見

ミラーさん、今年もさくらがさきました。ひまがあったら、見に来ませんか。とてもきれいですよ。
ありがとうございます。ぜひ見たいです。
じゃ、今週末はどうですか。
それでは、日曜日に見に行きます。

日本では、お花見の時、さくらの木の下で、おべんとうを食べたり、お酒を飲んだりすることになっていますね。
じゃ、おべんとうを作って、お酒を持って行きましょう。
ええと、そぼろべんとうは、とりのひき肉とたまごとしょうゆとさとうで作ります。
フムフム。ごはんをたいて、ひき肉をいためて…。
食

ミラーさん、いらっしゃい。
こんにちは。これ、さくらの下で食べようと思って、作って来ました。あのう、さくらはどこですか。
ハハハ、私のさくらはぼんさいなので、この下で食べるのはちょっと難しいですね。

1. 日本では、春になると、何をしますか。
2. 日本では、お花見の時、何をしますか。
3. ミラーさんはさくらの木を見に行く前に、何をしましたか。
4. ミラーさんはどんな木だと思ったんですか。
5. この人のさくらの木はどうでしたか。

そぼろ	*seasoned minced meat*
とり	*chicken, bird*
ひき肉	*ground meat*
ごはんをたく	*to cook rice*
いためる	*to stir fry*
ぼんさい	*a dwarfed tree in a pot*

VIII. これは何ですか

1. テーブルの上に何がありましたか。
2. ミラーさんはソンさんが来た時に、何をしていましたか。
3. ミラーさんはどうしてコーヒーをこぼしてしまいましたか。
4. ソンさんはどうして「ミラーさん。これは何ですか」と言いましたか。
5. ソンさんが「これは何ですか」と言った時に、ミラーさんは何と答えましたか。
6. ミラーさんの答え方はてきとうでしたか。
7. どう答えたらいいですか。
8. Passive フォームか Causative フォームを使って文をかんせいしましょう。

   ソンさんはミラーさんに ＿＿＿＿＿＿＿＿＿＿ を ＿＿＿＿＿＿＿＿＿＿。

   ミラーさんはソンさんを＿＿＿＿＿＿＿＿＿＿＿＿＿＿＿＿＿＿＿＿。

IX.　映画を見るのが好きですか。「はい」の所に〇を書いて下さい。

映画名	もう見た	まだ見ていない	
		見ようと思う	見るつもりはない
1.　アメリカン・グラフィティ			
2.　アラビアのロレンス			
3.　イージー・ライダー			
4.　ウエスト・サイド物語			
5.　エデンの東			
6.　カサブランカ			
7.　ガンジー			
8.　ゴッド・ファーザー			
9.　サイコ			
10.　サウンド・オブ・ミュージック			
11.　サタデーナイト・フィーバー			
12.　ジュラシック・パーク			
13.　シンドラーのリスト			
14.　スーパーマン			
15.　スター・ウォーズ			
16.　卒業			
17.　タイタニック			
18.　タクシードライバー			
19.　ダンス・ウィズ・ウルブズ			
20.　ティファニーで朝食を			
21.　ドクトル・ジバゴ			
22.　バージニア・ウルフなんかこわくない			
23.　バック・トゥ・ザ・フューチャー			
24.　バットマン			
25.　ハリー・ポッター			
26.　ベン・ハー			
27.　プライベート・ライアン			
28.　ビューティフル・マインド			
29.　マイ・フェア・レディー			
30.　真夜中のカウボーイ			
31.　メリー・ポピンズ			
32.　モダン・タイムス			
33.　レイジングブル			
34.　レインマン			
35.　ロード・オブ・ザ・リング			
36.　ローマの休日			

X. 小説を読むのが好きですか。「はい」の所に〇を書いて下さい。

小説・作者の名前	もう読んだ	まだ読んでいない	
		読もうと思う	読むつもりはない
1. 『アンナ・カレーニナ』 レフ・トルストイ			
2. 『エマ』ジェーン・オースティン			
3. 『オセロ』 ウィリアム・シェイクスピア			
4. 『カラマーゾフの兄弟』 フョードル・ドストエフスキー			
5. 『ガリバー旅行記』 ジョナサン・スウィフト			
6. 『キリマンジャロの雪』 アーネスト・ヘミングウェイ			
7. 『クリシーの静かな日々』 ヘンリー・ミラー			
8. 『クリスマス・キャロル』 チャールズ・ディケンズ			
9. 『最後の一葉（ひとは）』オー・ヘンリー			
10. 『サロメ』オスカー・ワイルド			
11. 『サンクチュアリ』 ウィリアム・フォークナー			
12. 『ジェーン・エア』 シャーロット・ブロンテ			
13. 『セールスマンの死』 アーサー・ミラー			
14. 『チップス先生さようなら』 ジェイムズ・ヒルトン			
15. 『月と六ペンス』 サマセット・モーム			
16. 『ドン・キホーテ』 ミゲール・デ・セルバンテス			
17. 『ファウスト』ヨハン・ウォ ルフガング・フォン・ゲーテ			
18. 『ユリシーズ』 ジェイムズ・ジョイス			
19. 『レ・ミゼラブル』 ヴィクトル・ユーゴー			
20. 『ロリータ』 ウラジミール・ナボコフ			

XI. 次の市 (city) はどこですか。 (　　) の中にA～Tを書いて下さい。

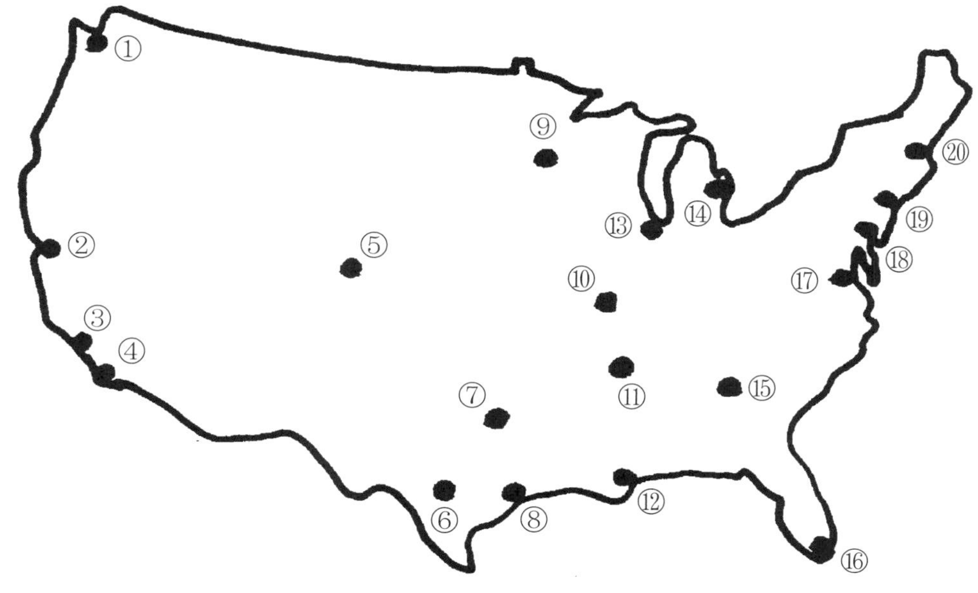

アトランタ	(A)	A.	Atlanta	(⑮)
サンアントニオ	(　　)	B.	Boston	(⑳)
サンディエゴ	(　　)	C.	Chicago	(⑬)
サンフランシスコ	(　　)	D.	Dallas	(⑦)
シアトル	(　　)	E.	Denver	(⑤)
シカゴ	(　　)	F.	Detroit	(⑭)
セントルイス	(　　)	G.	Houston	(⑧)
ダラス	(　　)	H.	Los Angeles	(③)
デトロイト	(　　)	I.	Memphis	(⑪)
デンバー	(　　)	J.	Miami	(⑯)
ニューオリンズ	(　　)	K.	Minneapolis	(⑨)
ニューヨーク	(　　)	L.	New Orleans	(⑫)
ヒューストン	(　　)	M.	New York	(⑲)
フィラデルフィア	(　　)	N.	Philadelphia	(⑱)
ボストン	(　　)	O.	San Antonio	(⑥)
マイアミ	(　　)	P.	San Diego	(④)
ミネアポリス	(　　)	Q.	San Francisco	(②)
メンフィス	(　　)	R.	Seattle	(①)
ロサンゼルス	(　　)	S.	St. Louis	(⑩)
ワシントン	(　　)	T.	Washington D.C.	(⑰)

XII.　ここに新しいPCがあります。このコンピューターを使って日本語を書くことができます。日本語を書きたい時はどうしますか。説明してみましょう。

A.　日本語でタイプしたい時は、Altキーと～キーをいっしょにおして下さい。いっしょにおすと、日本語モードになります。日本語モードになったら、書きたい言葉をローマ字でうって下さい。

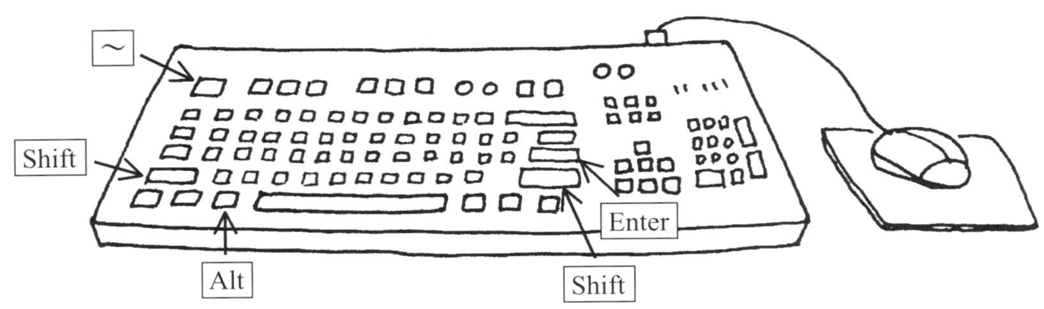

B.　ひらがなを書きたい時は、ローマ字でうつとひらがなが出ますから、Enterキーをおして下さい。

C.　漢字を書きたい時は、ローマ字でうってから、スペースバーをおして下さい。そして、使いたい漢字が出てくるまで何度もおして下さい。使いたい漢字が出たら、Enterキーをおします。こうして日本語を書くことができます。

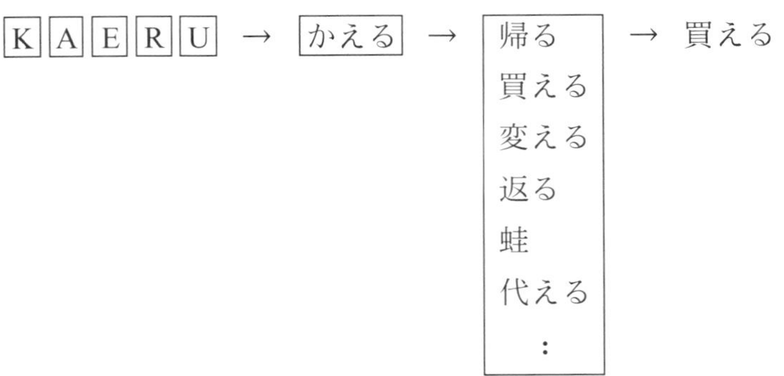

では、練習です。あなたは何を持っていますか。あなたが持っている物の使い方を友達に教えてあげましょう。

一年生の漢字 by Stroke Count

①	一	②	二	七	八	九	十	人	入	③	三	千	土	上	小
山	下	川	大	女	々	子	口	夕	④	五	六	日	月	火	水
分	木	今	中	父	円	手	方	文	元	少	午	友	化	予	切
犬	心	天	内	介	不	反	⑤	四	本	半	生	石	広	古	目
兄	母	去	冬	仕	外	末	出	白	左	右	写	田	用	正	冊
⑥	百	行	先	会	安	早	好	年	多	字	気	名	米	全	休
毎	有	色	忙	自	当	両	耳	同	回	考	地	伝	肉	死	成
次	⑦	何	来	私	見	車	弟	男	作	住	図	花	利	返	村
言	赤	近	足	医	社	困	冷	初	対	⑧	金	明	学	英	長
姉	妹	東	京	国	知	物	店	事	雨	取	画	始	受	供	使
夜	青	歩	卒	法	味	所	者	門	枚	招	注	泣	泳	⑨	昨
食	茶	待	後	音	背	前	便	秋	春	室	変	映	飛	洗	屋
度	急	単	乗	思	科	専	相	故	計	送	持	昼	客	⑩	時
家	留	高	帰	校	書	紙	院	員	料	夏	勉	酒	病	降	真
眠	旅	配	借	個	案	弱	笑	⑪	閉	部	理	都	週	教	宿
強	習	雪	終	授	転	動	問	符	魚	紹	悪	族	婚	⑫	買
晩	間	飲	番	開	朝	寒	達	絵	覚	期	葉	晴	復	運	貯
答	痛	着	暑	最	短	貸	遊	然	落	結	⑬	新	暗	話	漢
楽	働	電	寝	試	業	意	遠	辞	鉄	数	⑭	語	読	銀	聞
静	歌	練	駅	説	様	⑮	質	熱	調	談	⑯	館	頭	機	親
薬	⑰	濯	績	⑱	曜	題	験	顔	難	⑲	願				

TOTAL: 313!

私達の話はこれで終わりです。
みなさんといっしょに日本語の勉強ができて、とても楽しかったです。

どうもありがとうございました。

さようなら。
お元気で。

Appendix A Grammar Notes by Lesson

PART I

第一課

1a	Daily Expressions	
1b	Classroom Expressions	
1c	Self Introduction	
1d	List of College Majors	
1e	Hiragana Syllabary	
1f	The Moraic Consonant ん	
1g	Vowel Devoicing	
1h	Long Vowels	
1i	Long Consonants	
1j	Pitch Accent	

第二課

2a	X は Y です	"X is Y"
2b	X は Y ではありません／じゃありません	"X is not Y"
2c	Questions	
2d	Personal Pronouns	
2e	NOUN の NOUN	
2f	こ・そ・あ Demonstratives; ど Interrogatives	
2g	も	"also"
2h	Katakana Syllabary	

第三課

3a	Existential Verbs	
3b	Topic Marker は	
3c	Location Marker に	
3d	なにか／だれか／どなたか／どこかに + Affirmative Predicate なにも／だれも／どなたも／どこにも + Negative Predicate	
3e	NOUN1 と NOUN2	(NOUN1 and NOUN2)
3f	Final Particle よ	
3g	Numbers	

第四課

4a	Verb Conjugation: Pre- ますフォーム	
4b	Object Marker を	
4c	Beautifiers お and ご	
4d	で: Location Marker for Action Verbs	
4e	Instrument Marker で	"by means of"
4f	Direction / Goal Marker へ・に	
4g	Time Marker に	
4h	と "with"; ひとりで "by oneself"	
4i	A から B まで	"from A to B; from A as far as B"
4j	Pre- ますフォーム + ましょう	"Let's do ~"
	Pre- ますフォーム + ましょうか	"Shall we do ~?"
4k	Verbal Nouns	
4l	Final Particle ね	
4m	Days of the Week	
4n	Time	

第五課

5a	Object Marker に	
5b	Past Tense (Polite Speech)	
5c	Verb Conjugation: Dictionary フォーム	
5d	Dictionary フォーム + つもりです	"I intend / plan to do ~"
5e	X は Y があります	"X has Y"
5f	CLAUSE1 から CLAUSE2	"Because C1, C2; C1, so C2"
5g	どうしてですか	"Why is / was it so?"
5h	NOUN1 や NOUN2 など	"NOUN1 and NOUN2 among other things"
5i	もう "already"; まだ "yet"	
5j	Months of the Year	

第六課

6a	Verb Conjugation: Negative フォーム	
6b	Plain フォーム vs. Polite フォーム	
6c	ないフォーム + つもりです	"I intend / plan not to do ~"
6d	Pre- ますフォーム + ませんか	"Won't you do ~?; Would you like to do ~?"
6e	Pre- ますフォーム + に + 行く／来る／かえる	"go / come / return in order to do ~"
6f	Dictionary フォーム + ことができる	"can; be able to do ~"
6g	Plain フォーム + のです／んです	"It is the case that ~"
6h	Negative Scope Marker は	

6i	Answers to Negative Yes-No Questions	
6j	Nationalities (Examples)	
6k	Languages (Examples)	

第七課

7a	い -Adjectives	
7b	な -Adjectives	
7c	Antonyms (Opposite Terms)	
7d	Multiple Adjectives	
7e	は - が Construction	
7f	X で Y がある	"There is Y in / at X"
7g	Degree Adverbs	
7h	が	"but"
7i	X はどうですか／いかがですか	"How is X?"
7j	X はどんな Y ですか	"What kind of Y is X?"
7k	こちら／そちら／あちら	"this / that direction"

第八課

8a	Verb Conjugation: てフォーム	
8b	てフォーム + 下さい	"Please do ~"
	てフォーム + 下さいませんか	"Would you please do ~?"
8c	ないフォーム + で下さい	"Please don't do ~"
	ないフォーム + で下さいませんか	"Would you please not do ~?"
8d	てフォーム + いる	"be VERB-ing"
8e	まだ	"still"
8f	X はどうですか／いかがですか	"How about X?"
8g	Counting People	
8h	かぞく	

第九課

9a	X は Y が好きです／きらいです／上手です／下手です／とくいです "X likes / hates / is good at / is bad at / good at Y"	
9b	Nominalization	
9c	Comparative	
9d	Superlative	
9e	X を下さい／下さいませんか	"Please give me X"
9f	Counters	
9g	X にする	"decide on X/make something X"

第十課

10a	Verb Conjugation: たフォーム	
10b	たフォーム + ことがある	"X has had the experience of VERB-ing"
10c	てフォーム + いる	"X has VERB-ed"
10d	Transitive vs. Intransitive Verbs	
10e	Indirect Object Marker に	
10f	Verbs of Wearing Clothing	
10g	かかる	"It takes time/expense"
10h	NOUN ぐらい; NOUN ごろ (に)	"about/approximately ~"

第十一課

11a	Noun Modification by Verbs
11b	Past Tense of い-Adjectives
11c	Past Tense of です
11d	Noun Modification by Adjectives
11e	Object Marker が
11f	Sequential Voicing

第十二課

12a	X がほしいです	"I/We want X"
	X はほしくありません	"I/We don't want X" (formal)
	X はほしくないです	"I/We don't want X" (less formal)
12b	X は Y をほしがっている	"X wants Y"
12c	Pre-ますフォーム + たいです/	"I/We want to do ~"
	たくありません/たくないです	"I/We don't want to do ~"
12d	X は Pre-ますフォーム + たがっている	"X wants to do ~"
12e	どうして/なぜ	"Why ~"
	Plain フォーム + からだ	"It is because ~"
12f	Material Marker で	
12g	Quantifiers	

第十三課

13a	Verb Conjugation: Potential フォーム	
13b	CLAUSE1 時に CLAUSE2	"When C1, C2"
13c	VERBAL NOUN + に行く	"go for VERBAL NOUN"
13d	Deriving Adverbs from Adjectives	
13e	Relative Time	
13f	Days of the Month	

13g	Japanese Calendar	
13h	手紙の書き方	

第十四課

14a	CLAUSE1 ので CLAUSE2	"Because C1, C2; C1, so C2"
14b	Subject of a Subordinate Clause	
14c	Dictionary フォーム + ことにする	"I/We have decided to do ~"
	ないフォーム + ことにする	"I/We have decided not to do ~"
14d	Dictionary フォーム + ことになる	"It'll become that X does ~"
	ないフォーム + ことになる	"It'll become that X does not do ~"
14e	Dictionary フォーム + ことになった	"It was decided that X does ~"
	ないフォーム + ことになった	"It was decided that X does not do ~"
	Dictionary フォーム + ことになっている	"It's been decided that X does ~"
	ないフォーム + ことになっている	"It's been decided that X does not do ~"
14f	てフォーム + みる	"I'll try to do ~; I'll do ~ and see what it's like"
14g	Dictionary フォーム + ために	"in order to do ~"

PART II

第十五課

15a	VERB1 Pre- ますフォーム + ながら VERB2	"X does V2 while doing V1"
15b	CLAUSE1 て CLAUSE2	"C1, and C2"
15c	CLAUSE1 てから CLAUSE2	"After C1, C2"
	= てフォーム + から CLAUSE2	
15d	VERB1 Negative フォーム + ないで VERB2	"X does V2 without doing V1"
15e	てフォーム + しまう	"finish VERB-ing"
15f	VERB1- たり VERB2- たりする	"do V1 and V2, among other things"
15g	Anaphoric それ	

第十六課

16a	てフォーム + もいいですか	"May X do ~?; Is it okay to ~?"
	てフォーム + もいい	"X may do ~; It's okay to ~"
	てフォーム + はいけない	"X may not do ~; It's not okay to ~"
16b	Negative フォーム + なくてはいけない	"X must do ~"
16c	Negative フォーム + なくてもいい	"X need not do ~"
16d	Pre- ますフォーム + やすい	"easy to do ~"
	Pre- ますフォーム + にくい	"difficult / uncomfortable to do ~"
16e	X までに	"by X (time)"

第十七課

17a	ADJECTIVE / NOUN + なる	"become ADJECTIVE / NOUN"
17b	List of Professions	
17c	ADJECTIVE / NOUN + する	"make X ADJECTIVE / NOUN"
17d	CLAUSE1 と CLAUSE2	"When / If / Whenever C1, C2"
17e	Plain フォーム + でしょう	"It's probably the case that ~"
17f	NOUN 中	"throughout NOUN; in the middle of NOUN"
17g	色 (Color Terms)	

第十八課

18a	CLAUSE1 Dictionary フォーム + 前に CLAUSE2	"Before C1, C2"
18b	CLAUSE1 たフォーム + 後で CLAUSE2	"After C1, C2"
18c	Dictionary / ないフォーム + ようにする	"I make an effort (not) to do VERB; I make things so that ~"
18d	Dictionary / Potential / ないフォーム + ようになる	"It's gotten so that ~; It's become (im) possible that ~"
18e	Pre- ますフォーム + 始める Pre- ますフォーム + 終わる	"begin / start VERB-ing" "finish VERB-ing"
18f	Transitive and Intransitive Verbs	

第十九課

19a	Verb Honorifics	
19b	Adjective and Nominal Honorifics	
19c	CLAUSE1 たフォーム + ら CLAUSE2 = CLAUSE1 たら CLAUSE2	"After C1, C2; If C1, C2"

第二十課

20a	Direct and Indirect Quotations	
20b	Indirect Questions	
20c	Plain フォーム + と思う	"I think that ~"
20d	Verb Conjugation: Volitional フォーム	
20e	Volitional フォーム + と思う	"I think I'm going to do ~"

第二十一課

21a	Verb Conjugation: ばフォーム	
21b	CLAUSE1 ば CLAUSE2	"If C1, C2"

21c	～そうだ	"It looks (like) ~"
21d	てフォーム＋行く／来る／帰る	"do ~ and go / come / go back"
21e	NOUN (Quantity) + も	"as many / as much as NOUN"
21f	NOUN + しか + Negative	"only NOUN"
21g	Parts of the Body	
21h	Expressions of Illness	

第二十二課

22a	CLAUSE1 のに CLAUSE2	"Although / Even though C1, C2"
22b	CLAUSE + そうだ	"I heard that ~; It is said that ~"
22c	Plain フォーム＋かも知れない	"It possibly / may / might be ~"
22d	X と同じぐらい ADJECTIVE	as ADJECTIVE as X"
	X ほど (は) ADJECTIVE – neg	"not as ADJECTIVE as X"

第二十三課

23a	Verbs of Giving and Receiving	
23b	たフォーム＋方がいい	"It'd be better if X did ~; X had better do ~"
23c	ないフォーム＋方がいい	"It'd be better not to do ~; X had better not to do ~"
23d	たフォーム＋らいいですか	"What / how should I do ~?"
	たフォーム＋らどうですか	"How about VERB-ing?; Why not try VERB-ing?"

第二十四課

24a	てフォーム＋クレル	"X does a favor for me (or my in-group)"
	てフォーム＋モラウ	"I (or my in-group) receive a favor from Y"
	てフォーム＋アゲル	"X does a favor for Z"
24b	NOUN のために	"for NOUN"
24c	てフォーム＋おく	"do ~ in advance"
24d	てフォーム＋ある	"~ has been done; ~ was done and kept that way"

第二十五課

25a	Verb Conjugation: Passive フォーム	
25b	Simple (Direct) Passive Construction	
25c	Adversity (Indirect) Passive Construction	
25d	Pre- ますフォーム ＋ すぎる	"to do ~ excessively"
25e	ADJECTIVE + すぎる	"too ADJECTIVE"
25f	DURATION に X	"X per DURATION"

第二十六課

26a	Verb Conjugation: Causative フォーム	
26b	Causative Construction	
26c	CLAUSE1 なら CLAUSE2	"If (you say/think that) C1, then C2"
26d	てフォーム + ばかりいる	"do nothing but VERB"
26e	NOUN ばかり VERB	"VERB nothing but NOUN"
26f	まだ + てフォーム + いない	"have not done ~ yet"

第二十七課

Review

Appendix B　Verb/Adjective/Copula Conjugation

上: Plain フォーム　　下: Polite フォーム

		う verb	る verb		Irregular Verb	
Non-Past	Affirmative	会う	いる	食べる	来る	する
		会います	います	食べます	来ます	します
	Negative	会わない	いない	食べない	来ない	しない
		会いません	いません	食べません	来ません	しません
Past	Affirmative	会った	いた	食べた	来た	した
		会いました	いました	食べました	来ました	しました
	Negative	会わなかった	いなかった	食べなかった	来なかった	しなかった
		会いませんでした	いませんでした	食べませんでした	来ませんでした	しませんでした
Other Verbs		開く　買う 聞く　知る 住む　作る 飲む　話す 待つ　帰る	おきる かりる きる できる 見る	教える かんがえる しらべる ねる はじめる		

		う verb	る verb		Irregular Verb	
Negative フォーム	a	読ま (ない)	見 (ない)	食べ (ない)	来 (ない)	し (ない)
Passive フォーム	a	読まれる	見られる	食べられる	来られる	される
Causative フォーム	a	読ませる	見させる	食べさせる	来させる	させる
Pre- ますフォーム	i	読み (ます)	見 (ます)	食べ (ます)	来 (ます)	し (ます)
Dictionary フォーム	u	読む	見る	食べる	来る	する
Potential フォーム	e	読める	見られる	食べられる	来られる	できる
ばフォーム	e	読め (ば)	見れ (ば)	食べれ (ば)	来れ (ば)	すれ (ば)
Volitional フォーム	o	読もう	見よう	食べよう	来よう	しよう
てフォーム		読んで	見て	食べて	来て	して
たフォーム		読んだ	見た	食べた	来た	した

う verb Dictionary フォーム	Final Syllable	てフォーム	たフォーム
会う	う	会って	会った
書く	く	書いて	書いた
およぐ	ぐ	およいで	およいだ
話す	す	話して	話した
待つ	つ	待って	待った
しぬ	ぬ	しんで	しんだ
よぶ	ぶ	よんで	よんだ
飲む	む	飲んで	飲んだ
帰る	る	帰って	帰った

上: Plain フォーム 下: Polite フォーム

	い -adjective	な -adjective	Nominal Predicate
Non-past Affirmative	長い	元気だ	学生だ
	長いです	元気です	学生です
Non-past Negative	長くない	元気じゃない	学生じゃない
	長くないです 長くありません	元気じゃないです 元気じゃありません	学生じゃないです 学生じゃありません
Past Affirmative	長かった	元気だった	学生だった
	長かったです	元気でした	学生でした
Past Negative	長くなかった	元気じゃなかった	学生じゃなかった
	長くなかったです 長くありませんでした	元気じゃなかったです 元気じゃありませんでした	学生じゃなかったです 学生じゃありませんでした

Appendix C Kanji by Lesson

Lesson	Reading	Kanji
3	いち	一
	きゅう・く	九
	ご	五
	さん	三
	し・よん	四
	しち・なな	七
	じゅう	十
	せん	千
	に	二
	はち	八
	ひゃく	百
	ろく	六
4	かようび	火曜日
	きんようび	金曜日
	げつようび	月曜日
	～じ	～時
	すいようび	水曜日
	どようび	土曜日
	なに・なん	何
	なにか・なんか	何か
	なにも	何も
	なんじ	何時
	なんぷん	何分
	なんようび	何曜日
	にちようび	日曜日
	にほん	日本
	はん	半
	～ふん・ぷん	～分
	もくようび	木曜日
5	あした	明日
	いく	行く
	いま	今
	うえ	上
	がくせい	学生
	～がつ	～月
	きのう	昨日
	きょう	今日
	くる	来る
	こやま	小山
	した	下
	せんせい	先生
	ほん	本
	わたし	私
6	あう	会う
	うち	家
	えいご	英語
	かう	買う
	～ご	～語
	こんばん	今晩
	～じん	～人
	たべる	食べる
	ちゅうかん	中間
	なにご	何語
	にほんご	日本語
	にほんじん	日本人
	のむ	飲む
	みる	見る
	やまもと	山本
	りゅうがくせい	留学生
7	あかるい	明るい
	あたらしい	新しい
	いしかわ	石川
	おおきい	大きい
	おかね	お金
	くらい	暗い
	くるま	車
	だいがく	大学
	たかい	高い
	ちいさい	小さい
	ながい	長い
	はいる	入る
	ひろい	広い
	ふるい	古い
	め	目
	やすい	安い
	やました	山下
7	あに	兄
	あね	姉

	いもうと	妹
	おかあさん	お母さん
	おとうさん	お父さん
	おとうと	弟
	おとこ	男
	おにいさん	お兄さん
	おねえさん	お姉さん
	おんな	女
	かえる	帰る
	きょうだい	兄弟
	ください	下さい
	こうこうせい	高校生
	だいがくせい	大学生
	ちち	父
	とうきょう	東京
	～にん	～人
	はは	母
	はやい	早い
	ひと	人
	ひとり	一人
	ふたり	二人
	ふるかわ	古川
9	いちばん	一番
	いつつ	五つ
	～えん	～円
	おちゃ	お茶
	かく	書く
	～かげつ	～か月
	ここのつ	九つ
	じかん	時間
	～じかん	～時間
	じょうず	上手
	すき	好き
	ちゅうごく	中国
	つくる	作る
	とお	十
	なか	中
	ななつ	七つ
	～ねん	～年
	はなし	話
	はなす	話す
	ひとつ	一つ

	ふたつ	二つ
	へた	下手
	ほう	方
	～ほん・ぽん・ぼん	～本
	まつ	待つ
	みっつ	三つ
	むっつ	六つ
	やすかわ	安川
	やっつ	八つ
	よっつ	四つ
	よむ	読む
10	あく	開く
	あさ	朝
	おおい	多い
	がっこう	学校
	かんじ	漢字
	ぎんこう	銀行
	ことし	今年
	しまる	閉まる
	しる	知る
	すむ	住む
	てがみ	手紙
	としょかん	図書館
	なかやま	中山
	はやかわ	早川
	ひがしアジア	東アジア
	まえ	前
	わかる	分かる
11	うしろ	後ろ
	えいぶんがく	英文学
	おおどおり	大どおり
	おんがく	音楽
	がくぶ	学部
	かた	方
	かみ	紙
	きく	聞く
	げんき	元気
	こづつみ	小づつみ
	しずか	静か
	しんぶん	新聞
	せ	背
	だいがくいんせい	大学院生

	つき	月
	て	手
	ときどき	時々
	なまえ	名前
	～ねんせい	～年生
	ひがしやま	東山
	ひとびと	人々
	ほんばこ	本ばこ
12	あたま	頭
	かいもの	買い物
	きょねん	去年
	けさ	今朝
	こめ	米
	すこし	少し
	ぜんぶ	全部
	だいすき	大好き
	たべもの	食べ物
	たんじょうび	たんじょう日
	てんいん	店員
	はな	花
	べんり	便利
	みず	水
	みせ	店
	よみもの	読み物
	らいねん	来年
	りゅうがく	留学
	りょうり	料理
13	あき	秋
	あきやま	秋山
	かえす	返す
	かきかた	書き方
	きょうと	京都
	ごご	午後
	ごぜん	午前
	こんげつ	今月
	こんしゅう	今週
	さむい	寒い
	さらいげつ	さ来月
	さらいしゅう	さ来週
	さらいねん	さ来年
	しゅうまつ	週まつ
	しょうがっこう	小学校

	せんげつ	先月
	せんしゅう	先週
	せんせんげつ	先々月
	せんせんしゅう	先々週
	たのしい	楽しい
	たのしみ	楽しみ
	ちゅうがっこう	中学校
	とき	時
	ともだち	友達
	なつ	夏
	はる	春
	はるやすみ	春休み
	ふゆ	冬
	ふゆやすみ	冬休み
	ぶん	文
	へんじ	返事
	らいげつ	来月
	らいしゅう	来週
	わたしたち	私達
14	あめ	雨
	おしえる	教える
	きょうしつ	教室
	くに	国
	しごと	仕事
	～しゅうかん	～週間
	しゅくだい	宿題
	たいへん	大変
	とる	取る
	なつめ	夏目
	はたらく	働く
	べんきょう	勉強
	まいあさ	毎朝
	まいしゅう	毎週
	まいにち	毎日
	まいばん	毎晩
	やすみ	休み
	やすむ	休む
	ゆうめい	有名
	らく	楽
15	あがる	上がる
	うた	歌
	うたう	歌う

	え	絵
	えいが	映画
	おぼえる	覚える
	かいわ	会話
	きっさてん	きっさ店
	きむら	木村
	こどもたち	こども達
	こんがっき	今学期
	さくぶん	作文
	じ	字
	しんじゅく	新宿
	でんき	電気
	でんしゃ	電車
	でんわ	電話
	ならう	習う
	ねる	寝る
	はいる（おふろに）	入る
	はじめる	始める
	はるかわ	春川
	ひ	日
	ひこうき	飛行機
	びじゅつかん	びじゅつ館
	みっかめ	三日目
	むらやま	村山
16	あらう	洗う
	いう	言う
	うける	受ける
	おてあらい	お手洗い
	おとな	大人
	がいこく	外国
	がいこくじん	外国人
	き	気
	ききとり	聞き取り
	きまつしけん	期末しけん
	けんぶつ	見物
	ことば	言葉
	こども	子供
	さけ	酒
	しゅうまつ	週末
	せんたくき	洗濯機
	そと	外
	だす	出す

	つかいかた	使い方
	つかう	使う
	つれてくる	つれて来る
	にんき	人気
	よなか	夜中
	よる	夜
	ろっぽんぎ	六本木
17	あお	青
	あおい	青い
	あか	赤
	あかい	赤い
	あける	開ける
	いし	石
	いちねんじゅう	一年中
	いろ	色
	おはなみ	お花見
	かわ	川
	き	木
	きいろ	き色
	きいろい	き色い
	きもち	気もち
	くすりや	くすり屋
	このは	木の葉
	しけん	試験
	～じゅう・～ちゅう	～中
	しょくじ	食事
	しろ	白
	しろい	白い
	せんがっき	先学期
	たぶん	多分
	ちゅうがくせい	中学生
	つよい	強い
	でる	出る
	はれる	晴れる
	ひだり	左
	ひとばんじゅう	一晩中
	びょういん	病院
	びょうき	病気
	ふる（あめが）	降る
	へや	部屋
	まいとし・まいねん	毎年
	まんなか	まん中

	みぎ	右
	みどりいろ	みどり色
	～や	～屋
	ゆき	雪
18	あおき	青木
	あげる	上げる
	あと	後
	あるく	歩く
	いそぐ	急ぐ
	いれる	入れる
	いろいろ	色々
	えいがかん	映画館
	おえる	終える
	おと	音
	おわる	終わる
	がいこくご	外国語
	きこく	帰国
	こんど	今度
	しめる	閉める
	じゅぎょう	授業
	そつぎょう	卒業
	たんご	単語
	～ど	～度
	ねぼう	寝ぼう
	のる	乗る
	はじまる	始まる
	はじめ	始め
	ふくしゅう	復習
	ぶんか	文化
	ぶんぽう	文法
	まいつき	毎月
	まなぶ	学ぶ
	よしゅう	予習
	らいがっき	来学期
	れんしゅう	練習
19	いそがしい	忙しい
	うごく	動く
	うんてん	運転
	うんどう	運動
	げんごがく	言語学
	さき	先
	しつもん	質問
	じてんしゃ	自転車
	しゃしん	写真
	すくない	少ない
	たなか	田中
	ちば	千葉
	ちょきん	貯金
	どうぶつ	動物
	ねむい	眠い
	ねむる	眠る
	～ねんまえ	～年前
	はんぶん	半分
	ぶつりがく	物理学
	ほんとう	本当
	みせる	見せる
	むらかみ	村上
	めしあがる	めし上がる
	もんだい	問題
	やまだ	山田
	りょかん	旅館
	りょこう	旅行
20	あじ	味
	いみ	意味
	うまれる	生まれる
	えき	駅
	おもう	思う
	かざん	火山
	きって	切手
	きょうかしょ	教科書
	けんがく	見学
	こたえ	答え
	こたえる	答える
	こんしゅうまつ	今週末
	じぶん	自分
	じゅうしょ	住所
	しんせつ	親切
	だいじ	大事
	たいしかん	大使館
	ちかい	近い
	ちかく	近く
	でかける	出かける
	とおい	遠い
	ところ	所

	へん	変
	やま	山
	ようい	用意
	ようじ	用事
	りょうしん	両親
21	あし	足
	あたる	当たる
	いかだいがくいん	医科大学院
	いしゃ	医者
	いたい	痛い
	いぬ	犬
	うかる	受かる
	うわぎ	上着
	かお	顔
	かおいろ	顔色
	かぜぐすり	かぜ薬
	きぶん	気分
	きる	着る
	くすり	薬
	くすりや	薬屋
	くち	口
	こんや	今夜
	さがる	下がる
	しんぱい	心配
	せいぶつがく	生物学
	せなか	背中
	たりる	足りる
	つく	着く
	てんらんかい	てんらん会
	なかむら	中村
	にほんが	日本画
	ねつ	熱
	ひきうける	ひき受ける
	みみ	耳
22	あつい	暑い
	いっしょうけんめい	一生けんめい
	えいこくじん	英国人
	おなじ	同じ
	～かい	～回
	かがく	化学
	きっぷ	切符
	さいきん	最近

	さいご	最後
	しょうせつ	小説
	しんりがく	心理学
	せつめい	説明
	せんもん	専門
	たいせつ	大切
	ただしい	正しい
	ちゅうとう	中東
	てんき	天気
	とおやま	遠山
	にほんしゅ	日本酒
	まにあう	間にあう
	みじかい	短い
	みずぎ	水着
	みつかる	見つかる
	むずかしい	難しい
	ゆうがた	夕方
	ゆうしょく	夕食
	ゆうべ	夕べ
23	あいて	相手
	あかちゃん	赤ちゃん
	あとで	後で
	あんぜん	安全
	いけん	意見
	おしょうがつ	お正月
	おちゅうげん	お中元
	おとしだま	お年だま
	おわり	終わり
	かいしゃ	会社
	かす	貸す
	かりる	借りる
	くださる	下さる
	～こ	～個
	このあいだ	この間
	こまる	困る
	～さつ	～冊
	じこ	事故
	じしょ	辞書
	しらべる	調べる
	そうだん	相談
	たかだ	高田
	とけい	時計

	にゅうがく	入学
	にゅうしゃ	入社
	～まい	～枚
	まさこ	正子
	めぐすり	目薬
24	あそぶ	遊ぶ
	あんしん	安心
	おくる	送る
	かいてん	開店
	かんがえ	考え
	かんがえる	考える
	きもち	気持ち
	きもの	着物
	きる	切る
	きんじょ	近所
	さかな	魚
	しょうかい	紹介
	しょうたい	招待
	しんねん	新年
	ちず	地図
	ちゃわん	茶わん
	つたえる	伝える
	つめたい	冷たい
	てつだう	手伝う
	てんちょう	店長
	にく	肉
	はこぶ	運ぶ
	ひやす	冷やす
	へいてん	閉店
	もつ	持つ
	やすだ	安田
	わるい	悪い
25	おとこのこ	男の子
	おねがい	お願い
	およぐ	泳ぐ
	おんがくかい	音楽会
	おんなのこ	女の子
	がくぶせい	学部生
	かしだす	貸し出す
	がっき	学期
	かりだす	借り出す
	けいかく	計画

	さくしゃ	作者
	しぜん	自然
	しぬ	死ぬ
	しゃちょう	社長
	せいせき	成績
	せかいじゅう	せかい中
	ぜんぜん	全然
	ちかてつ	地下鉄
	ちゅうい	注意
	ちゅうもん	注文
	つぎ	次
	とぶ	飛ぶ
	なく	泣く
	はなび	花火
	はりだす	はり出す
	ひ	火
	ひる	昼
	ひるね	昼寝
	まえだ	前田
	めざましどけい	めざまし時計
	ものがたり	物語
	よわい	弱い
	わらう	笑う
26	わるぐち	悪口
	あきち	あき地
	あんない	案内
	いいわけ	言いわけ
	いえだ	家田
	えいかいわ	英会話
	おきゃくさま	お客様
	おちる	落ちる
	おや	親
	がいしょく	外食
	かぞく	家族
	かわもと	川本
	けっこん	結婚
	さいしょ	最初
	しゅうじ	習字
	じゅけん	受験
	すいえい	水泳
	すうがく	数学
	せんせいがた	先生方

せんもんがっこう	専門学校
とうぜん	当然
ならいごと	習い事
ねぶそく	寝不足
はんたい	反対
ふあん	不安
ぶちょう	部長
ふべん	不便
ほんだ	本田
ようし	用紙
よふかし	夜ふかし

Appendix D　Kanji by あいうえお

あ	あいて	相手	23
	あう	会う	6
	あお	青	17
	あおい	青い	17
	あおき	青木	18
	あか	赤	17
	あかい	赤い	17
	あかちゃん	赤ちゃん	23
	あがる	上がる	15
	あかるい	明るい	7
	あき	秋	13
	あきち	あき地	26
	あきやま	秋山	13
	あく	開く	10
	あける	開ける	17
	あげる	上げる	18
	あさ	朝	10
	あし	足	21
	あじ	味	20
	あした	明日	5
	あそぶ	遊ぶ	24
	あたま	頭	12
	あたらしい	新しい	7
	あたる	当たる	21
	あつい	暑い	22
	あと	後	18
	あとで	後で	23
	あに	兄	8
	あね	姉	8
	あめ	雨	14
	あらう	洗う	16
	あるく	歩く	18
	あんしん	安心	24
	あんぜん	安全	23
	あんない	案内	26
い	いいわけ	言いわけ	26
	いう	言う	16
	いえだ	家田	26
	いかだいがくいん	医科大学院	21
	いく	行く	5
	いけん	意見	23
	いし	石	17
	いしかわ	石川	7
	いしゃ	医者	21
	いそがしい	忙しい	19
	いそぐ	急ぐ	18
	いたい	痛い	21
	いち	一	3
	いちねんじゅう	一年中	17
	いちばん	一番	9
	いっしょうけんめい	一生けんめい	22
	いつつ	五つ	9
	いぬ	犬	21
	いま	今	5
	いみ	意味	20
	いもうと	妹	8
	いれる	入れる	18
	いろ	色	17
	いろいろ	色々	18
う	うえ	上	5
	うける	受ける	16
	うごく	動く	19
	うしろ	後ろ	11
	うた	歌	15
	うたう	歌う	15
	うち	家	6
	うまれる	生まれる	20
	うわぎ	上着	21
	うんてん	運転	19
	うんどう	運動	19
え	え	絵	15
	えいが	映画	15
	えいかいわ	英会話	26
	えいがかん	映画館	18
	えいご	英語	6
	えいこくじん	英国人	22
	えいぶんがく	英文学	11
	えき	駅	20

	～えん	～円	9
お	おえる	終える	18
	おおい	多い	10
	おおきい	大きい	7
	おおどおり	大どおり	11
	おかあさん	お母さん	8
	おかね	お金	7
	おきゃくさま	お客様	26
	おくる	送る	24
	おしえる	教える	14
	おしょうがつ	お正月	23
	おちゃ	お茶	9
	おちゅうげん	お中元	23
	おちる	落ちる	26
	おてあらい	お手洗い	16
	おと	音	18
	おとうさん	お父さん	8
	おとうと	弟	8
	おとこ	男	8
	おとこのこ	男の子	25
	おとしだま	お年だま	23
	おとな	大人	16
	おなじ	同じ	22
	おにいさん	お兄さん	8
	おねえさん	お姉さん	8
	おねがい	お願い	25
	おはなみ	お花見	17
	おぼえる	覚える	15
	おもう	思う	20
	おや	親	26
	およぐ	泳ぐ	25
	おわり	終わり	23
	おわる	終わる	18
	おんがく	音楽	11
	おんがくかい	音楽会	25
	おんな	女	8
	おんなのこ	女の子	25
か	～かい	～回	22
	がいこく	外国	16
	がいこくご	外国語	18
	がいこくじん	外国人	16
	かいしゃ	会社	23

	がいしょく	外食	26
	かいてん	開店	24
	かいもの	買い物	12
	かいわ	会話	15
	かう	買う	6
	かえす	返す	13
	かえる	帰る	8
	かお	顔	21
	かおいろ	顔色	21
	かがく	化学	22
	かきかた	書き方	13
	かく	書く	9
	がくせい	学生	5
	がくぶ	学部	11
	がくぶせい	学部生	25
	～かげつ	～か月	9
	かざん	火山	20
	かしだす	貸し出す	25
	かす	貸す	23
	かぜぐすり	かぜ薬	21
	かぞく	家族	26
	かた	方	11
	～がつ	～月	5
	がっき	学期	25
	がっこう	学校	10
	かみ	紙	11
	かようび	火曜日	4
	かりだす	借り出す	25
	かりる	借りる	23
	かわ	川	17
	かわもと	川本	26
	かんがえ	考え	24
	かんがえる	考える	24
	かんじ	漢字	10
き	き	気	16
	き	木	17
	きいろ	き色	17
	きいろい	き色い	17
	ききとり	聞き取り	16
	きく	聞く	11
	きこく	帰国	18
	きっさてん	きっさ店	15

	きって	切手	20
	きっぷ	切符	22
	きのう	昨日	5
	きぶん	気分	21
	きまつしけん	期末しけん	16
	きむら	木村	15
	きもち	気もち	17
		気持ち	24
	きもの	着物	24
	きゅう	九	3
	きょう	今日	5
	きょうかしょ	教科書	20
	きょうしつ	教室	14
	きょうだい	兄弟	8
	きょうと	京都	13
	きょねん	去年	12
	きる	着る	21
	きる	切る	24
	ぎんこう	銀行	10
	きんじょ	近所	24
	きんようび	金曜日	4
く	く	九	3
	くすり	薬	21
	くすりや	くすり屋	17
		薬屋	21
	ください	下さい	8
	くださる	下さる	23
	くち	口	21
	くに	国	14
	くらい	暗い	7
	くる	来る	5
	くるま	車	7
け	けいかく	計画	25
	けさ	今朝	12
	けっこん	結婚	26
	げつようび	月曜日	4
	けんがく	見学	20
	げんき	元気	11
	げんごがく	言語学	19
	けんぶつ	見物	16
こ	～こ	～個	23
	ご	五	3
	～ご	～語	6
	こうこうせい	高校生	8
	ごご	午後	13
	ここのつ	九つ	9
	ごぜん	午前	13
	こたえ	答え	20
	こたえる	答える	20
	こづつみ	小づつみ	11
	ことし	今年	10
	ことば	言葉	16
	こども	子供	16
	こどもたち	こども達	15
	このあいだ	この間	23
	このは	木の葉	17
	こまる	困る	23
	こめ	米	12
	こやま	小山	5
	こんがっき	今学期	15
	こんげつ	今月	13
	こんしゅう	今週	13
	こんしゅうまつ	今週末	20
	こんど	今度	18
	こんばん	今晩	6
	こんや	今夜	21
さ	さいきん	最近	22
	さいご	最後	22
	さいしょ	最初	26
	さかな	魚	24
	さがる	下がる	21
	さき	先	19
	さくしゃ	作者	25
	さくぶん	作文	15
	さけ	酒	16
	～さつ	～冊	23
	さむい	寒い	13
	さらいげつ	さ来月	13
	さらいしゅう	さ来週	13
	さらいねん	さ来年	13
	さん	三	3
し	し	四	3
	じ	字	15
	～じ	～時	4

	じかん	時間	9
	～じかん	～時間	9
	しけん	試験	17
	じこ	事故	23
	しごと	仕事	14
	じしょ	辞書	23
	しずか	静か	11
	しぜん	自然	25
	した	下	5
	しち	七	3
	しつもん	質問	19
	じてんしゃ	自転車	19
	しぬ	死ぬ	25
	じぶん	自分	20
	しまる	閉まる	10
	しめる	閉める	18
	しゃしん	写真	19
	しゃちょう	社長	25
	じゅう	十	3
	～じゅう	～中	17
	～しゅうかん	～週間	14
	しゅうじ	習字	26
	じゅうしょ	住所	20
	しゅうまつ	週まつ	13
		週末	16
	じゅぎょう	授業	18
	しゅくだい	宿題	14
	じゅけん	受験	26
	しょうかい	紹介	24
	しょうがっこう	小学校	13
	じょうず	上手	9
	しょうせつ	小説	22
	しょうたい	招待	24
	しょくじ	食事	17
	しらべる	調べる	23
	しる	知る	10
	しろ	白	17
	しろい	白い	17
	～じん	～人	6
	しんじゅく	新宿	15
	しんせつ	親切	20
	しんねん	新年	24

	しんぱい	心配	21
	しんぶん	新聞	11
	しんりがく	心理学	22
す	すいえい	水泳	26
	すいようび	水曜日	4
	すうがく	数学	26
	すき	好き	9
	すくない	少ない	19
	すこし	少し	12
	すむ	住む	10
せ	せ	背	11
	せいせき	成績	25
	せいぶつがく	生物学	21
	せかいじゅう	せかい中	25
	せつめい	説明	22
	せなか	背中	21
	せん	千	3
	せんがっき	先学期	17
	せんげつ	先月	13
	せんしゅう	先週	13
	せんせい	先生	5
	せんせいがた	先生方	26
	ぜんぜん	全然	25
	せんせんげつ	先々月	13
	せんせんしゅう	先々週	13
	せんたくき	洗濯機	16
	ぜんぶ	全部	12
	せんもん	専門	22
	せんもんがっこう	専門学校	26
そ	そつぎょう	卒業	18
	そうだん	相談	23
	そと	外	16
た	だいがく	大学	7
	だいがくいんせい	大学院生	11
	だいがくせい	大学生	8
	だいじ	大事	20
	たいしかん	大使館	20
	だいすき	大好き	12
	たいせつ	大切	22
	たいへん	大変	14
	たかい	高い	7
	たかだ	高田	23

	だす	出す	16
	ただしい	正しい	22
	たなか	田中	19
	たのしい	楽しい	13
	たのしみ	楽しみ	13
	たぶん	多分	17
	たべもの	食べ物	12
	たべる	食べる	6
	たりる	足りる	21
	たんご	単語	18
	たんじょうび	たんじょう日	12
ち	ちいさい	小さい	7
	ちかい	近い	20
	ちかく	近く	20
	ちかてつ	地下鉄	25
	ちず	地図	24
	ちち	父	8
	ちば	千葉	19
	ちゃわん	茶わん	24
	～ちゅう	～中	17
	ちゅうい	注意	25
	ちゅうがくせい	中学生	17
	ちゅうがっこう	中学校	13
	ちゅうかん	中間	6
	ちゅうごく	中国	9
	ちゅうとう	中東	22
	ちゅうもん	注文	25
	ちょきん	貯金	19
つ	つかいかた	使い方	16
	つかう	使う	16
	つき	月	11
	つぎ	次	25
	つく	着く	21
	つくる	作る	9
	つたえる	伝える	24
	つめたい	冷たい	24
	つよい	強い	17
	つれてくる	つれて来る	16
て	て	手	11
	でかける	出かける	20
	てがみ	手紙	10
	てつだう	手伝う	24
	でる	出る	17
	てんいん	店員	12
	てんき	天気	22
	でんき	電気	15
	でんしゃ	電車	15
	てんちょう	店長	24
	てんらんかい	てんらん会	21
	でんわ	電話	15
と	～ど	～度	18
	とうきょう	東京	8
	とうぜん	当然	26
	どうぶつ	動物	19
	とお	十	9
	とおい	遠い	20
	とおやま	遠山	22
	とき	時	13
	ときどき	時々	11
	とけい	時計	23
	ところ	所	20
	としょかん	図書館	10
	とぶ	飛ぶ	25
	ともだち	友達	13
	どようび	土曜日	4
	とる	取る	14
な	なか	中	9
	ながい	長い	7
	なかむら	中村	21
	なかやま	中山	10
	なく	泣く	25
	なつ	夏	13
	なつめ	夏目	14
	なな	七	3
	ななつ	七つ	9
	なに	何	4
	なにか	何か	4
	なにご	何語	6
	なにも	何も	4
	なまえ	名前	11
	ならいごと	習い事	26
	ならう	習う	15
	なん	何	4
	なんか	何か	4

	なんじ	何時	4
	なんぷん	何分	4
	なんようび	何曜日	4
に	に	二	3
	にく	肉	24
	にちようび	日曜日	4
	にほん	日本	4
	にほんが	日本画	21
	にほんご	日本語	6
	にほんしゅ	日本酒	22
	にほんじん	日本人	6
	にゅうがく	入学	23
	にゅうしゃ	入社	23
	～にん	～人	8
	にんき	人気	16
ね	ねつ	熱	21
	ねぶそく	寝不足	26
	ねぼう	寝ぼう	18
	ねむい	眠い	19
	ねむる	眠る	19
	ねる	寝る	15
	～ねん	～年	9
	～ねんせい	～年生	11
	～ねんまえ	～年前	19
の	のむ	飲む	6
	のる	乗る	18
は	はいる	入る	7
	はいる（おふろに）	入る	15
	はこぶ	運ぶ	24
	はじまる	始まる	18
	はじめ	始め	18
	はじめる	始める	15
	はたらく	働く	14
	はち	八	3
	はな	花	12
	はなし	話	9
	はなす	話す	9
	はなび	花火	25
	はは	母	8
	はやい	早い	8
	はやかわ	早川	10
	はりだす	はり出す	25
	はる	春	13
	はるかわ	春川	15
	はるやすみ	春休み	13
	はれる	晴れる	17
	はん	半	4
	はんたい	反対	26
	はんぶん	半分	19
ひ	ひ	日	15
	ひ	火	25
	ひがしアジア	東アジア	10
	ひがしやま	東山	11
	ひきうける	ひき受ける	21
	ひこうき	飛行機	15
	びじゅつかん	びじゅつ館	15
	ひだり	左	17
	ひと	人	8
	ひとつ	一つ	9
	ひとばんじゅう	一晩中	17
	ひとびと	人々	11
	ひとり	一人	8
	ひゃく	百	3
	ひやす	冷やす	24
	びょういん	病院	17
	びょうき	病気	17
	ひる	昼	25
	ひるね	昼寝	25
	ひろい	広い	7
ふ	ふあん	不安	26
	ふくしゅう	復習	18
	ふたつ	二つ	9
	ふたり	二人	8
	ぶちょう	部長	26
	ぶつりがく	物理学	19
	ふべん	不便	26
	ふゆ	冬	13
	ふゆやすみ	冬休み	13
	ふる（あめが）	降る	17
	ふるい	古い	7
	ふるかわ	古川	8
	～ふん・ぷん	～分	4
	ぶん	文	13
	ぶんか	文化	18

	ぶんぽう	文法	18
へ	へいてん	閉店	24
	へた	下手	9
	へや	部屋	17
	へん	変	20
	べんきょう	勉強	14
	へんじ	返事	13
	べんり	便利	12
ほ	ほう	方	9
	ほん	本	5
	~ほん・ぽん・ぼん	~本	9
	ほんだ	本田	26
	ほんとう	本当	19
	ほんばこ	本ばこ	11
ま	~まい	~枚	23
	まいあさ	毎朝	14
	まいしゅう	毎週	14
	まいつき	毎月	18
	まいとし	毎年	17
	まいにち	毎日	14
	まいねん	毎年	17
	まいばん	毎晩	14
	まえ	前	10
	まえだ	前田	25
	まさこ	正子	23
	まつ	待つ	9
	まなぶ	学ぶ	18
	まにあう	間にあう	22
	まんなか	まん中	17
み	みぎ	右	17
	みじかい	短い	22
	みず	水	12
	みずぎ	水着	22
	みせ	店	12
	みせる	見せる	19
	みっかめ	三日目	15
	みつかる	見つかる	22
	みっつ	三つ	9
	みどりいろ	みどり色	17
	みみ	耳	21
	みる	見る	6
む	むずかしい	難しい	22

	むっつ	六つ	9
	むらかみ	村上	19
	むらやま	村山	15
め	め	目	7
	めぐすり	目薬	23
	めざましどけい	めざまし時計	25
	めしあがる	めし上がる	19
も	もくようび	木曜日	4
	もつ	持つ	24
	ものがたり	物語	25
	もんだい	問題	19
や	~や	~屋	17
	やすい	安い	7
	やすかわ	安川	9
	やすだ	安田	24
	やすみ	休み	14
	やすむ	休む	14
	やっつ	八つ	9
	やま	山	20
	やました	山下	7
	やまだ	山田	19
	やまもと	山本	6
ゆ	ゆうがた	夕方	22
	ゆうしょく	夕食	22
	ゆうべ	夕べ	22
	ゆうめい	有名	14
	ゆき	雪	17
よ	ようい	用意	20
	ようし	用紙	26
	ようじ	用事	20
	よしゅう	予習	18
	よっつ	四つ	9
	よなか	夜中	16
	よふかし	夜ふかし	26
	よみもの	読み物	12
	よむ	読む	9
	よる	夜	16
	よわい	弱い	25
	よん	四	3
ら	らいがっき	来学期	18
	らいげつ	来月	13
	らいしゅう	来週	13

	らいねん	来年	12
	らく	楽	14
り	りゅうがく	留学	12
	りゅうがくせい	留学生	6
	りょうしん	両親	20
	りょうり	料理	12
	りょかん	旅館	19
	りょこう	旅行	19
れ	れんしゅう	練習	18
ろ	ろく	六	3
	ろっぽんぎ	六本木	16
わ	わかる	分かる	10
	わたし	私	5
	わたしたち	私達	13
	わらう	笑う	25
	わるい	悪い	24
	わるぐち	悪口	25

Appendix E Kanji by Stroke Count

Count	L3	L4	L5	L6	L7	L8	L9	L10	L11	L12	L13	L14
1	一											
2	九七十二八			人	入							
3	三千	土	上小山下		川大	女			々			
4	五六	火日月水分木	今	中		父	円手方		文元	少	午友	
5	四	本半	生		石広古目	兄母				去	冬	仕
6	百		行先	会	安	早	好年	多字	気名	米全	休	毎有
7		何	来私	見	車	弟男	作	住図		花利	返	
8		金	明学	英	長	姉妹東京	国	知		店物	事	雨取
9			昨	食			茶待	前	後音背	便	秋春	室変
10		時		家留	高	帰校	書	紙	院	員料	夏	勉
11								閉	部	理	都週	教宿強
12				買晩間飲			番	開朝			寒達	
13					新暗		話	漢	楽			働
14				語			読	銀	聞静			
15												
16								館		頭		
17												
18		曜										題
19												
Total	12	13	13	13	13	13	13	13	13	13	13	13

Count	L15	L16	L17	L18	L19	L20	L21	L22	L23	L24	L25	L26
1												
2												
3		子					口	夕				
4				化予		切	犬心	天		介		内不反
5		外末出	白左右		写田	用		正	冊			
6			色		忙自当	両	耳	同回		考地伝肉	死成次	
7	村	言	赤			近	足医		社困	冷		初対
8	画始	受供使夜	青	歩卒法		味所	者	門	枚	招	泳注泣	
9	映飛	洗	屋	度急単乗		思科		専	相故計	送持	昼	客
10		酒	病降		真眠旅		配		借個		弱笑	案
11	習		雪	終授	転動問			符		魚紹悪		族婚
12	絵覚期	葉	晴	復	運貯	答	痛着	暑最短	貸	遊	然	落結
13	電寝		試	業		意遠			辞		鉄	数
14	歌			練		駅		説				様
15					質		熱		調談			
16	機					親	薬					
17		濯									績	
18			験				顔	難				
19											願	
Total	13	13	13	14	14	13	13	13	13	13	13	13

Appendix F Vocabulary List (Japanese to English)

品詞	Parts of speech	単語課	Lesson where the word is introduced
漢字	Kanji	漢字課	Lesson where the kanji is introduced
反対語・対語	Antonym/A pair of words		
X	The kanji is used, but not taught.		
Adj irreg	Irregular adjective	N proper	Proper noun
Conj	Conjunction	N verbal	Verbal noun
Interject	Interjection		

	日本語 Japanese	英語 English	品詞	単語課	漢字	漢字課	反対語・対語
	CD プレーヤー	CD player	Noun	12			
	E メール	email	Noun	9			
	T シャツ	T-shirt	Noun	9			
あ	アーティスト	artist	Noun	17			
	アームストロング	Armstrong	N proper	11			
	アイスクリーム	ice cream	Noun	15			
	あいて	partner, opponent	Noun	23	相手	23	
	アイロン	iron	Noun	24			
	あう	meet	Verb う	4	会う	6	
	あお	blue	Noun	17	青	17	
	あおい	blue	Adj い	17	青い	17	
	あおき	Aoki	N proper	18	青木	18	
	あか	red	Noun	17	赤	17	
	あかい	red	Adj い	17	赤い	17	
	あかちゃん	baby	Noun	23	赤ちゃん	23	
	あがる	step up	Verb う	15	上がる	15	
	あかるい	bright, cheerful	Adj い	7	明るい	7	くらい
	あき	autumn	Noun	12	秋	13	
	あきち	vacant lot	Noun	18	あき地	26	
	あきはばら	Akihabara	N proper	13	秋葉原	X	
	あきやま	Akiyama	N proper	13	秋山	13	
	あく	open (intransitive)	Verb う	10	開く	10	しまる
	あける	open (transitive)	Verb る	17	開ける	17	しめる
	あげる	raise	Verb る	14	上げる	18	
	あげる	give	Verb る	23	上げる	23	もらう

あさ	morning	Noun	5	朝	10	ばん
あさくさ	Asakusa	N proper	13	浅草	X	
あさごはん	breakfast	Noun	4	朝ごはん	10	ばんごはん
あさって	day after tomorrow	Noun	13			おととい
あし	foot, leg	Noun	7	足	21	
あじ	taste	Noun	20	味	20	
あしくび	ankle	Noun	21	足くび	21	
あした	tomorrow	Noun	4	明日	5	きのう
あそこ	place over there	Pronoun	2			ここ
あそび	play	Noun	26	遊び	26	
あそぶ	play	Verb う	6	遊ぶ	24	
あたたかい	warm	Adj い	17			
あたま	head	Noun	7	頭	12	
あたらしい	new	Adj い	7	新しい	7	ふるい
あたる	hit (intransitive)	Verb う	21	当たる	21	
あちら	that direction	Pronoun	7			
あつい	hot	Adj い	11	暑い	22	さむい
あと	remaining	Noun	18	後	18	
あとで	after	Conj	18	後で	18	まえに
あとで	afterwards, later	Adv	23	後で	23	
アドバイス（する）	advice	N verbal	23			
アトランタ	Atlanta	N proper	27			
あなた	you	Pronoun	2			
あに	elder brother (plain)	Noun	8	兄	8	おとうと
アニメ	animated cartoon	Noun	23			
あね	elder sister (plain)	Noun	8	姉	8	いもうと
あの + NOUN	that NOUN (over there)	Adj irreg	2			
アパート	apartment	Noun	2			
あびる	take (a shower)	Verb る	13			
あぶない	dangerous	Adj い	22			あんぜん（な）
アフリカ	Africa	N proper	12			
あまい	sweet	Adj い	11			からい
あまり	(not) much	Adv	7			
あむ	knit	Verb う	24			
あめ	rain	Noun	8	雨	14	
アメリカ	America	N proper	5			
アメリカじん	American people	Noun	6	アメリカ人	6	
あやまる	apologize	Verb う	26			
あらう	wash	Verb う	14	洗う	16	よごす
アラスカ	Alaska	N proper	11			
ある	exist (things)	Verb う	3			ない
あるいて	on foot	Phrase	4	歩いて	18	

あるく	walk	Verb う	8	歩く	18	
あれ	that one	Pronoun	2			これ
あんしん（する）	relief	N verbal	24	安心	24	しんぱい
あんぜん（な）	safe	Adj な	23	安全	23	きけん（な）
あんない（する）	guide	N verbal	26	案内	26	
あんなに	so many, so much	Adv	20			

い

い	stomach	Noun	21			
いい	good	Adj い	7			わるい
いいえ	no	Adv	2			はい
いいわけ	excuse	Noun	26	言いわけ	26	
いう	say, speak, talk	Verb う	11	言う	16	
(もんくを) いう	complain	Verb う	26	言う	16	
いえ	no	Adv	26			
いえだ	Ieda	N proper	26	家田	26	
いかが	how (respectful)	Adv	7			
いかだいがくいん	medical school	Noun	21	医科大学院	21	
イギリス	England	N proper	9			
いく	go	Verb う	4	行く	5	くる
いくら	how much	Adv	10			
いけん	opinion	Noun	23	意見	23	
いし	stone	Noun	17	石	17	
いしかわ	Ishikawa	N proper	2	石川	7	
いしゃ	medical doctor	Noun	16	医者	21	
～いじょう	more than X	Suffix	19			
いじわる（な）	mean	Adj な	7			しんせつ(な)、やさしい
いす	chair	Noun	3			
いそがしい	busy	Adj い	10	忙しい	19	ひま（な）
いそぐ	hurry	Verb う	18	急ぐ	18	
いたい	painful	Adj い	12	痛い	21	
いただく	receive (respectful)	Verb う	8			
いたまえ	cook	Noun	17	板前	X	
いためる	to stir fry	Verb る	27			
イタリアりょうり	Italian cuisine	Noun	9	料理	12	
いち	one	Noun	3	一	3	
いちがつ	January	N proper	5	一月	5	
いちにちめ	first day	Noun	15	一日目	15	
いちねんせい	first-year student	Noun	2	一年生	11	
いちねんじゅう	all year round	Adv	17	一年中	17	
いちばん	first, best, number one	Noun	9	一番	9	
いつ	when	Adv	4			
いつか	someday, sometime	Adv	23			

	いつかめ	fifth day	Noun	15	五日目	15	
	いっしょうけんめい(に)	with all one's might	Phrase	21	一生けんめい	22	
	いっしょに	together	Phrase	4			
	いつつ	five things	Noun	9	五つ	9	
	いつつめ	fifth	Noun	17	五つ目	17	
	いつでも	anytime	Adv	16			
	いつも	always	Adv	7			
	イベント	event	Noun	20			
	いぬ	dog	Noun	3	犬	21	
	いぬごや	doghouse	Noun	3	犬ごや	21	
	いま	now	Noun	4	今	5	
	いまでも	still now, even now	Adv	18	今でも	18	
	いみ	meaning	Noun	12	意味	20	
	いもうと	younger sister (plain)	Noun	8	妹	8	あね
	いもうとさん	younger sister (resp)	Noun	8	妹さん	8	おねえさん
	いや（な）	annoying, unpleasant	Adj な	25			
	イヤリング	earrings	Noun	10			
	いらっしゃい	welcome (casual)	Phrase	24			
	いらっしゃる	exist (honorific)	Verb う	3			
	いらっしゃる	come, go (honorific)	Verb う	19			
	いる	exist (people, animals)	Verb る	3			
	いれる	turn on (a switch), put into	Verb る	17	入れる	18	
	いれる	put into	Verb る	18	入れる	18	だす
	(おちゃを) いれる	make (tea)	Verb る	24	入れる	24	
	いろ	color	Noun	17	色	17	
	いろいろ（な）	various, many kinds of	Adj な	12	色々	18	
	インストール（する）	installation	N verbal	19			
	インターネット	Internet	N proper	16			
	インタビュー（する）	interview	N verbal	10			
う	ウィスキー	whisky	Noun	9			
	ウィルソン	Wilson	N proper	7			
	ううん	no (casual)	Adv	6			うん
	うえ	on, above	Noun	3	上	5	した
	ウェイター	waiter	Noun	9			
	うえき	garden plant, tree	Noun	23	うえ木	23	
	うえの	Ueno	N proper	15	上野	X	
	ウェブ	Web	N proper	21			
	ウォン	Wong	N proper	2			
	うかる	pass / succeed at (exam, class, etc.)	Verb う	21	受かる	21	おちる

	（しけんを） うける	take (exam)	Verb る	13	受ける	16	
	うごく	move	Verb う	18	動く	19	とまる
	うしろ	back, behind	Noun	3	後ろ	11	まえ
	うた	song	Noun	8	歌	15	
	うたう	sing	Verb う	8	歌う	15	
	うち	house, home	Noun	3	家	6	
	うちゅうひこうし	astronaut	Noun	17	宇宙飛行士	X	
	うっかり	carelessly	Adv	15			
	うっかりする	forget to do something carelessly	V irreg	15			
	うつす	copy	Verb う	25			
	うなぎ	eel	Noun	12			
	うまれる	be born	Verb る	20	生まれる	20	しぬ
	うるさい	noisy	Adj い	7			しずか（な）
	うれしい (1st person)	happy, pleased	Adj い	13			
	うわぎ	jacket	Noun	21	上着	21	
	うん	yes (casual)	Adv	5			ううん
	うんてん（する）	drive	N verbal	11	運転	19	
	うんどう（する）	exercise	N verbal	4	運動	19	
え	え	picture, drawing	Noun	9	絵	15	
	えいが	movie	Noun	4	映画	15	
	えいかいわ	English conversation	Noun	26	英会話	26	
	えいがかん	movie theater	Noun	18	映画館	18	
	えいご	English	Noun	2	英語	6	
	えいこくじん	British (person)	Noun	22	英国人	22	
	えいぶんがく	English literature	Noun	11	英文学	11	
	エイミー	Amy	N proper	2			
	えき	station	Noun	4	駅	20	
	エグザミナー	Examiner	N proper	2			
	えさ	feed, pet food	Noun	23			
	エッセー	essay	Noun	11			
	エネルギー	energy	Noun	25			
	えらぶ	choose, select	Verb う	24			
	エルビス	Elvis	N proper	11			
	～えん	X Yen	Counter	9	～円	9	
	エンジニア	engineer	Noun	17			
	えんそう（する）	music performance	N verbal	17			
	えんぴつ	pencil	Noun	2			
	えんりょ（する）	reservation, hesitation	N verbal	19			
お	おい	nephew (plain)	Noun	8			めい
	おいごさん	nephew (respectful)	Noun	8			めいごさん
	おいしい	delicious	Adj い	7			まずい

おいしゃさん	medical doctor	Noun	16	お医者さん	21	
おうぼ（する）	application	N verbal	26			
おえる	finish (transitive)	Verb る	18	終える	18	はじめる
おおい	many, plenty	Adj い	10	多い	10	すくない
おおきい	big, large	Adj い	7	大きい	7	ちいさい
オークランド	Oakland	N proper	5			
おおさか	Osaka	N proper	7	大阪	X	
オーストラリア	Australia	N proper	22			
おおぜい	many (people)	Noun	18			
オーダー（する）	order	N verbal	9			
おおどおり	boulevard	Noun	11	大どおり	11	
オートバイ	motorcycle	Noun	14			
オーバー	overcoat	Noun	22			
おおや（さん）	landlord	Noun	18			テナント
おかあさん	mother (respectful)	Noun	8	お母さん	8	おとうさん
おかげさまで	thanks to X	Phrase	18			
おかし	snack	Noun	11			
おかね	money	Noun	6	お金	7	
おかんじょう	check	Noun	9			
おきゃくさま	guest (respectful)	Noun	18	お客様	26	
おきゃくさん	guest	Noun	18	お客さん	26	
おきる	wake up, get up	Verb る	5			ねる
おくさん	wife (respectful)	Noun	8			ごしゅじん
おくりもの	present	Noun	14	おくり物	14	
おくる	send	Verb う	10	送る	24	
おくれる	be late for	Verb る	14			まにあう
おこさん	child (respectful)	Noun	8	お子さん	16	
おこす	wake up (transitive)	Verb う	25			
おこめ	uncooked rice	Noun	12	お米	12	
おこる	get angry	Verb う	17			
おごる	treat someone to something	Verb う	24			
おさけ	liquor, Japanese sake	Noun	5	お酒	16	
おさしみ	raw fish	Noun	6			
おさとう	sugar	Noun	12			
おさら	dish	Noun	14			
おじ	uncle (plain)	Noun	8			おば
おじいさん	grandfather (respect)	Noun	8			おばあさん
おじいさん	old man	Noun	24			おばあさん
おしえる	teach	Verb る	5	教える	14	ならう
おしえる	tell, inform	Verb る	24	教える	14	
おしお	salt	Noun	12			

おじさん	uncle (respectful)	Noun	8			おばさん
おじさん	middle-aged man	Noun	24			おばさん
おしゃべり（する）	chat	N verbal	19			
おしょうがつ	(1st month of) New Year	N proper	14	お正月	23	
おす	vinegar	Noun	11			
おす	push	Verb う	17			
おすし	sushi	Noun	4			
おせいぼ	year-end present	Noun	23			
おせわになる	be cared for	Phrase	15			
おせんべい	rice cracker	Noun	19			
おせんべつ	good-bye present	Noun	23			
おそい	slow, late	Adj い	11			はやい
おそうしき	funeral ceremony	Noun	14			
おそくまで	until late	Phrase	19			
おだいば	Odaiba	N proper	16	お台場	X	
おちつく	calm down	Verb う	17			
おちゃ	tea	Noun	4	お茶	9	
おちゃ	tea ceremony	Noun	18	お茶	18	
おちゅうげん	midyear present	Noun	23	お中元	23	
(しけんに) おちる	fail (exam)	Verb る	15	落ちる	26	うかる
おっしゃる	say (honorific)	Verb う	19			
おつり	change	Noun	12			
おてあらい	toilet, lavatory, restroom	Noun	3	お手洗い	16	
おてら	Buddhist temple	Noun	13			
おてんき	weather	Noun	13	お天気	22	
おと	sound	Noun	18	音	18	
おとうさん	father (respectful)	Noun	8	お父さん	8	おかあさん
おとうと	younger brother (plain)	Noun	8	弟	8	あに
おとうとさん	younger brother (resp)	Noun	8	弟さん	8	おにいさん
おとこ	male	Noun	2	男	8	おんな
おとこのこ	boy	Noun	25	男の子	25	おんなのこ
おとしだま	new year's gift money	Noun	23	お年だま	23	
おととい	day before yesterday	Noun	13			あさって
おととし	year before last	Noun	13			さらいねん
おとな	adult	Noun	16	大人	16	こども
おどる	dance	Verb う	13			
おどろく	get surprised	Verb う	19			
おなか	stomach	Noun	9			
おなじ	same	Adj irreg	22	同じ	22	ちがう（V う）
おなまえ	name (respectful)	Noun	1	お名前	11	
おにいさん	elder brother (respect)	Noun	8	お兄さん	8	おとうとさん

おねえさん	elder sister (respectful)	Noun	8	お姉さん	8	いもうとさん
おねがい（する）	favor, request	N verbal	9	お願い	25	
おば	aunt (plain)	Noun	8			おじ
おばあさん	grandmother (respect)	Noun	8			おじいさん
おばあさん	old woman	Noun	24			おじいさん
おばさん	aunt (respectful)	Noun	8			おじさん
おばさん	middle-aged woman	Noun	24			おじさん
おはし	chopsticks	Noun	4			
おはなみ	flower viewing	Noun	17	お花見	17	
オフィス	office	Noun	3			
オフィスアワー	office hours	Noun	10			
おふろ	bath	Noun	14			
おべんとう	box lunch	Noun	14			
おぼえる	memorize	Verb る	12	覚える	15	わすれる
おまごさん	grandchild (respectful)	Noun	8			
おまつり	festival	Noun	13			
おまわりさん	police(wo)man	Noun	20			
おみせ	store, shop	Noun	6	お店	12	
おみやげ	gift	Noun	13			
おめでとう（ございます）	congratulations	Phrase	24			
おもい	heavy	Adj い	14			かるい
おもう	think	Verb う	20	思う	20	
おもしろい	interesting	Adj い	7			つまらない
おもしろい	funny, amusing	Adj い	26			つまらない
おもち	rice cake	Noun	14			
おや	parent(s)	Noun	26	親	26	
およぐ	swim	Verb う	6	泳ぐ	25	
おりる	get off (train, airplane)	Verb る	17			のる
おれい（する）	gratitude	N verbal	27			
オレンジ	orange	Noun	9			
（おかねを）おろす	withdraw (money)	Verb う	18			
おわり	end	Noun	23	終わり	23	
おわる	finish (intransitive)	Verb う	18	終わる	18	はじまる
おんがく	music	Noun	9	音楽	11	
おんがくかい	music concert	Noun	25	音楽会	25	
おんな	female	Noun	2	女	8	おとこ
おんなのこ	girl	Noun	25	女の子	25	おとこのこ

か

か	or	Particle	15			
カーテン	curtain, drapes	Noun	24			
ガールフレンド	girlfriend	Noun	26			ボーイフレンド
～かい	X times	Counter	22	～回	22	

かいぎ	meeting	Noun	18			
かいけいし	accountant	Noun	20			
がいこく	foreign country	Noun	11	外国	16	
がいこくご	foreign language	Noun	18	外国語	18	
がいこくじん	foreigner	Noun	16	外国人	16	
かいしゃ	company	Noun	14	会社	23	
かいしゃいん	company employee, office worker	Noun	17	会社員	23	
がいしょく（する）	eating out	N verbal	26	外食	26	
かいてん（する）	opening a store	N verbal	24	開店	24	へいてん
かいもの（する）	shopping	N verbal	4	買い物	12	
かいわ	conversation	Noun	15	会話	15	
かう	buy	Verb う	5	買う	6	
かえす	return	Verb う	6	返す	13	かりる
かえる	go home, return	Verb う	4	帰る	8	でかける
かえる	change	Verb る	17			
かえる	frog	Noun	25			
かお	face	Noun	15	顔	21	
かおいろ	face color, complexion	Noun	21	顔色	21	
かがく	chemistry	Noun	22	化学	22	
かがくしゃ	scientist	Noun	17	科学者	X	
かかる	take (time, expense)	Verb う	10			
かぎ	key	Noun	15			
かきかた	way of writing	Noun	13	書き方	13	
かきなおす	rewrite, revise	Verb う	23	書きなおす	23	
かく	write	Verb う	4	書く	9	けす
かく	draw	Verb う	9			けす
がくせい	student	Noun	1	学生	5	
がくぶ	academic department	Noun	11	学部	11	
がくぶせい	undergraduate student	Noun	25	学部生	25	
〜かげつ	X month(s)	Counter	9	〜か月	9	
(アイロンを) かける	iron	Verb る	24			
(かぎを) かける	lock (with a key)	Verb る	24			あける
(めがねを) かける	wear (glasses)	Verb る	10			はずす
かさ	umbrella	Noun	6			
かざん	volcano	Noun	20	火山	20	
かしだす	lend out	Verb う	25	貸し出す	25	かりだす
かす	lend	Verb う	8	貸す	23	かりる
かぜ	a cold	Noun	14			
かぜぐすり	cold medicine	Noun	21	かぜ薬	21	
かぞく	family (plain)	Noun	8	家族	26	
かた	person (respectful)	Noun	2	方	11	

かた	shoulder	Noun	21			
～がた	polite plural marker (people)	Suffix	26	～方	26	
かたい	tough, hard	Adj い	11			やわらかい
カタカナ	katakana	Noun	2			ひらがな
かたち	shape	Noun	23			
かたづける	straighten (clean) up	Verb る	18			
カタログ	catalogue	Noun	24			
(～に) かつ	win (a game)	Verb う	22			まける
～がつ	Xth month	Suffix	5	～月	5	
がっかりする	be disappointed	V irreg	23			
がっき	semester, academic term	Noun	25	学期	25	
がっこう	school	Noun	10	学校	10	
かつどう (する)	activity	N verbal	25			
かど	corner	Noun	17			
かない	wife (plain)	Noun	8			しゅじん
かなざわ	Kanazawa	N proper	22	金沢	X	
かなしい	sad	Adj い	17			うれしい
カナダ	Canada	N proper	6			
カナダじん	Canadian people	Noun	6	カナダ人	6	
かならず	be sure to do something	Adv	21			
かなり	fairly	Adv	22			
かに	crab	Noun	20			
かね	money	Noun	6	金	7	
かのじょ	she	Pronoun	26			かれ
かばん	briefcase	Noun	3			
かびん	vase	Noun	21			
カフェテリア	cafeteria	Noun	4			
かぶき	kabuki	Noun	15			
かぶる	wear (hat, cap)	Verb う	10			とる
かべ	wall	Noun	21			
かみ	hair	Noun	7			
かみ	paper	Noun	11	紙	11	
かむ	bite	Verb う	25			
カメラ	camera	Noun	3			
かゆい	itchy	Adj い	21			
かようび	Tuesday	N proper	4	火曜日	4	
から	from	Particle	4			
から	because	Conj	5			
から	since	Particle	15			
からい	hot, spicy, salty	Adj い	19			あまい
カラオケ	karaoke	Noun	12			

からだ	body	Noun	26			
かりだす	check out	Verb う	25	借り出す	25	かしだす
カリフォルニア	California	N proper	3			
かりる	borrow	Verb る	6	借りる	23	かえす、かす
かるい	light (weight)	Adj い	14			おもい
かれ	he	Pronoun	26			かのじょ
カレーライス	curry rice	Noun	9			
かわ	river	Noun	17	川	17	
かわいい	cute	Adj い	9			
かわいそう（な）	pitiable, pitiful	Adj な	26			
かわく	get dry	Verb う	16			
かわもと	Kawamoto	N proper	26	川本	26	
かんがえ	thought	Noun	24	考え	24	
かんがえかた	way of thinking	Noun	20	考え方	24	
かんがえる	think	Verb る	11	考える	24	
かんこくご	Korean language	Noun	6	かんこく語	6	
かんこくじん	Korean people	Noun	6	かんこく人	6	
かんごし	nurse	Noun	17	看護師	X	
かんじ	Chinese characters	Noun	10	漢字	10	
かんせい（する）	completion	N verbal	19			
かんたん（な）	easy	Adj な	9			むずかしい
がんばる	do one's best	Verb う	6			
き	tree	Noun	17	木	17	
キーホルダー	key holder	Noun	17			
きいろ	yellow	Noun	17	き色	17	
きいろい	yellow	Adj い	17	き色い	17	
きえる	turn off (intransitive)	Verb る	10			つく
ききとり	listening	Noun	16	聞き取り	16	
きく	listen, ask	Verb う	5	聞く	11	
きけん（な）	dangerous	Adj な	25			あんぜん（な）
きこえる	be audible	Verb る	25	聞こえる	25	
きこく（する）	returning to one's home country	N verbal	18	帰国	18	
きせつ	season	Noun	22			
きた	north	Noun	20			
ギター	guitar	Noun	9			
きたない	dirty	Adj い	7			きれい（な）
きっさてん	café, coffee shop	Noun	15	きっさ店	15	
きって	postage stamp	Noun	15	切手	20	
きっと	surely	Adv	20			
きっぷ	ticket	Noun	13	切符	22	
きのう	yesterday	Noun	5	昨日	5	あした

	きびしい	severe, strict	Adj い	26			
	きぶん	feelings, mood	Noun	21	気分	21	
	きまつしけん	final exam	Noun	16	期末	16	
					試験	17	
	キム	Kim	N proper	4			
	きむら	Kimura	N proper	3	木村	15	
	きめる	decide	Verb る	23			
	きもち	feelings, mood	Noun	17	気持ち	24	
	きもの	kimono	Noun	18	着物	24	
	キャンパス	campus	Noun	6			
	キャンプ（する）	camping	N verbal	20			
	きゅう	nine	Noun	3	九	3	
	ぎゅうにく	beef	Noun	12	ぎゅう肉	24	
	きょう	today	Noun	4	今日	5	
	きょうかしょ	textbook	Noun	9	教科書	20	
	きょうし	teacher	Noun	17	教師	X	
	きょうしつ	classroom	Noun	3	教室	14	
	きょうだい	siblings	Noun	8	兄弟	8	
	きょうと	Kyoto	N proper	2	京都	13	
	きょねん	last year	Noun	8	去年	12	らいねん
	きらい（な）	dislike	Adj な	9			すき（な）
	きらう	hate	Verb う	26			
	きる	wear (dress, shirt, suit)	Verb る	10	着る	21	ぬぐ
	きる	cut, chop	Verb う	24	切る	24	つなげる
	きれい（な）	clean, beautuful	Adj な	7			きたない
	きをつける	be careful	Phrase	16	気をつける	16	
	きをつける	pay attention to	Phrase	23	気をつける	23	
	きんこ	safe	Noun	26			
	ぎんこう	bank	Noun	3	銀行	10	
	ぎんざ	Ginza	N proper	15	銀座	X	
	きんじょ	neighborhood	Noun	19	近所	24	
	きんようび	Friday	N proper	4	金曜日	4	
く	く	nine	Noun	3	九	3	
	グアム	Guam	N proper	22			
	くうこう	airport	Noun	13			
	くがつ	September	N proper	5	九月	5	
	くさ	grass	Noun	25			
	くしゃみ（する）	sneeze	N verbal	21			
	くすり	medicine	Noun	16	薬	21	
	くすりや	drug store	Noun	16	薬屋	21	
	ください	please give	Phrase	8	下さい	8	
	くださる	give	Verb う	23	下さる	23	

くだもの	fruit	Noun	9			
くち	mouth	Noun	7	口	21	
くつ	shoes	Noun	6			
クッキー	cookie	Noun	11			
グッスリ	deep sleep (sound symbolic)	Adv	25			
くに	country	Noun	14	国	14	
くび	neck	Noun	21			
くらい	dark	Adj い	7	暗い	7	あかるい
～ぐらい	about, approximately	Suffix	10			
クラシック	classical music	Noun	9			
クラス	class	Noun	2			
クラスメート	classmate	Noun	9			
クラッカー	cracker	Noun	24			
クラブ	club	Noun	11			
クラブ	club, disco	Noun	20			
グランドキャニオン	Grand Canyon	N proper	22			
クリスマス	Christmas	N proper	16			
くる	come	V irreg	4	来る	5	いく
グループ	group	Noun	14			
くるま	car	Noun	2	車	7	
クレジットカード	credit card	Noun	25			
くれる	give	Verb る	23			あげる
くろ	black	Noun	17			
くろい	black	Adj い	17			
くわしい	detailed	Adj い	19			

け

けいかく（する）	plan	N verbal	25	計画	25	
けいざい	economy	Noun	20			
けいざいアナリスト	economic analyst	Noun	17	経済アナリスト	X	
けいざいがく	economics	Noun	2	けいざい学	11	
けいざいてき（な）	economical	Adj な	20			
けいさつ	police	Noun	23			
げいじゅつか	artist	Noun	17	芸術家	X	
けいたいでんわ	cellular phone	Noun	16	電話	15	
ケーキ	cake	Noun	7			
ゲーム	game	Noun	18			
けさ	this morning	Noun	12	今朝	12	こんばん
けしゴム	eraser	Noun	23			
けす	turn off	Verb う	14			つける
けす	erase	Verb う	18			かく
けっか	result	Noun	24			
けっこう（な）	fine, nice, wonderful	Adj な	8			だめ（な）

	けっこん（する）	marriage	N verbal	19	結婚	26	りこん（する）
	けっこんしき	wedding ceremony	Noun	14	結婚しき	26	
	げつようび	Monday	N proper	4	月曜日	4	
	けれども	but	Conj	18			
	けんか（する）	quarrel	N verbal	15			
	けんがく（する）	study tour	N verbal	20	見学	20	
	げんかん	entrance	Noun	15			
	げんき	high spirits, good health	Noun	25	元気	25	
	げんき（な）	energetic	Adj な	7	元気	11	
	けんきゅう（する）	research	N verbal	20			
	げんこう	draft	Noun	22			
	げんごがく	linguistics	Noun	19	言語学	19	
	げんじものがたり	The Tale of Genji	N proper	25	源氏物語	X	
	けんちくか	architect	Noun	17	建築家	X	
	けんどう	kendo	Noun	14			
	けんぶつ（する）	sightseeing	N verbal	16	見物	16	
こ	〜こ	X unit(s)	Counter	9	〜個	23	
	ご	five	Noun	3	五	3	
	〜ご	suffix (language)	Suffix	6	〜語	6	
	こうえん	park	Noun	6			
	こうえん（する）	lecture	N verbal	20			
	ごうか（な）	deluxe, luxurious, gorgeous	Adj な	24			
	こうぎ（する）	lecture	N verbal	15			
	こうこう	high school	Noun	8	高校	8	
	こうこうせい	high school student	Noun	8	高校生	8	
	こうすい	perfume	Noun	23			
	こうつう	transportation	Noun	26			
	こうつうじこ	traffic accident	Noun	22	事故	23	
	こうばん	police box	Noun	20			
	コース	course	Noun	7			
	コート	coat	Noun	15			
	コーヒー	coffee	Noun	4			
	コーラ	cola	Noun	4			
	ごかい（する）	misunderstanding	N verbal	27			
	ごかぞく	family (respectful)	Noun	8	ご家族	26	
	ごがつ	May	N proper	5	五月	5	
	ごきょうだい	siblings (respectful)	Noun	8	ご兄弟	8	
	こくばん	blackboard	Noun	18			
	ゴクンと	swallowing (sound symbolic)	Adv	25			
	ここ	here	Pronoun	2			そこ、あそこ

ごご	afternoon, P.M.	Noun	4	午後	13	ごぜん
ここのかめ	ninth day	Noun	15	九日目	15	
ここのつ	nine things	Noun	9	九つ	9	
ここのつめ	ninth	Noun	17	九つ目	17	
こし	waist, hips	Noun	21			
ごしゅじん	husband (respectful)	Noun	8			おくさん
こしょう（する）	breakdown	N verbal	22			なおる
こする	rub	Verb う	17			
ごぜん	morning, A.M.	Noun	4	午前	13	ごご
ごせんもん	major, speciality (resp)	Noun	1	ご専門	22	
ごぞんじだ	know (honorific)	Phrase	19			
こたえ	answer	Noun	16	答え	20	
こたえる	answer	Verb る	15	答える	20	しつもんする
ごちそうする	treat someone to something	V irreg	24			
こちら	this direction	Pronoun	7			そちら、あちら
こづつみ	parcel	Noun	11	小づつみ	11	
こと	matter, affair	Noun	16			
こと	koto (Japanese musical instrument)	Noun	24			
ことし	this year	Noun	8	今年	10	
ことば	language, word	Noun	16	言葉	16	
こども	child (plain)	Noun	8	子供	16	おとな
こどもたち	children	Noun	15	子供達	16	おとなたち
ことわる	decline	Verb う	25			ひきうける
この + NOUN	this NOUN	Adj irreg	2			その、あの
このあいだ	some time ago, the other day	Phrase	12	この間	23	
このは	leaf of a tree	Noun	17	木の葉	17	
ごはん	(cooked) rice, meal	Noun	4			
コピー（する）	copy	N verbal	4			
こぼす	spill	Verb う	18			
こまる	get in trouble	Verb う	15	困る	23	
こむ	get crowded	Verb う	21			すく
こむぎこ	wheat flour	Noun	12			
こめ	uncooked rice	Noun	12	米	12	
こやま	Koyama	N proper	3	小山	5	
ごらんになる	see, watch (honorific)	Verb う	19			
ごりょうしん	parents (respectful)	Noun	8	ご両親	20	
ゴルフ	golf	Noun	6			
これ	this one	Pronoun	2			それ、あれ
これから	now, from now on	Phrase	4			

	～ごろ	about, approximately	Suffix	10			
	ころす	kill	Verb う	25			
	コロンブス	Columbus	N proper	11			
	こわい	threatening, scary	Adj い	19			
	こわす	break (transitive)	Verb う	18			しゅうり（する）、つくる、なおす
	こわれる	break (intransitive)	Verb る	15			なおる
	こんがっき	this semester	Noun	15	今学期	15	
	こんげつ	this month	Noun	13	今月	13	
	コンサート	concert	Noun	22			
	こんしゅう	this week	Noun	12	今週	13	
	こんしゅうまつ	this weekend	Noun	20	今週末	20	
	こんど	next time	Noun	6	今度	18	
	こんばん	this evening	Noun	5	今晩	6	けさ
	コンピューター	computer	Noun	2			
	コンピューターショップ	computer store	Noun	18			
	コンピュータープログラマー	computer programmer	Noun	17			
	こんや	this evening	Noun	21	今夜	21	けさ
さ	サービス（する）	service	N verbal	11			
	～さい	X year(s) old	Counter	14			
	サイエンス	science	Noun	2			
	さいきん	recently	Noun	14	最近	22	むかし
	さいご	final, last	Noun	22	最後	22	さいしょ
	さいしょ	first	Noun	15	最初	26	さいご
	さいふ	purse, wallet	Noun	25			
	さいよう（する）	employment, adoption	N verbal	24			
	サイン（する）	signboard, sign	N verbal	24			
	さがす	search for	Verb う	14			
	さかな	fish	Noun	6	魚	24	
	さがる	come down, fall	Verb う	21	下がる	21	あがる
	さかん（な）	flourishing	Adj な	25			
	さきに	ahead, before	Adv	15	先に	19	
	さく	bloom	Verb う	17			
	さくしゃ	author	Noun	25	作者	25	
	さくぶん	composition, writing	Noun	15	作文	15	
	さくら	cherry blossom/tree	Noun	13			
	さけ	liquor, Japanese sake	Noun	5	酒	16	
	さけ	salmon	Noun	12			
	さしあげる	give	Verb る	23	さし上げる		いただく
	さしみ	raw fish	Noun	6			

(かさを) さす	put up (an umbrella)	Verb う	22			
(めぐすりを) さす	apply (eye drops)	Verb う	23			
さそう	invite	Verb う	20			
～さつ	counter (bound things)	Counter	9	～冊	23	
さっか	writer, novelist	Noun	17	作家	X	
さっき	a little while ago	Adv	22			
ざっし	magazine	Noun	2			
さとう	sugar	Noun	12			
さびしい	lonely	Adj い	13			
サボる	cut classes	Verb う	26			
～さま	suffix (honored person)	Suffix	13	～様	26	
(めを) さます	wake up	Verb う	17			
さむい	cold	Adj い	11	寒い	13	あつい
さめる	get cold	Verb る	18			
さら	dish	Noun	14			
さらいげつ	month after next	Noun	13	さ来月	13	せんせんげつ
さらいしゅう	week after next	Noun	13	さ来週	13	せんせんしゅう
さらいねん	year after next	Noun	13	さ来年	13	おととし
サラダ	salad	Noun	24			
サラリーマン	company employee	Noun	14			
さわる	touch	Verb う	16			
さん	three	Noun	3	三	3	
サンアントニオ	San Antonio	N proper	27			
さんか (する)	participation	N verbal	26			
さんがつ	March	N proper	5	三月	5	
サングラス	sunglasses	Noun	10			
サンディエゴ	San Diego	N proper	4			
さんにん	three persons	Counter	8	三人	8	
ざんねん (な)	regrettable, regret	Adj な	6			
さんねんせい	third-year student	Noun	2	三年生	11	
サンフランシスコ	San Francisco	N proper	2			
さんぽ (する)	stroll	N verbal	13			

し

し	four	Noun	3	四	3	
～じ	X o'clock	Suffix	4	～時	4	
じ	letter, character	Noun	15	字	15	
しあい	match, game	Noun	22			
シアトル	Seattle	N proper	27			
しあわせ (な)	happy	Adj な	26			
ジーンズ	jeans	Noun	10			
シェークスピア	Shakespeare	N proper	11			
シェフ	cook	Noun	17			
しお	salt	Noun	12			

しかくい	square	Adj い	21			まるい
シカゴ	Chicago	N proper	3			
しがつ	April	N proper	5	四月	5	
しかる	scold	Verb う	25			ほめる
～じかん	X hour(s)	Counter	9	～時間	9	
じかん	time	Noun	10	時間	10	
しけん	test, examination	Noun	6	試験	17	
じこ	accident	Noun	23	事故	23	
しごと（する）	job	N verbal	8	仕事	14	
じしょ	dictionary	Noun	2	辞書	23	
しずか（な）	quiet	Adj な	7	静か	11	うるさい
しぜん	nature	Noun	25	自然	25	
した	under, below	Noun	3	下	5	うえ
しち	seven	Noun	3	七	3	
しちがつ	July	N proper	5	七月	5	
じつは	to tell the truth	Phrase	13			
しっぱい（する）	mistake	N verbal	20			
しつもん（する）	question	N verbal	6	質問	19	こたえる
しつれい（な）	impolite	Adj な	7			
じてんしゃ	bicycle	Noun	4	自転車	19	
しながわ	Shinagawa	N proper	15	品川	X	
しぬ	die	Verb う	8	死ぬ	25	うまれる
しぶや	Shibuya	N proper	20	渋谷	X	
じぶん	oneself	Pronoun	20	自分	20	
しまる	close (intransitive)	Verb う	10	閉まる	10	あく
ジミー	Jimmy	N proper	2			
ジム	gymnasium	Noun	4			
しめきり	deadline	Noun	16			
しめる	close (transitive)	Verb る	18	閉める	18	あける
じゃあ	well then	Adv	5			
ジャーナリスト	journalist	Noun	17			
じゃがいも	potato	Noun	12			
しゃしん	photograph	Noun	2	写真	19	
ジャズ	Jazz	Noun	9			
しゃちょう	company president	Noun	25	社長	25	
シャツ	shirt	Noun	17			
ジャック	Jack	N proper	10			
ジャパン	Japan	N proper	11			
シャワー	shower	Noun	13			
シャンペン	champagne	Noun	24			
じゅう	ten	Noun	3	十	3	

～じゅう	in the middle of, throughout	Suffix	17	～中	17	
じゅういちがつ	November	N proper	5	十一月	5	
しゅうがくりょこう	school excursion	Noun	20	旅行	19	
じゅうがつ	October	N proper	5	十月	5	
～しゅうかん	X week(s)	Counter	14	～週間	14	
しゅうかん	custom	Noun	14			
しゅうじ	calligraphy	Noun	26	習字	26	
じゅうしょ	address	Noun	20	住所	20	
しゅうしょく（する）	getting a job	N verbal	19			
しゅうしょくしけん	employment exam	Noun	22	試験	17	
ジュース	juice	Noun	8			
じゅうどう	judo	Noun	19			
じゅうにがつ	December	N proper	5	十二月	5	
しゅうまつ	weekend	Noun	4	週まつ	13	
				週末	16	
しゅうり（する）	repair	N verbal	18			こわす
しゅうりや	repair store	Noun	18	しゅうり屋	18	
じゅぎょう	class	Noun	12	授業	18	
じゅく	cramming school	Noun	26			
しゅくだい	homework	Noun	4	宿題	14	
じゅけん（する）	taking an exam	N verbal	26	受験	26	
しゅじん	husband (plain)	Noun	8			かない
しゅっせき（する）	attendance	N verbal	21			
しゅっぱつ（する）	departure	N verbal	18			とうちゃく（する）
しゅふ	housewife	Noun	17	主婦	X	
シュミット	Schmidt	N proper	8			
じゅんばん	order	Noun	15			
じゅんび（する）	preparation	N verbal	24			
しょうかい（する）	introduction	N verbal	14	紹介	24	
しょうがくきん	scholarship (money)	Noun	19			
しょうがつ	(1st month of) New Year	N proper	14	正月	23	
しょうがっこう	elementary school	Noun	13	小学校	13	
しょうじ	shoji screen	Noun	21			
じょうし	one's superior	Noun	23			
じょうず（な）	good at	Adj な	9	上手	9	へた（な）
しょうせつ	novel	Noun	11	小説	22	
しょうせつか	writer, novelist	Noun	17	小説家	X	
しょうたい（する）	invitation	N verbal	24	招待	24	
しょうたいじょう	invitation letter	Noun	24	招待じょう	24	
じょうだん	joke	Noun	19			

しょうゆ	soy sauce	Noun	12			
しょうらい	in the future	Noun	20			
ショートパンツ	shorts	Noun	10			
ジョーンズ	Jones	N proper	4			
ジョギング（する）	jogging	N verbal	5			
しょくじ（する）	meal	N verbal	17	食事	17	
ショッピングセンター	shopping center/mall	Noun	19			
しょどう	calligraphy	Noun	19			
じょゆう	actress	Noun	17	女優	X	
ジョン	John	N proper	11			
しらべる	check	Verb る	14	調べる	23	
しる	get to know	Verb う	10	知る	10	
しろ	white	Noun	17	白	17	
しろい	white	Adj い	17	白い	17	
シン	Singh	N proper	7			
～じん	suffix (nationality)	Suffix	6	～人	6	
しんおおさか	Shin-Osaka	N proper	10	新大阪	X	
しんかんせん	Japanese bullet train	N proper	4			
しんごう	traffic light	Noun	17			
じんじゃ	Shinto shrine	Noun	13			
しんじゅく	Shinjuku	N proper	15	新宿	15	
しんせき	relatives	Noun	23			
しんせつ（な）	kind	Adj な	7	親切	20	いじわる（な）
しんねん	new year	Noun	24	新年	24	
しんぱい（する）	anxiety, concern, worry	N verbal	19	心配	21	あんしん（する）
シンフォニー	symphony	Noun	22			
しんぶん	newspaper	Noun	2	新聞	11	
しんりがく	psychology	Noun	22	心理学	22	

す

す	vinegar	Noun	11			
すいえい（する）	swimming	N verbal	26	水泳	26	
すいせんじょう	recommendation letter	Noun	24			
スイッチ	switch	Noun	17			
すいようび	Wednesday	N proper	4	水曜日	4	
すう	inhale	Verb う	16			
すうがく	mathematics	Noun	6	数学	26	
スーツ	suit	Noun	10			
スーツケース	suitcase	Noun	13			
スーパー	supermarket	Noun	4			
スープ	soup	Noun	24			
スカート	skirt	Noun	10			
スカーフ	scarf	Noun	15			
すき（な）	like	Adj な	9	好き	9	きらい（な）

スキー	ski	Noun	6			
スキット	skit	Noun	13			
すきやき	Sukiyaki	Noun	9			
すく	become empty	Verb う	9			こむ
すぐ	immediately, soon	Adv	5			
すくない	very few/little	Adj い	19	少ない	19	おおい
スクリーン	screen (of a computer)	Noun	17			
スケジュール	schedule	Noun	18			
スケッチ（する）	sketch	N verbal	16			
すごい	teriffic	Adj い	11			
すこし	a little	Adv	6	少し	11	たくさん
すし	sushi	Noun	4			
すずしい	cool	Adj い	11			あたたかい
ずっと	continuously, all the time	Adv	15			
ずっと	much more	Adv	26			
すっぱい	sour	Adj い	20			
ステーキ	steak	Noun	5			
すてき（な）	superb, splendid	Adj な	18			
ステレオ	stereo (set)	Noun	11			
ストレス	stress	Noun	25			
スニーカー	sneakers	Noun	10			
スパイ	spy	Noun	25			
スパゲティ	spaghetti	Noun	6			
スピーカー	speaker	Noun	24			
スピーチ（する）	speech	N verbal	18			
スペインご	Spanish language	Noun	6	スペイン語	6	
スポーツ	sport	Noun	9			
スポーツ・インストラクター	sports instructor	Noun	17			
スポーツせんしゅ	athlete	Noun	17	～選手	X	
ズボン	trousers, pants	Noun	10			
スミス	Smith	N proper	7			
すむ	start living somewhere	Verb う	10	住む	10	
すもう	sumo wrestling	Noun	10			
すり	pickpocket	Noun	25			
する	do	V irreg	4			
する	wear (accessory)	V irreg	10			とる、はずす
すると	then	Conj	25			
すわる	sit down	Verb う	10			たつ

せ

せ	body height	Noun	7	背	11	
せいきょう	co-op	Noun	14			
ぜいきん	tax	Noun	19			

せいじ	politics	Noun	20			
せいじか	politician	Noun	17	政治家	X	
せいじてき（な）	political	Adj な	20			
せいせき	grade	Noun	14	成績	25	
せいぶつがく	biology	Noun	11	生物学	21	
せいぼ	year-end present	Noun	23			
セーター	sweater	Noun	10			
セール	sale	Noun	7			
せかいじゅう	all over the world	Phrase	25	せかい中	25	
せき	cough	Noun	21			
せき	seat	Noun	22			
セクハラ	sexual harassment	Noun	26			
ぜったいに	absolutely	Adv	16			
せつめい（する）	explanation	N verbal	16	説明	22	
せつやく（する）	saving, thrift	N verbal	20			
せなか	back (body)	Noun	21	背中	21	
ぜひ	by all means	Adv	14			
せまい	narrow, small	Adj い	7			ひろい
せわ（する）	care	N verbal	18			
せわになる	be cared for	Phrase	15			
せん	thousand	Noun	3	千	3	
せんがっき	last semester	Noun	17	先学期	17	らいがっき
せんげつ	last month	Noun	13	先月	13	らいげつ
せんしゅ	sports player	Noun	11			
せんしゅう	last week	Noun	5	先週	13	らいしゅう
せんせい	teacher	Noun	1	先生	5	
ぜんぜん	(not) at all	Adv	7	全然	25	
せんせんげつ	month before last	Noun	13	先々月	13	さらいげつ
せんせんしゅう	week before last	Noun	13	先々週	13	さらいしゅう
せんたく（する）	laundry	N verbal	12	洗濯	16	
せんたくき	washing machine	Noun	16	洗濯機	16	
セント	cent(s)	Noun	9			
セントルイス	St, Louis	N proper	27			
せんぱい	one's senior	Noun	19			
ぜんぶ	all	Adv	12	全部	12	
せんべい	rice cracker	Noun	19			
せんべつ	good-bye present	Noun	23			
せんもん	major, speciality	Noun	1	専門	22	
せんもんがっこう	vocational school	Noun	26	専門学校	26	
せんもんてき（な）	professional	Adj な	20	専門	22	
そ						
そう	so	Adv	24			
そうじ（する）	clean	N verbal	9			

そうしき	funeral ceremony	Noun	14			
そうだん（する）	consultation	N verbal	18	相談	23	
そうりつ（する）	establishment, founding	N verbal	25			
そこ	there	Pronoun	2			ここ
そこ	bottom	Noun	11			
そして	and then	Conj	4			
そちら	that direction	Pronoun	7			こちら
そつぎょう（する）	graduation	N verbal	13	卒業	18	にゅうがく（する）
そつぎょうしき	graduation ceremony	Noun	23	卒業しき	18	
ソックス	socks	Noun	10			
そっと	softly	Adv	26			
そと	outside	Noun	3	外	16	なか
その + NOUN	that NOUN	Adj irreg	2			この
そふ	grandfather (plain)	Noun	8			そぼ
ソファー	sofa	Noun	3			
ソフト	software	Noun	24			
そぼ	grandmother (plain)	Noun	8			
そぼろ	minced meat	Noun	27			
そら	sky	Noun	22			
そる	shave	Verb う	18			
それ	that one	Pronoun	2			これ
それから	after that	Phrase	4			
それじゃ	well then (casual)	Conj	6			
それで	therefore, so that	Conj	8			
それでは	well then (formal)	Adv	18			
それなのに	nevertheless	Adv	26			
それに	besides, moreover, in addition to that	Conj	20			
そろばん	abacus	Noun	26			
ソン	Son	N proper	2			
そんなに	that much	Adv	26			
た ターキー	turkey	Noun	24			
タイ	Thailand	N proper	11			
〜だい	counter (cars, TV, etc.)	Counter	9			
ダイエット（する）	diet	N verbal	12			
たいおんけい	thermometer	Noun	21			
だいがく	college, university	Noun	2	大学	7	
だいがくいんせい	graduate student	Noun	2	大学院生	11	
だいがくせい	undergraduate student	Noun	2	大学生	8	
だいく	carpenter	Noun	17	大工	X	
たいこ	Japanese drum	Noun	22			

だいじ（な）	important	Adj な	20	大事	20	
たいしかん	embassy	Noun	20	大使館	20	
だいじょうぶ（な）	alright, okay	Adj な	12			
だいすき（な）	like very much	Adj な	12	大好き	12	
たいせつ（な）	important	Adj な	22	大切	22	
だいとうりょう	president of a country	Noun	22			
タイプ	typing	N verbal	22			
だいぶつ	great statue of Buddha	Noun	15			
たいへん（な）	tough	Adj な	5	大変	14	らく（な）
タイムズ	Times	N proper	2			
ダウンタウン	downtown	Noun	4			
たおれる	fall over	Verb る	21			
たかい	expensive, high	Adj い	7	高い	7	やすい
たかだ	Takada	N proper	23	高田	23	
たからもの	treasure	Noun	18	たから物	18	
（ごはんを）たく	to cook (rice)	Verb う	27			
たくさん	a lot, many	Adj irreg	5			すこし
タクシー	taxi	Noun	8			
たしかに	undoubtedly	Adv	16			
たす	add	Verb う	17			ひく
だす	submit, send out (HW, letter)	Verb う	16	出す	16	
だす	serve, put out	Verb う	24	出す	24	
たすかる	be saved	Verb う	19			
たすける	help	Verb る	13			
ただ	free of charge	Noun	25			
たたく	pat	Verb う	25			
ただしい	correct	Adj い	17	正しい	22	まちがっている（V う）
たたみ	tatami mat	Noun	17			
～たち	plural marker (people)	Suffix	2	～達	13	
たつ	stand up	Verb う	10			すわる
たつ	be built	Verb う	18			
たてもの	building	Noun	20	たて物	20	
たとえば	for example	Phrase	21			
たなか	Tanaka	N proper	3	田中	19	
たのしい	enjoyable, pleasant	Adj い	9	楽しい	13	
たのしみにする	look forward to	Phrase	4	楽しみ	13	
たのしむ	enjoy	Verb う	26	楽しむ	26	
たのむ	ask, request	Verb う	25			
タバコ	tobacco, cigarette	Noun	16			
たぶん	perhaps, probably	Adv	17	多分	17	

たべもの	food	Noun	9	食べ物	12	
たべる	eat	Verb る	4	食べる	6	
タホ	Tahoe	N proper	5			
たまご	egg	Noun	12			
たまに	once in a while	Adv	26			
たまねぎ	onion	Noun	12			
たまる	accumulate	Verb う	25			
だめ（な）	no good	Adj な	11			いい、けっこう（な）
ダラス	Dallas	N proper	27			
たりる	be sufficient	Verb る	19	足りる	21	
だれ	who	Pronoun	2			
だれか	someone	Pronoun	3			だれも
だれも	anyone	Pronoun	3			だれか
たんい	unit(s)	Noun	16			
たんけんか	explorer	Noun	17	探検家	X	
タンゴ	Tango	N proper	13			
たんご	vocabulary, word	Noun	14	単語	18	
たんじょうび	birthday	Noun	12	たんじょう日	12	
ダンス（する）	dance	N verbal	11			
だんだん	gradually	Adv	18			
たんてい	private detective	Noun	24			

ち

ち	blood	Noun	11			
ちいさい	small	Adj い	7	小さい	7	おおきい
チーズ	cheese	Noun	24			
チーズケーキ	cheesecake	Noun	21			
チーム	team	Noun	11			
ちえ	wisdom, intelligence	Noun	11			
チェン	Chen	N proper	5			
ちかい	near	Adj い	7	近い	20	とおい
ちがい	difference	Noun	20			
ちがう	be different	Verb う	19			おなじ
ちがう	be wrong	Verb う	19			
ちかく	vicinity	Noun	3	近く	20	
ちかてつ	subway	Noun	15	地下鉄	25	
ちから	power	Noun	11			
ちこく（する）	being late for something	N verbal	22			
ちず	map	Noun	9	地図	24	
ちち	father (plain)	Noun	8	父	8	はは
ちちのひ	Father's Day	N proper	23	父の日	23	
ちば	Chiba	N proper	19	千葉	19	
チャイナタウン	Chinatown	Noun	5			

ちゃわん	tea cup	Noun	24	茶わん	24	
ちゃわんむし	thick custard soup	Noun	24	茶わんむし	24	
～ちゃん	suffix (child's name)	Suffix	23			
ちゃんと	properly	Adv	26			
～ちゅう	in the middle of, throughout	Suffix	17	～中	17	
ちゅうい (する)	warning	N verbal	18	注意	25	
ちゅうかがい	Chinatown	Noun	19			
ちゅうがくせい	junior high school student	Noun	17	中学生	17	
ちゅうがっこう	junior high school	Noun	13	中学校	13	
ちゅうかりょうり	Chinese cuisine	Noun	9	料理	12	
ちゅうかん	midterm	Noun	6	中間	6	
ちゅうげん	midyear present	Noun	23	中元	23	
ちゅうごく	China	N proper	9	中国	9	
ちゅうごくご	Chinese language	Noun	6	中国語	9	
ちゅうごくじん	Chinese people	Noun	6	中国人	9	
ちゅうとう	Middle East	N proper	22	中東	22	
ちゅうもん (する)	order	N verbal	21	注文	25	
ちょきん (する)	savings	N verbal	18	貯金	19	
ちょきんばこ	piggy bank	Noun	25	貯金ばこ	19	
チョコレート	chocolate	Noun	12			
ちょっと	a little	Adv	7			たくさん

つ

～つ	X unit(s)	Counter	9			
ツアー・ガイド	tour guide	Noun	17			
つえ	cane	Noun	11			
つかいかた	usage, way to use	Noun	13	使い方	16	
つかう	use	Verb う	6	使う	16	
つかれる	get tired	Verb る	5			
つき	moon	Noun	11	月	11	
つぎ	next	Noun	15	次	25	
つきあたり	the end of a street	Noun	17			
つく	turn on (intransitive)	Verb う	10			きえる
つく	arrive	Verb う	15	着く	21	(X を) でる
つくえ	desk	Noun	3			
つくりかた	way of making	Noun	13	作り方	13	
つくる	make	Verb う	5	作る	9	こわす
つける	turn on (transitive)	Verb る	14			けす
つたえる	tell, inform	Verb る	24	伝える	24	
つづく	continue	Verb う	23			
つなげる	connect (transitive)	Verb る	23			きる
つまらない	trivial, trifle, boring	Adj い	7			おもしろい

	つめたい	cold	Adj い	19	冷たい	24	あつい
	つもり	intention	Noun	5			
	つよい	strong	Adj い	17	強い	17	よわい
	つれていく	take along (person, animal)	Verb う	21	つれて行く	21	つれてくる
	つれてくる	bring (person, animal)	V irreg	16	つれて来る	16	つれていく
て	て	hand, arm	Noun	7	手	11	
	ていしゅつ（する）	submission	N verbal	21			
	ディズニー	Disney	N proper	11			
	ディズニーランド	Disneyland	N proper	14			
	ていねい（な）	polite, courteous	Adj な	19			
	ていねい（な）	thorough, careful, meticulous	Adj な	22			
	デート	date	Noun	26			
	テープ	tape	Noun	6			
	テーブル	table	Noun	3			
	でかける	go out	Verb る	15	出かける	20	かえる
	てがみ	letter	Noun	3	手紙	10	
	テキスト	textbook	Noun	2			
	てきとう（な）	appropriate	Adj な	19			
	できる	be able to	Verb る	6			
	できる	can do, come to being, be done	Verb る	17			
	できるだけ	as much as possible	Phrase	14			
	てくび	wrist	Noun	21	手くび	21	
	デザート	dessert	Noun	9			
	デザイナー	designer	Noun	17			
	デジタルカメラ	digital camera	Noun	23			
	ですから	therefore, so	Conj	6			
	テスト（する）	quiz, examination	N verbal	5			
	てつだい	help, assistance	Noun	18	手伝い	24	
	てつだう	help, assist	Verb う	24	手伝う	24	
	てつや（する）	staying up all night	N verbal	22			
	デトロイト	Detroit	N proper	11			
	テナント	tenant	Noun	18			おおや（さん）
	テニス	tennis	Noun	4			
	デパート	department store	Noun	4			
	てぶくろ	gloves	Noun	24	手ぶくろ	24	
	でも	but	Conj	4			
	デモ	demonstration	Noun	7			
	てら	Buddhist temple	Noun	13			
	（～に）でる	attend, enter (a contest)	Verb る	12	出る	17	やすむ

(～を) でる	leave (some place)	Verb る	15	出る	17	(～に) つく
(～を) でる	come out, go out	Verb る	18	出る	18	はいる
(はなが) でる	have a runny nose	Verb る	21	出る	21	
(ほしが) でる	be out	Verb る	22	出る	22	
テレビ	TV	Noun	4			
テレビきょく	TV station	Noun	20			
てん	points, score	Noun	14			
～てん	X point(s)	Counter	15			
てんいん	store clerk	Noun	12	店員	12	
てんき	weather	Noun	13	天気	22	
でんき	electricity, electric light	Noun	10	電気	15	
でんきや	electric appliance shop	Noun	18	電気屋	18	
てんきよほう	weather forecast	Noun	22	天気よほう	22	
でんしゃ	train	Noun	4	電車	15	
でんしレンジ	microwave oven	Noun	12			
てんちょう	shop/branch manager	Noun	24	店長	24	てんいん
デンバー	Denver	N proper	27			
てんぷら	tempura	Noun	5			
てんらんかい	exhibition	Noun	21	てんらん会	21	
でんわ (する)	telephone	N verbal	10	電話	15	

と

と	door	Noun	17			
～ど	X time(s)	Counter	16	～度	18	
～ど	X degree	Counter	21	～度	21	
ドア	door	Noun	10			
ドイツご	German language	Noun	6	ドイツ語	6	
ドイツじん	German people	Noun	6	ドイツ人	6	
ドイル	Doyle	N proper	3			
どう	how	Adv	7			
どういう + NOUN	what kind of	Phrase	20			
とうきょう	Tokyo	N proper	7	東京	8	
とうきょうタワー	Tokyo Tower	N proper	20	東京タワー	20	
どうして	why	Adv	5			
とうぜん	a matter of course	Noun	26	当然	26	
どうぞ	please	Adv	9			
とうちゃく (する)	arrival	N verbal	15			しゅっぱつ (する)
とうふ	tofu	Noun	12			
どうぶつ	animal	Noun	19	動物	19	
どうろ	street	Noun	21			
とお	ten things	Noun	9	十	9	
とおい	far	Adj い	7	遠い	20	ちかい
とおかめ	tenth day	Noun	15	十日目	15	

とおやま	Toyama	N proper	22	遠山	22	
とおり	street	Noun	11			
とき	time, when	Noun	13	時	13	
ときどき	sometimes	Adv	11	時々	11	
とくい（な）	good at	Adj な	9			へた（な）
とくに	especially	Adv	18			
とけい	watch, clock	Noun	3	時計	23	
どこ	where	Pronoun	2			
どこかに	somewhere	Adv	3			どこにも
どこにも	anywhere	Adv	3			どこかに
とこや	barbershop	Noun	18	とこ屋	18	
ところ	place	Noun	16	所	20	
ところで	by the way	Adv	8			
としょかん	library	Noun	2	図書館	10	
とても	very	Adv	7			
とどく	reach, arrive	Verb う	19			
とどける	deliver	Verb る	20			
どなた	who (respectful)	Pronoun	2			
どなたか	someone (respectful)	Pronoun	3			どなたも
どなたも	anyone (respectful)	Pronoun	3			どなたか
となり	next to	Noun	3			
とにかく	anyway	Adv	21			
どの + NOUN	which NOUN	Adj irreg	2			
どのぐらい	how long, how much	Adv	10			
とぶ	fly	Verb う	25	飛ぶ	25	
とまる	stay over night	Verb う	14			
とまる	stop (intransitive)	Verb う	23			うごく
とめる	stop (transitive)	Verb る	25			
ともだち	friend	Noun	4	友達	13	
どようび	Saturday	N proper	4	土曜日	4	
ドライブ（する）	drive	N verbal	19			
トラック	truck	Noun	22			
とり	chicken	Noun	27			
とりにく	chicken	Noun	12	とり肉	24	
とる	take	Verb う	5	取る	14	
（しゃしんを）とる	take (a picture)	Verb う	8			
とる	take something away	Verb う	26	取る	26	
ドル	dollar	Noun	5			
どれ	which one	Pronoun	2			
トレーナー	sweatshirt	Noun	10			
どろぼう	thief	Noun	25			
とんかつ	pork cutlet	Noun	5			

な

ドンドン	rapidly (sound symbolic)	Adv	22			
どんな + NOUN	what kind of	Adj irreg	7			
なおす	fix, repair, cure, put straight, correct	Verb う	21			こわす
なおる	be repaired	Verb う	19			こしょう（する）、こわれる
なおる	recover	Verb う	21			
なか	inside	Noun	3	中	9	そと
ながい	long	Adj い	7	長い	7	みじかい
なかむら	Nakamura	N proper	21	中村	21	
なかやま	Nakayama	N proper	10	中山	10	
なく	cry	Verb う	25	泣く	25	わらう
なくす	lose	Verb う	16			
なくなる	run out of	Verb う	19			
なごや	Nagoya	N proper	10	名古屋	X	
なさる	do (honorific)	Verb う	9			
なぜ	why	Adv	12			
なつ	summer	Noun	13	夏	13	
なつめ	Natsume	N proper	14	夏目	14	
なつやすみ	summer vacation	Noun	6	夏休み	13	
など	etc.	Particle	5			
なな	seven	Noun	3	七	3	
ななつ	seven things	Noun	9	七つ	9	
ななつめ	seventh	Noun	17	七つ目	17	
なに	what	Pronoun	3	何	4	
なにか	something	Pronoun	3	何か	4	なにも
なにご	what language	Pronoun	6	何語	6	
なにも	anything	Pronoun	3	何も	4	なにか
なのかめ	seventh day	Noun	15	七日目	15	
なまえ	name	Noun	1	名前	11	
なら	Nara	N proper	13	奈良	X	
ならいごと	lesson, practice, class	Noun	26	習い事	26	
ならう	learn	Verb う	12	習う	15	
なれる	become used to	Verb る	18			
なん	what	Pronoun	2	何	4	
なんか	something	Pronoun	4	何か	4	なにも
なんがつ	which month	Pronoun	5	何月	5	
なんじ	what hour	Pronoun	4	何時	4	
なんにん	how many people	Pronoun	8	何人	8	
なんねんせい	what-year student	Pronoun	2	何年生	11	
なんぷん	what minute	Pronoun	4	何分	4	

	なんようび	which day of the week	Pronoun	4	何曜日	4	
に	に	two	Noun	3	二	3	
	ニール	Neil	N proper	11			
	にがい	bitter	Adj い	16			
	にがつ	February	N proper	5	二月	5	
	にぎやか（な）	lively	Adj な	7			しずか（な）
	にく	meat	Noun	11	肉	24	
	にちようび	Sunday	N proper	4	日曜日	4	
	にっけい	of Japanese ancestry	Noun	11	日系	X	
	にねんせい	second-year student	Noun	2	二年生	11	
	にほん	Japan	N proper	2	日本	4	
	にほんが	Japanese painting	Noun	21	日本画	21	
	にほんご	Japanese language	Noun	1	日本語	6	
	にほんしゅ	Japanese sake	Noun	22	日本酒	22	
	にほんじん	Japanese people	Noun	6	日本人	6	
	にほんじんてき（な）	Japanese	Adj な	20	日本人	6	
	にほんまち	Japantown	Noun	4	日本まち	4	
	にほんりょうり	Japanese cuisine	Noun	5	日本料理	12	
	にもつ	baggage	Noun	25			
	ニューオリンズ	New Orleans	N proper	27			
	にゅうがく（する）	entering school	N verbal	23	入学	23	そつぎょう（する）
	にゅうしゃ（する）	entering company	N verbal	23	入社	23	
	ニュース	news	Noun	22			
	ニューヨーク	New York	N proper	2			
	にる	resemble	Verb る	22			
	にわ	garden	Noun	12			
	～にん	counter (people)	Counter	8	～人	8	
	にんき	popularity	Noun	16	人気	16	
	にんじん	carrot	Noun	12			
ぬ	ぬう	sew	Verb う	24			
	ヌエン	Nguyen	N proper	10			
	ぬぐ	take off (clothes, shoes)	Verb う	14			
	ぬすむ	steal	Verb う	25			きる、はく
ね	ねぎ	green onion	Noun	12			
	ネクタイ	necktie	Noun	10			
	ねこ	cat	Noun	3			
	ねつ	fever	Noun	21	熱	21	
	ネックレス	necklace	Noun	10			
	ねぶそく	not having enough sleep	Noun	26	寝不足	26	
	ねぼうする	oversleep	V irreg	12	寝ぼうする	18	
	ねむい	sleepy	Adj い	14	眠い	19	

	ねむる	sleep	Verb う	14	眠る	19	おきる
	ねる	go to bed, lie down	Verb る	5	寝る	15	おきる
	～ねん	X year(s)	Counter	9	～年	9	
	～ねんまえ	X years ago	Suffix	19	～年前	19	
の	のうぎょうけいえいしゃ	farmer	Noun	17	農業経営者	X	
	ノート	notebook	Noun	3			
	ノック（する）	knock	N verbal	18			
	のど	throat	Noun	16			
	のぼる	climb	Verb う	20			
	のみもの	drinks	Noun	9	飲み物	12	
	のむ	drink	Verb う	4	飲む	6	
	のり	laver	Noun	12			
	のりまき	norimaki	Noun	12			
	のる	ride, get on	Verb う	13	乗る	18	おりる
は	は	tooth	Noun	15			
	バー	bar	Noun	21			
	バークレー	Berkeley	N proper	2			
	パーティー	party	Noun	6			
	ハート	heart	Noun	23			
	パートナー	partner	Noun	10			
	バーベキュー	barbecue	Noun	20			
	はい	yes	Adv	2			いいえ
	～はい	counter (cup(s), bowl(s), glass(es))	Counter	9			
	ハイキング	hiking	Noun	20			
	ハイヒール	high heeled shoes	Noun	10			
	はいゆう	actor	Noun	17	俳優	X	
	はいる	enter	Verb う	7	入る	7	でる
	（おふろに）はいる	take (a bath)	Verb う	15	入る	15	でる
	パイロット	pilot	Noun	17			
	ばか	stupid	Adj な	25			
	はかい（する）	destruction	N verbal	25			
	はかた	Hakata	N proper	10	博多	X	
	はかる	measure	Verb う	21			
	はく	wear (shoes, socks, trousers)	Verb う	10			ぬぐ
	パク	Pak	N proper	3			
	はくりょくがある	powerful	Phrase	22			
	はげます	encourage	Verb う	26			
	はこ	box	Noun	11			
	はこぶ	carry	Verb う	14	運ぶ	24	

はし	chopsticks	Noun	4			
はじまる	start (intransitive)	Verb う	18	始まる	18	おわる
はじめ	first, beginning	Noun	18	始め	18	さいご
はじめて	for the first time	Adv	10	始めて	15	
はじめる	start (transitive)	Verb る	10	始める	15	おえる、やめる
パジャマ	pajamas	Noun	24			
ばしょ	location, place	Noun	12			
はしる	run	Verb う	13			
バス	bus	Noun	4			
はずかしい	ashamed, embarrassed	Adj い	20			
バスケットボール	basketball	Noun	9			
はずす	take off (accessories)	Verb う	15			する
パスタ	pasta	Noun	24			
パスポート	passport	Noun	14			
パソコン	personal computer	Noun	26			
バター	butter	Noun	12			
はたらく	work	Verb う	13	働く	14	
はち	eight	Noun	3	八	3	
はちがつ	August	N proper	5	八月	5	
ばつ	batsu(cross)	Noun	22			
はっこう（する）	publication, printing (newspapers, magazines, etc.)	N verbal	25			
はっぴょう（する）	presentation	N verbal	25			
はで（な）	flamboyant	Adj な	22			
はな	flower	Noun	6	花	12	
はな	nose	Noun	7			
はなし	talk, story	Noun	9	話	9	
はなす	speak, chat	Verb う	6	話す	9	
はなび	fireworks	Noun	25	花火	25	
はなみ	flower viewing	Noun	17	花見	17	
はは	mother (plain)	Noun	8	母	8	ちち
はははのひ	Mother's Day	N proper	23	母の日	23	
ハムレット	Hamlet	N proper	11			
はやい	early	Adj い	8	早い	8	おそい
はやい	fast	Adj い	9			おそい
はやかわ	Hayakawa	N proper	3	早川	10	
はらう	pay	Verb う	16			
はりだす	post	Verb う	25	はり出す	25	
はる	spring	Noun	13	春	13	
はる	paste	Verb う	15			

はるかわ	Harukawa	N proper	15	春川	15	
はるやすみ	spring vacation	Noun	13	春休み	13	
バレエ	ballet	Noun	26			
はれる	clear up	Verb る	17	晴れる	17	（あめが）ふる
バレンタインデー	Valentine's Day	N proper	23			
ハワイ	Hawaii	N proper	11			
はん	half	Noun	4	半	4	
パン	bread	Noun	12			
ばん	evening	Noun	5	晩	6	あさ
ばんごう	number	Noun	19			
はんこう（する）	rebellion, defiance	N verbal	26			
ばんごはん	dinner, supper	Noun	4	晩ごはん	6	あさごはん
ハンサム	handsome	Adj な	9			
はんたい（する）	opposition	N verbal	22	反対	26	
ハンドアウト	handout	Noun	9			
ハンドバッグ	handbag	Noun	16			
ハンバーガー	hamberger	Noun	5			
パンフレット	pamphlet	Noun	22			
はんぶん	half	Noun	19	半分	19	

ひ

ひ	day	Noun	15	日	15	
ひ	spark, fire	Noun	25	火	25	
ピアノ	piano	Noun	6			
ピーシー（PC）	PC	Noun	16			
ヒーター	heater	Noun	14			
ビートルズ	The Beatles	N proper	13			
ビーフジャーキー	beef jerky	Noun	23			
ビール	beer	Noun	4			
ひがしアジア	East Asia	N proper	10	東アジア	10	
ひがしやま	Higashiyama	N proper	11	東山	11	
ひきうける	undertake	Verb る	21	ひき受ける	21	ことわる
ひきにく	ground meat	Noun	27	ひき肉	27	
ひく	play (musical instrument)	Verb う	6			
ひく	subtract	Verb う	17			たす
ひく	run over	Verb う	25			
（かぜを）ひく	catch (cold)	Verb う	14			
（じしょを）ひく	look up (dictionary)	Verb う	15			
ひくい	low, short (height)	Adj い	7			たかい
ピクニック	picnic	Noun	6			
ひげ	beard, mustache	Noun	18			
ひこうき	airplane	Noun	4	飛行機	15	
ひざ	knee	Noun	21			
ピザ	pizza	Noun	11			

びじゅつかん	art museum	Noun	15	びじゅつ館	15	
ひしょ	secretary	Noun	17	秘書	X	
ビタミン	vitamin	Noun	18			
ひだり	left	Noun	17	左	17	みぎ
びっくりする	get surprised	V irreg	19			
ひっこし（する）	housemoving	N verbal	24			
ビデオ	video	Noun	11			
ビデオゲーム	video game	Noun	26			
ひと	person	Noun	2	人	8	
ひどい	terrible	Adj い	26			
ひとつ	one thing	Noun	9	一つ	9	
ひとつめ	first	Noun	17	一つ目	17	
ひとばんじゅう	all through the night	Adv	17	一晩中	17	
ひとびと	people	Noun	11	人々	11	
ひとり	one person	Counter	8	一人	8	
ひとりで	by oneself	Phrase	4	一人で	8	
ひま（な）	leisure, not busy	Adj な	12			いそがしい
ひゃく	hundred	Noun	3	百	3	
ひやす	cool, chill (transitive)	Verb う	23	冷やす	24	
ヒューストン	Houston	N proper	27			
ひよう	expense	Noun	10			
びょういん	hospital	Noun	16	病院	17	
びょうき	illness	Noun	13	病気	17	
びようし	hairdresser	Noun	17	美容師	X	
ひょうばん	reputation	Noun	14			
ひらがな	hiragana	Noun	1			カタカナ
ひる	noon	Noun	25	昼	25	よる
ビル	building	Noun	2			
ひるごはん	lunch	Noun	4	昼ごはん	25	
ひるね（する）	nap	N verbal	13	昼寝	25	
ヒルマン	Hillman	N proper	18			
ひろい	spacious, wide	Adj い	7	広い	7	せまい
ひろしま	Hiroshima	N proper	10	広島	X	

ふ

ふあん（な）	uneasy	Adj な	26	不安	26	
フィラデルフィア	Philadelphia	N proper	27			
ブーツ	boots	Noun	23			
ふうとう	envelope	Noun	15			
ふうふ	married couple	Noun	26			
ふくざつ（な）	complicated	Adj な	19			
ふくしゅう（する）	review	N verbal	6	復習	18	よしゅう（する）
ふじさん	Mt. Fuji	N proper	12	富士山	X	

ふたつ	two things	Noun	9	二つ	9	
ふたつめ	second	Noun	17	二つ目	17	
ふたり	two persons	Counter	8	二人	8	
ぶちょう	department head	Noun	26	部長	26	
ふつかめ	second day	Noun	15	二日目	15	
ぶつりがく	physics	Noun	19	物理学	19	
ふとる	become fat	Verb う	14			
ふね	boat, ship	Noun	11			
ふべん（な）	inconvenient	Adj な	7	不便	26	べんり（な）
ふまじめ（な）	not serious	Adj な	7			まじめ（な）
ふむ	step on	Verb う	25			
ふゆ	winter	Noun	8	冬	13	
ふゆやすみ	winter vacation	Noun	6	冬休み	13	
フライトアテンダント	flight attendant	Noun	17			
ブラウス	blouse	Noun	10			
ブラウン	Brown	N proper	2			
ブラスバンド	brass band	Noun	18			
フラッシュカード	flash card	Noun	14			
プラン	plan	Noun	4			
フランスご	French language	Noun	6	フランス語	6	
フランスじん	French people	Noun	6	フランス人	6	
プリン	pudding	Noun	24			
プリンター	printer	Noun	13			
ふる	fall	Verb う	8	降る	17	やむ、はれる
ふる	jilt, dump (a significant other)	Verb う	26			
ふるい	old	Adj い	7	古い	7	あたらしい
ブルース	blues	Noun	11			
ふるかわ	Furukawa	N proper	8	古川	8	
ふるさと	hometown	Noun	17			
プレスリー	Presley	N proper	11			
プレゼント（する）	present	N verbal	10			
ふろ	bath	Noun	14			
プログラム	program	Noun	3			
プロジェクト	project	Noun	21			
～ふん	X minute(s)	Suffix	4	～分	4	
ぶん	sentence	Noun	13	文	13	
～ぷん	X minute(s)	Suffix	4	～分	4	
ふんか（する）	eruption	N verbal	20			
ぶんか	culture	Noun	18	文化	18	
ぶんがく	literature	Noun	5	文学	11	
ぶんかてき（な）	cultural	Adj な	20	文化	18	

	ぶんぽう	grammar	Noun	13	文法	18	
へ	ペア	pair	Noun	19			
	へいてん（する）	closing a store	N verbal	24	閉店	24	かいてん（する）
	へえ	Oh	Interject	4			
	ページ	page	Noun	18			
	へた（な）	bad at	Adj な	9	下手	9	じょうず(な)、とくい（な）
	ベッド	bed	Noun	3			
	へび	snake	Noun	25			
	へや	room	Noun	3	部屋	17	
	ペラペラ	fluently (sound symbolic)	Adv	25			
	ベランダ	balcony	Noun	20			
	ペレス	Perez	N proper	11			
	ペロっと	rapid eating (sound symbolic)	Adv	25			
	へん	vicinity	Noun	22			
	ペン	pen	Noun	2			
	へん（な）	strange	Adj な	20	変	20	
	べんきょう（する）	study	N verbal	4	勉強	14	
	べんごし	lawyer	Noun	17	弁護士	X	
	べんごし	lawyer	Noun	20			
	へんじ（する）	reply	N verbal	13	返事	13	
	ベンチ	bench	Noun	17			
	べんとう	box lunch	Noun	14			
	べんり（な）	convenient	Adj な	7	便利	12	ふべん（な）
ほ	ほう	direction, side, way	Noun	9	方	9	
	ぼう	stick, pole	Noun	21			
	ぼうし	hat, cap	Noun	10			
	ボーイフレンド	boyfriend	Noun	26			
	ボーッとする	become absentminded	V irreg	18			
	ボート	boat	Noun	20			
	ホームズ	Holmes	N proper	3			
	ホームステイ（する）	homestay	N verbal	13			
	ホール	hall	Noun	22			
	ボール	ball	Noun	16			
	ボールペン	ballpoint pen	Noun	2			
	ほか	other (than something)	Noun	10			
	ぼく	I (typically by boys)	Pronoun	17			
	ほし	star	Noun	22			
	ほしい	want, desire	Adj い	12			

ほしがる	show signs of desire	Verb う	12			
ホストファミリー	host family	Noun	13			
ボストン	Boston	N proper	9			
ボタン	button (of a switch)	Noun	16			
ホチキス	stapler	Noun	24			
ポップコーン	popcorn	Noun	12			
ホテル	hotel	Noun	16			
ホノルル	Honolulu	N proper	10			
ほめる	praise	Verb る	25			しかる
ほん	book	Noun	2	本	5	
～ほん	counter (long things)	Counter	9	～本	9	
ぼんさい	dwarfed tree in a pot	Noun	27			
ほんだ	Honda	N proper	26	本田	26	
ほんとうに	really, truly	Adv	18	本当	19	
ほんばこ	bookshelf	Noun	11	本ばこ	11	
ほんや	bookstore	Noun	3	本屋	17	
ほんやくか	translator	Noun	17	翻訳家	X	

ま

～まい	counter (flat things)	Counter	9	～枚	23	
まいあさ	every morning	Noun	11	毎朝	14	
マイアミ	Miami	N proper	27			
マイク	microphone	Noun	25			
まいしゅう	every week	Noun	14	毎週	14	
まいつき	every month	Noun	18	毎月	18	
まいとし	every year	Noun	17	毎年	17	
まいにち	everyday	Noun	11	毎日	14	
まいねん	every year	Noun	17	毎年	17	
まいばん	every evening	Noun	11	毎晩	14	
マイル	mile	Noun	13			
まえ	front	Noun	3	前	10	うしろ
まえだ	Maeda	N proper	7	前田	25	
まえに	before	Conj	18	前に	18	あとで
まがる	turn (intransitive)	Verb う	17			
マグカップ	mug	Noun	9			
マクドナルド	McDonald's	N proper	5			
(～に) まける	lose (a game)	Verb る	22			かつ
まご	grandchild (plain)	Noun	8			
まさこ	Masako	N proper	23	正子	23	
まじめ (な)	serious	Adj な	7			ふまじめ (な)
まず	first of all	Adv	16			
まずい	not tasty, yucky	Adj い	7			おいしい
また	again	Adv	6			
まだ	yet	Adv	5			もう

まだ	still	Adv	8			もう
まち	town, city	Noun	4			
まちがい	mistake	Noun	23			
まつ	wait	Verb う	8	待つ	9	
マッキントッシュ	Macintosh	N proper	16			
まっすぐ（な）	straight	Adj な	17			
まつり	festival	Noun	13			
まで	to, up to	Particle	4			から
までに	by X (time)	Particle	16			
まど	window	Noun	10			
まなぶ	learn, study	Verb う	18	学ぶ	18	おしえる
まにあう	make it in time	Verb う	22	間にあう	22	おくれる
マニュアル	manual	Noun	17			
マネージャー	manager	Noun	16			
マリーナ	marina	Noun	24			
まるい	round	Adj い	21			しかくい
まんが	comic strip	Noun	23			
まんてん	perfect score	Noun	22			
まんなか	(dead) center	Noun	17	まん中	17	

み

ミーティング	meeting	Noun	16			
みえる	be visible	Verb る	25	見える	25	
みがく	brush, polish	Verb う	15			
みかん	mandarin orange	Noun	23			
みぎ	right	Noun	17	右	17	ひだり
みじかい	short (length)	Adj い	7	短い	22	ながい
みず	water	Noun	12	水	12	
みずうみ	lake	Noun	20			
みずぎ	bathing suit, swimsuit	Noun	22	水着	22	
みせ	shop	Noun	6	店	12	
みせる	show	Verb る	19	見せる	19	
みち	way, road, street	Noun	17			
みっかめ	third day	Noun	15	三日目	15	
みつかる	be find	Verb う	22	見つかる	22	
ミッキーマウス	Mickey Mouse	N proper	11			
みっつ	three things	Noun	9	三つ	9	
みっつめ	third	Noun	17	三つ目	17	
みどり	green	Noun	17			
みどりいろ	green color	Noun	17	みどり色	17	
みなさん	everyone (respectful)	Noun	12			
ミネアポリス	Minneapolis	N proper	27			
みみ	ear	Noun	7	耳	21	
みやげ	gift	Noun	13			

	ミュージシャン	musician	Noun	17			
	ミラー	Miller	N proper	2			
	みる	see, watch	Verb る	4	見る	6	
	ミルク	milk	Noun	15			
	みんな	everyone (plain)	Noun	13			
む	むいかめ	sixth day	Noun	15	六日目	15	
	むかし	old days	Noun	20			さいきん
	むし	insect	Noun	25			
	むす	steam	Verb う	24			
	むずかしい	difficult	Adj い	7	難しい	22	やさしい
	むすこ（さん）	son	Noun	26			むすめ（さん）
	むすめ（さん）	daughter	Noun	26			むすこ（さん）
	むっつ	six things	Noun	9	六つ	9	
	むっつめ	sixth	Noun	17	六つ目	17	
	むらかみ	Murakami	N proper	19	村上	19	
	むらやま	Murayama	N proper	15	村山	15	
	むりやり	forcefully, against one's will	Adv	26			
め	め	eye	Noun	7	目	7	
	めい	niece (plain)	Noun	8			おい
	めいごさん	niece (respectful)	Noun	8			おいごさん
	めがね	glasses	Noun	10			
	メキシコじん	Mexican people	Noun	6	メキシコ人	6	
	めぐすり	eye drops	Noun	23	目薬	23	
	めざましどけい	alarm clock	Noun	25	時計	25	
	めしあがる	eat (honorific)	Verb う	19	めし上がる	19	
	めずらしい	rare	Adj い	23			
	メモ（する）	memo	N verbal	24			
	めんせつ（する）	interview	N verbal	24			
	メンフィス	Memphis	N proper	27			
も	も	also	Particle	2			
	もう	already	Adv	5			まだ
	もう	more	Adv	18			
	もういちど	once more	Phrase	16	一度	18	
	もうすぐ	soon	Phrase	5			
	モーツアルト	Mozart	N proper	20			
	もくようび	Thursday	N proper	4	木曜日	4	
	もし	if	Adv	19			
	もしもし	hello (on the phone)	Interject	10			
	もち	rice cake	Noun	14			
	もちろん	of course	Adv	6			
	もつ	have, hold	Verb う	8	持つ	24	

	もっていく	take along (thing)	Verb う	21	持って行く	24	もってくる
	もってくる	bring (thing)	V irreg	19	持って来る	24	もっていく
	もっと	more	Adv	16			
	モニター	monitor	Noun	14			
	もの	thing	Noun	26	物	26	
	もらう	receive	Verb う	11			あげる
	もり	woods	Noun	17			
	もんく	complaint	Noun	26			
	もんげん	curfew	Noun	16			
	もんだい	problem	Noun	16	問題	19	
や	や	and	Particle	5			
	～や	X shop	Suffix	17	～屋	17	
	やく	bake, broil	Verb う	24			
	やくす	translate	Verb う	24			
	やくそく（する）	promise	N verbal	22			
	やさい	vegetable	Noun	12			
	やさしい	easy, gentle	Adj い	7			むずかしい
	やすい	cheap, inexpensive	Adj い	7	安い	7	たかい
	やすかわ	Yasukawa	N proper	8	安川	9	
	やすだ	Yasuda	N proper	24	安田	24	
	やすみ	day off	Noun	14	休み	14	
	やすむ	take a day off, rest	Verb う	14	休む	14	
	やっつ	eight things	Noun	9	八つ	9	
	やっつめ	eighth	Noun	17	八つ目	17	
	やっと	finally	Adv	17			
	やま	mountain	Noun	20	山	20	
	やました	Yamashita	N proper	7	山下	7	
	やまだ	Yamada	N proper	3	山田	19	
	やまもと	Yamamoto	N proper	6	山本	6	
	やむ	stop (raining)	Verb う	15			
	やめる	quit doing something	Verb る	14			はじめる
	やりかた	way of doing something	Noun	21	やり方	21	
	やる	do, try	Verb う	14			
	やる	do	Verb う	22			
	やる	give	Verb う	23			もらう
	やわらかい	soft	Adj い	11			かたい
	ヤング	Young	N proper	3			
ゆ	ゆうがた	evening	Noun	22	夕方	22	あさ
	ゆうしょく	dinner	Noun	22	夕食	22	
	ゆうびんきょく	post office	Noun	3			
	ゆうべ	last night	Noun	14	夕べ	22	
	ゆうめい（な）	famous	Adj な	14	有名	14	

ゆき	snow	Noun	13	雪	17	
ゆきだるま	snowman	Noun	13	雪だるま	17	
ゆずる	give up, hand over	Verb う	24			
ゆっくり	leisurely	Adv	21			
ゆっくりする	relax	Adv	21			
ゆどうふ	tofu in hot broth	Noun	26			
ユニバーシティー	university	Noun	22			
ゆびわ	ring	Noun	10			
ゆれる	jolt	Verb る	15			

よ

ようい（する）	preparation	N verbal	20	用意	20	
ようかめ	eighth day	Noun	15	八日目	15	
ようかん	sweet adzukibean paste	Noun	12			
ようし	form	Noun	26	用紙	26	
ようじ	business, an errand	Noun	16	用事	20	
ようふく	(Western-style) clothes	Noun	16			
ヨーロッパ	Europe	N proper	10			
よく	well	Adv	10			
よく	often, frequently	Adv	18			
よこ	side	Noun	3			
よごす	stain, soil	Verb う	25			あらう
よこはま	Yokohama	N proper	8	横浜	X	
よしゅう（する）	preparatory study	N verbal	14	予習	18	ふくしゅう（する）
ヨセミテ	Yosemite	N proper	3			
よっかめ	fourth day	Noun	15	四日目	15	
よっつ	four things	Noun	9	四つ	9	
よっつめ	fourth	Noun	17	四つ目	17	
よてい	plan	Noun	26			
よていひょう	schedule	Noun	22			
よなか	middle of night	Noun	16	夜中	16	
よねんせい	fouth-year student	Noun	2	四年生	11	
よぶ	call, summon	Verb う	8			
よぶ	invite	Verb う	12			
よふかし（する）	staying up late at night	N verbal	26	夜ふかし	26	
よみかた	way of reading	Noun	13	読み方	13	
よみもの	readings	Noun	12	読み物	12	
よむ	read	Verb う	4	読む	9	
よやく（する）	reservation	N verbal	18			
よる	night	Noun	15	夜	16	
よろこぶ (3rd person)	be happy, pleased	Verb う	13			
よわい	weak	Adj い	25	弱い	25	つよい
よん	four	Noun	3	四	3	

ら	らいがっき	next semester	Noun	18	来学期	18	せんがっき
	らいげつ	next month	Noun	13	来月	13	せんげつ
	らいしゅう	next week	Noun	11	来週	13	せんしゅう
	ライトきょうだい	Wright Brothers	N proper	11	ライト兄弟	11	
	らいねん	next year	Noun	12	来年	12	きょねん
	ラウール	Raoul	N proper	4			
	らく（な）	easy, simple, comfortable, relaxed	Adj な	14	楽	14	たいへん（な）
	らくに	easily, smoothly	Adv	18	楽	14	
	ラジオ	radio	Noun	3			
	ラップトップ	laptop	Noun	12			
	ラブレター	love letter	Noun	25			
	ラボ	laboratory	Noun	7			
り	リーダー	leader	Noun	21			
	りこん（する）	divorce	N verbal	26			けっこん（する）
	りっぱ（な）	splendid	Adj な	18			
	リムジン	airport shuttle bus	Noun	15			
	りゅうがく（する）	studying abroad	N verbal	12	留学	12	
	りゅうがくせい	foreign student	Noun	6	留学生	6	
	りょう	dormitory	Noun	2			
	りょうし	fisherman	Noun	17	漁師	X	
	りょうしん	parents (plain)	Noun	8	両親	20	
	りょうり（する）	cuisine, cooking	N verbal	5	料理	12	
	りょかん	Japanese-style inn	Noun	15	旅館	19	
	りょこう（する）	trip, travel	N verbal	13	旅行	19	
	りれきしょ	résumé	Noun	24			
	リン	Lin	N proper	3			
	リンカーン	Lincoln	N proper	11			
	りんご	apple	Noun	9			
る	ルイス	Lewis	N proper	7			
	ルームメート	roommate	Noun	3			
れ	れい	example	Noun	4	例	X	
	れいぞうこ	refrigerator	Noun	12			
	れきし	history	Noun	20			
	れきしてき（な）	historical	Adj な	20			
	レジ	cash register	Noun	12			
	レシピ	recipe	Noun	15			
	レストラン	restaurant	Noun	5			
	レノン	Lennon	N proper	11			
	レモネード	lemonade	Noun	24			
	れんしゅう（する）	practice	N verbal	9	練習	18	

	れんらく（する）	contact	N verbal	19			
	れんらくをとる	contact, communicate	Phrase	19	取る	14	
ろ	ローン	loan	Noun	18			
	ろく	six	Noun	3	六	3	
	ろくがつ	June	N proper	5	六月	5	
	ロサンゼルス	Los Angeles	N proper	9			
	ロシアご	Russian language	Noun	6	ロシア語	6	
	ロス	Los Angeles	N proper	9			
	ロック	rock	Noun	9			
	ろっぽんぎ	Roppongi	N proper	16	六本木	16	
	ろんぶん	thesis, article	Noun	21			
わ	わあ	Wow	Interject	4			
	ワープロ	word processor	Noun	26			
	ワイシャツ	dress shirt	Noun	10			
	ワイン	wine	Noun	5			
	わかい	young	Adj い	16			
	わかる	understand	Verb う	10	分かる	10	
	ワシントン	Washington, D.C.	N proper	27			
	わすれる	forget	Verb る	15			
	わたし	I, me	Pronoun	1	私	5	
	わたしたち	we	Pronoun	2	私達	13	
	わたす	hand over	Verb う	25			
	ワトソン	Watson	N proper	3			
	わらう	smile, laugh, laugh at	Verb う	25	笑う	25	なく
	わるい	bad	Adj い	11	悪い	24	いい
	わるぐち	slander, (Lit.) bad mouth	Noun	25	悪口	25	
	ワンピース	dress	Noun	10			

Appendix G Vocabulary List (English to Japanese)

品詞 (ひんし)	Parts of speech	単語課 (たんごか)	Lesson where the word is introduced
漢字 (かんじ)	Kanji	漢字課 (かんじか)	Lesson where the kanji is introduced
反対語・対語 (はんたいご・ついご)	Antonym/A pair of words		
X	The kanji is used, but not taught.		
Adj irreg	Irregular adjective	N proper	Proper noun
Conj	Conjunction	N verbal	Verbal noun
Interject	Interjection		

	英語 English	日本語 Japanese	品詞	単語課	漢字	漢字課	反対語・対語
A	affair	こと	Noun	16			
	a little	すこし	Adv	6	少し	11	たくさん
	a little	ちょっと	Adv	7			たくさん
	a little while ago	さっき	Adv	22			
	a lot	たくさん	Adj irreg	5			すこし、ちょっと
	A.M.	ごぜん	Noun	4	午前	13	ごご
	abacus	そろばん	Noun	26			
	able to (to be)	できる	Verb る	6			
	about	～ぐらい	Suffix	10			
	about (time)	～ごろ	Suffix	10			
	above	うえ	Noun	3	上	5	した
	(become) absentminded	ボーッとする	V irreg	18			
	absolutely	ぜったいに	Adv	16			
	academic department	がくぶ	Noun	11	学部	11	
	academic term	がっき	Noun	25	学期	25	
	accident	じこ	Noun	23	事故	23	
	(traffic) accident	こうつうじこ	Noun	22	事故	23	
	accountant	かいけいし	Noun	20			
	accumulate	たまる	Verb う	25			
	activity	かつどう（する）	N verbal	25			
	actor	はいゆう	Noun	17	俳優	X	
	actress	じょゆう	Noun	17	女優	X	
	add	たす	Verb う	17			ひく
	address	じゅうしょ	Noun	20	住所	20	

adult	おとな	Noun	16	大人	16	
advice	アドバイス（する）	N verbal	23			
Africa	アフリカ	N proper	12			
after	あとで	Conj	18	後で	18	まえに
after that	それから	Phrase	4			
afternoon	ごご	Noun	4	午後	13	ごぜん
afterwards	あとで	Adv	23	後で	23	
again	また	Adv	6			
against one's will	むりやり	Adv	26			
(a little while) ago	さっき	Adv	22			
ahead	さきに	Adv	15	先に	19	
airplane	ひこうき	Noun	4	飛行機	15	
airport	くうこう	Noun	13			
airport shuttle bus	リムジン	Noun	15			
Akihabara	あきはばら	N proper	13	秋葉原	X	
Akiyama	あきやま	N proper	13	秋山	13	
alarm clock	めざましどけい	Noun	25	時計	25	
Alaska	アラスカ	N proper	11			
all	ぜんぶ	Adv	12	全部	12	
all over the world	せかいじゅう	Phrase	25	せかい中	25	
all the time	ずっと	Adv	15			
all through the night	ひとばんじゅう	Adv	17	一晩中	17	
all year round	いちねんじゅう	Adv	17	一年中	17	
already	もう	Adv	5			まだ
alright	だいじょうぶ（な）	Adj な	12			
also	も	Particle	2			
always	いつも	Adv	7			
America	アメリカ	N proper	5			
American people	アメリカじん	Noun	6	アメリカ人	6	
amusing	おもしろい	Adj い	26			つまらない
Amy	エイミー	N proper	2			
and	や	Particle	5			
and then	そして	Conj	4			
(get) angry	おこる	Verb う	17			
animal	どうぶつ	Noun	19	動物	19	
animated cartoon	アニメ	Noun	23			
ankle	あしくび	Noun	21	足くび	21	
annoying	いや（な）	Adj な	25			
answer	こたえ	Noun	16	答え	20	
answer	こたえる	Verb る	15	答える	20	しつもんする
anxiety	しんぱい（する）	N verbal	19	心配	21	あんしん（する）
anyone	だれも	Pronoun	3			

anyone (respectful)	どなたも	Pronoun	3			
anything	なにも	Pronoun	3	何も	4	
anytime	いつでも	Adv	16			
anyway	とにかく	Adv	21			
anywhere	どこにも	Adv	3			
Aoki	あおき	N proper	18	青木	18	
apartment	アパート	Noun	2			
apologize	あやまる	Verb う	26			
apple	りんご	Noun	9			
application	おうぼ（する）	N verbal	26			
appropriate	てきとう（な）	Adj な	19			
approximately	～ぐらい	Suffix	10			
approximately (time)	～ごろ	Suffix	10			
April	しがつ	N proper	5	四月	5	
architect	けんちくか	Noun	17	建築家	X	
arm	て	Noun	7	手	11	
Armstrong	アームストロング	N proper	11			
arrival	とうちゃく（する）	N verbal	15			しゅっぱつ（する）
arrive	つく	Verb う	15	着く	21	(Xを) でる
arrive	とどく	Verb う	19			
art museum	びじゅつかん	Noun	15	びじゅつ館	15	
article, thesis	ろんぶん	Noun	21			
artist	アーティスト	Noun	17			
artist	げいじゅつか	Noun	17	芸術家	X	
as much as possible	できるだけ	Phrase	14			
Asakusa	あさくさ	N proper	13	浅草	X	
ashamed	はずかしい	Adj い	20			
ask	きく	Verb う	5	聞く	11	
ask	たのむ	Verb う	25			
assist	てつだう	Verb う	24	手伝う	24	
assistance	てつだい	Noun	18	手伝い	24	
astronaut	うちゅうひこうし	Noun	17	宇宙飛行士	X	
(not) at all	ぜんぜん	Adv	7	全然	25	
athlete	スポーツせんしゅ	Noun	17	～選手	X	
Atlanta	アトランタ	N proper	27			
attend	でる（～に）	Verb る	12	出る	17	やすむ
attendance	しゅっせき（する）	N verbal	21			
(pay) attention to	きをつける	Phrase	23	気をつける	23	
(be) audible	きこえる	Verb る	25	聞こえる	25	
August	はちがつ	N proper	5	八月	5	
aunt (plain)	おば	Noun	8			

	aunt (respectful)	おばさん	Noun	8			
	Australia	オーストラリア	N proper	22			
	author	さくしゃ	Noun	25	作者	25	
	autumn	あき	Noun	12	秋	13	はる
B	baby	あかちゃん	Noun	23	赤ちゃん	23	
	back	うしろ	Noun	3	後ろ	11	まえ
	back (body)	せなか	Noun	21	背中	21	
	bad	わるい	Adj い	11	悪い	24	いい
	bad at	へた（な）	Adj な	9	下手	9	じょうず（な）
	bad mouth	わるぐち	Noun	25	悪口	25	
	baggage	にもつ	Noun	25			
	bake	やく	Verb う	24			
	balcony	ベランダ	Noun	20			
	ball	ボール	Noun	16			
	ballet	バレエ	Noun	26			
	ballpoint pen	ボールペン	Noun	2			
	bank	ぎんこう	Noun	3	銀行	10	
	bar	バー	Noun	21			
	barbecue	バーベキュー	Noun	20			
	barbershop	とこや	Noun	18	とこ屋	18	
	basketball	バスケットボール	Noun	9			
	bath	（お）ふろ	Noun	14			
	bathing suit	みずぎ	Noun	22	水着	22	
	batsu(cross)	ばつ	Noun	22			まる
	(The) Beatles	ビートルズ	N proper	13			
	beard	ひげ	Noun	18			
	beautuful	きれい（な）	Adj な	7			きたない
	because	から	Conj	5			
	become empty	すく	Verb う	9			こむ
	become fat	ふとる	Verb う	14			
	become used to	なれる	Verb る	18			
	bed	ベッド	Noun	3			
	beef	ぎゅうにく	Noun	12	ぎゅう肉	24	
	beef jerky	ビーフジャーキー	Noun	23			
	beer	ビール	Noun	4			
	before	さきに	Adv	15	先に	19	
	before	まえに	Conj	18	前に	18	あとで
	beginning	はじめ	Noun	18	始め	18	さいご
	behind	うしろ	Noun	3	後ろ	11	まえ
	below	した	Noun	3	下	5	うえ
	bench	ベンチ	Noun	17			
	Berkeley	バークレー	N proper	2			

besides	それに	Conj	20			
best	いちばん	Noun	9	一番	9	
bicycle	じてんしゃ	Noun	4	自転車	19	
big	おおきい	Adj い	7	大きい	7	ちいさい
biology	せいぶつがく	Noun	11	生物学	21	
bird	とり	Noun	27			
birthday	たんじょうび	Noun	12	たんじょう日	12	
bite	かむ	Verb う	25			
bitter	にがい	Adj い	16			
black	くろ	Noun	17			
black	くろい	Adj い	17			
blackboard	こくばん	Noun	18			
blood	ち	Noun	11			
bloom	さく	Verb う	17			
blouse	ブラウス	Noun	10			
blue	あお	Noun	17	青	17	
blue	あおい	Adj い	17	青い	17	
blues	ブルース	Noun	11			
boat	ふね	Noun	11			
boat	ボート	Noun	20			
body	からだ	Noun	26			
body height	せ	Noun	7	背	11	
book	ほん	Noun	2	本	5	
bookshelf	ほんばこ	Noun	11	本ばこ	11	
bookstore	ほんや	Noun	3	本屋	17	
boots	ブーツ	Noun	23			
boring	つまらない	Adj い	7			おもしろい
(be) born	うまれる	Verb る	20	生まれる	20	しぬ
borrow	かりる	Verb る	6	借りる	23	かえす、かす
Boston	ボストン	N proper	9			
bottom	そこ	Noun	11			
boulevard	おおどおり	Noun	11	大どおり	11	
(X) bound thing(s)	～さつ	Counter	9			
box	はこ	Noun	11			
box lunch	（お）べんとう	Noun	14			
boy	おとこのこ	Noun	25	男の子	25	おんなのこ
boyfriend	ボーイフレンド	Noun	26			ガールフレンド
branch/shop manager	てんちょう	Noun	24	店長	24	てんいん
brass band	ブラスバンド	Noun	18			
bread	パン	Noun	12			
break (intransitive)	こわれる	Verb る	15			なおる

	break (transitive)	こわす	Verb う	18			しゅうり（する）、つくる、なおす
	breakdown	こしょう（する）	N verbal	22			なおる
	breakfast	あさごはん	Noun	4	朝ごはん	10	
	briefcase	かばん	Noun	3			
	bright	あかるい	Adj い	7	明るい	7	くらい
	bring (person, animal)	つれてくる	V irreg	16	つれて来る	16	つれていく
	bring (thing)	もってくる	V irreg	19	持って来る	24	もっていく
	British (person)	えいこくじん	Noun	22	英国人	22	
	broil	やく	Verb う	24			
	Brown	ブラウン	N proper	2			
	brush	みがく	Verb う	15			
	Buddhist temple	（お）てら	Noun	13			
	building	ビル	Noun	2			
	building	たてもの	Noun	20	たて物	20	
	(be) built	たつ	Verb う	18			
	bus	バス	Noun	4			
	business	ようじ	Noun	16	用事	20	
	busy	いそがしい	Adj い	10	忙しい	19	ひま（な）
	but	でも	Conj	4			
	but	けれども	Conj	18			
	butter	バター	Noun	12			
	button	ボタン	Noun	16			
	buy	かう	Verb う	5	買う	6	
	by all means	ぜひ	Adv	14			
	by oneself	ひとりで	Phrase	4	一人で	8	
	by the way	ところで	Adv	8			
	by X (time)	までに	Particle	16			
C	café	きっさてん	Noun	15	きっさ店	15	
	cafeteria	カフェテリア	Noun	4			
	cake	ケーキ	Noun	7			
	California	カリフォルニア	N proper	3			
	call	よぶ	Verb う	8			
	calligraphy	しゅうじ	Noun	26	習字	26	
	calligraphy	しょどう	Noun	19			
	calm down	おちつく	Verb う	17			
	camera	カメラ	Noun	3			
	camping	キャンプ（する）	N verbal	20			
	campus	キャンパス	Noun	6			
	can do	できる	Verb る	17			
	Canada	カナダ	N proper	6			

Canadian people	カナダじん	Noun	6	カナダ人	6	
cane	つえ	Noun	11			
cap	ぼうし	Noun	10			
car	くるま	Noun	2	車	7	
care	せわ（する）	N verbal	18			
(be) cared for	（お）せわになる	Phrase	15			
careful	ていねい（な）	Adj な	22			
(be) careful	きをつける	Phrase	16	気をつける	16	
carelessly	うっかり	Adv	15			
carpenter	だいく	Noun	17	大工	X	
carrot	にんじん	Noun	12			
carry	はこぶ	Verb う	14	運ぶ	24	
cash register	レジ	Noun	12			
cat	ねこ	Noun	3			
catalogue	カタログ	Noun	24			
catch (cold)	ひく	Verb う	14			
CD player	ＣＤプレーヤー	Noun	12			
cellular phone	けいたいでんわ	Noun	16	電話	15	
(X) cent(s)	～セント	Counter	9			
(dead) center	まんなか	Noun	17	まん中	17	
chair	いす	Noun	3			
champagne	シャンペン	Noun	24			
change	おつり	Noun	12			
change	かえる	Verb る	17			
character	じ	Noun	15	字	15	
chat	はなす	Verb う	6	話す	9	
chat	おしゃべり（する）	N verbal	19			
cheap	やすい	Adj い	7	安い	7	たかい
check	おかんじょう	Noun	9			
check	しらべる	Verb る	14	調べる	23	
check out	かりだす	Verb う	25	借り出す	25	かしだす
cheerful	あかるい	Adj い	7	明るい	7	くらい
cheese	チーズ	Noun	24			
cheesecake	チーズケーキ	Noun	21			
chemistry	かがく	Noun	22	化学	22	
Chen	チェン	N proper	5			
cherry blossom/tree	さくら	Noun	13			
Chiba	ちば	N proper	19	千葉	19	
Chicago	シカゴ	N proper	3			
chicken	とり	Noun	27			
chicken	とりにく	Noun	12	とり肉	24	
child (plain)	こども	Noun	8	子供	16	おとな

child (respectful)	おこさん	Noun	8	お子さん	16	
children	こどもたち	Noun	15	子供達	16	おとなたち
chill	ひやす	Verb う	23	冷やす	24	
China	ちゅうごく	N proper	9	中国	9	
Chinatown	チャイナタウン	Noun	5			
Chinatown	ちゅうかがい	Noun	19			
Chinese characters	かんじ	Noun	10	漢字	10	
Chinese cuisine	ちゅうかりょうり	Noun	9	料理	12	
Chinese language	ちゅうごくご	Noun	6	中国語	9	
Chinese people	ちゅうごくじん	Noun	6	中国人	9	
chocolate	チョコレート	Noun	12			
choose	えらぶ	Verb う	24			
chop	きる	Verb う	24	切る	24	
chopsticks	(お) はし	Noun	4			
Christmas	クリスマス	N proper	16			
cigarette	タバコ	Noun	16			
city	まち	Noun	4			
class	クラス	Noun	2			
class	じゅぎょう	Noun	12	授業	18	
class, lesson, practice,	ならいごと	Noun	26	習い事	26	
classical music	クラシック	Noun	9			
classmate	クラスメート	Noun	9			
classroom	きょうしつ	Noun	3	教室	14	
clean	きれい (な)	Adj な	7			きたない
clean	そうじ (する)	N verbal	9			
clean (straighten) up	かたづける	Verb る	18			
clear up	はれる	Verb る	17	晴れる	17	(あめが) ふる
climb	のぼる	Verb う	20			
clock	とけい	Noun	3			
close (intransitive)	しまる	Verb う	10	閉まる	10	あく
close (transitive)	しめる	Verb る	18	閉める	18	あける
closing a store	へいてん (する)	N verbal	24	閉店	24	かいてん (する)
(Western-style) clothes	ようふく	Noun	16			
club	クラブ	Noun	11			
club, disco	クラブ	Noun	20			
coat	コート	Noun	15			
coffee	コーヒー	Noun	4			
coffee shop	きっさてん	Noun	15	きっさ店	15	
cola	コーラ	Noun	4			
cold	かぜ	Noun	14			
cold	さむい	Adj い	11	寒い	13	あつい

cold	つめたい	Adj い	19	冷たい	24	あつい
(get) cold	さめる	Verb る	18			
cold medicine	かぜぐすり	Noun	21	かぜ薬	21	
college	だいがく	Noun	2	大学	7	
color	いろ	Noun	17	色	17	
Columbus	コロンブス	N proper	11			
come	くる	V irreg	4	来る	5	いく
come (honorific)	いらっしゃる	Verb う	19			
come to being	できる	Verb る	17			
come out	(～を) でる	Verb る	18	出る	18	はいる
comfortable	らく (な)	Adj な	14	楽	14	たいへん (な)
comic strip	まんが	Noun	23			
communicate	れんらくをとる	Phrase	19	取る	14	
company	かいしゃ	Noun	14	会社	23	
company employee	かいしゃいん	Noun	17	会社員	23	
company president	しゃちょう	Noun	25	社長	25	
complain	もんくをいう	Phrase	26	言う	16	
complaint	もんく	Noun	26			
completion	かんせい (する)	N verbal	19			
complexion	かおいろ	Noun	21	顔色	21	
complicated	ふくざつ (な)	Adj な	19			かんたん (な)
composition	さくぶん	Noun	15	作文	15	
computer	コンピューター	Noun	2			
computer programmer	コンピュータープログラマー	Noun	17			
computer store	コンピューターショップ	Noun	18			
concern	しんぱい (する)	N verbal	19	心配	21	あんしん (する)
concert	おんがくかい	Noun	25	音楽会	25	
concert	コンサート	Noun	22			
congratulations	おめでとう (ございます)	Phrase	24			
connect (transitive)	つなげる	Verb る	23			きる
consultation	そうだん (する)	N verbal	18	相談	23	
contact	れんらく (する)	N verbal	19			
contact	れんらくをとる	Phrase	19	取る	14	
continue	つづく	Verb う	23			
continuously	ずっと	Adv	15			
convenient	べんり (な)	Adj な	7	便利	12	ふべん (な)
conversation	かいわ	Noun	15	会話	15	
cook	いたまえ	Noun	17	板前	X	

cook	シェフ	Noun	17			
cook (rice)	（ごはんを）たく	Verb う	27			
cooked rice	ごはん	Noun	4			
cookie	クッキー	Noun	11			
cooking	りょうり（する）	N verbal	5	料理	12	
cool	すずしい	Adj い	11			あたたかい
cool, chill (transitive)	ひやす	Verb う	23	冷やす	24	
come down	さがる	Verb う	21	下がる	21	あがる
co-op	せいきょう	Noun	14			
copy	うつす	Verb う	25			
copy	コピー（する）	N verbal	4			
corner	かど	Noun	17			
correct	ただしい	Adj い	17	正しい	22	まちがっている（V う）
correct	なおす	Verb う	21			
cough	せき	Noun	21			
country	くに	Noun	14	国	14	
course	コース	Noun	7			
courteous	ていねい（な）	Adj な	19			
cracker	クラッカー	Noun	24			
crab	かに	Noun	20			
cramming school	じゅく	Noun	26			
credit card	クレジットカード	Noun	25			
(get) crowded	こむ	Verb う	21			すく
cry	なく	Verb う	25	泣く	25	わらう
cuisine	りょうり（する）	N verbal	5	料理	12	
cultural	ぶんかてき（な）	Adj な	20	文化	18	
culture	ぶんか	Noun	18	文化	18	
cure	なおす	Verb う	21			こわす
curfew	もんげん	Noun	16			
curry rice	カレーライス	Noun	9			
curtain	カーテン	Noun	24			
(thick) custard soup	ちゃわんむし	Noun	24	茶わんむし	24	
custom	しゅうかん	Noun	14			
cut	きる	Verb う	24	切る	24	
cut classes	サボる	Verb う	26			
cute	かわいい	Adj い	9			
D Dallas	ダラス	N proper	27			
dance	ダンス（する）	N verbal	11			
dance	おどる	Verb う	13			
dangerous	あぶない	Adj い	22			あんぜん（な）
dangerous	きけん（な）	Adj な	25			あんぜん（な）

dark	くらい	Adj い	7	暗い	7	あかるい
date	デート	Noun	26			
daughter	むすめ（さん）	Noun	26			むすこ（さん）
day	ひ	Noun	15	日	15	
day after tomorrow	あさって	Noun	13			おととい
day before yesterday	おととい	Noun	13			
day off	やすみ	Noun	14	休み	14	
dead center	まんなか	Noun	17	まん中	17	
deadline	しめきり	Noun	16			
December	じゅうにがつ	N proper	5	十二月	5	
decide	きめる	Verb る	23			
decline	ことわる	Verb う	25			ひきうける
deep sleep (sound symbolic)	グッスリ	Adv	25			
defiance	はんこう（する）	N verbal	26			
definitely	たしかに	Adv	16			
(X) degree	～ど	Counter	21	～度	21	
delicious	おいしい	Adj い	7			まずい
deliver	とどける	Verb る	20			
deluxe	ごうか（な）	Adj な	24			
demonstration	デモ	Noun	7			
Denver	デンバー	N proper	27			
(academic) department	がくぶ	Noun	11	学部	11	
department head	ぶちょう	Noun	26	部長	26	
department store	デパート	Noun	4			
departure	しゅっぱつ（する）	N verbal	18			とうちゃく（する）
designer	デザイナー	Noun	17			
desire	ほしい	Adj い	12			
desk	つくえ	Noun	3			
dessert	デザート	Noun	9			
destruction	はかい（する）	N verbal	25			
detailed	くわしい	Adj い	19			
(private) detective	たんてい	Noun	24			
Detroit	デトロイト	N proper	11			
dictionary	じしょ	Noun	2	辞書	23	
die	しぬ	Verb う	8	死ぬ	25	うまれる
diet	ダイエット（する）	N verbal	12			
difference	ちがい	Noun	20			
(be) different	ちがう	Verb う	19			おなじ
difficult	むずかしい	Adj い	7	難しい	22	やさしい
digital camera	デジタルカメラ	Noun	23			

dinner	ばんごはん	Noun	4	晩ごはん	6	あさごはん
dinner	ゆうしょく	Noun	22	夕食	22	
direction	ほう	Noun	9	方	9	
dirty	きたない	Adj い	7			きれい（な）
(be) disappointed	がっかりする	V irreg	23			
disco	クラブ	Noun	20			
dish	（お）さら	Noun	14			
dislike	きらい（な）	Adj な	9			すき（な）
Disney	ディズニー	N proper	11			
Disneyland	ディズニーランド	N proper	14			
divorce	りこん（する）	N verbal	26			けっこん（する）
do	する	V irreg	4			
do	やる	Verb う	14			
do (honorific)	なさる	Verb う	9			
do one's best	がんばる	Verb う	6			
dog	いぬ	Noun	3	犬	21	
doghouse	いぬごや	Noun	3	犬ごや	21	
dollar	ドル	Noun	5			
(be) done	できる	Verb る	17			
door	ドア	Noun	10			
door	と	Noun	17			
dormitory	りょう	Noun	2			
downtown	ダウンタウン	Noun	4			
Doyle	ドイル	N proper	3			
draft	げんこう	Noun	22			
drapes	カーテン	Noun	24			
draw	かく	Verb う	9			けす
drawing	え	Noun	9	絵	15	
dress	ワンピース	Noun	10			
dress shirt	ワイシャツ	Noun	10			
drink	のむ	Verb う	4	飲む	6	
drinks	のみもの	Noun	9	飲み物	12	
drive	うんてん（する）	N verbal	11	運転	19	
drive	ドライブ（する）	N verbal	19			
drug store	くすりや	Noun	16	薬屋	21	
(Japanese) drum	たいこ	Noun	22			
(get) dry	かわく	Verb う	16			
dump (a significant other)	ふる	Verb う	26			
dwarfed tree in a pot	ぼんさい	Noun	27			

E

ear	みみ	Noun	7	耳	21	
early	はやい	Adj い	8	早い	8	おそい

earrings	イヤリング	Noun	10			
easily	らくに	Adv	18	楽	14	
East Asia	ひがしアジア	N proper	10	東アジア	10	
easy	やさしい	Adj い	7			むずかしい
easy	かんたん（な）	Adj な	9			むずかしい
easy	らく（な）	Adj な	14	楽	14	たいへん（な）
eat	たべる	Verb る	4	食べる	6	
eat (honorific)	めしあがる	Verb う	19	めし上がる	19	
eating out	がいしょく（する）	N verbal	26	外食	26	
economic analyst	けいざいアナリスト	Noun	17	経済アナリスト	X	
economical	けいざいてき（な）	Adj な	20			
economics	けいざいがく	Noun	2	けいざい学	11	
economy	けいざい	Noun	20			
eel	うなぎ	Noun	12			
egg	たまご	Noun	12			
eight	はち	Noun	3	八	3	
eight things	やっつ	Noun	9	八つ	9	
eighth	やっつめ	Noun	17	八つ目	17	
eighth day	ようかめ	Noun	15	八日目	15	
elder brother (plain)	あに	Noun	8	兄	8	おとうと
elder brother (resp)	おにいさん	Noun	8	お兄さん	8	
elder sister (plain)	あね	Noun	8	姉	8	いもうと
elder sister (respect)	おねえさん	Noun	8	お姉さん	8	
electric appliance shop	でんきや	Noun	18	電気屋	18	
electric light	でんき	Noun	10	電気	15	
electricity	でんき	Noun	10	電気	15	
elementary school	しょうがっこう	Noun	13	小学校	13	
Elvis	エルビス	N proper	11			
email	E メール	Noun	9			
embarrassed	はずかしい	Adj い	20			
embassy	たいしかん	Noun	20	大使館	20	
employment	さいよう（する）	N verbal	24			
employment exam	しゅうしょくしけん	Noun	22	試験	17	
(become) empty	すく	Verb う	9			こむ
encourage	はげます	Verb う	26			
end	おわり	Noun	23	終わり	23	
end of a street	つきあたり	Noun	17			
energetic	げんき（な）	Adj な	7	元気	11	
energy	エネルギー	Noun	25			
engineer	エンジニア	Noun	17			
England	イギリス	N proper	9			
English	えいご	Noun	2	英語	6	

English conversation	えいかいわ	Noun	26	英会話	26	
English literature	えいぶんがく	Noun	11	英文学	11	
enjoy	たのしむ	Verb う	26	楽しむ	26	
enjoyable	たのしい	Adj い	9	楽しい	13	
enter	はいる	Verb う	7	入る	7	でる
enter (a contest)	(〜に) でる	Verb る	12	出る	17	
entering company	にゅうしゃ (する)	N verbal	23	入社	23	
entering school	にゅうがく (する)	N verbal	23	入学	23	そつぎょう (する)
entrance	げんかん	Noun	15			
envelope	ふうとう	Noun	15			
erase	けす	Verb う	18			かく
eraser	けしゴム	Noun	23			
errand	ようじ	Noun	16	用事	20	
eruption	ふんか (する)	N verbal	20			
especially	とくに	Adv	18			
essay	エッセー	Noun	11			
establishment	そうりつ (する)	N verbal	25			
etc.	など	Particle	5			
Europe	ヨーロッパ	N proper	10			
even now	いまでも	Adv	18	今でも	18	
evening	ばん	Noun	5	晩	6	あさ
evening	ゆうがた	Noun	22	夕方	22	あさ
event	イベント	Noun	20			
every evening	まいばん	Noun	11	毎晩	14	
every month	まいつき	Noun	18	毎月	18	
every morning	まいあさ	Noun	11	毎朝	14	
every week	まいしゅう	Noun	14	毎週	14	
every year	まいとし、まいねん	Noun	17	毎年	17	
everyday	まいにち	Noun	11	毎日	14	
everyone (respectful)	みなさん	Noun	12			
everyone (plain)	みんな	Noun	13			
examination	テスト (する)	N verbal	5			
examination	しけん	Noun	6	試験	17	
Examiner	エグザミナー	N proper	2			
example	れい	Noun	4	例	X	
(for) example	たとえば	Phrase	21			
excuse	いいわけ	Noun	26	言いわけ	26	
exercise	うんどう (する)	N verbal	4	運動	19	
exhibition	てんらんかい	Noun	21	てんらん会	21	
exist (people, animals)	いる	Verb る	3			
exist (honorific)	いらっしゃる	Verb う	3			

exist (things)	ある	Verb う	3			ない
expense	ひよう	Noun	10			
expensive	たかい	Adj い	7	高い	7	やすい
explanation	せつめい（する）	N verbal	16	説明	22	
explorer	たんけんか	Noun	17	探検家	X	
eye	め	Noun	7	目	7	
eye drops	めぐすり	Noun	23	目薬	23	
F face	かお	Noun	15	顔	21	
face color	かおいろ	Noun	21	顔色	21	
fail (exam)	（しけんに）おちる	Verb る	15	落ちる	26	うかる
fairly	かなり	Adv	22			
fall	ふる	Verb う	8	降る	17	やむ、はれる
fall, come down	さがる	Verb う	21	下がる	21	あがる
fall over	たおれる	Verb る	21			
family (plain)	かぞく	Noun	8	家族	26	
family (respectful)	ごかぞく	Noun	8	ご家族	26	
famous	ゆうめい（な）	Adj な	14	有名	14	
far	とおい	Adj い	7	遠い	20	ちかい
farmer	のうぎょうけいえいしゃ	Noun	17	農業経営者	X	
fast	はやい	Adj い	9			おそい
(become) fat	ふとる	Verb う	14			
father (plain)	ちち	Noun	8	父	8	
father (respectful)	おとうさん	Noun	8	お父さん	8	
Father's Day	ちちのひ	N proper	23	父の日	23	
favor	おねがい（する）	N verbal	9	お願い	25	
February	にがつ	N proper	5	二月	5	
feed, pet food	えさ	Noun	23			
feelings	きぶん	Noun	21	気分	21	
feelings	きもち	Noun	17	気もち	17	
female	おんな	Noun	2	女	8	
festival	（お）まつり	Noun	13			
fever	ねつ	Noun	21	熱	21	
(very) few	すくない	Adj い	19	少ない	19	おおい
fifth	いつつめ	Noun	17	五つ目	17	
fifth day	いつかめ	Noun	15	五日目	15	
final	さいご	Noun	22	最後	22	さいしょ
final exam	きまつしけん	Noun	16	期末	16	
				試験	17	
finally	やっと	Adv	17			
fine	けっこう（な）	Adj な	8			だめ（な）
finish (intransitive)	おわる	Verb う	18	終わる	18	はじまる

finish (transitive)	おえる	Verb る	18	終える	18	はじめる
fire	ひ	Noun	25	火	25	
fireworks	はなび	Noun	25	花火	25	
first	いちばん	Noun	9	一番	9	
first	さいしょ	Noun	15	最初	26	さいご
first	はじめ	Noun	18	始め	18	さいご
first	ひとつめ	Noun	17	一つ目	17	
first day	いちにちめ	Noun	15	一日目	15	
first of all	まず	Adv	16			
first-year student	いちねんせい	Noun	2	一年生	11	
fish	さかな	Noun	6	魚	24	
fisherman	りょうし	Noun	17	漁師	X	
five	ご	Noun	3	五	3	
five things	いつつ	Noun	9	五つ	9	
fix	なおす	Verb う	21			こわす
flamboyant	はで（な）	Adj な	22			
flash card	フラッシュカード	Noun	14			
flight attendant	フライトアテンダント	Noun	17			
flourishing	さかん（な）	Adj な	25			
flower	はな	Noun	6	花	12	
flower viewing	（お）はなみ	Noun	17	（お）花見	17	
fluently (sound symbolic)	ペラペラ	Adv	25			
fly	とぶ	Verb う	25	飛ぶ	25	
food	たべもの	Noun	9	食べ物	12	
foot	あし	Noun	7	足	21	
for example	たとえば	Phrase	21			
for the first time	はじめて	Adv	10	始めて	15	
forcefully	むりやり	Adv	26			
foreign country	がいこく	Noun	11	外国	16	
foreign language	がいこくご	Noun	18	外国語	18	
foreign student	りゅうがくせい	Noun	6	留学生	6	
foreigner	がいこくじん	Noun	16	外国人	16	
forget	わすれる	Verb る	15			おぼえる
forget to do something carelessly	うっかりする	V irreg	15			
form	ようし	Noun	26	用紙	26	
(be) found	みつかる	Verb う	22	見つかる	22	
founding	そうりつ（する）	N verbal	25			
four	し・よん	Noun	3	四	3	
four things	よっつ	Noun	9	四つ	9	
fourth	よっつめ	Noun	17	四つ目	17	

fourth day	よっかめ	Noun	15	四日目	15	
fourth-year student	よねんせい	Noun	2	四年生	11	
free of charge	ただ	Noun	25			
French language	フランスご	Noun	6	フランス語	6	
French people	フランスじん	Noun	6	フランス人	6	
frequently	よく	Adv	18			
Friday	きんようび	N proper	4	金曜日	4	
friend	ともだち	Noun	4	友達	13	
frog	かえる	Noun	25			
from	から	Particle	4			
from now on	これから	Phrase	4			
front	まえ	Noun	3	前	10	
fruit	くだもの	Noun	9			
funeral ceremony	（お）そうしき	Noun	14			
funny	おもしろい	Adj い	26			つまらない
Furukawa	ふるかわ	N proper	8	古川	8	

G

game, match	しあい	Noun	22			
garden	にわ	Noun	12			
garden plant	うえき	Noun	23	うえ木	23	
gentle	やさしい	Adj い	7			むずかしい
German language	ドイツご	Noun	6	ドイツ語	6	
German people	ドイツじん	Noun	6	ドイツ人	6	
get angry	おこる	Verb う	17			
get crowded	こむ	Verb う	21			すく
get dry	かわく	Verb う	16			
get in trouble	こまる	Verb う	15	困る	23	
get off (train, airplane)	おりる	Verb る	17			のる
get on	のる	Verb う	13			おりる
get tired	つかれる	Verb る	5			
get to know	しる	Verb う	10	知る	10	
get up	おきる	Verb る	5			ねる
getting a job	しゅうしょく（する）	N verbal	19			
gift	（お）みやげ	Noun	13			
Ginza	ぎんざ	N proper	15	銀座	X	
girl	おんなのこ	Noun	25	女の子	25	おとこのこ
girlfriend	ガールフレンド	Noun	26			ボーイフレンド
give	あげる	Verb る	23	上げる	23	もらう
give	くださる	Verb う	23	下さる	23	
give	くれる	Verb る	23			あげる
give	さしあげる	Verb る	23	さし上げる		いただく
give	やる	Verb う	23			もらう

give up, hand over	ゆずる	Verb う	24			
glasses	めがね	Noun	10			
gloves	てぶくろ	Noun	24	手ぶくろ	24	
go	いく	Verb う	4	行く	5	くる
go (honorific)	いらっしゃる	Verb う	19			
go home	かえる	Verb う	4	帰る	8	でかける
go out	でかける	Verb る	15	出かける	20	かえる
go out	(～を) でる	Verb る	18	出る	18	はいる
go to bed	ねる	Verb る	5	寝る	15	おきる
golf	ゴルフ	Noun	6			
good	いい	Adj い	7			わるい
good at	じょうず (な)	Adj な	9	上手	9	へた (な)
good at	とくい (な)	Adj な	9			へた (な)
good-bye present	(お) せんべつ	Noun	23			
good health	げんき	Noun	25	元気	25	
gorgeous	ごうか (な)	Adj な	24			
grade	せいせき	Noun	14	成績	25	
gradually	だんだん	Adv	18			
graduate student	だいがくいんせい	Noun	2	大学院生	11	
graduation	そつぎょう (する)	N verbal	13	卒業	18	にゅうがく (する)
graduation ceremony	そつぎょうしき	Noun	23	卒業しき	18	
grammar	ぶんぽう	Noun	13	文法	18	
Grand Canyon	グランドキャニオン	N proper	22			
grandchild (plain)	まご	Noun	8			
grandchild (respect)	おまごさん	Noun	8			
grandfather (plain)	そふ	Noun	8			そぼ
grandfather (respect)	おじいさん	Noun	8			おばあさん
grandmother (plain)	そぼ	Noun	8			そふ
grandmother (resp)	おばあさん	Noun	8			おばあさん
grass	くさ	Noun	25			
gratitude	おれい (する)	N verbal	27			
great statue of Buddha	だいぶつ	Noun	15			
green	みどり	Noun	17			
green color	みどりいろ	Noun	17	みどり色	17	
green onion	ねぎ	Noun	12			
ground meat	ひきにく	Noun	27	ひき肉	27	
group	グループ	Noun	14			
Guam	グアム	N proper	22			
guest (respectful)	おきゃくさま	Noun	18	お客様	26	
guest	おきゃくさん	Noun	18	お客さん	26	
guide	あんない (する)	N verbal	26	案内	26	

guitar	ギター	Noun	9			
gymnasium	ジム	Noun	4			
H hair	かみ	Noun	7			
hairdresser	びようし	Noun	17	美容師	X	
Hakata	はかた	N proper	10	博多	X	
half	はん	Noun	4	半	4	
half	はんぶん	Noun	19	半分	19	
hall	ホール	Noun	22			
hamburger	ハンバーガー	Noun	5			
Hamlet	ハムレット	N proper	11			
hand	て	Noun	7	手	11	
hand over, give up	ゆずる	Verb う	24			
hand over	わたす	Verb う	25			
handbag	ハンドバッグ	Noun	16			
handout	ハンドアウト	Noun	9			
handsome	ハンサム	Adj な	9			
happy	うれしい (1st person)	Adj い	13			
happy	しあわせ（な）	Adj な	26			
(be) happy	よろこぶ (3rd person)	Verb う	13			
hard	かたい	Adj い	11			やわらかい
Harukawa	はるかわ	N proper	15	春川	15	
hat	ぼうし	Noun	10			
hate	きらう	Verb う	26			
have	もつ	Verb う	8			
Hawaii	ハワイ	N proper	11			
Hayakawa	はやかわ	N proper	3	早川	10	
he	かれ	Pronoun	26			かのじょ
head	あたま	Noun	7	頭	12	
heart	ハート	Noun	23			
heater	ヒーター	Noun	14			
heavy	おもい	Adj い	14			かるい
(body) height	せ	Noun	7	背	11	
hello (on the phone)	もしもし	Interject	10			
help	たすける	Verb る	13			
help	てつだい	Noun	18	手伝い	24	
help	てつだう	Verb う	24	手伝う	24	
here	ここ	Pronoun	2			そこ、あそこ
hesitation	えんりょ（する）	N verbal	19			
Higashiyama	ひがしやま	N proper	11	東山	11	
high (height)	たかい	Adj い	7	高い	7	ひくい
high heeled shoes	ハイヒール	Noun	10			
high school	こうこう	Noun	8	高校	8	

high school student	こうこうせい	Noun	8	高校生	8	
high spirits	げんき	Noun	25	元気	25	
hiking	ハイキング	Noun	20			
Hillman	ヒルマン	N proper	18			
hips, waist	こし	Noun	21			
Hiroshima	ひろしま	N proper	10	広島	X	
historical	れきしてき（な）	Adj な	20			
history	れきし	Noun	20			
hit (intransitive)	あたる	Verb う	21	当たる	21	
hold	もつ	Verb う	8			
Holmes	ホームズ	N proper	3			
home	うち	Noun	3	家	6	
(going) home country	きこく（する）	N verbal	18	帰国	18	
hometown	ふるさと	Noun	17			
homestay	ホームステイ（する）	N verbal	13			
homework	しゅくだい	Noun	4	宿題	14	
Honda	ほんだ	N proper	26	本田	26	
Honolulu	ホノルル	N proper	10			
hospital	びょういん	Noun	16	病院	17	
host family	ホストファミリー	Noun	13			
hot	あつい	Adj い	11	暑い	22	さむい
hot (spicy)	からい	Adj い	19			
hotel	ホテル	Noun	16			
house	うち	Noun	3	家	6	
housemoving	ひっこし（する）	N verbal	24			
housewife	しゅふ	Noun	17	主婦	X	
Houston	ヒューストン	N proper	27			
how	どう	Adv	7			
how (respectful)	いかが	Adv	7			
how long	どのぐらい	Adv	10			
how many people	なんにん	Pronoun	8	何人	8	
how much	いくら、どのぐらい	Adv	10			
hundred	ひゃく	Noun	3	百	3	
hurry	いそぐ	Verb う	18	急ぐ	18	
husband (plain)	しゅじん	Noun	8			かない
husband (respectful)	ごしゅじん	Noun	8			おくさん

I

I (typically by boys)	ぼく	Pronoun	17			
I	わたし	Pronoun	1	私	5	
ice cream	アイスクリーム	Noun	15			
Ieda	いえだ	N proper	26	家田	26	
if	もし	Adv	19			
illness	びょうき	Noun	13	病気	17	

impolite	しつれい（な）	Adj な	7			
important	だいじ（な）	Adj な	20	大事	20	
important	たいせつ（な）	Adj な	22	大切	22	
in addition to that	それに	Conj	20			
in the future	しょうらい	Noun	20			
in the middle of	～じゅう、～ちゅう	Suffix	17	～中	17	
(make) it in time	まにあう	Verb う	22	間にあう	22	おくれる
inconvenient	ふべん（な）	Adj な	7	不便	26	べんり（な）
inexpensive	やすい	Adj い	7	安い	7	たかい
inform	おしえる	Verb る	24	教える	14	
inform	つたえる	Verb る	24	伝える	24	
inhale	すう	Verb う	16			
(Japanese-style) inn	りょかん	Noun	15	旅館	19	
insect	むし	Noun	25			
inside	なか	Noun	3	中	9	そと
installation	インストール（する）	N verbal	19			
intelligence	ちえ	Noun	11			
intention	つもり	Noun	5			
interesting	おもしろい	Adj い	7			つまらない
Internet	インターネット	N proper	16			
interview	インタビュー（する）	N verbal	10			
interview	めんせつ（する）	N verbal	24			
introduction	しょうかい（する）	N verbal	14	紹介	24	
invitation	しょうたい（する）	N verbal	24	招待	24	
invitation letter	しょうたいじょう	Noun	24	招待じょう	24	
invite	よぶ	Verb う	12			
invite	さそう	Verb う	20			
iron	アイロン	Noun	24			
iron	アイロンをかける	Phrase	24			
Ishikawa	いしかわ	N proper	2	石川	7	
Italian cuisine	イタリアりょうり	Noun	9	料理	12	
itchy	かゆい	Adj い	21			

J

Jack	ジャック	N proper	10			
jacket	うわぎ	Noun	21	上着	21	
January	いちがつ	N proper	5	一月	5	
Japan	にほん	N proper	2	日本	4	
Japan	ジャパン	N proper	11			
Japanese	にほんじんてき（な）	Adj な	20	日本人	6	
(of) Japanese ancestry	にっけい	Noun	11	日系	X	
Japanese bullet train	しんかんせん	N proper	4			
Japanese cuisine	にほんりょうり	Noun	5	日本料理	12	
Japanese drum	たいこ	Noun	22			

Japanese language	にほんご	Noun	1	日本語	6	
Japanese painting	にほんが	Noun	21	日本画	21	
Japanese people	にほんじん	Noun	6	日本人	6	
Japanese pop music	J ポップ	Noun	23			
Japanese sake	にほんしゅ	Noun	22	日本酒	22	
Japanese-style inn	りょかん	Noun	15	旅館	19	
Japantown	にほんまち	Noun	4	日本まち	4	
Jazz	ジャズ	Noun	9			
jeans	ジーンズ	Noun	10			
jilt	ふる	Verb う	26			
Jimmy	ジミー	N proper	2			
job	しごと（する）	N verbal	8	仕事	14	
jogging	ジョギング（する）	N verbal	5			
John	ジョン	N proper	11			
joke	じょうだん	Noun	19			
jolt	ゆれる	Verb る	15			
Jones	ジョーンズ	N proper	4			
journalist	ジャーナリスト	Noun	17			
judo	じゅうどう	Noun	19			
juice	ジュース	Noun	8			
July	しちがつ	N proper	5	七月	5	
June	ろくがつ	N proper	5	六月	5	
junior high school	ちゅうがっこう	Noun	13	中学校	13	
junior high school student	ちゅうがくせい	Noun	17	中学生	17	
K						
kabuki	かぶき	Noun	15			
Kanazawa	かなざわ	N proper	22	金沢	X	
Kawamoto	かわもと	N proper	26	川本	26	
key	かぎ	Noun	15			
key holder	キーホルダー	Noun	17			
kill	ころす	Verb う	25			
Kim	キム	N proper	4			
kimono	きもの	Noun	18	着物	24	
Kimura	きむら	N proper	3	木村	15	
kind	しんせつ（な）	Adj な	7	親切	20	いじわる（な）
knee	ひざ	Noun	21			
knit	あむ	Verb う	24			
knock	ノック（する）	N verbal	18			
know (honorific)	ごぞんじだ	Phrase	19			
Korean language	かんこくご	Noun	6	かんこく語	6	
Korean people	かんこくじん	Noun	6	かんこく人	6	
Koyama	こやま	N proper	3	小山	5	

Kyoto	きょうと	N proper	2	京都	13	
L laboratory	ラボ	Noun	7			
lake	みずうみ	Noun	20			
landlord	おおや（さん）	Noun	18			テナント
language	ことば	Noun	16	言葉	16	
laptop	ラップトップ	Noun	12			
large	おおきい	Adj い	7	大きい	7	ちいさい
last	さいご	Noun	22	最後	22	さいしょ
last month	せんげつ	Noun	13	先月	13	らいげつ
last night	ゆうべ	Noun	14	夕べ	22	
last semester	せんがっき	Noun	17	先学期	17	らいがっき
last week	せんしゅう	Noun	5	先週	13	らいしゅう
last year	きょねん	Noun	8	去年	12	らいねん
late	おそい	Adj い	11			はやい
(be) late for	おくれる	Verb る	14			まにあう
(being) late for something	ちこく（する）	N verbal	22			
later	あとで	Adv	23	後で	23	
laugh (at)	わらう	Verb う	25	笑う	25	なく
laundry	せんたく（する）	N verbal	12	洗濯	16	
lavatory	おてあらい	Noun	3	お手洗い	16	
laver	のり	Noun	12			
lawyer	べんごし	Noun	17	弁護士	X	
lawyer	べんごし	Noun	20			
leader	リーダー	Noun	21			
leaf of a tree	このは	Noun	17	木の葉	17	
learn	ならう	Verb う	12	習う	15	
learn	まなぶ	Verb う	18	学ぶ	18	おしえる
leave (some place)	（～を）でる	Verb る	15	出る	17	（～に）つく
lecture	こうえん（する）	N verbal	20			
lecture	こうぎ（する）	N verbal	15			
left	ひだり	Noun	17	左	17	みぎ
leg	あし	Noun	7			
leisure	ひま（な）	Adj な	12			いそがしい
leisurely	ゆっくり	Adv	21			
lemonade	レモネード	Noun	24			
lend	かす	Verb う	8	貸す	23	かりる
lend out	かしだす	Verb う	25	貸し出す	25	かりだす
Lennon	レノン	N proper	11			
lesson, practice, class	ならいごと	Noun	26	習い事	26	
letter	てがみ	Noun	3	手紙	10	
letter, character	じ	Noun	15	字	15	

Lewis	ルイス	N proper	7			
library	としょかん	Noun	2	図書館	10	
lie down	ねる	Verb る	5	寝る	15	おきる
light (weight)	かるい	Adj い	14			おもい
like	すき（な）	Adj な	9	好き	9	きらい（な）
like very much	だいすき（な）	Adj な	12	大好き	12	
Lin	リン	N proper	3			
Lincoln	リンカーン	N proper	11			
linguistics	げんごがく	Noun	19	言語学	19	
liquor	（お）さけ	Noun	5	（お）酒	16	
listen	きく	Verb う	5	聞く	11	
listening	ききとり	Noun	16	聞き取り	16	
literature	ぶんがく	Noun	5	文学	11	
(a) little	すこし	Adv	6	少し	12	たくさん
(a) little	ちょっと	Adv	7			たくさん
(a) little while ago	さっき	Adv	22			
(very) little	すくない	Adj い	19	少ない	19	おおい
lively	にぎやか（な）	Adj な	7			しずか（な）
loan	ローン	Noun	18			
location	ばしょ	Noun	12			
lock (with a key)	（かぎを）かける	Verb る	24			あける
lonely	さびしい	Adj い	13			
long	ながい	Adj い	7	長い	7	みじかい
look forward to	たのしみにする	Phrase	4	楽しみ	13	
look up (dictionary)	ひく	Verb う	15			
Los Angeles	ロサンゼルス／ロス	N proper	9			
lose	なくす	Verb う	16			
lose (a game)	（～に）まける	Verb る	22			かつ
(a) lot	たくさん	Adv	5			
love letter	ラブレター	Noun	25			
low (height)	ひくい	Adj い	7			たかい
lunch	ひるごはん	Noun	4	昼ごはん	25	
luxurious	ごうか（な）	Adj な	24			

M

Macintosh	マッキントッシュ	N proper	16			
Maeda	まえだ	N proper	7	前田	25	
magazine	ざっし	Noun	2			
major	せんもん	Noun	1	専門	22	
major (respectful)	ごせんもん	Noun	1	ご専門	22	
make (tea)	（おちゃを）いれる	Verb る	24	入れる	24	
make	つくる	Verb う	5	作る	9	こわす
make it in time	まにあう	Verb う	22	間にあう	22	おくれる
male	おとこ	Noun	2	男	8	

manager	マネージャー	Noun	16			
mandarin orange	みかん	Noun	23			
manual	マニュアル	Noun	17			
many	おおい	Adj い	10	多い	10	すくない
many	たくさん	Adv	5			すこし、ちょっと
many (people)	おおぜい	Noun	18			
many kinds of	いろいろ（な）	Adj な	12			
map	ちず	Noun	9	地図	24	
March	さんがつ	N proper	5	三月	5	
marina	マリーナ	Noun	24			
marriage	けっこん（する）	N verbal	19	結婚	26	りこん（する）
married couple	ふうふ	Noun	26			
Masako	まさこ	N proper	23	正子	23	
match, game	しあい	Noun	22			
mathematics	すうがく	Noun	6	数学	26	
matter	こと	Noun	16			
(a) matter of course	とうぜん	Noun	26	当然	26	
May	ごがつ	N proper	5	五月	5	
McDonald's	マクドナルド	N proper	5			
me	わたし	Pronoun	1	私	5	
meal	ごはん	Noun	4			
meal	しょくじ（する）	N verbal	17	食事	17	
mean	いじわる（な）	Adj な	7			しんせつ（な）、やさしい
meaning	いみ	Noun	12	意味	20	
measure	はかる	Verb う	21			
meat	にく	Noun	11	肉	24	
medical doctor	いしゃ、おいしゃさん	Noun	16	医者	21	
medical school	いかだいがくいん	Noun	21	医科大学院	21	
medicine	くすり	Noun	16	薬	21	
meet	あう	Verb う	4	会う	6	
meeting	かいぎ	Noun	18			
meeting	ミーティング	Noun	16			
memo	メモ（する）	N verbal	24			
memorize	おぼえる	Verb る	12	覚える	15	わすれる
Memphis	メンフィス	N proper	27			
meticulous	ていねい（な）	Adj な	22			
Mexican people	メキシコじん	Noun	6	メキシコ人	6	
Miami	マイアミ	N proper	27			
Mickey Mouse	ミッキーマウス	N proper	11			
microphone	マイク	Noun	25			

microwave oven	でんしレンジ	Noun	12			
Middle East	ちゅうとう	N proper	22	中東	22	
(in the) middle of	～じゅう、～ちゅう	Suffix	17	～中	17	
middle of night	よなか	Noun	16	夜中	16	
middle-aged man	おじさん	Noun	24			おばさん
middle-aged woman	おばさん	Noun	24			おじさん
midterm	ちゅうかん	Noun	6	中間	6	
midyear present	（お）ちゅうげん	Noun	23	（お）中元	23	
(with all one's) might	いっしょうけんめい（に）	Phrase	21	一生けんめい	22	
mile	マイル	Noun	13			
milk	ミルク	Noun	15			
Miller	ミラー	N proper	2			
minced meat	そぼろ	Noun	27			
Minneapolis	ミネアポリス	N proper	27			
mistake	しっぱい（する）	N verbal	20			
mistake	まちがい	Noun	23			
misunderstanding	ごかい（する）	N verbal	27			
Monday	げつようび	N proper	4	月曜日	4	
money	（お）かね	Noun	6	お金	7	
monitor	モニター	Noun	14			
(X) month(s)	～かげつ	Counter	9	～か月	9	
month after next	さらいげつ	Noun	13	さ来月	13	せんせんげつ
month before last	せんせんげつ	Noun	13	先々月	13	さらいげつ
mood	きぶん	Noun	21	気分	21	
mood	きもち	Noun	17	気もち	17	
moon	つき	Noun	11	月	11	
more	もっと	Adv	16			
more	もう	Adv	18			
moreover	それに	Conj	20			
more than X	～いじょう	Suffix	19			
morning	ごぜん	Noun	4	午前	13	ごご
morning	あさ	Noun	5	朝	10	ばん
mother (plain)	はは	Noun	8	母	8	ちち
mother (respectful)	おかあさん	Noun	8	お母さん	8	おとうさん
Mother's Day	はははのひ	N proper	23	母の日	23	
motorcycle	オートバイ	Noun	14			
mountain	やま	Noun	20	山	20	
mouth	くち	Noun	7	口	21	
move	うごく	Verb う	18	動く	19	とまる
movie	えいが	Noun	4	映画	15	
movie theater	えいがかん	Noun	18	映画館	18	

(house) moving	ひっこし（する）	N verbal	24			
Mozart	モーツアルト	N proper	20			
MP3 player	MP3 プレーヤー	Noun	23			
Mt. Fuji	ふじさん	N proper	12	富士山	X	
much more	ずっと	Adv	26			
mug	マグカップ	Noun	9			
Murakami	むらかみ	N proper	19	村上	19	
Murayama	むらやま	N proper	15	村山	15	
music	おんがく	Noun	9	音楽	11	
music concert	おんがくかい	Noun	25	音楽会	25	
music performance	えんそう（する）	N verbal	17			
musician	ミュージシャン	Noun	17			
mustache	ひげ	Noun	18			

N

Nagoya	なごや	N proper	10	名古屋	19	
Nakamura	なかむら	N proper	21	中村	21	
Nakayama	なかやま	N proper	10	中山	10	
name	なまえ	Noun	1	名前	11	
name (respectful)	おなまえ	Noun	1	お名前	11	
nap	ひるね（する）	N verbal	13	昼寝	25	
Nara	なら	N proper	11	奈良	X	
narrow	せまい	Adj い	7			ひろい
Natsume	なつめ	N proper	14	夏目	14	
nature	しぜん	Noun	25	自然	25	
near	ちかい	Adj い	7	近い	20	とおい
neck	くび	Noun	21			
necklace	ネックレス	Noun	10			
necktie	ネクタイ	Noun	10			
neighborhood	きんじょ	Noun	19	近所	24	
Neil	ニール	N proper	11			
nephew (plain)	おい	Noun	8			めい
nephew (respectful)	おいごさん	Noun	8			めいごさん
nevertheless	それなのに	Adv	26			
new	あたらしい	Adj い	7	新しい	7	ふるい
New Orleans	ニューオリンズ	N proper	27			
(1st month of) New Year	（お）しょうがつ	N proper	14	（お）正月	23	
new year	しんねん	Noun	24	新年	24	
new year's gift money	おとしだま	Noun	23	お年だま	23	
New York	ニューヨーク	N proper	2			
news	ニュース	Noun	22			
newspaper	しんぶん	Noun	2	新聞	11	
next	つぎ	Noun	15	次	25	
next month	らいげつ	Noun	13	来月	13	せんげつ

	next semester	らいがっき	Noun	18	来学期	18	せんがっき
	next time	こんど	Noun	6	今度	18	
	next to	となり	Noun	3			
	next week	らいしゅう	Noun	11	来週	13	せんしゅう
	next year	らいねん	Noun	12	来年	12	きょねん
	Nguyen	ヌエン	N proper	10			
	nice	けっこう（な）	Adj な	8			だめ（な）
	niece (plain)	めい	Noun	8			おい
	niece (respectful)	めいごさん	Noun	8			おいごさん
	night	よる	Noun	15	夜	16	あさ
	nine	きゅう・く	Noun	3	九	3	
	nine things	ここのつ	Noun	9	九つ	9	
	ninth	ここのつめ	Noun	17	九つ目	17	
	ninth day	ここのかめ	Noun	15	九日目	15	
	no	いいえ	Adv	2			はい
	no	いえ	Adv	26			
	no (casual)	ううん	Adv	6			うん
	no good	だめ（な）	Adj な	11			いい、けっこう（な）
	noisy	うるさい	Adj い	7			しずか（な）
	noon	ひる	Noun	25	昼	25	よる
	north	きた	Noun	20			
	nose	はな	Noun	7			
	(not) at all	ぜんぜん	Adv	7			
	not busy	ひま（な）	Adj な	12			いそがしい
	not having enough sleep	ねぶそく	Noun	26	寝不足	26	
	(not) much	あまり	Adv	7			
	not serious	ふまじめ（な）	Adj な	7			まじめ（な）
	notebook	ノート	Noun	3			
	novel	しょうせつ	Noun	11	小説	22	
	novelist	さっか	Noun	17	作家	X	
	novelist	しょうせつか	Noun	17	小説家	X	
	November	じゅういちがつ	N proper	5	十一月	5	
	now	いま	Noun	4	今	5	
	now	これから	Phrase	4			
	number	ばんごう	Noun	19			
	number one	いちばん	Noun	9	一番	9	
	nurse	かんごし	Noun	17	看護師	X	
O	Oakland	オークランド	N proper	5			
	October	じゅうがつ	N proper	5	十月	5	
	Odaiba	おだいば	N proper	16	お台場	X	
	of course	もちろん	Adv	6			

office	オフィス	Noun	3			
office hours	オフィスアワー	Noun	10			
office worker	かいしゃいん	Noun	17	会社員	23	
often	よく	Adv	18			
oh	へえ	Interject	4			
okay	だいじょうぶ（な）	Adj な	12			
old	ふるい	Adj い	7	古い	7	あたらしい
old days	むかし	Noun	20			さいきん
old man	おじいさん	Noun	24			おばあさん
old woman	おばあさん	Noun	24			おじいさん
on	うえ	Noun	3	上	5	した
on foot	あるいて	Phrase	4	歩いて	18	
once in a while	たまに	Adv	26			
once more	もういちど	Phrase	16	一度	18	
one	いち	Noun	3	一	3	
one person	ひとり	Noun	8	一人	8	
one thing	ひとつ	Noun	9	一つ	9	
(with all) one's might	いっしょうけんめい（に）	Phrase	21	一生けんめい	22	
oneself	じぶん	Pronoun	20	自分	20	
onion	たまねぎ	Noun	12			
open (intransitive)	あく	Verb う	10	開く	10	しまる
open (transitive)	あける	Verb る	17	開ける	17	しめる
opening a store	かいてん（する）	N verbal	24	開店	24	へいてん
opinion	いけん	Noun	23	意見	23	
opponent	あいて	Noun	23	相手	23	
opposition	はんたい（する）	N verbal	22	反対	26	
or	か	Particle	15			
orange	オレンジ	Noun	9			
order	オーダー（する）	N verbal	9			
order	じゅんばん	Noun	15			
order	ちゅうもん（する）	N verbal	21	注文	25	
Osaka	おおさか	N proper	7	大阪	X	
other (than something)	ほか	Noun	10			
(be) out	（ほしが）でる	Verb る	22	出る	22	
outside	そと	Noun	3	外	16	なか
overcoat	オーバー	Noun	22			
oversleep	ねぼうする	V irreg	12	寝ぼうする	18	

P

P.M.	ごご	Noun	4	午後	13	ごぜん
page	ページ	Noun	18			
painful	いたい	Adj い	12	痛い	21	
pair	ペア	Noun	19			

pajamas	パジャマ	Noun	24			
Pak	パク	N proper	3			
pamphlet	パンフレット	Noun	22			
pants	ズボン	Noun	10			
paper	かみ	Noun	11	紙	11	
parcel	こづつみ	Noun	11	小づつみ	11	
parent(s)	おや	Noun	26	親	26	
parents (plain)	りょうしん	Noun	8	両親	20	
parents (respectful)	ごりょうしん	Noun	8	ご両親	20	
park	こうえん	Noun	6			
participation	さんか（する）	N verbal	26			
partner	あいて	Noun	23	相手	23	
partner	パートナー	Noun	10			
party	パーティー	Noun	6			
pass (exam, class, etc.)	うかる	Verb う	21	受かる	21	おちる
passport	パスポート	Noun	14			
pasta	パスタ	Noun	24			
paste	はる	Verb う	15			
pat	たたく	Verb う	25			
pay	はらう	Verb う	16			
pay attention to	きをつける	Phrase	23	気をつける	23	
PC	ピーシー（PC）	Noun	16			
pen	ペン	Noun	2			
pencil	えんぴつ	Noun	2			
people	ひとびと	Noun	11	人々	11	
Perez	ペレス	N proper	11			
perfect score	まんてん	Noun	22			
(music) performance	えんそう（する）	N verbal	17			
perfume	こうすい	Noun	23			
perhaps	たぶん	Adv	17	多分	17	
person	ひと	Noun	2	人	8	
person (respectful)	かた	Noun	2	方	11	
personal computer	パソコン	Noun	26			
pet food	えさ	Noun	23			
Philadelphia	フィラデルフィア	N proper	27			
photograph	しゃしん	Noun	2	写真	19	
physics	ぶつりがく	Noun	19	物理学	19	
piano	ピアノ	Noun	6			
pickpocket	すり	Noun	25			
picnic	ピクニック	Noun	6			
picture	え	Noun	9	絵	15	
piggy bank	ちょきんばこ	Noun	25	貯金ばこ	25	

pilot	パイロット	Noun	17			
pitiable, pitiful	かわいそう（な）	Adj な	26			
pizza	ピザ	Noun	11			
place	ばしょ	Noun	12			
place	ところ	Noun	16	所	20	
place over there	あそこ	Pronoun	2			ここ
plan	けいかく（する）	N verbal	25	計画	25	
plan	プラン	Noun	4			
plan	よてい	Noun	26			
play	あそび	Noun	26	遊び	26	
play	あそぶ	Verb う	6	遊ぶ	24	
play (musical instrument)	ひく	Verb う	6			
pleasant	たのしい	Adj い	9	楽しい	13	
please	どうぞ	Adv	9			
please give	ください	Phrase	8	下さい	8	
(to be) pleased	うれしい (1st person)	Adj い	13			
(to be) pleased	よろこぶ (3rd person)	Verb う	13			
plenty	おおい	Adj い	10	多い	10	すくない
plural marker (people)	～たち	Suffix	2	～達	13	
points	てん	Noun	14			
(X) point(s)	～てん	Counter	15			
pole, stick	ぼう	Noun	21			
police	けいさつ	Noun	23			
police box	こうばん	Noun	20			
police(wo)man	おまわりさん	Noun	20			
polish	みがく	Verb う	15			
polite	ていねい（な）	Adj な	19			
polite plural marker (people)	～がた	Suffix	26	～方	26	
political	せいじてき（な）	Adj な	20			
politician	せいじか	Noun	17	政治家	X	
politics	せいじ	Noun	20			
popcorn	ポップコーン	Noun	12			
popularity	にんき	Noun	16	人気	16	
pork cutlet	とんかつ	Noun	5			
post	はりだす	Verb う	25	はり出す	25	
post office	ゆうびんきょく	Noun	3			
postage stamp	きって	Noun	15	切手	20	
potato	じゃがいも	Noun	12			
power	ちから	Noun	11			
powerful	はくりょくがある	Phrase	22			
practice, class, lesson	ならいごと	Noun	26	習い事	26	

	practice	れんしゅう（する）	N verbal	9	練習	18	
	praise	ほめる	Verb る	25			しかる
	preparation	じゅんび（する）	N verbal	24			
	preparation	ようい（する）	N verbal	20	用意	20	
	preparatory study	よしゅう（する）	N verbal	14	予習	18	ふくしゅう（する）
	present	プレゼント（する）	N verbal	10			
	present	おくりもの	Noun	14	おくり物	14	
	presentation	はっぴょう（する）	N verbal	25			
	president of a country	だいとうりょう	Noun	22			
	Presley	プレスリー	N proper	11			
	printer	プリンター	Noun	13			
	printing (newspapers, magazines)	はっこう（する）	N verbal	25			
	private detective	たんてい	Noun	24			
	probably	たぶん	Adv	17	多分	17	
	problem	もんだい	Noun	16	問題	19	
	professional	せんもんてき（な）	Adj な	20	専門	22	
	program	プログラム	Noun	3			
	project	プロジェクト	Noun	21			
	promise	やくそく（する）	N verbal	22			
	properly	ちゃんと	Adv	26			
	psychology	しんりがく	Noun	22	心理学	22	
	publication (newspapers, magazines)	はっこう（する）	N verbal	25			
	pudding	プリン	Noun	24			
	purse	さいふ	Noun	25			
	push	おす	Verb う	17			
	put into	いれる	Verb る	17	入れる	18	だす
	put into	（めぐすりを）さす	Verb う	23			
	put out, serve	だす	Verb う	24	出す	24	
	put straight	なおす	Verb う	21			
	put up (an umbrella)	（かさを）さす	Verb う	22			
Q	quarrel	けんか（する）	N verbal	15			
	question	しつもん（する）	N verbal	6	質問	19	こたえる
	quiet	しずか（な）	Adj な	7	静か	11	うるさい
	quit doing something	やめる	Verb る	14			はじめる
R	radio	ラジオ	Noun	3			
	rain	あめ	Noun	8	雨	14	
	raise	あげる	Verb る	14	上げる	18	もらう
	Raoul	ラウール	N proper	4			

rapid eating (sound symbolic)	ペロっと	Adv	25			
rapidly (sound symbolic)	ドンドン	Adv	22			
rare	めずらしい	Adj い	23			
raw fish	(お) さしみ	Noun	6			
reach	とどく	Verb う	19			
read	よむ	Verb う	4	読む	9	
readings	よみもの	Noun	12	読み物	12	
really	ほんとうに	Adv	18	本当	19	
rebellion	はんこう(する)	N verbal	26			
receive	もらう	Verb う	11			あげる
receive (respectful)	いただく	Verb う	8			さしあげる
recently	さいきん	Noun	14	最近	22	むかし
recipe	レシピ	Noun	15			
recommendation letter	すいせんじょう	Noun	24			
recover	なおる	Verb う	21			
red	あか	Noun	17	赤	17	
red	あかい	Adj い	17	赤い	17	
refrigerator	れいぞうこ	Noun	12			
regret	ざんねん (な)	Adj な	6			
regrettable	ざんねん (な)	Adj な	6			
relatives	しんせき	Noun	23			
relax	ゆっくりする	V irreg	21			
relaxed	らく (な)	Adj な	14	楽	14	たいへん (な)
relief	あんしん (する)	N verbal	24	安心	24	しんぱい (する)
remaining	あと	Noun	18	後	18	
repair	しゅうり (する)	N verbal	18			こわす
repair	なおす	Verb う	21			こわす
repair store	しゅうりや	Noun	18	しゅうり屋	18	
(be) repaired	なおる	Verb う	19			こしょう (する)、こわれる
reply	へんじ (する)	N verbal	13	返事	13	
reputation	ひょうばん	Noun	14			
request	おねがい (する)	N verbal	9	お願い	25	
request	たのむ	Verb う	25			
research	けんきゅう (する)	N verbal	20			
resemble	にる	Verb る	22			
reservation, hesitation	えんりょ (する)	N verbal	19			
reservation	よやく (する)	N verbal	18			
rest	やすむ	Verb う	14	休む	14	
restaurant	レストラン	Noun	5			

restroom	おてあらい	Noun	3	お手洗い	16	
result	けっか	Noun	24			
résumé	りれきしょ	Noun	24			
return	かえす	Verb う	6	返す	13	かりる
return	かえる	Verb う	4	帰る	8	でかける
returning to one's home country	きこく(する)	N verbal	18	帰国	18	
review	ふくしゅう (する)	N verbal	6	復習	18	よしゅう (する)
revise	かきなおす	Verb う	23	書きなおす	23	
rewrite	かきなおす	Verb う	23	書きなおす	23	
(cooked) rice	ごはん	Noun	4			
(uncooked) rice	(お) こめ	Noun	12	お米	12	
rice bowl	ちゃわん	Noun	24	茶わん	24	
rice cake	(お) もち	Noun	14			
rice cracker	(お) せんべい	Noun	19			
ride	のる	Verb う	13	乗る	18	おりる
right	みぎ	Noun	17	右	17	ひだり
ring	ゆびわ	Noun	10			
river	かわ	Noun	17	川	17	
road	みち	Noun	17			
rock	ロック	Noun	9			
room	へや	Noun	3	部屋	17	
roommate	ルームメート	Noun	3			
Roppongi	ろっぽんぎ	N proper	16	六本木	16	
round	まるい	Adj い	21			しかくい
rub	こする	Verb う	17			
run	はしる	Verb う	13			
run out of	なくなる	Verb う	19			
run over	ひく	Verb う	25			
(have a) runny nose	はながでる	Phrase	21	出る	21	
Russian language	ロシアご	Noun	6	ロシア語	6	

S

sad	かなしい	Adj い	17			うれしい
safe	あんぜん (な)	Adj な	23	安全	23	きけん (な)
safe	きんこ	Noun	26			
sake	(お) さけ	Noun	5	お酒	16	
(Japanese) sake	にほんしゅ	Noun	22	日本酒	22	
salad	サラダ	Noun	24			
sale	セール	Noun	7			
salmon	さけ	Noun	12			
salt	(お) しお	Noun	12			
salty	からい	Adj い	19			あまい

same	おなじ	Adj irreg	22	同じ	22	ちがう（V う）
San Antonio	サンアントニオ	N proper	27			
San Diego	サンディエゴ	N proper	4			
San Francisco	サンフランシスコ	N proper	2			
Saturday	どようび	N proper	4	土曜日	4	
(be) saved	たすかる	Verb う	19			
saving, thrift	せつやく（する）	N verbal	20			
savings	ちょきん（する）	N verbal	18	貯金	19	
say	いう	Verb う	11	言う	16	
say (honorific)	おっしゃる	Verb う	19			
scarf	スカーフ	Noun	15			
scary	こわい	Adj い	19			
schedule	スケジュール	Noun	18			
schedule	よていひょう	Noun	22			
Schmidt	シュミット	N proper	8			
scholarship (money)	しょうがくきん	Noun	19			
school	がっこう	Noun	10	学校	10	
school excursion	しゅうがくりょこう	Noun	20	旅行	19	
science	サイエンス	Noun	2			
scientist	かがくしゃ	Noun	17	科学者	X	
scold	しかる	Verb う	25			ほめる
score	てん	Noun	14			
screen (of a computer)	スクリーン	Noun	17			
search for	さがす	Verb う	14			
season	きせつ	Noun	22			
seat	せき	Noun	22			
Seattle	シアトル	N proper	27			
second	ふたつめ	Noun	17	二つ目	17	
second day	ふつかめ	Noun	15	二日目	15	
second-year student	にねんせい	Noun	2	二年生	11	
secretary	ひしょ	Noun	17	秘書	X	
see	みる	Verb る	4	見る	6	
see (honorific)	ごらんになる	Verb う	19			
select	えらぶ	Verb う	24			
semester	がっき	Noun	25	学期	25	
send	おくる	Verb う	10	送る	24	
send out (HW, letter)	だす	Verb う	16	出す	16	
(one's) senior	せんぱい	Noun	19			
sentence	ぶん	Noun	13	文	13	
September	くがつ	N proper	5	九月	5	
serious	まじめ（な）	Adj な	7			ふまじめ（な）
serve, put out	だす	Verb う	24	出す	24	

service	サービス（する）	N verbal	11			
seven	しち・なな	Noun	3	七	3	
seven things	ななつ	Noun	9	七つ	9	
seventh	ななつめ	Noun	17	七つ目	17	
seventh day	なのかめ	Noun	15	七日目	15	
severe	きびしい	Adj い	26			
sew	ぬう	Verb う	24			
sexual harassment	セクハラ	Noun	26			
Shakespeare	シェークスピア	N proper	11			
shape	かたち	Noun	23			
shave	そる	Verb う	18			
she	かのじょ	Pronoun	26			かれ
Shibuya	しぶや	N proper	20	渋谷	X	
Shinagawa	しながわ	N proper	15	品川	X	
Shinjuku	しんじゅく	N proper	15	新宿	15	
Shin-Osaka	しんおおさか	N proper	10	新大阪	X	
Shinto shrine	じんじゃ	Noun	13			
ship	ふね	Noun	11			
shirt	シャツ	Noun	17			
shoes	くつ	Noun	6			
shoji screen	しょうじ	Noun	21			
shop	（お）みせ	Noun	6	（お）店	12	
(X) shop	～や	Suffix	17	～屋	17	
shop/branch manager	てんちょう	Noun	24	店長	24	てんいん
shopping	かいもの（する）	N verbal	4	買い物	12	
shopping center/mall	ショッピングセンター	Noun	19			
short (height)	ひくい	Adj い	7			たかい
short (length)	みじかい	Adj い	7	短い	22	ながい
shorts	ショートパンツ	Noun	10			
shoulder	かた	Noun	21			
show	みせる	Verb る	19	見せる	19	
show signs of desire	ほしがる	Verb う	12			
shower	シャワー	Noun	13			
siblings	きょうだい	Noun	8	兄弟	8	
siblings (respectful)	ごきょうだい	Noun	8	ご兄弟	8	
side	よこ	Noun	3			
side	ほう	Noun	9	方	9	
sign, signboard	サイン（する）	N verbal	24			
sightseeing	けんぶつ（する）	N verbal	16	見物	16	
simple	らく（な）	Adj な	14	楽	14	たいへん（な）
since	から	Particle	15			
sing	うたう	Verb う	8	歌う	15	

Singh	シン	N proper	7			
sit down	すわる	Verb う	10			たつ
six	ろく	Noun	3	六	3	
six things	むっつ	Noun	9	六つ	9	
sixth	むっつめ	Noun	17	六つ目	17	
sixth day	むいかめ	Noun	15	六日目	15	
sketch	スケッチ（する）	N verbal	16			
ski	スキー	Noun	6			
skirt	スカート	Noun	10			
skit	スキット	Noun	13			
sky	そら	Noun	22			
slander	わるぐち	Noun	25	悪口	25	
sleep	ねむる	Verb う	14	眠る	19	おきる
sleepy	ねむい	Adj い	14	眠い	19	
slow	おそい	Adj い	11			はやい
small	せまい	Adj い	7			ひろい
small	ちいさい	Adj い	7	小さい	7	おおきい
smile	わらう	Verb う	25	笑う	25	なく
Smith	スミス	N proper	7			
smoothly	らくに	Adv	18	楽	14	
snack	おかし	Noun	11			
snake	へび	Noun	25			
sneakers	スニーカー	Noun	10			
sneeze	くしゃみ（する）	N verbal	21			
snow	ゆき	Noun	13	雪	17	
snowman	ゆきだるま	Noun	13	雪だるま	17	
so	ですから	Conj	6			
so	そう	Adv	24			
so many, so much	あんなに	Adv	20			
so that	それで	Conj	8			
socks	ソックス	Noun	10			
sofa	ソファー	Noun	3			
soft	やわらかい	Adj い	11			かたい
softly	そっと	Adv	26			
software	ソフト	Noun	24			
soil	よごす	Verb う	25			あらう
some time ago	このあいだ	Phrase	12	この間	23	
someday	いつか	Adv	23			
someone	だれか	Pronoun	3			だれも
someone (respectful)	どなたか	Pronoun	3			どなたも
something	なにか・なんか	Pronoun	3	何か	4	なにも
sometime	いつか	Adv	23			

sometimes	ときどき	Adv	11	時々	11	いつも
somewhere	どこかに	Adv	3			どこにも
Son	ソン	N proper	2			
son	むすこ（さん）	Noun	26			むすめ（さん）
song	うた	Noun	8	歌	15	
soon	すぐ・もうすぐ	Adv	5			
sound	おと	Noun	18	音	18	
soup	スープ	Noun	24			
sour	すっぱい	Adj い	20			
soy sauce	（お）しょうゆ	Noun	12			
spacious	ひろい	Adj い	7	広い	7	せまい
spaghetti	スパゲティ	Noun	6			
Spanish language	スペインご	Noun	6	スペイン語	6	
spark	ひ	Noun	25	火	25	
speak	はなす	Verb う	6	話す	9	
speak	いう	Verb う	11	言う	16	
speaker	スピーカー	Noun	24			
speciality	せんもん	Noun	1			
speciality (respectful)	ごせんもん	Noun	1			
speech	スピーチ（する）	N verbal	18			
spicy	からい	Adj い	19			
spill	こぼす	Verb う	18			
splendid	すてき（な）、 りっぱ（な）	Adj な	18			
sport	スポーツ	Noun	9			
sports instructor	スポーツ・ インストラクター	Noun	17			
sports player	せんしゅ	Noun	11			
spring	はる	Noun	13	春	13	
spring vacation	はるやすみ	Noun	13	春休み	13	
spy	スパイ	Noun	25			
square	しかくい	Adj い	21			まるい
St, Louis	セントルイス	N proper	27			
stain	よごす	Verb う	25			あらう
stamp, postage	きって	Noun	15	切手	20	
stand up	たつ	Verb う	10			すわる
stapler	ホチキス	Noun	24			
star	ほし	Noun	22			
start (intransitive)	はじまる	Verb う	18	始まる	18	おわる
start (transitive)	はじめる	Verb る	10	始める	15	おえる、やめる
start living somewhere	すむ	Verb う	10	住む	10	
station	えき	Noun	4	駅	20	

stay over night	とまる	Verb う	14			
staying up all night	てつや（する）	N verbal	22			
staying up late at night	よふかし（する）	N verbal	26	夜ふかし	26	
steak	ステーキ	Noun	5			
steal	ぬすむ	Verb う	25			
steam	むす	Verb う	24			
step on	ふむ	Verb う	25			
step up	あがる	Verb う	15	上がる	15	
stereo (set)	ステレオ	Noun	11			
stick, pole	ぼう	Noun	21			
still	まだ	Adv	8			もう
still now	いまでも	Adv	18	今でも	18	
stir fry	いためる	Verb る	27			
stomach	い	Noun	21			
stomach	おなか	Noun	9			
stone	いし	Noun	17	石	17	
stop (intransitive)	とまる	Verb う	23			うごく
stop (transitive)	とめる	Verb る	25			
stop (raining)	やむ	Verb う	15			ふる
store	（お）みせ	Noun	6	（お）店	12	
store clerk	てんいん	Noun	12	店員	12	
story	はなし	Noun	9	話	9	
straight	まっすぐ（な）	Adj な	17			
straighten (clean) up	かたづける	Verb る	18			
strange	へん（な）	Adj な	20	変	20	
street	どうろ	Noun	21			
street	とおり	Noun	11			
street	みち	Noun	17			
stress	ストレス	Noun	25			
strict	きびしい	Adj い	26			
stroll	さんぽ（する）	N verbal	13			
strong	つよい	Adj い	17	強い	17	よわい
student	がくせい	Noun	1	学生	5	
study	べんきょう（する）	N verbal	4	勉強	14	
study	まなぶ	Verb う	18	学ぶ	18	おしえる
studying abroad	りゅうがく（する）	N verbal	12	留学	12	
study tour	けんがく（する）	N verbal	20	見学	20	
stupid	ばか	Adj な	25			
submission	ていしゅつ（する）	N verbal	21			
submit (HW, letter)	だす	Verb う	16	出す	16	
subtract	ひく	Verb う	17			たす
subway	ちかてつ	Noun	15	地下鉄	25	

succeed at (exam, class, etc.)	うかる	Verb う	21	受かる	21	おちる
(be) sufficient	たりる	Verb る	19	足りる	21	
sugar	(お) さとう	Noun	12			
suit	スーツ	Noun	10			
suitcase	スーツケース	Noun	13			
summer	なつ	Noun	13	夏	13	
summer vacation	なつやすみ	Noun	6	夏休み	13	
summon	よぶ	Verb う	8			
Sunday	にちようび	N proper	4	日曜日	4	
sunglasses	サングラス	Noun	10			
superb	すてき (な)	Adj な	18			
(one's) superior	じょうし	Noun	23			
supermarket	スーパー	Noun	4			
supper	ばんごはん	Noun	4	晩ごはん	6	あさごはん
(be) sure to do something	かならず	Adv	21			
surely	きっと	Adv	20			
(get) surprised	おどろく	Verb う	19			
(get) surprised	びっくりする	V irreg	19			
swallowing (sound symbolic)	ゴクンと	Adv	25			
sweater	セーター	Noun	10			
sweatshirt	トレーナー	Noun	10			
sweet	あまい	Adj い	11			からい
swim	およぐ	Verb う	6	泳ぐ	25	
swimming	すいえい (する)	N verbal	26	水泳	26	
swimsuit	みずぎ	Noun	22	水着	22	
switch	スイッチ	Noun	17			
symphony	シンフォニー	Noun	22			

T

table	テーブル	Noun	3			
Tahoe	タホ	N proper	5			
Takada	たかだ	N proper	23	高田	23	
take	とる	Verb う	5	取る	14	
take (picture)	(しゃしんを) とる	Verb る	8			
take (shower)	(シャワーを) あびる	Verb る	13			
take (exam)	(しけんを) うける	Verb る	13	受ける	16	
take (time, expense)	かかる	Verb う	10			
take along (person, animal)	つれていく	Verb う	21	つれて行く	21	つれてくる
take (a bath)	(おふろに) はいる	Verb う	15	入る	15	でる
take a day off	やすむ	Verb う	14	休む	14	

take along (thing)	もっていく	Verb う	21	持って行く	24	もってくる
take off (clothes, shoes)	ぬぐ	Verb う	14			きる、はく
take off (accessories)	はずす	Verb う	15			する
take something away	とる	Verb う	26	取る	26	
taking an exam	じゅけん（する）	N verbal	26	受験	26	
(The) Tale of Genji	げんじものがたり	N proper	25	源氏物語	X	
talk	はなし	Noun	9	話	9	
talk	いう	Verb う	11	言う	16	
Tanaka	たなか	N proper	3	田中	19	
Tango	タンゴ	N proper	13			
tape	テープ	Noun	6			
taste	あじ	Noun	20	味	20	
tatami mat	たたみ	Noun	17			
tax	ぜいきん	Noun	19			
taxi	タクシー	Noun	8			
tea	おちゃ	Noun	4	お茶	9	
(make) tea	（おちゃを）いれる	Verb る	24	入れる	24	
tea ceremony	おちゃ	Noun	18	お茶	18	
teach	おしえる	Verb る	5	教える	14	ならう
teacher	せんせい	Noun	1	先生	5	
teacher	きょうし	Noun	17	教師	X	
team	チーム	Noun	11			
telephone	でんわ（する）	N verbal	10	電話	15	
tell	おしえる	Verb る	24	教える	14	
tell	つたえる	Verb る	24	伝える	24	
ten	じゅう	Noun	3	十	3	
ten things	とお	Noun	9	十	9	
tenant	テナント	Noun	18			おおや（さん）
tennis	テニス	Noun	4			
tenth day	とおかめ	Noun	15	十日目	15	
teriffic	すごい	Adj い	11			
terrible	ひどい	Adj い	26			
test	しけん	Noun	6	試験	17	
textbook	テキスト	Noun	2			
textbook	きょうかしょ	Noun	9	教科書	20	
Thailand	タイ	N proper	11			
thanks to X	おかげさまで	Phrase	18			
that direction	あちら	Pronoun	7			こちら
that direction	そちら	Pronoun	7			こちら
that much	そんなに	Adv	26			
that NOUN	その + NOUN	Adj irreg	2			この
that NOUN (over there)	あの + NOUN	Adj irreg	2			この

that one	あれ	Pronoun	2			これ
that one	それ	Pronoun	2			これ
the other day	このあいだ	Phrase	12			
then	すると	Conj	25			
there	そこ	Pronoun	2			ここ
therefore	ですから	Conj	6			
therefore	それで	Conj	8			
thermometer	たいおんけい	Noun	21			
thesis, article	ろんぶん	Noun	21			
thick custard soup	ちゃわんむし	Noun	24	茶わんむし	24	
thief	どろぼう	Noun	25			
thing	もの	Noun	26	物	26	
think	おもう	Verb う	20	思う	20	
think	かんがえる	Verb る	11	考える	24	
third	みっつめ	Noun	17	三つ目	17	
third day	みっかめ	Noun	15	三日目	15	
third-year student	さんねんせい	Noun	2	三年生	11	
this direction	こちら	Pronoun	7			あちら
this evening	こんばん	Noun	5	今晩	6	けさ
this evening	こんや	Noun	21	今夜	21	けさ
this month	こんげつ	Noun	13	今月	13	
this morning	けさ	Noun	12	今朝	12	こんばん
this NOUN	この + NOUN	Adj irreg	2			その、あの
this one	これ	Pronoun	2			それ、あれ
this semester	こんがっき	Noun	15	今学期	15	
this week	こんしゅう	Noun	12	今週	13	
this weekend	こんしゅうまつ	Noun	20	今週末	20	
this year	ことし	Noun	8	今年	10	
thousand	せん	Noun	3	千	3	
threatening	こわい	Adj い	19			
three	さん	Noun	3	三	3	
three persons	さんにん	Noun	8	三人	8	
three things	みっつ	Noun	9	三つ	9	
thrift, saving	せつやく（する）	N verbal	20			
throat	のど	Noun	16			
thorough	ていねい（な）	Adj な	22			
throughout	～じゅう、～ちゅう	Suffix	17	～中	17	
thought	かんがえ	Noun	24	考え	24	
Thursday	もくようび	N proper	4	木曜日	4	
ticket	きっぷ	Noun	13	切符	22	
time	じかん	Noun	10	時間	10	
time	とき	Noun	13	時	13	

(X) time(s)	～かい	Counter	22	～回	22	
(X) time(s)	～ど	Counter	16	～度	18	
Times	タイムズ	N proper	2			
to	まで	Particle	4			から
to tell the truth	じつは	Phrase	13			
tobacco	タバコ	Noun	16			
today	きょう	Noun	4	今日	5	
tofu in hot broth	ゆどうふ	Noun	26			
together	いっしょに	Phrase	4			
toilet	おてあらい	Noun	3	お手洗い	16	
Tokyo	とうきょう	N proper	7	東京	8	
Tokyo Tower	とうきょうタワー	N proper	20	東京タワー	20	
tomorrow	あした	Noun	4	明日	5	きのう
tooth	は	Noun	15			
touch	さわる	Verb う	16			
tough	たいへん（な）	Adj な	5	大変	14	らく（な）
tough	かたい	Adj い	11			やわらかい
tour guide	ツアー・ガイド	Noun	17			
town	まち	Noun	4			
Toyama	とおやま	N proper	22	遠山	22	
traffic accident	こうつうじこ	Noun	22	事故	23	
traffic light	しんごう	Noun	17			
train	でんしゃ	Noun	4	電車	15	
translate	やくす	Verb う	24			
translator	ほんやくか	Noun	17	翻訳家	X	
transportation	こうつう	Noun	26			
travel	りょこう（する）	N verbal	13	旅行	19	
treasure	たからもの	Noun	18	たから物	18	
treat someone to something	おごる	Verb う	24			
treat someone to something (formal)	ごちそうする	V irreg	24			
tree	うえき	Noun	23	うえ木	23	
tree	き	Noun	17	木	17	
trifle	つまらない	Adj い	7			
trip	りょこう（する）	N verbal	13	旅行	19	
trivial	つまらない	Adj い	7			
trousers	ズボン	Noun	10			
truck	トラック	Noun	22			
truly	ほんとうに	Adv	18	本当	19	
try	やる	Verb う	14			
T-shirt	Tシャツ	Noun	9			

	Tuesday	かようび	N proper	4	火曜日	4	
	turkey	ターキー	Noun	24			
	turn (intransitive)	まがる	Verb う	17			
	turn off (transitive)	けす	Verb う	14			つける
	turn off (intransitive)	きえる	Verb る	10			つく
	turn on (intransitive)	つく	Verb う	10			きえる
	turn on (transitive)	つける	Verb る	14			けす
	turn on (a switch)	いれる	Verb る	17	入れる	18	
	TV	テレビ	Noun	4			
	TV station	テレビきょく	Noun	20			
	two	に	Noun	3	二	3	
	two persons	ふたり	Noun	8	二人	8	
	two things	ふたつ	Noun	9	二つ	9	
	typing	タイプ	N verbal	22			
U	Ueno	うえの	N proper	15	上野	X	
	umbrella	かさ	Noun	6			
	uncle (plain)	おじ	Noun	8			おば
	uncle (respectful)	おじさん	Noun	8			おばさん
	uncooked rice	（お）こめ	Noun	12	（お）米	12	
	under	した	Noun	3	下	5	うえ
	undergraduate student	がくぶせい	Noun	25	学部生	25	
	undergraduate student	だいがくせい	Noun	2	大学生	8	
	understand	わかる	Verb う	10	分かる	10	
	undertake	ひきうける	Verb る	21	ひき受ける	21	ことわる
	undoubtedly	たしかに	Adv	16			
	uneasy	ふあん（な）	Adj な	26	不安	26	
	unit(s)	たんい	Noun	16			
	(X) unit(s)	〜こ	Counter	9	〜個	23	
	university	だいがく	Noun	2	大学	7	
	university	ユニバーシティー	Noun	22			
	unpleasant	いや（な）	Adj な	25			
	untasty	まずい	Adj い	7			おいしい
	until late	おそくまで	Phrase	19			
	up to	まで	Particle	4			から
	usage	つかいかた	Noun	13	使い方	16	
	use	つかう	Verb う	6	使う	16	
	(become) used to	なれる	Verb る	18			
V	vacant lot	あきち	Noun	18	あき地	26	
	Valentine's Day	バレンタインデー	N proper	23			
	various	いろいろ（な）	Adj な	12	色々	18	
	vase	かびん	Noun	21			
	vegetable	やさい	Noun	12			

	very	とても	Adv	7			
	vicinity	ちかく	Noun	3	近く	20	
	vicinity	へん	Noun	22			
	video	ビデオ	Noun	11			
	video game	ビデオゲーム	Noun	26			
	vinegar	（お）す	Noun	11			
	(be) visible	みえる	Verb る	25	見える	25	
	vitamin	ビタミン	Noun	18			
	vocabulary	たんご	Noun	14	単語	18	
	vocational school	せんもんがっこう	Noun	26	専門学校	26	
	volcano	かざん	Noun	20	火山	20	
W	waist, hips	こし	Noun	21			
	wait	まつ	Verb う	8	待つ	9	
	waiter	ウェイター	Noun	9			
	wake up (intransitive)	おきる	Verb る	5			ねる
	wake up (transitive)	おこす	Verb う	25			
	wake up	（めを）さます	Verb う	17			
	walk	あるく	Verb う	8	歩く	18	
	wall	かべ	Noun	21			
	wallet	さいふ	Noun	25			
	want	ほしい	Adj い	12			
	warm	あたたかい	Adj い	17			すずしい
	warning	ちゅうい（する）	N verbal	18	注意	25	
	wash	あらう	Verb う	14	洗う	16	よごす
	washing machine	せんたくき	Noun	16	洗濯機	16	
	Washington, D.C.	ワシントン	N proper	27			
	watch	とけい	Noun	3	時計	23	
	watch	みる	Verb る	4	見る	6	
	watch (respectful)	ごらんになる	Verb う	19			
	water	みず	Noun	12	水	12	
	Watson	ワトソン	N proper	3			
	way	ほう	Noun	9	方	9	
	way, road, street	みち	Noun	17			
	way of doing something	やりかた	Noun	21	やり方	21	
	way of making	つくりかた	Noun	13	作り方	13	
	way of reading	よみかた	Noun	13	読み方	13	
	way of thinking	かんがえかた	Noun	20	考え方	24	
	way of writing	かきかた	Noun	13	書き方	13	
	way to use	つかいかた	Noun	13	使い方	16	
	we	わたしたち	Pronoun	2	私達	13	
	weak	よわい	Adj い	25	弱い	25	つよい
	wear (accessory)	する	V irreg	10			とる、はずす

wear (dress, shirt, suit)	きる	Verb る	10	着る	21	ぬぐ
wear (glasses)	（めがねを）かける	Verb る	10			はずす
wear (hat, cap)	かぶる	Verb う	10			とる
wear (shoes, socks, trousers)	はく	Verb う	10			ぬぐ
weather	（お）てんき	Noun	13	（お）天気	22	
weather forecast	てんきよほう	Noun	22	天気よほう	22	
Web	ウェブ	N proper	21			
wedding ceremony	けっこんしき	Noun	14	結婚しき	26	
Wednesday	すいようび	N proper	4	水曜日	4	
week after next	さらいしゅう	Noun	13	さ来週	13	せんせんしゅう
week before last	せんせんしゅう	Noun	13	先々週	13	さらいしゅう
weekend	しゅうまつ	Noun	4	週まつ	13	
				週末	16	
welcome (casual)	いらっしゃい	Phrase	24			
well	よく	Adv	10			
well then (casual)	じゃ	Conj	5			
well then (casual)	それじゃ	Conj	6			
well then (formal)	それでは	Conj	18			
Western-style clothes	ようふく	Noun	16			
what	なに・なん	Pronoun	2	何	4	
what hour	なんじ	Pronoun	4	何時	4	
what kind of	どういう + NOUN	Phrase	20			
what kind of	どんな + NOUN	Adj irreg	7			
what language	なにご	Pronoun	6	何語	6	
what minute	なんぷん	Pronoun	4	何分	4	
what-year student	なんねんせい	Pronoun	2	何年生	11	
wheat flour	こむぎこ	Noun	12			
when	いつ	Adv	4			
when	とき	Noun	13	時	13	
where	どこ	Pronoun	2			
which day of the week	なんようび	Pronoun	4	何曜日	4	
which month	なんがつ	Pronoun	5	何月	5	
which NOUN	どの + NOUN	Adj irreg	2			
which one	どれ	Pronoun	2			
whisky	ウィスキー	Noun	9			
white	しろ	Noun	17	白	17	
white	しろい	Adj い	17	白い	17	
who	だれ	Pronoun	2			
who (respectful)	どなた	Pronoun	2			
why	どうして	Adv	5			
why	なぜ	Adv	12			

wide	ひろい	Adj い	7	広い	7	せまい
wife (plain)	かない	Noun	8			しゅじん
wife (respectful)	おくさん	Noun	8			ごしゅじん
Wilson	ウィルソン	N proper	7			
win (a game)	(〜に) かつ	Verb う	22			まける
window	まど	Noun	10			
wine	ワイン	Noun	5			
winter	ふゆ	Noun	8	冬	13	
winter vacation	ふゆやすみ	Noun	6	冬休み	13	
wisdom	ちえ	Noun	11			
with all one's might	いっしょうけんめい(に)	Phrase	21	一生けんめい	22	
withdraw (money)	(おかねを) おろす	Verb う	18			
wonderful	けっこう (な)	Adj な	8			だめ (な)
Wong	ウォン	N proper	2			
woods	もり	Noun	17			
word	たんご	Noun	14	単語	18	
word	ことば	Noun	16	言葉	16	
word processor	ワープロ	Noun	26			
work	はたらく	Verb う	13	働く	14	
worry	しんぱい (する)	N verbal	19	心配	21	あんしん (する)
wow	わあ	Interject	4			
Wright Brothers	ライトきょうだい	N proper	11	ライト兄弟	11	
wrist	てくび	Noun	21	手くび	21	
write	かく	Verb う	4	書く	9	けす
writer, novelist	さっか	Noun	17	作家	X	
writer, novelist	しょうせつか	Noun	17	小説家	X	
writing	さくぶん	Noun	15	作文	15	

Y

(be) wrong	ちがう	Verb う	19			
Yamada	やまだ	N proper	3	山田	19	
Yamamoto	やまもと	N proper	6	山本	6	
Yamashita	やました	N proper	7	山下	7	
Yasuda	やすだ	N proper	24	安田	24	
Yasukawa	やすかわ	N proper	8	安川	9	
year after next	さらいねん	Noun	13	さ来年	13	おととし
year before last	おととし	Noun	13			さらいねん
year-end present	(お) せいぼ	Noun	23			
(X) years ago	〜ねんまえ	Suffix	19	〜年前	19	
yellow	きいろ	Noun	17	き色	17	
yellow	きいろい	Adj い	17	き色い	17	
yes	はい	Adv	2			いいえ
yes (casual)	うん	Adv	5			ううん

yesterday	きのう	Noun	5	昨日	5	あした
yet	まだ	Adv	5			もう
Yokohama	よこはま	N proper	8	横浜	X	
Yosemite	ヨセミテ	N proper	3			
you	あなた	Pronoun	2			
Young	ヤング	N proper	3			
young	わかい	Adj い	16			
younger brother (plain)	おとうと	Noun	8	弟	8	あに
younger brother (resp)	おとうとさん	Noun	8	弟さん	8	おにいさん
younger sister (plain)	いもうと	Noun	8	妹	8	あね
younger sister (resp)	いもうとさん	Noun	8	妹さん	8	おねえさん
yucky	まずい	Adj い	7			おいしい

Appendix H　Predicates by Category

い -Adjectives

17	あおい	blue
17	あかい	red
7	あかるい	bright, cheerful
17	あたたかい	warm
7	あたらしい	new
11	あつい	hot
22	あぶない	dangerous
11	あまい	sweet
7	いい	good
10	いそがしい	busy
12	いたい	painful
7	うるさい	noisy
13	うれしい (1st person)	happy, pleased
7	おいしい	delicious
10	おおい	many, plenty
7	おおきい	big, large
11	おそい	slow, late
14	おもい	heavy
7	おもしろい	interesting
26	おもしろい	funny, amusing
11	かたい	tough, hard
17	かなしい	sad
21	かゆい	itchy
19	からい	hot, salty
14	かるい	light (weight)
9	かわいい	cute
17	きいろい	yellow
7	きたない	dirty
26	きびしい	severe, strict
7	くらい	dark
17	くろい	black
19	くわしい	detailed
19	こわい	threatening, scary
13	さびしい	lonely
11	さむい	cold
21	しかくい	square
17	しろい	white
19	すくない	very few/little
11	すごい	teriffic
11	すずしい	cool
20	すっぱい	sour
7	せまい	narrow, small
7	たかい	expensive, high
17	ただしい	correct
9	たのしい	enjoyable, pleasant
7	ちいさい	small
7	ちかい	near
7	つまらない	trivial, trifle, boring
19	つめたい	cold
17	つよい	strong
7	とおい	far
7	ながい	long
16	にがい	bitter
14	ねむい	sleepy
20	はずかしい	ashamed, embarrassed
8	はやい	early
9	はやい	fast
7	ひくい	low, short (height)
26	ひどい	terrible
7	ひろい	spacious, wide
7	ふるい	old
12	ほしい	want, desire
7	まずい	not tasty, yucky
21	まるい	round
7	みじかい	short (length)
7	むずかしい	difficult
23	めずらしい	rare
7	やさしい	easy, gentle
7	やすい	cheap, inexpensive
11	やわらかい	soft
25	よわい	weak
16	わかい	young
11	わるい	bad

な -Adjectives

23	あんぜん	safe
7	いじわる	mean
25	いや	annoying
12	いろいろ	various, many kinds of
26	かわいそう	pitiable, pitiful
9	かんたん	easy
25	きけん	dangerous
9	きらい	dislike
7	きれい	clean, beautuful
20	けいざいてき	economical
8	けっこう	fine, nice, wonderful
7	げんき	energetic
24	ごうか	deluxe, luxurious, gorgeous
25	さかん	flourishing
6	ざんねん	regrettable, regret
26	しあわせ	happy
7	しずか	quiet
7	しつれい	impolite
9	じょうず	good at
7	しんせつ	kind
9	すき	like
18	すてき	superb, splendid
20	せいじてき	political
20	せんもんてき	professional
20	だいじ	important
12	だいじょうぶ	alright, okay
12	だいすき	like very much
22	たいせつ	important
5	たいへん	tough
11	だめ	no good
19	ていねい	polite, courteous
22	ていねい	thorough, careful, meticulous
19	てきとう	appropriate
9	とくい	good at
7	にぎやか	lively
20	にほんじんてき	Japanese
25	ばか	stupid
22	はで	flamboyant
9	ハンサム	handsome
12	ひま	leisure, not busy
26	ふあん	uneasy
19	ふくざつ	complicated
7	ふべん	inconvenient
7	ふまじめ	not serious
20	ぶんかてき	cultural
9	へた	bad at
20	へん	strange
7	べんり	convenient
7	まじめ	serious
17	まっすぐ	straight
14	ゆうめい	famous
14	らく	easy, simple, comfortable, relaxed
18	りっぱ	splendid
20	れきしてき	historical

Verbal Nouns

23	アドバイス	advice
24	あんしん	relief
26	あんない	guide
19	インストール	installation
10	インタビュー	interview
11	うんてん	drive
4	うんどう	exercise
17	えんそう	music performance
19	えんりょ	reservation, hesitation
26	おうぼ	application
9	オーダー	order
19	おしゃべり	chat
9	おねがい	favor, request
27	おれい	gratitude
26	がいしょく	eating out
24	かいてん	opening a store
4	かいもの	shopping
25	かつどう	activity
19	かんせい	completion
18	きこく	returning to one's home country

20	キャンプ	camping
21	くしゃみ	sneeze
25	けいかく	plan
19	けっこん	marriage
15	けんか	quarrel
20	けんがく	study tour
20	けんきゅう	research
16	けんぶつ	sightseeing
20	こうえん	lecture
15	こうぎ	lecture
27	ごかい	misunderstanding
22	こしょう	breakdown
4	コピー	copy
11	サービス	service
24	さいよう	employment
24	サイン	sign
26	さんか	participation
13	さんぽ	stroll
8	しごと	job
20	しっぱい	mistake
6	しつもん	question
19	しゅうしょく	getting a job
18	しゅうり	repair
26	じゅけん	taking an exam
21	しゅっせき	attendance
18	しゅっぱつ	departure
24	じゅんび	preparation
14	しょうかい	introduction
24	しょうたい	invitation
5	ジョギング	jogging
17	しょくじ	meal
19	しんぱい	anxiety, concern, worry
26	すいえい	swimming
16	スケッチ	sketch
18	スピーチ	speech
16	せつめい	explanation
20	せつやく	saving, thrift
18	せわ	care
12	せんたく	laundry
9	そうじ	clean
18	そうだん	consultation
25	そうりつ	establishment, founding
13	そつぎょう	graduation
12	ダイエット	diet
22	タイプ	typing
11	ダンス	dance
22	ちこく	being late for something
18	ちゅうい	warning
21	ちゅうもん	order
18	ちょきん	savings
21	ていしゅつ	submission
5	テスト	test, examination
22	てつや	staying up all night
10	でんわ	telephone
15	とうちゃく	arrival
19	ドライブ	drive
23	にゅうがく	entering school
23	にゅうしゃ	entering company
18	ノック	knock
25	はかい	destruction
25	はっこう	publication, print
25	はっぴょう	presentation
26	はんこう	rebellion, defiance
22	はんたい	opposition
24	ひっこし	housemoving
13	ひるね	nap
6	ふくしゅう	review
10	プレゼント	present
24	へいてん	closing a store
4	べんきょう	study
13	へんじ	reply
13	ホームステイ	homestay
24	メモ	memo
24	めんせつ	interview
22	やくそく	promise
20	ようい	preparation
14	よしゅう	preparatory study
26	よふかし	staying up late at night
18	よやく	reservation
26	りこん	divorce

12	りゅうがく	studying abroad
5	りょうり	cuisine, cooking
13	りょこう	trip, travel
9	れんしゅう	practice
19	れんらく	contact

う Verbs

4	あう	meet
15	あがる	step up
10	あく	open (intran)
6	あそぶ	play
21	あたる	hit (intran)
24	あむ	knit
26	あやまる	apologize
14	あらう	wash
3	ある	exist (things)
8	あるく	walk
11	いう	say, speak, talk
26	（もんくを） いう	complain, make (a complaint)
4	いく	go
18	いそぐ	hurry
8	いただく	receive
3	いらっしゃる	exist
19	いらっしゃる	come, go
21	うかる	pass (exam, class, etc.)
18	うごく	move (intran)
8	うたう	sing
25	うつす	copy
24	えらぶ	choose, select
10	おくる	send
25	おこす	wake (someone) up
17	おこる	get angry
24	おごる	treat someone to something
17	おす	push
17	おちつく	calm down
19	おっしゃる	say
13	おどる	dance
19	おどろく	get surprised
20	おもう	think
6	およぐ	swim
18	（おかねを） おろす	withdraw (money)
18	おわる	finish (intran)
5	かう	buy
6	かえす	return
4	かえる	go home, return
10	かかる	take (time, expense)
23	かきなおす	rewrite, revise
4	かく	write
9	かく	draw
25	かしだす	lend out
8	かす	lend
22	かつ	win
10	かぶる	wear (hat, cap)
25	かむ	bite
25	かりだす	check out
16	かわく	get dry
6	がんばる	do one's best
5	きく	listen, ask
26	きらう	hate
24	きる	cut, chop
23	くださる	give
18	けす	erase
14	けす	turn off
17	こする	rub
25	ことわる	decline
18	こぼす	spill
15	こまる	get in trouble
21	こむ	get crowded
19	ごらんになる	see, watch
25	ころす	kill
18	こわす	break (tran)
14	さがす	search for
21	さがる	go down
17	さく	bloom
22	（かさを） さす	put up (an umbrella)
23	（めぐすりを） さす	apply (eye drops)
20	さそう	invite
26	サボる	cut classes
17	（めを） さます	wake up
16	さわる	touch
25	しかる	scold

8	しぬ	die
10	しまる	close (intran)
10	しる	get to know
16	すう	inhale
9	すく	become empty
10	すむ	start living somewhere
10	すわる	sit down
18	そる	shave
17	たす	add
16	だす	submit, send out
24	だす	serve, put out
19	たすかる	be saved
25	たたく	pat
18	たつ	be built (intran)
10	たつ	stand up
26	たのしむ	enjoy
25	たのむ	ask, request
25	たまる	accumulate
19	ちがう	be wrong, different
6	つかう	use
10	つく	turn on (intran)
15	つく	arrive
5	つくる	make
23	つづく	continue (intran)
21	つれていく	take along (person, animal)
24	てつだう	help, assist
19	とどく	reach, arrive (intran)
25	とぶ	fly
14	とまる	stay over night
23	とまる	stop (intran)
5	とる	take
8	(しゃしんを) とる	take (a picture)
26	とる	take s.t. away
21	なおす	fix, repair, put straight, correct (tran)
19	なおる	be repaired (intran)
21	なおる	recover (intran)
25	なく	cry
16	なくす	lose (tran)
19	なくなる	run out of (intran)
9	なさる	do
12	ならう	learn
24	ぬう	sew
14	ぬぐ	take off
25	ぬすむ	steal
14	ねむる	sleep
20	のぼる	climb
4	のむ	drink
13	のる	ride, get on
7	はいる	enter
15	(おふろに) はいる	take (a bath)
21	はかる	measure
10	はく	wear (shoes, socks, trousers)
26	はげます	encourage
14	はこぶ	carry, transport
18	はじまる	start (intran)
13	はしる	run
15	はずす	take off (accessories)
13	はたらく	work
6	はなす	speak, chat
16	はらう	pay
25	はりだす	post
15	はる	paste
6	ひく	play (musical instrument)
14	(かぜを) ひく	catch (a cold)
15	(じしょを) ひく	look up (dictionary)
17	ひく	subtract
25	ひく	run over
23	ひやす	cool, chill
14	ふとる	become fat
25	ふむ	step on
8	ふる	fall
26	ふる	jilt, dump
12	ほしがる	show signs of desire
17	まがる	turn
8	まつ	wait
18	まなぶ	learn, study
22	まにあう	make it in time

15	みがく	brush, polish
22	みつかる	be found (intran)
24	むす	steam
19	めしあがる	eat
8	もつ	have, hold
21	もっていく	take along (thing)
11	もらう	receive
24	やく	bake, broil
24	やくす	translate
14	やすむ	take a day off
15	やむ	stop (raining)
14	やる	do, try
23	やる	give
24	ゆずる	give up, hand over
25	よごす	stain, soil
8	よぶ	call, summon
12	よぶ	invite
4	よむ	read
13	よろこぶ (3rd person)	be happy, pleased
10	わかる	understand
25	わたす	hand over
25	わらう	smile, laugh, laugh at

る Verbs

17	あける	open (tran)
14	あげる	raise
23	あげる	give
13	(シャワーを) あびる	take (a shower)
3	いる	exist (people, animals)
17	いれる	turn on (a switch), put into
24	(おちゃを) いれる	make (tea)
13	(しけんを) うける	take (an exam)
20	うまれる	be born
18	おえる	finish (intran)
5	おきる	wake up, get up
14	おくれる	late for (to be)
5	おしえる	teach
24	おしえる	tell, inform
15	(しけんに) おちる	fail (an exam)
12	おぼえる	memorize
17	おりる	get off
17	かえる	change (tran)
24	(アイロンを) かける	iron, use (an iron)
24	(かぎを) かける	lock (with a key)
10	(めがねを) かける	wear (glasses)
18	かたづける	straighten (clean) up
6	かりる	borrow
11	かんがえる	think
10	きえる	turn off (tran)
25	きこえる	be audible
23	きめる	decide
10	きる	wear (dress, shirt, suit)
23	くれる	give
15	こたえる	answer
15	こわれる	break (intran)
23	さしあげる	give
18	さめる	get cold
18	しめる	close (tran)
14	しらべる	check
21	たおれる	fall over
13	たすける	help
4	たべる	eat
19	たりる	be sufficient
5	つかれる	get tired
14	つける	turn on (tran)
24	つたえる	tell, inform
23	つなげる	connect (tran)
15	でかける	go out
6	できる	able to do (to be)
17	できる	can do, come to being, be done
12	(〜に) でる	attend, enter (a contest)
15	(〜を) でる	leave (some place)
18	(〜を) でる	come out, go out
21	(はなが) でる	have a runny nose
22	(ほしが) でる	come out (stars)

20	とどける	deliver
25	とめる	stop
18	なれる	become used to
22	にる	resemble
5	ねる	go to bed, lie down
10	はじめる	start (tran)
17	はれる	clear up
21	ひきうける	undertake
25	ほめる	praise
22	(〜に) まける	lose (a game)
25	みえる	be visible
19	みせる	show
4	みる	see, watch
14	やめる	quit doing something
15	ゆれる	jolt
15	わすれる	forget

Irregular Verbs

15	うっかりする	forget to do s.t. carelessly
23	がっかりする	be disappointed
4	くる	come
24	ごちそうする	treat someone to something
4	する	do
10	する	wear (accessories)
16	つれてくる	bring (person, animal)
12	ねぼうする	oversleep
19	びっくりする	get surprised
18	ボーッとする	become absentminded
19	もってくる	bring (a thing)
21	ゆっくりする	relax

Appendix I Subject Index

KN: Kanji note UN: Usage note

	Entry	Ref.
	が subject marker	3a
	～か（と）・かどうか（と） whether	20b
	かい kanji radical	19KN
	かえる *go back*	4UN
	(～て) かえる *do ~ and go back*	21d
	かおをする *look (face)*	21c
	かかる *take time / expense*	10g
	かぎ・かぎかっこ punctuation symbol	20a
	かぞく family	8h
	かねへん kanji radical	25KN
	かべにみみあり～ proverb	21g
	かまえ kanji radical	8KN
	～かもしれない *it may be ~*	22c
	から: A から B まで *from A to B; from A as far as B*	4i
	～から *because / so*	5f
	(～て) から *after*	15c
	(Plain フォーム+) からだ *it is because ~*	12e
	(introduction of) かんじ	3KN
	(radicals of) かんじ	8KN
	(readings of) かんじ	5KN
	(stroke counts of) かんじ	7KN
	(stroke order of) かんじ	7KN
	がんねん *first year*	13g
	かんむり kanji radical	8KN
き	きへん kanji radical	15KN
	ぎょうにんべん kanji radical	11KN
	(X は Y が) きらいだ *X hates Y*	9a
く	くさかんむり kanji radical	12KN
	(～て) ください *please do ~*	8b
	(～ないで) ください *please don't do ~*	8c
	(X を) ください・くださいませんか *please give me X*	9e
	(～て) くださいませんか *would you please do ~?*	8b
	(～ないで) くださいませんか *would you please not do ~?*	8c
	くてん punctuation symbol	20a
	～くなさそう negative of そうだ (い-Adj)	21c

	Entry	Ref.
	くにがまえ kanji radical	10KN
	～ぐらい *about/approximately ~*	10h
	(～て) くる *do ~ and come*	21d
	(～て) クレル *do a favor for me (or my in-group)*	24a
	くんよみ explanatory / instructional reading	5KN
け	けっこう *fine*	8UN
こ	ご-NOUN beautifier	4c
	こ demonstratives	2f
	ごえんりょなく～てください *please feel free to do ~*	19UN
	こころ kanji radical	20KN
	こざとへん kanji radical	17KN
	こ・そ・あ demonstratives	2f
	こちら *this direction*	7k
	こと *event*	23b
	(～た) ことがある *have had the experience of Verb-ing*	10b
	(Dictionary フォーム+) ことができる *can, be able to*	6f
	(Dictionary フォーム+) ことにする *have decided to do*	~14c
	(Dictionary フォーム+) ことになった *it was decided that X does ~*	14e
	(Dictionary フォーム+) ことになっている *it's been decided that X does ~*	14e
	(Dictionary フォーム+) ことになる *it'll become that X does ~*	14d
	～ごろ（に） *about / approximately ~*	10h
	ごんべん kanji radical	9KN
さ	さけづくり kanji radical	16KN
	さんずい kanji radical	16KN
し	しか *only ~*	21f
	したごころ kanji radical	20KN
	(～て) しまう *finish Verb-ing*	15e
	(X は Y) じゃありません *X is not Y*	2b
	～じゃなさそう・ではなさそう negative of そうだ (な-Adj / Noun)	21c
	(X は Y が) じょうずだ *X is good at Y*	9a

	しょうわ	13g
	しょくへん kanji radical	18KN
	しんにゅう・しんにょう kanji radical	13KN
す	(XはYが) すきだ *X likes Y*	9a
	(ADJECTIVE+) すぎる *too ADJECTIVE*	25e
	(Pre- ますフォーム+) すぎる *do ~ excessively*	25d
	すこし *a little*	7g
	(ADJ/NOUN+) する *make X ADJ/NOUN*	17c
	(Xに) する *decide on X/make something X*	9g
せ	ぜんぜん negative adverb	7g
そ	そ demonstratives	2f
	そういえば *if you say so*	23UN
	そうじゃない・そうではない negative of そうだ	21c
	そうだ *hear that ~; it is said that ~*	22b
	そうだ *it looks (like) ~*	21c
	そうに(も)ない negative of そうだ	21c
	そちら *that direction*	7k
た	〜たあとで *after*	18b
	〜たことがある *have had the experience of Verb-ing*	10b
	たいしょう	13g
	(Pre- ますフォーム+) たいです *want to do ~*	12c
	(Pre- ますフォーム+) たがっている *want to do ~*	12d
	(Pre- ますフォーム+) たくない *don't want to do ~*	12c
	たけかんむり kanji radical	22KN
	ただいま *I'm home*	15UN
	たフォーム	10a
	〜たほうがいい *it'd be better if X did ~;X had better do ~*	23b
	(Dictionary フォーム+) ために *in order to do ~*	14g
	(Xの) ために *for X*	24b
	〜たら *after*	19c

	〜たらいいですか *what should I do ~*	23d
	〜たらどうですか *why don't you do ~;what about Verb-ing*	23d
	〜たり〜たりする	15f
	たれ kanji radical	8KN
	だれか *someone*	3d
	だれも *anyone*	3d
ち	ちょっと *a little*	7g
	(X) ちゅう *throughout X; in the middle of X*	17f
つ	つくり kanji radical	8KN
	(Dictionary フォーム+) つもりだ *intend/plan to do ~*	5d
	(ないフォーム+) つもりだ *intend/plan not to do ~*	6c
て	で instrument marker	4e
	で location marker for action verbs	4d
	で material marker	12f
	て *and*	15b
	〜てアゲル *do a favor for X*	24a
	〜てある *have been done;* *was done and kept that way*	24d
	〜ていく・くる・かえる *do ~ and go/come/go back*	21d
	〜ている *be Verb-ing*	8d
	〜ている *have Verb-ed*	10c
	〜ておく *do ~ in advance*	24c
	てがみのかきかた letter format	13h
	〜てから *after*	15c
	できる *be able to do; be done; come to being*	17a
	〜てください *please do ~*	8b
	〜てくださいませんか *would you please do ~?*	8b
	〜てクレル *do a favor for me (or my in-group)*	24a
	〜てしまう *finish VERB-ing*	15e
	(Plain フォーム+) でしょう *It's probably the case that ~*	17e
	(past tense of) です (でした)	11c
	てへん kanji radical	24KN

	Entry	Lesson
	～てみる *try to do ~; do~ and see what it is like*	14f
	です: X は Y です *X is Y*	2a
	(X は Y) ではありません *X is not Y*	2b
	～てはいけない *may not do ~*	16a
	～てばかりいる *do nothing but ~*	26d
	てフォーム	8a
	てフォームソング	8a
	～てもいい *it's okay to do ~*	16a
	～てもいいですか *Is it okay to do ~?*	16a
	～てモラウ *receive a favor*	24a
	～てモラウ vs. adversity passive	25c
	でるくいはうたれる proverb	25b
と	と: X と Y *and*	3e
	と quotation marker	20a
	～と *when/if/whenever*	17d
	と *with*	4h
	ど interrogatives	2f
	どうがまえ kanji radical	22KN
	どうして *why*	12e
	どうしてですか *why is/was it so?*	5g
	(X は) どうですか *how about X?*	8f
	(X は) どうですか *how is X?*	7i
	(～たら) どうですか *why don't you do~; what about Verb-ing*	23d
	(Plain フォーム+) とおもう *I think that ~*	20c
	(Volitional フォーム+) とおもう *I think I'm going to do ~*	20e
	～ときに *when*	13b
	(X は Y が) とくいだ *X is good at Y*	9a
	どこかに *somewhere*	3d
	どこにも *anywhere*	3d
	どなたか *someone* (respectful)	3d
	どなたも *anyone* (respectful)	3d
	となり *next to*	3c
	どんな *what kind of*	7j
な	な-Adjectives	7b
	(Negative フォーム of) な-Adjectives	7b
	～ないことにする *have decided not to do ~*	14c

	Entry	Lesson
	～ないことになった *it was decided that X does not do ~*	14e
	～ないことになっている *it's been decided that X does not do ~*	14e
	～ないことになる *it'll become that X does not do ~*	14d
	～ないつもりだ *intend/plan not to do ~*	6c
	(Negative フォーム+) ないで *without*	15d
	～ないでください *please don't do ~*	8c
	～ないでくださいませんか *would you please not do ~?*	8c
	ないフォーム	6a
	～ないほうがいい *it'd be better not to do ~; had better not do ~*	23c
	～ないようにする *make an effort not to do ~*	18c
	～ないようになる *it's gotten so that ~; it's become impossible that ~*	18d
	なかったフォーム	10a
	ながら *while*	15a
	(Negative フォーム+) なくてはいけない *must do ~*	16b
	(Negative フォーム+) なくてもいい *need not do ~*	16c
	なぜ *why*	12e
	など: X や Y など *X and Y among other things*	5h
	なに interrogative pronoun	2d
	なにか *something*	3d
	なにも *anything*	3d
	なべぶた kanji radical	9KN
	～なら～ *if (you say/think that) C1, then C2*	26c
	(ADJ/NOUN +) なる *become ADJ/NOUN*	17a
に	に direction/goal marker	4f
	に indirect object marker	10e
	に location marker	3c
	に object marker	5a
	に time marker	4g

	に: DURATION に X "X per DURATION"	25f
	(Pre- ますフォーム+) に＋いく・くる・かえる *go / come / return in order to do ~*	6e
	(Pre- ますフォーム+) にくい *difficult / uncomfortable to do ~*	16d
	にすい kanji radical	24KN
	にょう kanji radical	8KN
	にる *become look-alike*	22a
	にんべん kanji radical	11KN
	(NOUN +) に＋いく *go for NOUN*	13c
ね	ね	4l
の	の: NOUN の NOUN	2e
	のぎへん kanji radical	15KN
	ので *because*	14a
	(Plain フォーム+) のです・んです *it is the case that ~*	6g
	～のに *although*	22a
は	は negative scope marker	6h
	は topic marker	3b
	～ば *If*	21b
	は - が construction	7e
	ばかり: NOUN ばかり VERB *VERB nothing but NOUN*	26e
	(～て) ばかりいる *do nothing but VERB*	26d
	(Pre- ますフォーム+) はじめる *begin / start Verb-ing*	18e
	はなよりだんご proverb	17UN
	ばフォーム	21a
ひ	ひとあし kanji radical	23KN
	ひとりで *by oneself*	4h
	ひとやね kanji radical	23KN
	ひへん kanji radical	8KN
	びょうき *illness*	21h
へ	へ direction / goal marker	4f
	へいせい	13g
	(X は Y が) へただ *X is bad at Y*	9a
	へん kanji radical	8KN
ほ	(～た) ほうがいい *it'd be better if X did ~; had better do ~*	23b
	(ないフォーム+) ほうがいい *it'd be better not to do ~;* *had better not do ~*	23c
	ほうへん kanji radical	26KN
	ぼくづくり kanji radical	26KN
	(X が) ほしい *want X*	12a
	(X は Y を) ほしがっている *X wants Y*	12b
	(X は) ほしくありません・ないです *don't want X*	12a
	ほど: X ほど (は) ADJ-neg *not as ADJ as X*	22d
ま	まあ interjection	19UN
	まえに *before*	18a
	まけるがかち proverb	22a
	(Pre- ますフォーム+) ましょう *let's do*	4j
	(Pre- ますフォーム+) ましょうか *shall we do ~?*	4j
	(Pre- ますフォーム+) ませんか *won't you do ~?; would you like to do ~?*	6d
	まだ *still*	8e
	まだ *yet*	5i
	まだ＋～ていない *have not done Verb yet*	26f
	まだれ kanji radical	12KN
	まで: A から B まで *from A to B; from A as far as B*	4i
	(X) までに *by X (time)*	16e
	まる punctuation symbol	20a
と	みえる *visible / can see*	25c
	(～て) みる *try to do ~; do ~ and see what it is like*	14f
め	めいじ	13g
も	も *also*	2g
	(X quantity +) も *as many / much as X*	21e
	もう *already*	5i
	もうすぐ *soon*	5UN
	ものがたり *tale*	25b
	(～て) モラウ *receive a favor*	24a
	もんがまえ kanji radical	10KN

や	や: X や Y など *X and Y among other things*	5h
	(Pre- ますフォーム+) やすい *easy to do ~*	16d
	やまいだれ kanji radical	21KN
よ	よ final particle	3f
	(Dictionary フォーム+) ようにする *make an effort to do ~;* *make things so that ~*	18c
	(ないフォーム+) ようにする *make an effort not to do ~*	18c
	(Dictionary フォーム+) ようになる *it's gotten so that ~;* *it's become possible that ~*	18d
	(Potential フォーム+) ようになる *it's gotten so that ~;* *it's become possible that ~*	18d
	(ないフォーム+) ようになる *it's gotten so that ~;* *it's become impossible that ~*	18d
	ようび days of the week	4m
	よこ *beside*	3c
	よつてん kanji radical	25KN
り	りっしんべん kanji radical	20KN
れ	れっか・れんが kanji radical	25KN
わ	わらう *laugh, laugh at*	25b
を	を object marker	4b
ん	ん moraic consonant	1f